501 MUST-SEE
NATURAL WONDERS

501 MUST-SEE
NATURAL WONDERS

Bounty
BOOKS

An Hachette UK Company
www.hachette.co.uk

First published in Great Britain in 2007 by Bounty Books,
a division of Octopus Publishing Group Ltd
Carmelite House
50 Victoria Embankment
London EC4Y 0DZ
www.octopusbooks.co.uk

First published in paperback in 2013
This revised edition published in 2016

ISBN: 978-0-7537-2984-7

A CIP catalogue record is available from the British Library

Printed and bound in China

10 9 8 7 6 5 4 3 2

Publisher: Samantha Warrington
Art Director: Miranda Snow
Managing Editor: Karen Rigden
Senior Production Manager: Peter Hunt
Packaged by The Urban Ant Ltd

CONTENTS

INTRODUCTION

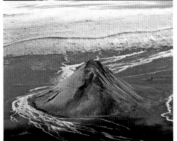

There really is no limit to the number of natural wonders on our planet Earth. While this book gives you the opportunity to read and learn about 501 of the most spectacular examples, there are an infinite number of natural wonders all around us. Whether it is the trees that grow in our woods, fields and parks, the plants (and weeds!) that thrive in our gardens and hedgerows, the ants' nests, the spiders' webs or the amazingly varied landscape of our countryside – virtually anywhere you look there is something 'naturally wonderful'.

Yet if it's the spectacular natural wonders you're after – and who isn't? – this is the book for you. Here you will find described the cave where 20 million bats roost, the remote Indian Ocean island that is home to 100,000 giant tortoises as well as the world's most active volcano, the longest cave system and the lake that is so deep that it would take all the world's rivers more than a year to refill it. Mountain ranges, deserts, gorges, rivers, glaciers, marshes, cliffs, waterfalls, coral reefs, tropical rainforests – there is a wealth of wonders here to exhaust even the most intrepid of armchair travellers.

While quite a few, such as Mount Everest, the Rock of Gibraltar and the Great Rift Valley, are world famous, even more are unfamiliar to most of us. Apart from locals or avid geographers, how many have even heard of Hungary's Hortobágy National Park or Japan's Shirakami-Sanchi Forest or the hauntingly beautiful Wrangel Island within the Arctic Circle? At the same time there are natural wonders here that we do know about, indeed probably some that we live quite close to and yet we still haven't seen them!

There is no doubt that many of the world's natural wonders are under threat – from desertification, pollution, the pressure from increasing human population or the effects of global warming. Only a rash or very optimistic individual would predict that all the 501 must-visit natural wonders in this book will still be there in the year 2100. In a hundred years, will you still be able to enjoy the sight of polar bears in Churchill? Will there be enough fish in Lake Victoria to feed the millions living on and near its shores? Will loggerhead turtles still be nesting on the Greek isle of Zakynthos? Will Lake Chad exist at all? The challenges that many natural wonders face in the future are very considerable – and nearly all of them are caused by man's existence on this planet. One can only hope that we are able to alter our behaviour in time.

Whilst one often reads nowadays about the harmful effects of global tourism, the result of tourists' visits to many natural wonders is generally a positive one. Many of the world's wildlife parks only exist because of the income they derive from tourism. There are many instances where tourists' interest in a natural wonder makes the local population realize its importance and its value to them. Frequently, too, these locals can gain an income – as guides or guards, or by providing accommodation, food or numerous other services to tourists. Many of the world's natural wonders, especially those in poorer countries, will only be preserved if there is a benefit to the 'host' countries. This can of course be in the form of grants or gifts from the richer countries, but the advantage of tourism, in this tough capitalist world, is that there is a benefit to both parties.

Despite the remoteness and inaccessibility of some of these natural wonders, if you have the determination, it is possible to visit virtually all of them. To obtain the most benefit from the experience, you should read as much as you can about your natural wonder, be aware of the potential problems, make a careful, realistic plan for the journey, ensure you take appropriate clothing and equipment etc. . . . and enough money. Don't expect comfortable beds, fine restaurants and an ATM on every corner.

Some places are scorchingly hot, some are freezing cold, some very high, at some you will be surrounded by mosquitoes, and at others you may be pursued by bears. Whether you choose to go to Denali in Alaska or the Tsingy of Bemaraha in Madagascar or the Scottish Highlands, make sure you go prepared.

So which of these 501 natural wonders are you going to visit first?

AMERICAS & THE CARIBBEAN

NIAGARA FALLS

Canada

Although they are not the highest or broadest falls in the world, Niagara are the best known. Lying across the border between Canada and the United States, they were formed towards the end of the last ice age, when the glaciers of the Laurentide ice sheet retreated, creating the Great Lakes. Water flowing from Lake Erie to Lake Ontario carved a gorge past the Niagara escarpment and over the millennia since, it has eroded the shale below the hard dolomitic rock at the top. The falls are currently retreating at a rate of about 1m (3ft) a year. On the American side of the border, the Niagara Falls carry about 10 per cent of the flow, while on the Canadian side, the Horseshoe Falls carry far more. The water flows at the astonishing rate of 56.3kph (35mph). The local tribespeople call the falls *onguiaahra*, a 'thundering noise', which may seem like an understatement when you are faced with the sheer noise of almost 185,000 cubic m (6,600,00 cubic ft) of water roaring into the gorge every minute. The *Maid of the Mist* takes visitors up the gorge to the base of the Horseshoe Falls for a truly dramatic, and wet, experience and photogenic views as the sun creates rainbows in the mists.

HOODOO MOUNTAIN

Canada

HOW TO GET THERE:
By privately chartered
helicopter from Stewart, or
try to arrange a lift with a
mining operation.
WHEN TO GO:
July to September.
NEAREST TOWN:
Stewart 100km (63 miles).

On the northern edge of the Iskut river in remote northwestern British Columbia rises the commanding, flat-topped volcano, Hoodoo Mountain. Few people are aware of the fact that both British Columbia and the Yukon are home to large regions of volcanic activity, and are situated within the volatile Pacific Ring of Fire. Hoodoo Mountain rises to the west of the Stikine volcanic belt, and is considered to be an active volcano that could erupt again. Its flat top has an icecap that is some 3–4km (2–2.5 miles) in diameter. The fact that it is flat suggests that it was formed beneath glacial ice, its earliest eruptions occurring some 100,000 years ago. Most of the volcanic deposits found here are lava flows, although there are also some pyroclastic rocks that prove it has also had one or more periods of explosive activity. The most recent lava flows seem to have originated from under the icecap.

CARIBOU MIGRATION

Canada

There are over 2.4 million caribou *(Rangifer tarandus)* in Canada and they are found from British Columbia in the west to Newfoundland in the east, and from the US border in the south to Ellesmere Island, north of the Arctic Circle. Half of these are barren-ground caribou, most of which live in eight large migratory herds that move from the tundra in the far north to the sparsely treed forests to the south. These summer and winter ranges can be as far as 500 miles apart and this migration is one of the greatest wildlife spectacles on Earth. In spring the caribou set off north to the open tundra, where they can feed well on various plants and grasses. These are the calving grounds and the newborns grow rapidly thanks to their mothers' super-rich milk. In four weeks they are weaned, and growing strong enough to travel south. Finally they set out, in their thousands, to travel the same route back to the edges of the boreal forests that provide some shelter from the bitter cold.

HOW TO GET THERE: Several tour companies take groups by light plane to tent base camps on the migration routes.
WHEN TO GO: August to mid-September.
NEAREST TOWN: Yellowknife, Northwest Territories would be one good starting point.

YOHO NATIONAL PARK

Canada

Yoho National Park is the smallest of four national parks that together make up the Canadian Rocky Mountain Parks World Heritage Site. Located in southeastern British Columbia on the western slopes of the Rocky Mountains, the park is a breathtaking region of snowy peaks – 28 of which are over 3,000m (9,900ft) – glacial lakes, waterfalls, wild rivers and deep, dark forest. In 1909 Charles Walcott of the Smithsonian Institution discovered a unique deposit of Cambrian-era fossils here. Approximately 120 soft-bodied marine species from 515 million years ago have been found, perfectly preserved from the time when warm, shallow seas washed over land that has long since been uplifted to a major mountain range. These simple life forms took on bizarre shapes, and the fossils found in the Burgess Shale have provided scientists with a mass of new information about the evolutionary process itself.

There are only two other known sites of these fossils in existence. These craggy mountains were a nightmare for the builders of the Canadian Pacific rail line, but resulted in two remarkable spiral tunnels that climb up inside the mountain towards Kicking Horse Pass. The mighty river of the same name is responsible for having gouged out a natural bridge through solid rock, and water erosion has also formed hoodoos – boulders balanced on pillars of glacial debris. Glacial melt produces the amazing colour that gave Emerald Lake its name, the Takakkaw Falls is the third-highest waterfall in the country and all these features are quite accessible either by car or by hiking some of the 400km (250 miles) of very well-maintained trails.

YOU SHOULD KNOW
An entry fee is payable.

HOW TO GET THERE:
By road.
WHEN TO GO:
Year-round, but July to October for guided hikes to the fossil beds.
NEAREST TOWNS:
Field, in the centre of the Park; Lake Louise 27km (17 miles).

HOW TO GET THERE:
By road from Chicago,
Detroit or Toronto.
WHEN TO GO:
Summer, but take
mosquito repellent.
NEAREST TOWNS:
There are numerous cities
and towns situated on the
shores of the lakes.

THE GREAT LAKES

Canada

North America's five Great Lakes – Erie, Huron, Michigan, Ontario and Superior – lie on the Canadian/US border and were carved out of the landscape by great glaciers during the last ice age, then filled with meltwater as the glaciers retreated. These interconnected lakes make up the largest body of fresh water on Earth, with a volume of 22,812 cubic km (5,473 cubic miles) and a total area of 151,681 sq km (94,250 sq miles), with their main outlet to the Atlantic being via the St Lawrence river. This link with the ocean led to their exploitation for heavy industry, particularly on the US side, but the successive advents of rail, road and air freight mean that they are far quieter than in their heyday. Away from the major cities there are quiet bays and peaceful countryside with stunning landscapes to explore. Concerted efforts are being made to preserve the wilderness areas, particularly in the various national parks that surround the lake shores, where it is possible to lose yourself for days.

MOUNT LOGAN AND KLUANE NATIONAL PARK

Canada

Kluane National Park is situated in the southwestern corner of the Yukon and, together with Tatshenshini–Alsek, Wrangell–St Elias and Glacier Bay Parks, was inscribed as a UNESCO World Heritage Site in 1979. It is famous as the site of Canada's highest peak, and North America's second-highest after Mount McKinley, Mount Logan, which stands at 5,950m (19,521ft). High mountains and mighty glaciers cover 80 per cent of the park's territory, some 22,000 sq km (8,490 sq miles). Mount Logan is part of the St Elias Mountains and it is still growing taller due to tectonic activity. Reputedly, it has the largest circumference of any mountain on the planet. A glaciated plateau covers the top of the Logan massif, and Mount Logan is the highest of the 12 peaks that rise from it. Ridges lead up to the plateau from every direction, but in order to climb here a license must be applied for at least three months in advance. Kluane National Park teems with flora and fauna, and some 150 species of birds live here.

HOW TO GET THERE: By air to Whitehorse, then by road to Haines Junction. Mount Logan is accessed by ski-equipped aircraft or helicopters.
WHEN TO GO: Mid-June to August.
NEAREST TOWN: Haines Junction is at the park boundary.

MIGUASHA NATIONAL PARK

Canada

Miguasha National Park is situated on the Gaspé Peninsula in the eastern Canadian province of Quebec. The peninsula is separated from the rest of the province by the St Lawrence river, which forms its northern boundary. Today the area supports aspen, birch and fir forests, but 370 million years ago the now austere southern coast of the peninsula was a tropical estuary, and a vast array of fish swam in the warm, tidal waters. These fish crawled from the water and evolved into tetrapods, the original four-legged, air-breathing land animals. Miguasha National Park contains the world's greatest number of fossils from the Devonion period, and was designated a UNESCO World Heritage Site in 1999. The coastal cliffs are made of ancient grey rock formed from layers of sandstone and silt. They hold the fossils of ancient species of flora and fauna, including one of the oldest flowering species on Earth. However, Miguasha is most famous for its 21 species of fish fossils. The Natural History Museum in the park has an excellent collection of fossils, and there is a fascinating clifftop trail with fabulous views over the Restigouche estuary, and steps leading to the beach.

HOW TO GET THERE:
By road.
WHEN TO GO:
The park is open all year.
NEAREST TOWNS:
Carleton 20km (12.5 miles)
or Campbellton,
New Brunswick.

GRIZZLY BEARS

Cariboo Chilcotin, Canada

HOW TO GET THERE:
Fly or drive from Vancouver.
NEAREST TOWNS:
Quesnel or Prince George.

The Cariboo Chilcotin coast is situated in British Columbia's central region, some 240km (150 miles) north of Vancouver. It stretches from the Pacific Ocean in the west to the Cariboo Mountains in the east, and encompasses three of British Columbia's national parks. Two major rivers cut through the area – the clear Chilcotin and the muddy Fraser – and countless other river systems and lakes contribute to the wild beauty here. The western side of the coastal range is the drier side. Here, the Fraser plateau was formed millions of years ago by an ice sheet that smoothed and flattened it, and the two rivers to the east and west gouged out the steep-sided valleys through which they flow. This is grizzly bear country. Grizzlies (Ursus arctos) are omnivores, eating plants and roots, newborn deer, elk, caribou and, in full summer, vast quantities of the salmon that swim upstream to spawn. A fully grown male bear can reach 2.8m (9ft) in length, 1.5m (5ft) at shoulder height and can weigh up to 800kg (1,750lb). They live alone for the most part, but will congregate at a good food source, such as the salmon runs, when each adult will eat up to a ton of fish over a six-week period.

DON'T MISS
A boat trip on one
of the tidal bores.

THE BAY OF FUNDY

Canada

HOW TO GET THERE:
By air to Halifax or Saint John,
then by road or rail.
WHEN TO GO:
Summer.
NEAREST TOWNS:
Saint John or Amherst.

This bay in southeastern Canada is famous for its extraordinary tidal range. Spring tides can reach as much as 16m (53ft) in Minas Basin, as 100 billion tonnes of water surge towards the head of the bay and beyond into the rivers, causing phenomena such as the tidal bore at Truro in Nova Scotia and the Reversing Falls in the St John river in New Brunswick. The waters are also very fast-moving, as the tide travels 280km (174 miles) in about six hours, and the currents swirl around the islands and underwater mountains, causing areas of turbulence, small waterspouts and whirlpools. If conditions are right, the feature called 'Old Sow' near the New Brunswick shore of Passamaquoddy Bay can form a single, large whirlpool within an area of churning water as much as 76m (250ft) across. The erosion caused by this mass of water being sucked in and out of the bay for thousands of years has formed a spectacular landscape of cliffs, sea stacks and sea caves, in places revealing fossils that have lain here for hundreds of millions of years. There is much wildlife in the area, but it is the big cetaceans for which the Bay of Fundy is most famous. Among frequent visitors here are finback, minke and sei whales, while blue and humpback whales and orca are spotted less often. However, it is the rare and endangered northern right whales that come here in summer that make this such a special place for wildlife-watching.

THE LAURENTIANS

Canada

The Laurentian Mountains are an outstandingly beautiful range in Quebec. This area of mountain and lakeland scenery was first colonized in the late 19th century and has been a popular attraction for outdoor enthusiasts for more than 60 years. These ancient mountains, ground down by glaciers, wind and water over millions of years, average between 300 and 520m (984 and 1,706ft) in height, with the highest being Mont Tremblant at 968m (3,175ft). The village and resort of the same name are at the centre of the winter skiing area. This land had long been a fruitful area for Amerindians to hunt wildlife and gather food and it is still rich in wildlife. Bird-watchers in particular are spoiled for choice by the range of birds here in the summer: it is best known as a haven for great northern divers, known locally as loons, whose eerie laughing and wailing are a constant background noise on the lakes in summer. The sugar maples that add red to the yellows, browns and golds of autumn in late September are tapped in spring, and in summer the area is popular for hiking, horse riding, cycling, fishing, rafting and kayaking. The landscape is spectacular and worth a visit at any time of year, whether it is blanketed in deep snow, just flushed with the greens of spring leaves or filled with birdsong in summer.

ORCAS

Canada

Orcas (*Orcinus orca*), commonly known as killer whales, are one of the world's best-known marine mammals. The world's fastest-swimming sea mammals, orcas are immediately recognizable by their black and white markings. One of the best places in the world to see them is off the coast of British Columbia, where a population known as the Southern Residents live. Their range stretches from Puget Sound, across the United States border and north to about halfway up Vancouver Island. A second population, the Northern Residents, inhabit the waters of northern British Columbia, but are not as well known. The Southern Residents support a huge whale-watching industry, but they are under threat, with numbers declining. The orcas are an indicator species that show the state of the marine environment, and unhappily, scientific studies show that these are some of the world's most contaminated marine mammals.

GROS MORNE NATIONAL PARK

Canada

The island of Newfoundland is the easternmost part of Canada, and situated on its rugged west coast is Gros Morne National Park – part of the Long Range Mountains that stretch the whole length of that side of the island. Some 20 times older than the Rocky Mountains, the peaks have been worn down over millennia by glaciation. Gros Morne National Park is an area of extraordinary natural beauty. It was declared a UNESCO World Heritage Site in 1987 not only for its visual impact but also because its topography reveals the major stages of the evolutionary history of the planet. Possibly its most spectacular feature is Western Brook Pond, a 30-km (19-mile) fjord-like structure. Western Brook Pond, however, was later cut off from the ocean, and is filled with pure, fresh, dark-blue water that cascades from the plateau above it.

GEORGIAN BAY ISLANDS NATIONAL PARK

Canada

DON'T MISS
Hiking the Cambrian trail on northern Beausoleil Island.

Georgian Bay Islands National Park stretches along the eastern shoreline of the bay, and is made up of 59 small islands and shoals. Within a 30,000-island archipelago, it is part of the world's largest group of freshwater islands and lies on the edge of the Canadian Shield. Known for the extraordinary variety of flora and fauna existing within an unusually small area, this beautiful region of fabulous vistas and crystal-clear waters is perfect for kayaking and canoeing, camping and hiking. Beausoleil Island, the largest in the park, is formed from hard shield rock that supports plant species such as juniper, red oak and white pine, twisted and buffeted by the wind. Scraped clean by the retreat of ancient glaciers, the barren rocks are lichen-covered and speckled with small bogs and ponds, enabling 33 species of amphibians and reptiles to live here – more than in any other part of the country. In summer, colourful wildflowers abound. Come autumn, the forests are aflame with reds and yellows as the leaves put on their magnificent display.

THE ROCKY MOUNTAINS

Canada

HOW TO GET THERE:
From Vancouver, Edmonton or Calgary.
WHEN TO GO:
Year-round.
NEAREST TOWNS:
There are many small towns located in the Rockies; the largest is Banff with a population of almost 8,000.

YOU SHOULD KNOW
If you are short of time you can take a two-day train tour through the Rockies. Travelling only in daylight, you are afforded spectacular views from the comfort of your seat.

The Rocky Mountains form part of an almost continuous chain of mountains that stretch from Alaska down practically the entire length of the West Coast of the Americas. The Canadian Rockies encompass a vast area that includes five national parks. Four of these, Banff, Jasper, Yoho and Kootenay, not only interlock with each other but also with three British Columbia provincial parks. Altogether these parks were declared a UNESCO World Heritage Site in 1984.

The Canadian Rockies are both older than, and geologically different from, the American Rockies. They are largely formed of sedimentary rock that has been severely glaciated, resulting in sharp, craggy-peaked mountains separated by broad valleys created by glaciers. The highest is the impressive Mount Robson, which stands at 3,954m (12,972ft). The backbone of the Canadian Rockies is the Continental Divide, which runs the length of the range and separates Alberta from British Columbia. The scenery is utterly spectacular on both sides of the mountains, although the parks of Banff and Jasper are the best known. Roads run parallel on both sides of the range, and there are four routes that cross over it. The most spectacular of these runs through Glacier National Park, with its awe-inspiring glacial peaks and vivid turquoise alpine lakes. The Rockies provide the opportunity to explore one of the most beautiful wilderness areas imaginable. Here you can hike, climb and horse-ride to your heart's content. The more adventurous can heli-hike through fabulous landscapes swathed in wildflowers during spring, or heli-ski in winter. Helicopters fly visitors up to lodge resorts and then ferry them to high mountain peaks for several different ski runs per day, each on virgin snow.

GREAT BEAR LAKE
Canada

Canada's Northwest Territories cover almost one-third of the country – an area of approximately 3 million sq km (1.88 million sq miles), with half of it lying north of the Arctic Circle. Great Bear Lake, the largest lake in the country, straddles the Arctic Circle, on the edge of the Canadian Shield. Visited by traders from the North West Company circa 1800, a trading post was subsequently set up, and in 1825 a British explorer began building a town on the southwest shore, now know as Deline, which is still inhabited. In the 1930s radium was discovered at the eastern side of the lake, and numerous mines, all long exhausted, were sited there.

HOW TO GET THERE:
By charter plane from Norman Wells. A landing strip serves all the camps on the lake. It is possible to canoe down the Great Bear river from Tulita.
WHEN TO GO:
June, July and August.
NEAREST TOWN:
Tulita 128km (80 miles).

Great Bear Lake drains to the west, where the Great Bear river flows down into Canada's longest river, the Mackenzie, which itself finally empties into the Beaufort Sea. The lake is about 320km (200 miles) long and its width varies from 40–177km (25–110 miles). Its shoreline is 2,719km (1,690 miles) around. Formed from pre-glacial valleys reshaped by ice during the Pleistocene age, and changed again when the ice melted, the lake has five 'arms' and contains numerous little islands. Great Bear Lake, which is frozen for eight months of the year, remains extraordinarily clear to a depth of about 31m (100ft). It is, of course, a freshwater lake, and its pristine waters teem with fish. Probably the world's biggest lake trout and grayling can be fished here, though hunting regulations, which also apply to anglers, ensure the conservation of the rich natural resources. The shoreline shelters a variety of wildlife, including elk and pine martens, as well as the grizzly bears from which it took its name.

DINOSAUR PROVINCIAL PARK

Canada

HOW TO GET THERE:
Two-hour drive east from Calgary.
WHEN TO GO:
Open all year except for weekends and holidays from October to May.
NEAREST TOWN:
Brooks 48km (30 miles).

Approximately 75 million years ago, this region was a subtropical wilderness consisting of dense forest and lush vegetation covering a coastal plain. Rivers ran east into a shallow, inland sea, producing a habitat perfect for numerous creatures, including sharks, crocodiles, marsupials and, of course, dinosaurs. This habitat was also perfect for the preservation of their fossilized skeletons. Situated in southern Alberta, Dinosaur Provincial Park is located in the valley of the Red Deer river, amidst the province's spectacular badlands. Not only is the scenery extraordinary, but also it contains some of the most important dinosaur fossil beds ever to have been found. Five trails meander through the park, enabling visitors to see the three separate habitats it encompasses. Gently rolling prairie grassland suddenly becomes eerie sandstone badlands, haunted by extraordinarily beautiful pinnacles and buttes carved by wind and water. Listed as a Natural World Heritage Site in 1979, the next 12 years produced a collection of over 23,000 fossils, including 300 dinosaur skeletons from almost 40 distinct species. In 1987, a field station of the Royal Tyrell Museum of Palaeontology was opened within the park to support the ongoing, long-term research and monitoring programmes that are in progress here. A visitor centre provides a wealth of fascinating information about the fossils and also the park's ecosystem.

NAHANNI NATIONAL PARK

Canada

HOW TO GET THERE:
By private air charter of floatplane or helicopter.
WHEN TO GO:
July or August.
NEAREST TOWN:
Fort Simpson 280km (175 miles).

This pristine wilderness park was one of the very first places in the world to be listed as a UNESCO World Heritage Site, in 1978. This reflects its remarkably beautiful and unusual nature. Nahanni's key feature is the wild and wonderful South Nahanni river that, uniquely amongst mountainous rivers, was formed when the region was still a wide, flat plain. As the mountains rose upwards, the river gouged four steep canyons to maintain its original winding course. About 300km (190 miles) of the river's length runs through Nahanni. The spectacular, vertical plunge of Virginia Falls drops 90m (292ft) – double that of the far more famous Niagara Falls. There are a number of unique features along the river and different types of habitat producing a rich diversity of flora. For example, there is an area of rare orchids near the falls. Nahanni is home to cave systems and lakes and wild white water that attract up to 1,000 adventurous visitors each year.

WOOD BUFFALO NATIONAL PARK

Canada

HOW TO GET THERE:
By plane from Edmonton to Fort Smith, then by plane or by road.
WHEN TO GO:
June to August.
NEAREST TOWNS:
Hay River, adjacent to the park, or Fort Smith in the NWT 280km (175 miles).

Wood Buffalo National Park was established in 1922. It is located on the boundary between Alberta and the Northwest Territories, and was designated a UNESCO World Heritage Site in 1983. It was created specifically to protect North America's largest free-roaming bison herd, some 2,500 animals, but it also contains the only natural nesting grounds of the critically endangered whooping crane. Wood Buffalo is Canada's largest national park, a boreal forest zone covering 44,807 sq km (17,300 sq miles). Within its boundaries there are fire-scarred forested uplands, a glacially eroded plateau, a major freshwater delta formed by three major rivers, salt plains and some of the best examples of karst topography in North America. It also contains the largest undisturbed grass and sedge meadows in North America, making it ideal bison country. The park has the longest tradition of native subsistence use in the country. It has been inhabited since the glaciers retreated, most recently by nomadic Micasew-Cree First Nation groups, some of whom still fish, hunt and trap here. The climate is one of long, cold winters and short, warm summers, and it is only frost-free in June, July and August.

There are 47 species of mammal here, including caribou, Arctic fox, black bear, moose, beaver and muskrat, and 227 bird species have been recorded, including peregrine falcons and bald eagles, as well as great grey and snowy owls. The bison are self-regulating and it is one of the few places left in the world where a genuine predator-versus-prey relationship exists between wolves and bison. The whooping cranes number some 140 individuals, of which there are 40 breeding pairs. The careful management and protection of these birds within the park, and the protection of their winter grounds in Texas, may have saved them from extinction.

POLAR BEARS AND CHURCHILL

Canada

HOW TO GET THERE: By plane or train from Winnipeg.
WHEN TO GO: October and November.

Churchill is found on the western shore of Hudson Bay, in northern Manitoba. Each autumn, thousands of visitors flock here, anxious to view the polar bears (*Ursus maritimus*) for which the town is internationally known. During the season you can expect to see up to 20 bears a day. However, come the end of November, both the polar bears and the visitors depart, leaving the 900 full-time residents to their bitter winter. This is a polar bear migration route. As they return from their summer on land, they congregate near Churchill waiting for the ice to form at sea so they can begin their annual seal hunt. In Churchill itself, bears are drawn to the municipal rubbish dumps. They are aggressive, dangerous animals, but troublesome bears are captured and transported to a safer – for everyone – location. Adult male polar bears are the world's largest terrestrial carnivore. Their apparently off-white fur is made of long, light, hollow, pigment-free hairs, specially adapted to maximize heat retention. Their huge feet, furred underneath to protect the pads from frostbite, spread their weight, thus enabling them to walk on ice that would not hold a human. Tragically, polar bears are seriously threatened by global warming.

YOU SHOULD KNOW

If you visit during summer, you can see the only remaining healthy population of beluga whales, which migrate here at this time.

THE GRAND CANYON

Arizona, USA

HOW TO GET THERE:
Highway 64 or rail from Williams.
WHEN TO GO:
The south rim is open all year but is busy in summer. The north rim is shut from mid-October to mid-May. The lower reaches of the canyon are extremely hot in summer.
NEAREST TOWN:
Williams 95km (60 miles).

Right: The Grand Canyon from Toroweap Point

The Grand Canyon, cut into layer after layer of the colourful sedimentary rocks of the Colorado plateau by the Colorado river and its tributaries, is one of the world's most spectacular landmarks. It lies within northern Arizona's Grand Canyon National Park, which was designated in 1919. The youngest rocks, at the top, were laid down by an inland sea some 260 million years ago, and a journey down into the canyon peels away millions of years of geological history as the different layers of rock are revealed. It is not just the sense of our planet's past that is awe-inspiring, it is the sheer size of the canyon, which is some 1.5km (1 mile) deep and has views that stretch across more than 16km (10 miles), a scale difficult to imagine until you are confronted with the reality of it.

HORSESHOE CRABS

Delaware, USA

At the mouth of the Delaware river, with New Jersey to the northeast and Delaware to the west and south, lies Delaware Bay. This is the largest spawning area in the world of the horseshoe crab *(Limulus polyphemus)*, an ancient creature more closely related to spiders and scorpions than to crabs. Sometimes referred to as 'living fossils', they evolved some 500 million years ago, and have changed very little since then. They look forbidding, growing up to 50cm (20in) in length, and covered with hard, curved shells. The fearsome tail, far from being a weapon, is used partly as a rudder and partly to right itself if flipped over. They have gills allowing them to breathe both underwater and, for brief periods, on land. Horseshoe crabs are extremely valuable in medical research. Most of what is known about human eye function, and malfunction, is as a result of studying their large, compound eyes. They also possess a brilliant immune system that traps bacteria in a clot of gel-like substance. Blood samples are taken for testing intravenous drugs and finding remedies for diseases that have become immune to antibiotics. All intravenous drugs used in hospitals have had a horseshoe crab test – the crabs themselves are left unharmed.

HOW TO GET THERE:
By road.
WHEN TO GO:
April to October.
NEAREST TOWN:
Dover, Delaware's capital, 13km (8 miles).

DON'T MISS
New Castle; Lewes; Delaware's beaches.

BLUEGRASS COUNTRY

Kentucky, USA

HOW TO GET THERE:
Fly to Lexington and hire a car, or drive.
WHEN TO GO:
Any time of year, but don't forget Derby Day is held on the first Saturday in May.
NEAREST TOWNS:
Towns and villages abound. The state capital is Frankfort.

Kentucky's Bluegrass Country is located in the north-central part of the state. It is a highly attractive area of rolling hills, elegant, antebellum mansions, picturesque villages, miles of stone and wooden fencing and horses galore. It is also peppered with historic Bourbon distilleries, including that of Jim Beam and Maker's Mark. The grass is not actually blue, but in spring it produces purple-blue buds which, seen from a distance, lend it a blue hue. The Kentucky river with its associated karst topography runs through the region. The Bluegrass region was first settled in the 1770s by wealthy families whose slaves helped create large estates, reminiscent of those in England – even the countryside looked somewhat similar. Lexington is the self-styled 'horse capital of the world', and indeed there are more thoroughbred breeding farms in the area than in any other part of the world. The calcium-rich bluegrass is good for the horses' bones, and horses provide Kentucky with a multimillion dollar industry. The Kentucky Derby, held annually at Louisville, is the USA's premier horserace.

BRACKEN CAVE BAT ROOST, SAN ANTONIO

Texas, USA

Ever since the end of the last ice age, some 10,000 years ago, Bracken Cave has been a home to bats. Today, during the summer months, an enormous colony of Mexican free-tailed bats (*Tadarida brasiliensis*) breed and rear their young here. These bats are widely distributed across the southern states of the USA, through Central America and most of western South America as far south as central Chile. Most of them, however, live in Mexico and Texas. Since 1992, Bat Conservation International (BCI) has been doing its best to buy up land around Bracken Cave in order to form a protection zone for the colony. Thanks to local landowners and various foundations, BCI has managed to acquire 280 hectares (692 acres) around the cave, upon which they intend to build an international centre for the study of bats. Bracken Cave contains the largest known concentration of mammals in the world. Each spring over 20 million Mexican free-tailed bats arrive from Mexico to breed, giving birth to one baby each, and leaving again in the late autumn. The sight of 20 million bats emerging from this cave at dusk is truly one of nature's most awesome wonders.

GLACIER BAY NATIONAL PARK AND PRESERVE

Alaska, USA

YOU SHOULD KNOW
You can stay in the small community of Gustavus that is adjacent to the park.

Situated on the Gulf of Alaska in the southeastern part of the country, Glacier Bay National Park and Preserve is an icy wonderland of snowy mountains and dazzling glaciers. It was designated a national monument in 1925, and added to the UNESCO World Heritage Site as part of a vast trans-border park system that includes Canada's Tatshenshini–Alsek and Kluane National Parks. The park covers 13,053 sq km (8,160 sq miles) and includes much of Mount Fairweather and the American section of the Alsek river as well as Glacier Bay itself. In 1794, Captain George Vancouver discovered Icy Strait, situated at the southern end of the bay. All he could find was an enormous glacier, but by 1879 John Muir, the naturalist, found that the glacier had retreated 80km (50 miles), leaving Glacier Bay in its wake. Today the park is formed from the largest group of high peaks on the continent, the largest ice fields outside the polar caps and 16 huge tidewater glaciers. These last are still retreating every year, and vast icebergs sheer off and plunge into the water.

PETRIFIED FOREST

Arizona, USA

HOW TO GET THERE:
By car.
WHEN TO GO:
Year-round, except
Christmas Day.
NEAREST TOWN:
Holbrook 19km (12 miles).

In 1906, President Theodore Roosevelt named the Petrified Forest a national monument, and archaeology shows that there has been a human presence here for over 2,000 years. This region was a trade route through to the Pacific Coast, and has been used by everyone from ancient Indians to the visitors of today. In the 1850s a surveyor for the transcontinental railroad brought back tales of 'trees turned to stone', and soon afterwards ranchers and farmers arrived, who mined the petrified wood for semiprecious stones. The Petrified Forest contains the remains of 225-million-year-old forests that were home to dinosaurs, giant fish-eating amphibians and large reptiles. This was once a floodplain, and the forests were washed into it and covered with volcanic ash and silt, slowing their decay. Silica-bearing water gradually seeped through and encased the trees, eventually crystallizing them into quartz. The region later flooded and sank, and during its next uplift, the trees cracked into giant logs. Even today erosion continues to break the logs and expose more beneath the surface of the ground. In some places 92m (300ft) of fossil-bearing material remains to be exposed. Scientists continue to study all aspects of this extraordinary area. The Rainbow Forest Museum has a fantastic collection of fossils, including dinosaurs, from the Triassic era, and throughout the area there are wonderful examples of rock art carved by early inhabitants.

DENALI (MT MCKINLEY)

Alaska, USA

HOW TO GET THERE:
By road to the park or plane to
the Kahiltna Glacier.
WHEN TO GO:
April, May and June are the
best climbing months.
NEAREST TOWNS:
Talkeetna 120km (75 miles);
Anchorage 209km (130 miles).

Denali, more generally known as Mt McKinley, is a majestic, towering, snow- and ice-clad mountain, flanked by five large glaciers. It is situated in the centre of the Alaska Mountain Range and utterly dominates Denali National Park, of which it is the centrepiece. This is the highest peak in North America, rising to 6,194m (20,320ft), and it has a larger bulk and rise than that of Mount Everest. More than 50 per cent of the mountain is covered with snow and ice, and it is a magnet for mountaineers. Technically it is not too difficult to climb, but conditions on the mountain are the worst in the world. Apart from the extreme cold – which can reach -71°C (-95°F) in winter – and ferocious winds exacerbated by its proximity to the jet stream, climbers face a severe risk of altitude sickness due to the high altitude. This is a dangerous mountain to climb: some 50 per cent of attempts fail to reach the summit.

THE EVERGLADES

Florida, USA

The Everglades National Park, in southern Florida, is the largest protected wilderness in the southeastern United States and was designated by President Truman in 1947 in order to protect it from land reclamation for agriculture. This stunning green, marshy landscape, with wide blue skies, is also a UNESCO World Heritage Site because of the importance of the habitat and animals it shelters. It is formed by the slow movement of fresh water southwards from the Orlando Kissimmee river system via the massive Lake Okeechobee. The park protects one-fifth of the original extent of the Everglades, of which about half remains. The wildlife in this lush, green landscape is justifiably famous: seemingly innumerable alligators and much rarer American crocodiles sun themselves on river banks or skulk beneath the water waiting for prey; the estuaries are full of such birds as egrets, spoonbills, wood storks and herons; while the endangered manatee may be seen around the coast and in estuaries. Although they contain both cypress and mangrove swamps, the Everglades are technically a very slow-moving river, known locally as the river of grass. This subtropical land also has broad swathes of sawgrass and internationally important areas of rock pineland. The main road through the park runs from Florida City on the east coast to Flamingo on the Gulf of Mexico and is known as 'Alligator Alley' because of the hundreds of these prehistoric animals that can be seen from the road. Short-distance walking trails, long-distance hiking routes, canoes and air-boat tours allow visitors to explore this beautiful and threatened landscape.

HOW TO GET THERE:
On State Road 9336 (Alligator Alley) from Florida City.
WHEN TO GO:
December to April is mild, relatively dry and mosquito-free.
NEAREST TOWN:
Florida City 15km (9 miles).

YOU SHOULD KNOW
The park headquarters is at the Ernest F. Coe Visitor Center, and there are visitor centres at Everglades City, Flamingo and Shark Valley.

THE SMOKY MOUNTAINS

Tennessee/North Carolina, USA

One of the most popular recreation areas of the eastern United States, the Smoky Mountains lie on the border between Tennessee and North Carolina. They are part of the Appalachians, the range that runs north–east/south–west from Maine to Georgia. Like the Blue Ridge Mountains in Virginia and the Blue Mountains of New South Wales in Australia, they get their name from the bluish haze, given off by trees, that hovers over them in summer. In summer, this beautiful area is a haven for hikers and walkers, and has some of the most stunning scenery and challenging ground to be found on the entire length of the 3,500-km (2,174-mile) Appalachian National Scenic Trail, the AT. At 2,030m (6,643ft), Clingmans Dome is the highest point on the AT, but the less adventurous can get to within 91m (300ft) of the summit by car to appreciate the magnificent views. The park is noted for the wealth of its wildflowers, including spectacular meadow flowers, orchids, rhododendrons and azaleas, and in autumn it nearly rivals the leaf colours of New England. Its most famous inhabitants are black bears. Other popular activities in the park are whitewater rafting and tubing in summer, and skiing during the brief winter season.

HOW TO GET THERE:
By road from Atlanta or Charlotte.
WHEN TO GO:
Any time of year.
NEAREST TOWN:
Gatlinburg.

CRATER LAKE

Oregon, USA

Some 7,700 years ago, a large volcano in what is now known as the Cascade Range produced an enormous eruption, 42 times more powerful than the 1980 eruption of Mount St Helens. The uppermost 1,538m (5,000ft) of the volcano collapsed to form a caldera that was subsequently sealed by lava flows and is now known as Crater Lake. The local Native American Klamath people considered the lake and its surroundings to be sacred, with the result that it remained undiscovered by white explorers until 1853. In 1902 Theodore Roosevelt designated the lake area a national park. The lake, known for its extraordinary, deep blue colour, lies high up, at over 1,846m (6,000 ft), and is the deepest in the United States. Remarkably, it has no inlets or outlets, and the exceedingly pure water comes from melted snow and rain.

CHESAPEAKE BAY

Virginia/Maryland/Delaware, USA

DON'T MISS
Annapolis, the 'sailing capital of the world'.

Chesapeake Bay was formed 10,000 years ago and is the largest estuary on the continent. Almost 320km (200 miles) long, it stretches from southern Virginia to northern Maryland and is a shallow, tidal area where salt water and fresh water come together. Historically renowned for its rich supply of seafood, particularly clams, crabs and oysters, it still yields a larger harvest of seafood than any other estuary in the country. The shoreline of Chesapeake Bay covers almost 19,000km (12,000 miles) – a glorious region of channels, waterways, farmland, historic towns, marinas and picturesque harbours. Find a tranquil haven in which to anchor, and enjoy silence broken only by birdcalls, eat crabs at a lively waterfront restaurant or search for fossilized sharks teeth at the foot of Calvert Cliffs – there is something here to appeal to everyone.

SAN ANDREAS FAULT, CARRIZO PLAIN

California, USA

The legendary San Andreas Fault is at least 16km (10 miles) deep and runs for some 1,280km (800 miles) through western and southern California. The fault is caused by the meeting and shifting of the Pacific and the North American plates and forms the boundary between the two. When the build-up of pressure breaks open the fault, earthquakes are the result. The San Andreas Fault is quite visible as a linear trough, particularly from the air, and on the ground it can be clearly seen on the Carrizo Plain. Here on this long, arid, treeless plain, geological research has been conducted since 1908, two years after the devastating San Francisco earthquake. Studies have shown that large earthquakes have occurred in this region roughly every 150 years for the past 1,500 years, making it a potential danger area – the last large quake was in 1857. Although it is impossible to prevent earthquakes, structures can be built to withstand them. Here on Carrizo Plain, streams can be seen turning sharply north as they cross the fault line. In the centre of the plain lies Soda Lake, which forms each winter and provides habitat for migratory birds. Having no outlet, the lake evaporates during summer, and the salts that are left are blown skyward in great white columns.

CADILLAC MOUNTAIN, ACADIA NATIONAL PARK

Maine, USA

Acadia National Park, off Maine's Atlantic Coast, comprises Mount Desert Island, parts of three smaller, neighbouring islands, and some of the mainland's Schoodic Peninsula. Mount Desert Island contains 17 mountains, including the famous Cadillac Mountain. Formed of pink granite and covered with pitch pine and spruce forests, its summit, between 7 October and 6 March of every year, is thought to be the first place in the USA to receive the sun's rays. From here, on a clear day, it is possible to see both Nova Scotia, lying over 160km (100 miles) to the east and, at a similar distance to the north, Maine's highest peak, Mount Katahdin. Views over the park itself are utterly delightful, and can be explored by following the glorious 43-km (27-mile) one-way Park Loop Road. The park is unique in that it exists largely thanks to private citizens who, realizing the dangers of overdevelopment, helped to create it. President Woodrow Wilson designated it a national monument in 1916, and in 1929 it was named Acadia.

THE BLACK HILLS

South Dakota, USA

The Black Hills of South Dakota are named for the dark, ponderosa pines that cover them. The area covers some 12,800 sq km (8,000 sq miles) and has been aptly described as 'an island of trees in a sea of grass'. The Hills are dotted with lush mountain meadows, and the southern edge is covered with a dry pine savannah due to the rain shadow of the higher elevations. In fact these are mountains rather than hills, with elevations of up to 2,154m (7,000ft). This legendary region contains a wealth of treasures, including one of the USA's most popular tourist attractions, Mount Rushmore. This high granite cliff is carved with the 18.5-m (60-ft) faces of four of the country's most influential presidents. Custer State Park, at the heart of the Black Hills, is a stunning area and is home to many species of wildlife, including bison. Drive the amazing Needles Highway that twists and turns through tunnels and around extraordinary rock formations. Needles Eye, a narrow rock spire standing almost 12.3m (40ft) high, can be found near the exit of one tunnel.

CAVE OF THE WINDS

Colorado, USA

Situated on the eastern slopes of the Rocky Mountains in the Pikes Peak region of Colorado, the Cave of the Winds is a vast, underground, limestone cave network. Still being explored and mapped, it is currently recognized as the fourth-longest cave in the world. So far over 195km (121 miles) of passages have been mapped, largely by volunteers. Serious exploration of the caves began in the 1890s, and the first official survey began in 1902. However the big breakthrough did not occur until the 1960s, with the discovery of a new passageway that was named the Spillway. This led to the realization that there was an enormous labyrinthine area to the west. The original caves and sinkholes were formed some 320 million years ago, but the major cave development occurred some 40–50 million years ago, after the uplift of the hills. There are a number of guided tours that lead you through this maze of rooms and passageways. Some, such as the Lantern Tour and the Explorer's Trip, are more adventurous than others. Whatever your choice, you can't fail to be awed and impressed by this extraordinary underground world.

THE PAINTED DESERT

Arizona, USA

HOW TO GET THERE:
By road.
WHEN TO GO:
Year-round, except
Christmas Day.
NEAREST TOWN:
Holbrook 64km (40 miles).

The Painted Desert is an area of multicoloured badlands that curves southeast from the Grand Canyon to the Petrified Forest National Park. It is roughly 256km (160 miles) in length, and between 16km (10 miles) and 64km (40 miles) wide. Part of the Chinle Formation, these hills are formed from layers of sediments of sandstone and mudstone deposited on what was once a huge flood plain. This high plateau is an arid region, with little vegetation, and it has been – and continues to be – heavily eroded by wind and water: the flat-topped mesas and buttes we see today will eventually be just another part of the rolling hills. Deep gullies have been carved through the hills, the tops of which have been softened and rounded as the soil is washed away, but it is this same erosion that enables us to see the fantastic banded colours that have given the region its name. These are the result of the different mineral content of the sediments, and the rate at which they were laid down. When the process is slow, oxides of aluminium and iron become highly concentrated, turning the soil orange, red and pink. When it occurs quickly, a lack of oxygen creates blues, lavenders and greys. Seen at sunset, the colours positively glow.

HOW TO GET THERE: By road.
WHEN TO GO: Throughout the year.
NEAREST TOWN: New York City 160km (100 miles).

THE CATSKILL MOUNTAINS

New York, USA

Situated northwest of New York City, the Catskill Mountains are actually a mature, dissected plateau region of the Appalachian Mountains. This is an area of some 9,600 sq km (6,000 sq miles) to the west of the Hudson river, and is made up of heavily wooded, rolling terrain studded with gorges and rivers, waterfalls and lakes that supply New York with water. Many of the peaks reach an elevation of 923m (3,000ft) and the highest, Slide Mountain, is a little over 1,230m (4,000ft). During the 1800s the area was quite rapidly developed as a centre for lumber, and bluestone and flagstone was excavated from the mountains. The first railway line was opened in 1828, adding to the speed of development. This in turn led to one of the earliest conservation movements, and from 1885 legislation was enacted to protect and preserve the area. This region has attracted holiday-makers from the city for over 100 years, and it contains resorts, attractive riverside towns and villages and outdoor recreation centres. There are endless recreational opportunities here, available at all times of year, including fly fishing in Beaverkill river, possibly the most famous trout river in the country, and many fashionable, arty towns such as Woodstock and Kingston to explore.

DON'T MISS
Kings Canyon
National Park.

GIANT REDWOODS

California, USA

Giant redwood trees, or sequoias, are the largest trees in the world, and possibly the largest living organisms on the planet. Members of the yew family, there are three distinct species: giant redwood, coastal redwood and dawn redwood.

HOW TO GET THERE:
By road.
WHEN TO GO:
Open all year.
NEAREST TOWN:
Visalia 78km (49 miles).

The first two types are to be found in California, and the last is native to China. Sequoias only grow in the Sierra Nevada mountains and are a breathtaking sight. Humboldt Redwood State Park contains the last virgin redwood groves in the world, and is both a World Heritage Site and part of an International Biosphere reserve.

These trees are up to 3,000 years old and grow to a height of over 91m (300ft), reaching up through the mist and fog of California's coastal climate to tower over the surrounding forest of firs and pines. The largest tree of all is named General Sherman, and is 83.8m (274.9ft) tall. Sequoias are not only tall, they are also broad: the trunk of Shrine Drive-Through Tree can indeed be driven through, and Tharp's Log is a cabin built out of one fallen, hollowed-out tree. Roads wind up into the Giant Forest where a new museum provides information about the trees and the efforts being made to protect them. The grandeur of these remarkable trees is truly one of nature's wonders. The lofty tranquillity of these groves gives the visitor a feeling of awe in the knowledge that the sequoias will still be standing here long after we have gone.

YOU SHOULD KNOW
An entrance fee is payable.

CAPE COD

Massachusetts, USA

The easternmost part of Massachusetts is the peninsula known as Cape Cod. Shaped like an arm flexing its muscles, it reaches 96km (60 miles) into the ocean. Attached to the mainland at the 'shoulder', the opening of the Cape Cod Canal in 1914 turned the peninsula into an island accessed by bridges. Around 18,000 years ago the Laurentide ice sheet was in retreat, and as it melted, so sea levels rose. Finally the sea was sufficiently high to start eroding the glacial deposits left on the peninsula, some of which were washed to the peninsula's northern tip, others to the south, where they formed islands. Cape Cod's Atlantic-facing shore is still being reshaped by the tides and the winds. Cape Cod has a population of about 230,000, but every summer thousands of visitors flock here from New England and further afield to enjoy the pleasant climate, beautiful beaches and delicious seafood. The nearby islands have attracted America's wealthiest and most aristocratic families for over 100 years. In 1961, John F. Kennedy was instrumental in getting federal protection for 64km (40 miles) of open beach and rippling sand dunes as well as 17,000 hectares (43,000 acres) of Outer Cape land, which is known as Cape Cod National Seashore. No doubt this area would otherwise have been heavily developed by now.

THE BADLANDS

South Dakota, USA

Southwest South Dakota's Badlands National Park is an area rich in human history and palaeontology. Its banded rocks, a mixture of sand, silt and clay and volcanic ash, were laid down one on top of the other in the Oligocene period, which lasted from 35.4 to 23.3 million years ago. The area was a vast floodplain, and the fossils uncovered here are the remains of animals caught in floods and quickly buried in sedimentary rocks. Over hundreds of thousands of years, the White river carved out a course in the soft rocks, at an average of 2.5cm (1in) a year, although at times erosion occurs much more rapidly. The Wall, the sheer cliff that marks the river's course, is continually moving northwards, exposing the harder, older rocks underneath, and leaving an eerie, beautiful land of isolated buttes, ridges, pinnacles and spires behind, particularly in the wind-sculpted forms of the Sage Creek Wilderness Area. This area was used as summer hunting grounds by Native Americans for some 11,000 years, and eventually saw some of the most bitter struggles between Native Americans and settlers. The Badlands are an area of stunning, if desolate, beauty that must be seen.

ADIRONDACK STATE PARK

New York, USA

HOW TO GET THERE:
More than 40 roads enter the park and there is also the Adirondack regional airport.
WHEN TO GO:
Year-round.
NEAREST TOWNS:
There are 105 towns and villages within the park's boundaries.

Situated in northeastern New York State lies a vast region of 2.5 million hectares (6.1 million acres): the Adirondack State Park. The largest park in the USA, it is a combination of publicly and privately owned land. The publicly owned portion, about 43 per cent, is constitutionally bound to remain 'forever wild'. To the northeast rise the Adirondack Mountains – 42 peaks reaching over 1,230m (4,000ft), 11 with alpine summits. People come here from all over the world to enjoy downhill and cross-country skiing, dog-sledding and other winter sports. The western and southern Adirondacks are made up of gentle hills, streams, lakes and ponds. There are 3,200km (2,000 miles) of hiking trails and 2,400km (1,500 miles) of rivers, so it comes as no surprise that some 7–10 million visitors come here annually.

GLACIER NATIONAL PARK

Montana, USA

This magnificent region of pristine wilderness is located in the northwest of Montana. There are no large cities anywhere nearby and few roads, but in 1921 construction began on the Going to the Sun Road, a staggering feat of engineering that took 11 years to complete. This is one of the most beautiful drives in North America – 80.5km (52 miles) from east to west, it crosses the Continental Divide at Logan Pass, in the northern Rocky Mountains. The Park contains over 1,120km (700 miles) of hiking trails, almost 1,600km (1,000 miles) of rivers and streams and 2,000 lakes. Altogether, 1,132 plant species have been identified here. The remoteness of the area makes it rich in wildlife, and it is a marvellous place to get away from it all. There are beautifully sited, historic lodges in which to relax after a hard day's hiking.

YOU SHOULD KNOW
Hunting is illegal, but regulated fishing is permitted. Snowmobiling is illegal, but cross-country skiing is permitted at lower elevations.

HOW TO GET THERE: By plane, train or road.
WHEN TO GO: June to September.
NEAREST TOWNS: West Glacier and East Glacier are both on the edges of the park, or Kalispell 40km (25 miles).

DEATH VALLEY

California, USA

Situated in southeastern California, Death Valley is a region of extremes. Even though its name suggests a barren, desolate place, over 1,000 plant species and many animals live here, having adapted successfully to the harsh environment. The oldest rocks here are about 1.7 billion years old, and the mountains that border the valley show an incredibly complex geological history. This is the hottest, driest place in the country, yet there are snowcapped, forested mountains here as well as sand dunes, stone desert and water-carved canyons. Very little rain falls, but when it does, the desert suddenly blooms with a million wildflowers. At night the temperature drops rapidly – during winter it dips below freezing. However, day temperatures in the summer months are regularly around 50°C (120°F), so be prepared. This is an unforgiving, inhospitable place, but it is also remarkably beautiful in its way, and there are various popular spots such as Zabriskie Point and Dante's View, where visitors come to watch the sun rise or set over this unique landscape.

CARLSBAD CAVERNS NATIONAL PARK

New Mexico, USA

Carlsbad Caverns, in the Chihuahuan Desert, was first designated a national monument in 1923. It became a national park in 1930 and a World Heritage Site in 1995. It was established to protect and preserve over 100 known caves that include the deepest limestone cave in the United States. The caves are the remains of a fossil reef in an inland sea that covered the region some 250 million years ago. When this evaporated, the reef was buried under mineral salts and gypsum. Millions of years later, the reef began to reappear as the area uplifted and corrosive gases from enormous oil and gas deposits beneath the reef began to dissolve the limestone and form the huge caverns that we can see today. Prehistoric Native Americans sheltered in Carlsbad Caverns more than 1,000 years ago. The caves are renowned for their stalactites, stalagmites and rare formations of calcite and aragonite.

Left: The Chinese Theater in Carlsbad Caverns

METEOR CRATER

Arizona, USA

Meteor Crater is a huge, almost circular hole in the arid Arizona desert. It is 1,200m (4,100ft) in diameter and 173m (570ft) deep, and has a rim of rocks and boulders rising some 45m (150ft) above the surrounding area. Although there are other, larger meteorite craters in the world, the studies made of this one provided the first proof of meteoritic impact upon the Earth's surface. Estimated to be some 50,000 years old, the meteorite, formed of nickel iron, was about 50m (165ft) across. It hit the ground at about 12.8km (8 miles) per second, and roughly half its bulk was vapourized as it ploughed through our atmosphere before impact. Even so, it will have produced an incredible explosion, in the region of 150 times the force of the atomic bombs at Hiroshima and Nagasaki. Daniel Moreau Barringer, a mining engineer, originally suggested that this was a meteorite crater in 1903. Prior to this it had been thought to be the result of volcanic activity. Barringer's company bought the crater and found that it had been caused by a violent impact. His conclusions were met with disbelief from the scientific community so he decided to prove it to them by digging up the remains of the meteorite, not knowing that it had disintegrated when it hit. He spent 26 years drilling for metallic iron without success, and in 1929 he died, his hypothesis still unproven. It was not until 1960 that Eugene M. Shoemaker found two forms of silica in the crater that can only be created through an impact event, and was able to conclusively confirm Barringer's theory.

YOU SHOULD KNOW

The crater is still owned and run by the Barringer family. An entry fee is payable. Visitors may not enter the crater itself.

HOW TO GET THERE:
By road.
WHEN TO GO:
October to May.
NEAREST TOWN:
Winslow 32km (20 miles).

SAINT FRANCOIS MOUNTAINS

Missouri, USA

The Saint Francois Mountains were formed by violent volcanic activity over 1.4 billion years ago. These low, rounded mountains rise over the Ozark plateau and contain some of the oldest visible igneous rock in the country. They are thought to have been the only area in the midwest that was never submerged by ancient seas, and the fossilized remains of reefs can still be seen at the base of the mountains. There are many marvellous natural features such as the Devil's Honeycomb, an area of igneous rhyolite that has formed unusual geometric honeycomb shapes Here, too, is Tam Sauk Mountain, at 540m (1,772ft) the highest point in Missouri, and easy to reach via a paved trail. Johnson's Shut-ins is a natural water park. Formed as the Black river carved its way through fractures within black and pink volcanic rocks, it is an area of deep waterholes, waterslides, whirlpools and cascades that attract so many visitors during summer that only a limited number of cars is allowed entry to the state park at any one time.

GREAT SALT LAKE

Utah, USA

DON'T MISS
The Bonneville Salt Flats.

The Great Salt Lake covers an area about 120km (75 miles) long and 56km (35 miles) wide, with an average depth of about 9m (30ft). The largest salt lake in the western hemisphere, it is the remains of the great Lake Bonneville, which covered most of western Utah, and receded after the end of the ice age. Ancient terraces carved by wave action can be seen as dark lines high up on the surrounding hills. Water from rivers and streams empties into the lake, bringing dissolved salt and other minerals with it, and as there is no outlet, constant evaporation concentrates the salt and leaves it there. Great Salt Lake is three to five times more saline than the ocean, and no fish inhabit it. However, several types of algae live in the lake, and brine shrimp that feed on algae thrive here. Antelope Island, a state park, is one of several islands in Great Salt Lake. It is popular for its clean, white-sand beaches, and for the fact that the warm water is so salty that it is impossible not to float. Wildlife is plentiful, but it is birdlife for which the area is known. There are several bird management areas and sanctuaries both around the shores and on some of the smaller islands.

YOSEMITE NATIONAL PARK

California, USA

HOW TO GET THERE:
By road from San Francisco or Fresno.
WHEN TO GO:
The park is open all year, although some approaches are shut during winter. The waterfalls are at their best in May.
NEAREST TOWN:
Mariposa 70km (43 miles).

YOU SHOULD KNOW
Black bears are effective scavengers: all food must be kept secure and covered so they cannot smell it.

Yosemite, high in California's Sierra Nevada, is a startlingly beautiful place, with iconic mountains and rock formations, stunning waterfalls, lush alpine meadows and forests filled with awe-inspiring trees. Features such as Half Dome and El Capitan are hauntingly familiar even to those who have never been here, largely because of the photographer Ansel Adams, who made documenting this valley his life's work.

Yosemite is one of the oldest national parks in the US, having been designated in 1890. This is a rock climber's paradise: the smooth face of Half Dome and the jagged granite of El Capitan provide even the most experienced with a challenge. But Yosemite is not just for the active: the views from along, and across, the valley floor are amazing. The three cascades of Yosemite Falls, one of the highest waterfalls in the world, drop a total of 740m (2,425ft), and in May, when the runoff is at its peak, the noise is overwhelming. One of the most popular areas of the valley for walkers is Mariposa Grove, where hundreds of giant sequoias reach high into the sky, making visitors feel very small indeed. The Tuolumne Meadows are worth a hike, especially in late spring and early summer when they are filled with typical alpine plants. The surrounding scenery, however, is stunning at any time of the year. Perhaps the best overview of the area can be obtained in summer from Glacier Point, about an hour's drive away from the main valley.

As well as rock-climbing, there is something to do all year, from skiing and snowboarding to fishing, hiking, rafting, horse-riding, bird-watching, stargazing at overnight camps and cycling. There is also an abundance of wildlife, including black bears and deer, bobcats, yellow-bellied marmots, Sierra Nevada bighorn sheep, coyotes, white-tailed hare, mountain beavers, grey foxes, martens and golden-mantled ground squirrels. Birds include spotted owls, Steller's jays, rosy finches, great grey owls, white-headed woodpeckers and northern goshawks. Whether you go to Yosemite for adventure or to simply gaze in awe at the magnificent landscape, Yosemite is a true must-see.

DEVILS TOWER

Wyoming, USA

DON'T MISS
Yellowstone
National Park.

HOW TO GET THERE:
By road.
WHEN TO GO:
May to October is
the best time.
NEAREST TOWN:
Hulett 16km (10 miles).

Devils Tower is a remarkable, monolithic rock formation that rises from the top of a forested area near the Belle Fourche river, in the wilderness of northeastern Wyoming. As the hill is some 182m (600ft) and Devils Tower is 263m (867ft), the whole eerie structure can be seen from 160km (100 miles) away. Formed by the intrusion of igneous material 50 million years ago, Devils Tower is a good example of columnar and horizontal fracturing. This occurred when the green-grey igneous rock cooled, causing the cracking that formed these multi-sided (often hexagonal) columns. The flat top was probably produced by molten rock meeting a layer of hard rock, forcing it to spread out. Originally Devils Tower would have been beneath overlying sedimentary rock – it is erosion that has worn away the nearby sandstone, allowing the tower to rise above the surrounding area. Rain and snow are still eroding the rocks at the base of the tower, but the tower itself is also being eroded, as can be seen in the broken columns, boulders and smaller rocks lying at its base. Devils Tower is sacred to several Native American peoples, including the Lakota Sioux, and in their legend the monolith was formed when three Sioux girls were attacked by a giant bear. The Great Spirit made the rock upon which they were standing rise up, out of the bear's reach and, in frustration, it clawed the rock, leaving the deep scoring that we see today. Every June visitors are requested to refrain from climbing the tower, in order that sacred ceremonies can be performed around the base.

ALABASTER CAVERNS

Oklahoma, USA

HOW TO GET THERE:
By road.
WHEN TO GO:
The park is open all
year round.
NEAREST TOWN:
Freedom 10km (6 miles).

The Alabaster Caverns are the centrepiece of the Alabaster Caverns State Park. The main cave is 1.2km (¾ mile) long, and is the largest natural gypsum cave open to the public in the world. The first known exploration of the caverns was made in 1898, although the area itself had previously been lived in. The underground cavern system was formed some 200 million years ago, when this area was an inland sea. Today a perennial stream flows through it. Geological evidence shows that this stream was once a mighty river that totally filled the cavern, and you can see weird and wonderful water-sculpted gypsum formations here. Gypsum caves tend to be large, and as you make your way through the entrance in the rock cliff, you find yourself in the first of a series of huge, beautifully lit rooms, 60m (195ft) in diameter and 23m (75ft) high. The walls are covered in thick, selenite crystals, a glass-like mineral, but many of the formations here are made of alabaster. Several types of alabaster are found here, including white, pink and the extremely rare black.

MOUNT WHITNEY

California, USA

Standing at 4,417m (14,491ft), Mount Whitney is not only the highest point in California but also the highest mountain in the United States, outside Alaska. Located in the northern Mohave Desert, the western slope is actually in Sequoia National Park, and the two faces, west and east, are utterly different from one another. This mountain is one of the most frequently climbed peaks in the country. The east face consists of almost sheer granite cliffs that plunge down to the Owens Valley, and provides a variety of climbs. The west slope is much easier, the most popular route being the Mount Whitney Trail. This is a 35-km (22-mile) trail, with camp sites along the way. Black bears are fairly common here, and backpackers must carry a bear-resistant canister with them, which can be rented from the visitors' centre. They are also advised to travel in large groups at night, with bright lights and loud whistles to warn off the bears. Most people take between two and four days to complete the hike. During summer the daytime temperatures can be hot, but at night they can drop below freezing at any time. In spring, ice axes and crampons may be necessary, but by July the trail should be snow-free.

HOW TO GET THERE: By road.
WHEN TO GO: Best from June to September.
NEAREST TOWN: Lone Pine 21km (13 miles).

AUTUMN COLOURS OF NEW ENGLAND

Connecticut/Rhode Island/Massachusetts/ Vermont/ New Hampshire/Maine, USA

HOW TO GET THERE:
By road from anywhere in the US eastern seaboard.
WHEN TO GO:
Early October is the most reliable time.

Every autumn, a vast area of the northeastern coastal United States – from Connecticut to Maine – turns vibrant shades of red, golden, russet, purple, yellow, orange, crimson and scarlet as the days shorten and temperatures begin to drop. This is a beautiful landscape at any time of year, but the changing colours of the leaves make this time of year a special time to visit. The leaves change colour as part of deciduous trees' preparation for winter. They do not need the leaves while they are dormant, so they cease the production of chlorophyll, the substance that photosynthesizes sunlight, water and chemicals to create energy and colours the leaves green. The dominant green of the leaves fades and the colours of other chemicals become visible. This prosaic explanation of the process belies the magical effect that it creates. Each species of tree has different chemicals in its leaves, so they all turn different colours, and the mixed woodlands become a spectacular patchwork of vivid hues: bronze hickories rub shoulders with scarlet maples, purplish-red dogwoods stand side by side with golden-yellow birch, and crimson sourwood provides a brilliant contrast to russet oak in what seems like nature's last glorious fling of the year. The most reliable time to observe this spectacle is early October, but exactly when the change takes place in any area is dependent on the weather, so 'tree peepers' need to be prepared to travel. A telephone service keeps people updated about the best locations.

HOW TO GET THERE:
By road.
WHEN TO GO:
Year-round.
NEAREST TOWN:
Custer 21km (13 miles).

JEWEL CAVE

South Dakota, USA

Jewel Cave was formed when stagnant, acid-rich water dissolved the existing limestone and enlarged the cracks that had appeared some 60 million years ago when the Black Hills were uplifted. In 1900, Frank and Albert Michaud passed through the Black Hills on their way home from the Alaskan gold rush. They had reached Hell Canyon when they heard a strange noise and discovered it was the sound of cold air forcing its way from a small hole in the hillside. On returning they dynamited their way in and found an amazing series of low caves that sparkled with jewel-like calcite crystals. For the next ten years, the Michauds tried unsuccessfully to turn the cave into a tourist attraction, but in 1908 President Roosevelt declared it a national monument. The family later sold its claim to the government. By 1939 various programmes had made the cave much more accessible, and a cabin and campground had been established. Since then over 208km (130 miles) of caves have been mapped, apparently a fraction of the site. Jewel Cave is now the third-longest cave in the world. It is beautifully decorated with gleaming calcite crystal spars, stalactites, stalagmites, flowstone and frostwork.

MAMMOTH CAVE

Kentucky, USA

DON'T MISS
Frozen Niagara;
Echo River.

HOW TO GET THERE:
By road.
WHEN TO GO:
Open all year, but best from May to September.
NEAREST TOWN:
Cave City 8km (5 miles).

Mammoth Cave National Park is situated in the Green river valley, a lovely area of limestone cliffs and hills draped with hardwood forest. Established in 1941 to protect the vast labyrinthine cave system that lies beneath those hills, it was designated a World Heritage Site in 1981 and, in 1990, an International Biosphere Reserve. As long as 12,000 years ago these caves were used by Ancient Indians, and archaeologists have found evidence that the region continued to be used and hunted by Native Americans until the first white settlers forced them off the land. This is the world's longest cave system. Unique geological circumstances have combined since the ice age to form a cave system of multiple levels, a complex, interconnected system with a few large passages and many smaller ones. Apart from the marvellous, multi-hued speleothems, including those made of sulphate that look like gold or white flowers growing from the walls, more than 200 animal species live in Mammoth Cave. There are 42 species of troglobites, animals that have adapted to a life of darkness, and the waters here are home to eyeless fish and cave shrimp. There are also flatworms and cave beetles that spend their entire life cycle here. Food is provided by the animals that come and go, such as rats, bats and crickets.

ANCIENT BRISTLECONE PINE FOREST

California, USA

Bristlecone pines are a small group of pine trees, one species of which, *Pinus longaeva*, contains the oldest living organism known to man. Nicknamed Methuselah, this tree is about 4,780 years old and is still growing. It stands, with many only marginally younger companions, in California's Ancient Bristlecone Pine Forest, itself an area of the Inyo National Forest in the White Mountains. The great age of these trees was discovered by Edmund Schulman, who found them growing in seemingly impossible locations at 3,048–3,354m (10,000–11,000ft). In 1957 Methuselah itself was found to be 4,723 years old. In the rain shadow of the Sierras, these mountains receive less than 30cm (12in) of precipitation annually, mainly as snow. The climate here is cold, dry and windy, and the soil quality is poor. The trees themselves are stunted and distorted, with large areas of deadwood and thin strips of living bark. There are two groves of ancient bristlecone pine, the Schulman Grove and the Patriarch Grove, home to the largest bristlecone pine in the world after which the grove is named.

HOW TO GET THERE:
By road.
WHEN TO GO:
Mid-May to November, depending on snowfall.
NEAREST TOWN:
Bishop 55km (34 miles).

ALASKA PENINSULA NATIONAL WILDLIFE REFUGE

Alaska, USA

HOW TO GET THERE:
Fly from Anchorage to King Salmon.
WHEN TO GO:
It is accessible all year round.
NEAREST TOWNS:
King Salmon is within the complex of national parks on the Alaska Peninsula. The refuge can be accessed by small aircraft or boat only. The visitor centre in King Salmon will assist you with air charter information and/or guides.

The Alaska Peninsula National Wildlife Refuge was established in 1980 in order to conserve the onshore and offshore wildlife, to provide for the continued subsistence of the various Alaska Native Peoples who inhabit the area, and to ensure water quality. This is a magnificent landscape of high mountain peaks, wide valleys, rolling tundra, glacial lakes and a rugged Pacific coastline of cliffs, fjords and sandy beaches. The Alaska Peninsula NWR also contains active volcanoes, including Mount Veniaminoff. This volcano is huge – its base has a 48-km (30-mile) diameter and the summit crater is 32km (20 miles) in circumference – and it last erupted between 1993 and 1995. It has the largest crater glacier in the country and is also the only known glacier in America with an active volcanic vent in its centre. The area supports plentiful wildlife and also supports the First Nation and Inuit peoples who live here.

DON'T MISS
Shenandoah National Park.

THE BLUE RIDGE MOUNTAINS

Virginia, USA

The Blue Ridge Mountains form the eastern rampart of the Appalachians, running from Pennsylvania to Georgia. They are made of ancient granite dating from some 1.2 billion years ago and lava flows up to 28m (90ft) deep from 570 million years ago. At one time these mountains were probably as high as the Rockies, but now their top elevation is just over 1,231m (4,000ft). The Blue Ridge Parkway, known as America's Favourite Drive, twists and turns for 750km (469 miles) from the Great Smoky Mountains National Park in the south to Shenandoah National Park to the north. It was enormously difficult to build, and it took some 50 years to complete. The landscape is stunning: endless vistas of forested mountains, valleys speckled with old farmsteads, wildflower-rich meadows and a wonderful variety of wildlife. The blue morning mists that rise from the forests give the Blue Ridge its name.

THE FINGER LAKES

New York, USA

HOW TO GET THERE:
By road.
WHEN TO GO:
Year-round, but between May and October to make the most of the lakes.
NEAREST TOWNS:
There are towns and villages around every lake.

To the northeast of New York City, on the far side of the Catskill Mountains, lies the region known as Finger Lakes. This was the heart of the Iroquois homeland, and legend has it that, as a reward for their courage in battle, the Great Spirit brought part of paradise down to Earth, the lakes being formed by the impression of his fingers. Geologically, the lakes were pre-glacial stream valleys. The deposits left behind when the glaciers retreated dammed these valleys and the lakes, parallel to each other and orientated from north to south, were born. Historic cities and towns such as Ithaca and Auburn can be found at the head and toe of most of the lakes. The southern ends of the lakes are particularly attractive, with steep hills and many lovely waterfalls. The longest and largest lakes, Cayuga and Seneca are both extremely deep, the latter reaching down to 188m (618ft). This is a fertile, beautiful region of rolling farmland and vineyards intersected by 11 lakes that drain north to Lake Ontario. Quaker, Amish and Mennonite families settled here during the 19th and 20th centuries, and dairy farms are common, as well as arable farms growing wheat, oats barley and soya beans. The region is probably best known for its vineyards, the first of which was planted in the 1860s. Today the number is approaching 100, and the white wines produced here are known throughout the country.

YELLOWSTONE NATIONAL PARK

Wyoming/Montana/Idaho, USA

During the first half of the 19th century, reports from hunters and mountain men of an area of the Rocky Mountains with mud pools, geysers, petrified forests and hot springs were dismissed as myths. However, after expeditions in 1869 and 1870 confirmed the tales, moves were quickly made to preserve this beautiful, otherworldly landscape, and the area was designated as Yellowstone National Park in 1872, the first national park in the world. The geothermal features are the result of water passing through extremely hot rock underground, which is still cooling down from a volcanic eruption thousands of years ago. In the 1960s and 1970s, it became apparent that the main feature of the park is a series of three giant volcanic calderas – craters formed when a massive volcano erupted and blew out so much material that the surface above collapsed. The most recent of these created a caldera roughly 85km (52 miles) by 45km (28 miles) and nearly 1km (3,300ft) deep, and blanketed most of North America in a deep layer of volcanic ash. It was the result of the eruption of a 'supervolcano' over a mantle plume (or hot spot), where material from the Earth's mantle gradually rises to its surface and pools until a cataclysmic explosion occurs. Smaller lava flows and steam eruptions occur every few thousand years, and there are frequent small earthquakes. At times, parts of the ground rise or fall over a period of years, which may be the result of the movement of magma or the build-up and gradual release of pressure below ground. As well as the geothermal features such as the Old Faithful geyser, Yellowstone has spectacular pristine landscapes and wildlife, including several thousand bison, as well as elk, grizzly bear, moose, mule deer, black bear, puma, wolverine and reintroduced wolf.

MONUMENT VALLEY

Arizona/Utah, USA

Monument Valley is not, strictly speaking, a valley at all, but a series of spectacular rock formations sculpted out of the Colorado plateau through the actions of rivers over millions of years. The shale, sandstone and siltstone formations, rising 300m (1,000ft) up from the desert floor in layers of browns, reds and greys, are among the most iconic sights of America's Wild West and have appeared in countless films. Among the best-known features are the East Mitten and West Mitten buttes, the North Window, John Ford's viewpoint, the Thumb, the Totem Pole, the Three Sisters and the Ear of Wind arch. The valley lies within the Navajo Nation Reservation in southeast Utah and is sacred to them. The most scenic areas are in the Monument Valley Navajo Tribal Park. Although much of the valley can be seen from the Valley Drive, a 27-km (17-mile) road, it is best experienced by guided tour, hike or horseback trail, especially as some areas such as Mystery Valley are accessible only with a Navajo guide. The Navajo have lived here for centuries, but the ancient cliff dwellings of their predecessors, the Anasazi, and age-old petroglyphs can also be seen. This colourful, desolate landscape leaves most visitors awestruck at its scale and beauty.

HOW TO GET THERE:
On Highway 163.
WHEN TO GO:
April to November.
NEAREST TOWN:
Bluff, Utah 105km (65 miles).

YOU SHOULD KNOW
Rock climbing is strictly forbidden.

OLYMPIC NATIONAL PARK

Washington, USA

The Olympic Peninsula protrudes into the Pacific Ocean at the far northwestern tip of Washington state, just to the south of Vancouver Island. Almost all of it is designated wilderness, and Olympic National Park covers 373,347 hectares (922,561 acres), having become an International Biosphere Reserve in 1976 and a World Heritage Site in 1981. The park naturally divides into three areas: the Pacific coastline, temperate rainforest and the Olympic Mountains that separate the peninsula from the land to the south. This isolation has resulted in many endemic flora and fauna. The mountains are topped with ancient glaciers, with the 2,428-m (7,965-ft) peak of Mount Olympus dominating the western half. The temperate rainforest is in the west of the park, and receives more rain than anywhere else in the country with the exception of Kauai in Hawaii. This is an amazing area of old growth forest, producing habitats for many different creatures. The coastal area is wild and wonderful. There are arches and sea stacks, tide pools full of shells and other marine life, and birds such as oyster catchers and bald eagles.

HOW TO GET THERE:
By bus or ferry to Port Angeles, then by car and on foot.
WHEN TO GO:
July to September.
NEAREST TOWN:
Port Angeles, on the northern edge of the park.

MOHAVE DESERT

California/Nevada/Utah/Arizona, USA

HOW TO GET THERE:
By road.
WHEN TO GO:
Spring and autumn are the best times.
NEAREST TOWNS:
There are towns and cities all over the region. The nearest town to the Joshua Tree National Park is Twentynine Palms, a three-hour drive from Los Angeles.

The Mohave Desert region is one of the country's most popular tourist areas. It contains four national parks: Death Valley, Grand Canyon, Joshua Tree and Zion, all of which are extremely beautiful. Here, too, are oases, sand dunes for off-road recreation and the lure of easy money in Las Vegas. There are also ghost towns to visit, the best known being Calico, an old silver-mining area. The Mohave Desert is the smallest and most arid of North America's deserts, covering some 35,000 sq km (22,000 sq miles). As a result of the surrounding mountains, the desert is in a rain shadow, receiving an average of less than 15cm (6in) of rain annually. However, it contains a large variety of habitats, flora and fauna, including some 200 plant species endemic to the Mohave. The best-known plant here, indeed the symbol of this desert, is the Joshua tree, a type of yucca. These only live at higher elevations, and indeed, they only live here.

CASCADE RANGE

British Columbia/Washington/Oregon/California, Canada/USA

The Cascade Range stretches for some 1,120km (700 miles) from southern British Columbia to northern California, about 160–240km (100–150 miles) inland. They are part of the Pacific Rim of Fire, and the section known as the High Cascades contains vast, snowcapped volcanoes including Mount Rainier, the highest peak at 4,434m (14,410ft), and Mount St Helens, the most notorious. The latter produced a major eruption in 1980, blowing up the northern part of the mountain, wiping out forests, and showering the northwest of the country with ash. The volcano continues to have minor eruptions, the last of which was in 2008. It became a national volcanic monument after 1980 in order to preserve the area and to enable scientists to study its recovery. The volcanoes stand alone in magnificent isolation, separated from each other by vast plateaux, but there are also many non-volcanic mountains in the range. Their sharp, rocky peaks seldom exceed 3,077m (10,000ft) but they receive extremely heavy snow and, together with many glaciers, provide excellent climbing. Thick forests of douglas fir and red alder cover the wetter, western slopes. The eastern side is much drier, reflected by forests of larch and ponderosa pine. There are roads and trails to all the most popular peaks, and routes to the summits of all the volcanoes. The Cascades include many national monuments, forests and wilderness areas as well as four national parks. The Oregon region in particular is a famous tourism area, containing Mount Hood, the Columbia river gorge and Crater Lake. Several million visitors come here each year during summer to hike, canoe, camp and climb, and during winter to enjoy excellent skiing on the many slopes.

HOW TO GET THERE:
By road.
WHEN TO GO:
The Cascade Range has wonderful recreational facilities and can be visited throughout the year.

YOU SHOULD KNOW
There are fascinating visitor centres at Mount St Helens enabling the public to see for themselves the devastated mountain and its recovery.

MOUNT RAINIER NATIONAL PARK

Washington, USA

DON'T MISS

Sunrise; the Ohanapecosh river; Longmire.

HOW TO GET THERE:
By car, or on a day trip by coach from Seattle.
WHEN TO GO:
The park is open year round, but July and August have the best of the weather.
NEAREST TOWN:
Ashford, at the Nisqually entrance to the park.

YOU SHOULD KNOW

Mount Rainier receives a huge amount of rain and snow each year, so go prepared.

Established in March 1889, Mount Rainer was the fifth national park to be formed in the USA, and it encompasses the whole of the mountain within its boundaries. It is, in fact, an episodically active volcano, rising suddenly from the surrounding landscape to a height of 4,392m (14,410ft). Mount Rainier is notable for the glaciers that radiate from its summit, of which 26 are named. One of the most accessible is Nisqually, which has advanced and retreated several times during the past 45 years, providing important indications of climatic change. The splendid, 149-km (93-mile) Wonderland Trail that encircles the mountain gives hikers superb views of the summit and the glaciers. The lower areas of the park are covered with old growth forests of cedar, fir and pine, which gradually give way to glorious subalpine wildflower meadows, valleys and waterfalls before reaching the snowline. The area is rich with wildlife, and over two million visitors come to this much-loved park each year. Numerous campsites and lodges enable visitors to explore some of the 480km (300 miles) of trails at their leisure. Paradise Valley, on the south slope of the mountain, is the most visited destination and should not be missed.

HOW TO GET THERE:
By air to Honolulu,
then by road.
WHEN TO GO:
March to November.
NEAREST TOWN:
Volcano is right at the
entrance to the park.

DON'T MISS
Crater Rim Drive;
Chain of Craters Road.

MAUNA LOA AND KILAUEA

Hawaii, USA

The Hawaiian islands are some of the most isolated on Earth, lying 2,000 miles from the nearest continental landmass. Mauna Loa and Kilauea are the Big Island's (Hawaii itself) southernmost volcanoes and together they form the Hawaii Volcanoes National Park. Mauna Loa and Kilauea are both very volatile, active volcanoes, and both are constantly monitored. Kilauea was thought to be a satellite vent of Mauna Loa, but they have been shown to have two separate magma chambers. Since 1984 they have been showing considerable seismic activity. Mauna Loa erupted at that time, since when the volcano has been inflating and the caldera walls moving further apart due to magma moving into a reservoir beneath the summit. Kilauea has been erupting for decades, sending lava flows down its sides from the summit and two other rift zones. Together these volcanoes have ensured that the Big Island continues to grow, year by year. Driving through this extraordinary, unpredictable landscape, with its steaming craters and lava flows, is an unforgettable experience.

DIAMOND HEAD CRATER, OAHU

Hawaii, USA

If you visit Waikiki, on the Hawaiian island of Oahu, you will instantly become aware of Diamond Head, the island's best-known landmark. With a height of 230m (760ft) and diameter of 1,060m (3,500ft), it dominates the city. From its summit, spectacular 360-degree views can be enjoyed. Formed over 200,000 years ago, the volcano is thought to have been extinct for about 150,000 years. When British sailors saw it from afar in the 1880s, they could see calcite crystals in the lava rock twinkling and shining in the sun. Thinking them to be diamonds, and imagining they would make their fortunes, the sailors gave it the name we know today. Diamond Head crater has been used militarily since the turn of the last century. During the First and Second World Wars it was heavily fortified, and a four-level underground command post was constructed within the crater walls. A switchback trail, classified as 'easy to moderate', ascends the inside slope of the crater until it reaches a series of steep steps and tunnels that bring you out onto the summit with its stupendous views of the island. Stepping out into the sunshine, the ground still sparkles, and one can only feel sympathy for those poor disappointed sailors.

HOW TO GET THERE: Bus or car from Waikiki.
WHEN TO GO: Year-round.
NEAREST TOWN: Waikiki is just beneath it.

NA PALI COAST, KAUAI

Hawaii, USA

HOW TO GET THERE:
Accessible only by foot on the hike from Ke'e beach to Kalalau Valley, or by boat.
WHEN TO GO:
Year-round.
NEAREST TOWN:
Ke'e beach at the start of the hike along the Na Pali coast.

YOU SHOULD KNOW

There is no entrance fee to the Na Pali coastal trail, but it costs non-residents US $20 to camp. Be very careful if swimming – ocean conditions can be dangerous, and there are no lifeguards

With its sandy beaches, giant waves and volcanic craters, Hawaii has plenty of breathtaking landscapes. But the drama and scale of the Na Pali coast of Kauai may top them all. This beautiful stretch of rugged coastline on the northwest shore literally means 'the cliffs', and much of the Na Pali coast is inaccessible due to its characteristic sheer cliffs that drop straight down, thousands of feet into the ocean. The lush green mountains ripple with scree slopes and ridges for more than 1,300m (4,264ft) before dipping into the Pacific. There are no roads, so the only way to access this amazing landscape is by boat or by hiking along the 17-km (11-mile) Kalalau trail. Sailing, rafting and hiking are the best ways to experience Na Pali's myriad of natural wonders. Kauai is the oldest inhabited Hawaiian island, and the remote location of the coastline, only accessible by water or strenuous foot trails, meant that the people that lived in these valleys were well protected. Native Hawaiians relied on canoes to access the Na Pali's numerous valleys, nearby Ni`ihau and outlying islands. Today, boat tours still offer the easiest way to explore this amazing coast.

ISLANDS OF THE SEA OF CORTEZ

Mexico

From the Colorado river delta in the north, to the tip of the Baja California peninsula, the emerald waters of the Sea of Cortez are studded by a chain of over 240 islands, great and small. Their natural beauty is enhanced by extraordinary diversities of terrain, habitat and even microclimate, from temperate wetlands and mountainous desert to tropical abundance. Each has evolved in unique symbiosis with its surrounding marine ecology – a relationship so fruitful that Jacques Cousteau called the Sea of Cortez 'the aquarium of the world'. Isla de Tiburon, due west of Hermosillo on the mainland, is the largest. It's an Eden for bird-watching, fishing, diving and walking; a truly pristine example of the high chaparral of mountain desert, with rare flora and fauna as unusual as they are beautiful. Isla Espiritu Sancto, off the coast of La Paz at the south of the peninsula, is a subtropical jewel, and typical of so many of the islands. It lies on the migration route of millions of birds, and of thousands of whales that come to Baja California to breed in the warm, shallow water. The islands are now protected, along with the surrounding seas, by World Heritage status.

POPOCATEPETL

Mexico

Its name is the Aztec word for 'smoking mountain', and Popocatepetl is one of Mexico's most active volcanoes. For the last 600 years, its eruptions have been relatively mild, with columns of ash rising only a few kilometres above the summit. But its position, 45km (28 miles) from Puebla and 70km (44 miles) from the heart of Mexico City, and its height of 5,465m (17,760ft), mean that its activities are a constant threat to some 40 million people living within its potential range. As recently as 2000 it roared back into life, melting snow into mudslides and hurling red-hot rocks down the nearest valleys. Popocatepetl is a particularly lovely volcano, with impressive green slopes marching steeply to the ring of snow and ice encircling the smoking crater. Almost symmetrical from every angle, it is as much an icon of modern Mexico as it was for the Aztecs and the colonial Spanish. The latter left their mark on the mountain: 14 well-preserved monasteries built by the early Franciscan, Dominican and Augustinian missionaries. They are among Mexico's best examples of colonial architecture, and provide a welcome destination and resting place for visitors to the volcano.

SIAN KA'AN BIOSPHERE

Mexico

The Sian Ka'an Biosphere Reserve is a 526,000-hectare (1.3 million-acre) park on the eastern side of the Yucatan Peninsula in the State of Quintana Roo. Set aside to preserve tropical forests, mangroves, savannas, cenotes (sink holes), coral reefs and more than 25 Mayan ruins, some of it is prohibited to any kind of human access. But the majority of this huge area is a playground for some of the world's most exotic ecotourism. Other than camping, it offers almost nowhere for people to stay except for a few specialist fishing lodges catering to its world-class saltwater-flats fishing opportunities. There are guided tours that will take you by boat round 'islands' of mangroves full of nesting birds, where roseate spoonbills, ibis and tri-coloured heron are common. Less so (but trust to luck) are jaguars, peccaries, manatees and spider monkeys. Then, heading inland where the salt of the lagoon turns into the fresh water of a coastal spring, blooming orchids and bromeliads cling to the mangrove trellis – and the guide passes out lifejackets for you to float downstream in the cool water. Of course you can drive yourself around the reserve – it's free to enter, but the roads will crack all but the sturdiest axle, and finding fuel beyond Tulum is a matter of chance.

HOW TO GET THERE:
By air to Cancun or Playa del Carmen.
WHEN TO GO:
November to May
NEAREST TOWNS:
Cancun, Playa del Carmen and Tulum.

CUEVA DE LA BOCA BAT ROOST

Mexico

HOW TO GET THERE:
By road from Monterrey.
WHEN TO GO:
April to November.
NEAREST TOWN:
Monterrey 23km (14 miles).

Situated close to Monterrey in the northeast, Cueva de la Boca is one of Mexico's most important bat caves, and the first to be bought solely in the interests of conservation. Its size and one-time population of 20 million bats has ensured its status as a tourist attraction. The same factors very nearly caused its destruction. Conservationists discovered that the bat populations of Cueva de la Boca and another nine of the major publicly accessible caves in northern Mexico had dropped by 90 per cent; la Boca had only 600,000 left. Hikers exploring the cave were inadvertently suffocating the bats with smoke from the makeshift torches they made from rags and plastic bottles. Happily, just two years after its purchase, the number of residents had risen to two million. The bats of la Boca travel more than 96km (60 miles) from their cave every night, eating around 15 tons of bugs before they return. They are the perfect pest control, discriminating their targets without damage to the rest of nature.

EL VIZCAÍNO BIOSPHERE RESERVE

Mexico

HOW TO GET THERE:
By air or boat to San Ignacio.
WHEN TO GO:
October to April.
NEAREST TOWNS:
Santa Rosalia (Sea of Cortez) and Guerrero Negro (Pacific).

This is Mexico's biggest and most dramatic reserve. It straddles the centre of the Baja California peninsula between the Pacific Ocean and the Sea of Cortez, and includes 450km (281 miles) of coast in its total of 25,000 sq km (15,625 sq miles). But apart from the 5-km (3-mile) deep littoral zone, animals and plants of El Vizcaíno have had to adapt to extreme desert conditions of little rain and intense winds, defining characteristics of an ecosystem that has produced thousands of endemic species unknown anywhere else on Earth. They roam an ancient landscape of as much cultural as natural significance: over 200 of the caves that pepper the Sierra contain the elaborate cave art of the Cochimi, who lived here 11,000 years ago. But Vizcaíno's greatest treasure is its whale sanctuaries. Grey whales travel over 8,000km (5,000 miles) from the Arctic Circle and some 900 calves are born each year within the reserve. With the threat of extinction lifted, the population has been restored to more than 27,000. Knowing they are safe, the whales tolerate boats and divers nearby. Nowhere else can you get so close.

CENOTES & THE UNDERGROUND RIVERS OF THE YUCATAN

Mexico

The whole Yucatan peninsula is like a giant limestone Swiss cheese. Hollowed out by millennia of tropical rainstorms, the porous rock has allowed an entire river system to evolve in its underground heart. About 560km (350 miles) of crisscrossing waterways have been mapped between Playa del Carmen and Tulum – just 10 per cent of the total. One twists and turns for 153km (96 miles), although the same river covers just 10km (6 miles) in a straight line. Gigantic meanders like these explain why fresh water is distributed so well across the peninsula. They are accessible via surface sinkwells, or 'cenotes'. They look like sunlit pools dotted randomly in the dense green, and many have steep walls as if a hole had been punched through the limestone. The Mayans believed the cenotes to be gateways to the 'Other World', and in one way they were right: each cenote connects to the only source of fresh water to be found. Descending into one is extraordinary, with the eerie beauty intensified by the faint green glow now far above. Real magic.

HOW TO GET THERE:
From Merida/Chichén Itzá (west) or Playa del Carmen (east).
WHEN TO GO:
November to May.
NEAREST TOWNS:
Cancun, Valladolid and Chichén Itzá are good regional bases.

YOU SHOULD KNOW
Open-water diving qualification is necessary for cavern (cenote) diving. Full-cave diving (defined as 'beyond sunlight') requires specialist training.

MONARCH BUTTERFLY SANCTUARIES

Mexico

HOW TO GET THERE:
By car/bus from Mexico City
(4hrs) west to Zitacuaro, then
north to Angangueo; then by
taxi with a guide, or a tough
hike north to El Rosario.
WHEN TO GO:
November to April.
NEAREST TOWN:
Angangueo 6km (4 miles).

Each November, as the North American summer ends, hundreds of millions of monarch butterflies stream south *en masse* to the mountains of Michoacan, west of Mexico City. They fill the sky with a blizzard of orange and black, and settle in such dense clusters that trees sag beneath their weight. Their destination is the group of Oyamel fir forests where they depend on a unique microclimate to overwinter. But the area is notorious for its poverty, and the surviving forests remain under relentless threat from logging. Only gradually are the local co-operatives coming to understand that ecotourism can provide them with a viable alternative income, and to support the three main bioreserves of El Rosario, El Capulin and Piedra Herrada. The awesome spectacle of up to 250 million monarchs is not necessarily a wilderness adventure. The butterflies share the small pueblos and mountain villages with the farmers, schoolchildren and storekeepers who live in the forests, as well as ecotourists. They settle everywhere, but you'll see them at their most dazzlingly prolific within the official sanctuaries. At El Rosario they carpet the forest floor in search of water, and you must step gingerly to avoid them. A sign enjoins you to *Guarda Silencio:* the same sign you see in Mexican churches. And they do indeed inspire holy awe.

HOW TO GET THERE:
By road from Morelia via
Uruapan and Angahuan.
WHEN TO GO:
Year-round.
NEAREST TOWN:
Angahuan 6km (4 miles).

PARICUTIN

Mexico

Paricutin is a volcano in the state of Michoacan. It is the youngest of more than 1,400 volcanic vents in Mexico, but it is unique because every phase of its formation has been witnessed. In 1943 it erupted suddenly in a cornfield, showering ash and stones on the farmer ploughing it. In a year it grew to a height of 336m (1,100ft), burying the villages of Paricutin and San Juan Parangaricutiro. The eruptions continued with diminishing violence over eight years, spreading layers of lava over 25 sq km (16 sq miles), and raising the summit to 424m (1,390ft); until in 1952, after a six-month display of renewed, explosive glory, they stopped forever. Paricutin is a monogenetic volcano, which means it will never erupt again. The cooled lava flow stands proud on the tranquil, fertile land. From Angahuan, the 16th-century town that overlooks Paracutin, a winding trail leads down the valley. Lush vegetation yields to the deep black, glittering, metallic ash. From the fluid waves of volcanic rock engulfing it, the walls and belltower of the church of San Juan Parangaricutiro emerge. Beyond, a steady 5-km (3-mile) climb brings you to the desolate cinders of the summit. The view is majestic.

CAVE OF CRYSTALS

Mexico

In 2000, a group of miners tunnelling in the Naica mine, in the Mexican state of Chihuahua, found an underground cavern almost 300m (984ft) below the surface containing giant selenite crystals. The size and beauty of these gypsum crystals is extraordinary – the cave's largest crystal found to date is 12m (39ft) in length, 4m (13ft) in diameter and 55 tons in weight. They were formed over a span of about half a million years in a hot-water solution, saturated with minerals. The floor of the cave is covered with perfectly faceted crystalline blocks, and huge crystal beams jut out from both the blocks and the floor. The cave is extremely hot, with air temperatures reaching up to 58°C (136°F) with 90 to 99 per cent humidity. The cave is relatively unexplored due to these factors. Without proper protection, people can only endure approximately ten minutes of exposure at a time. The caves are accessible today because the mining company's pumping operations keep them clear of water. If the pumping were stopped, the caves would again be submerged in water. However, the crystals deteriorate in air, so the Naica Project is attempting to visually document the crystals before they deteriorate further. While access is currently possible for short periods, the cave may be closed and flooded in the future to stop the crystals from disintegrating. It is an extraordinary sight, the caves as beautiful as they are dangerous.

HOW TO GET THERE:
By road.
WHEN TO GO:
See www.naica.com.mx.
NEAREST TOWN:
Naica, Chihuahua 135km
(84 miles).

YOU SHOULD KNOW
The cave is only accessible
with permits and suitable
equipment – see www.naica.
com.mx for details.

SEMUC CHAMPEY

Guatemala

HOW TO GET THERE:
By road, 7 hours from
Guatemala City and
3 hours from Coban.
WHEN TO GO:
Less hot and humid
in the dry season,
November to April.
NEAREST TOWN:
Lanquin 11km (7 miles).

YOU SHOULD KNOW

It is best to hire a guide
to take you through the
heavily forested terrain.
Tourists have died falling
into the river and then being
dragged down into the
tunnel under the bridge.

Semuc Champey means 'sacred water' in Mayan and it lives up to its name. It is quite unlike anything you have ever seen, in an idyllic mountain setting of tropical forest, full of wildlife, with radiantly coloured butterflies, hummingbirds and kingfishers darting around. You make your way through the forest along the Cahabon river to meet an extraordinary sight – a series of small ponds and pools, 1–4m (3–13ft) deep, fed by the waterfalls and streams that run down the mountainsides. They are a scintillating range of colours, varying in intensity from pale turquoise to deep emerald and violet. Then you realize that the river is running below you and that these pools are set in the dented surface of a natural limestone bridge that crosses the Cahabon river. It is an almost unbelievable sight and it is impossible not to be awestruck by its strange, overwhelming beauty. The torrential river beneath you spins wildly down, with a deafening noise as it is forcibly sucked into a limestone tunnel, only to re-emerge 350m (1,150ft) further on, where water from the top of the bridge cascades down in waterfalls to join it. It is a difficult spot to reach so it is worth spending one or two nights camping here. There are remarkably few tourists and you can spend your time swimming, diving from the mountainside into the pools and watching the abundant wildlife – 90 bird species alone. It is well worth making the journey, for it is arguably the most beautiful sight in the whole of Guatemala.

THE BLUE MOUNTAINS

Jamaica

The Blue Mountains are aptly named. They are enveloped in a permanent mist that, from a distance, suffuses them with a blue tint. They are renowned for their varied topography, biodiversity and staggering views, as well as the world's finest coffee, which is cultivated on the lower slopes. The mountains rise from foothills in a steeply inclined escarpment that sweeps along eastern Jamaica for 48km (28 miles). On a clear day, you can see Cuba from Blue Mountain Peak, the highest point in Jamaica at 2,256m (7,402ft). The heavily forested, rugged hinterland is scored with rapidly flowing rivers, streams and waterfalls. More than 760cm (300in) of rain a year falls here, providing water for almost half Jamaica's population. The terrain is so wild that parts of it are still uncharted.

BLUE LAGOON

Jamaica

Just outside Port Antonio, in the east of Jamaica, lies the beautiful swimming hole known as the Blue Lagoon. Almost surrounded by lush tropical greenery and steep cliffs, and separated from the Caribbean Sea by only a narrow strip of land, it is thought to be the crater of an extinct volcanic cone. Its blue and green, mineral-rich waters come from springs fed from higher up in the slopes of the Blue Mountain. In places the sides are steep, while in others the slope is shallow enough to allow you to walk into the lagoon. At their greatest depth, the waters are 56m (185ft) deep, and in places swimmers may feel warm or cold currents of water as they emerge from the springs: the warmer water is thought to have passed through rocks deep under the surface that are still warm from the last time the volcano erupted. Cooler currents may have passed through rock nearer the surface. In places, where the water is shallow, it can be seen bubbling out of the ground. Away from the hustle and bustle that characterizes other Jamaican attractions such as Kingston, this secluded spot is a must for any visit to the island.

THE SOUFRIÈRE HILLS

Montserrat

The Soufrière Hills are a series of lava domes, rising to 915m (3,000ft), in the southern half of the island of Montserrat. This 'Emerald Isle of the Caribbean' – named after the 17th-century Irish indentured workers who settled there – is one of the few places in the world where you can witness a live volcano at work. A grey, steaming plume of gas dramatically overshadows Montserrat's breathtaking scenery of tropical forest, sheer cliff-faces and sandy coves. At night, the gases emitted from the volcano's cone glow an eerie red in the darkness. The volcano was thought to be dormant until, in 1995, it started to erupt. The town of Plymouth, Montserrat's capital, was enveloped in a thick ash cloud and was evacuated. Eventually, in 1997, a massive flow of lava and boulders swept down from the volcano, set the town on fire and buried it 12m (40ft) deep. Two-thirds of the island is off-limits and all the remaining inhabitants have moved to the area in the north. There is a 34-sq-km (11-sq-mile) 'safe zone' from where you can see the apocalyptic scene at Plymouth. Among the remains, a church tower and the roofs of houses poke through the layer of volcanic debris – an extraordinary sight, reminiscent of Pompeii.

HOW TO GET THERE:
Scheduled air services or ferry from Antigua.
WHEN TO GO:
December to June (to avoid the rainy, hurricane season).
NEAREST TOWNS:
None – destroyed in volcanic eruption.

BASSE-TERRE

Guadeloupe

HOW TO GET THERE:
Fly to Pointe à Pitre, Grand-Terre.
WHEN TO GO:
January to June to avoid tropical storms and hurricanes.
NEAREST TOWN:
Basse-Terre.

DON'T MISS
Jacques Cousteau Marine Reserve on the Pigeon Islands; Sainte Marie de Capesterre.

Basse-Terre is a subtropical volcanically active island, widely recognized as one of the most spectacular rainforests in the West Indies. It is the larger of the two main islands of Guadeloupe, separated from Grande-Terre only by a narrow sea channel. Covered in dense, subtropical forest, the island has been shaped by four million years of volcanic activity. This led to the formation of La Soufrière about 250,000 years ago, still an active volcano today. The rainforest, full of flowers all year round, including orchids, bougainvillea, alamanda, hibiscus and lilies, and teeming with rivers and waterfalls, plunges steeply down to beaches of red or black sand. There are over 3,000 tree and plant species and thousands of colourful birds and butterflies. At higher altitudes there are wild pineapple trees, mosses and lichens.

DON'T MISS
Cayman Turtle Farm.

HELL

Grand Cayman

HOW TO GET THERE:
Scheduled flights to Owen
Roberts International Airport,
Grand Cayman.
WHEN TO GO:
Year-round. March and April
are the driest months.
NEAREST TOWN:
West Bay.

Located near West Bay, in Grand Cayman, Hell is an extraordinary field of ancient black rock, around 1.5 million years old and about half the size of a football pitch. Although it looks volcanic, it is in fact what is known as 'ironshore' – a spiky, porous combination of dolomite and limestone. This is a common enough rock, both on the Caymans and elsewhere, but it is extremely rare to find it in such a dramatic form. The stone is naturally white but has become gradually discoloured by acid-secreting algae, which have darkened and eroded the surface of the rock to form blackened, craggy shapes with sharp, jagged edges. At first sight, the field gives the impression of the charred remains of a huge fire. This 'hellfire' appearance is one of the possible explanations for the site's name. Another is that a visiting dignitary, on being shown around this strange place, exclaimed: 'This is what hell must look like,' and the name stuck. Hell is a major tourist attraction. There are so many visitors that they have had to be banned from walking around in the rock field itself and are restricted to viewing it from two large, purpose-built platforms. There is a small community near the field and, in 1962, a district post office was opened to accommodate innumerable requests from tourists that they should be able to send cards from the site, postmarked 'Hell'.

SEVEN MILE BEACH

Cayman Islands

HOW TO GET THERE:
Scheduled flights to Owen
Roberts International Airport.
WHEN TO GO:
Year-round but the drier
months of December to April
are high season.
NEAREST TOWN:
George Town.

DON'T MISS
Snorkelling in
Stingray City.

Seven Mile Beach is a crescent of immaculate coral-sand beach running along the western shore of Grand Cayman, the largest of the three Cayman Islands. The beach is world-renowned for its translucent aquamarine water, huge expanse of fine white sand, glorious sunsets, scented air from the Australian pines that grow in the hinterland and an ideal average winter temperature of 27°C (81°F). Not surprisingly, it recently received an award for being the 'Caribbean's Best Beach'. Although a consequence of its outstanding natural beauty is that it has become the most developed part of the island, this has its advantages in that there is something here to suit all tastes in the way of bars, restaurants, hotels and entertainment. There are extremely strict environmental laws to prevent the beach from being ruined by building development and it is so spacious that it feels remarkably uncrowded. Seven Mile belies its name, being in fact only 9km (5.5 miles) long and becoming progressively smaller due to constant erosion by the sea. However, it feels endless as you walk along this outstandingly beautiful stretch of shore, especially in the evenings when you can watch an amazing orange sun going down over the sparkling ocean, reflecting its colours in the darkening water. The whole beach is public property and you can walk its entire length unhindered. It has a completely relaxed atmosphere with few restrictions on behaviour; only nudity is forbidden. The unpolluted, clear sea is superb for both swimming and snorkelling, with many offshore reefs to explore, teeming with radiant tropical fish among the corals. Seven Mile is the epitome of the ideal beach holiday.

MOUNT PELÉE

Martinique

Mount Pelée ('Bald Mountain') is an active volcano on the island of Martinique, 24km (15 miles) northwest of the capital, Fort-De-France. It towers over the island at a height of 1,397m (4,583ft) and its ravined slopes sustain a magnificent tropical rainforest. Analysis of deposits has shown that more than 30 major eruptions have taken place in the past 5,000 years, making it one of the world's most dangerous volcanoes.

The original Carib inhabitants of the island called it 'Fire Mountain' (accurately, as it turned out) but it was renamed by French settlers who were struck by its barren cone, composed of hardened volcanic ash and lava, which stood out in such contrast to the luxuriant vegetation and flowers covering the rest of the island. The residents of Martinique lived in their tropical paradise for over 200 years unperturbed by minor eruptions. Nobody foresaw the terrible tragedy of 8 May 1902 when suddenly, after weeks of rumbling, a cloud of superheated gas, ash and rock shot down the mountainside at 160kph (100mph). It literally vapourized the colonial city of Saint Pierre, killing around 30,000 people in less than two minutes. There were only two known survivors, one of them a local villain who had been imprisoned and was protected by the thick walls of his cell. Saint Pierre, 'The Paris of the Caribbean', never regained its former status as the cultural and commercial capital of the French West Indies. Today an apparently docile Mount Pelée stands quietly over the town of Saint Pierre and the beautiful Martinique countryside. However, it could re-awaken at any time and is under constant watch by volcanologists.

HOW TO GET THERE:
Fly to Lamentin International Airport, ten minutes' drive from Fort-de-France, or ferries and catamarans from St Lucia, Guadeloupe and Dominica.
WHEN TO GO:
Warm sunny weather all year. April is the driest month, September the wettest.
NEAREST TOWN:
Morne Rouge.

TOBAGO CAYS

St Vincent and the Grenadines

Not to be confused with the island of Tobago, this cluster of five uninhabited islets in the Grenadines is straight out of *Robinson Crusoe*. The Tobago Cays are a 24-hectare (58-acre) desert-island haven of palm trees, pure white sandy beaches and secret rocky coves, set in crystal-clear shallow water. All except one of the islands are enclosed within a huge Horseshoe Reef, about 3km (2 miles) in diameter. They are renowned as a unique beauty spot and, despite their relative inaccessibility, have become the most popular anchorage of the Grenadines, attracting around 70,000 visitors a year with some of the finest snorkelling and diving in the world. On the seaward side of Horseshoe Reef, the deep ocean water is a dazzling emerald green, while the colours of the shallows (less than 4m/13ft deep) it harbours are simply spectacular – enchanting shades of blues and aquamarines sparkle with shoals of iridescent coloured fish. The 18-m (60-ft) reef wall, glowing with sponges and corals and teeming with myriad sea creatures, is a hunting ground for barracuda, sharks and turtles. The Tobago Cays have had a troubled history. From the 17th century onwards they passed through several families of private owners until eventually, in 1999, after some 15 years of negotiations, they were wrested from the hands of speculators and bought by the government to become the National Marine Park of St Vincent and the Grenadines. The mission of the park is to 'protect, conserve and improve the natural resources of the Tobago Cays and to be a natural heritage for the children of St Vincent and the Grenadines, and for the children of the world'.

HOW TO GET THERE:
Access by boat only.
Powerboat from Union Island.
WHEN TO GO:
December to May to avoid
the hurricane season.
NEAREST TOWN:
Clifton Harbour on Union
Island 10km (6 miles).

MUSTIQUE

St Vincent and the Grenadines

This privately owned tropical island, the 'Gem of the Caribbean', is renowned as a playground for the privileged. It is less well known that Mustique is a protected nature reserve and offshore conservation area of incredible beauty. The island was once used to cultivate sugar but was abandoned in the 19th century and allowed to revert to its natural state. Today the island is owned by the Mustique Company Ltd, a consortium of island homeowners set up to protect the island from development. There are fewer than 100 villas, most of them available for rent, and only two hotels. Around 500 people live permanently on the island and, even at peak season, the island population is never more than about 1,300. A perfect balance has been struck, so that the island is habitable at the same time as retaining all its natural, tranquil beauty.

GRENADA'S WATERFALLS

Grenada

It is not the height or the grandeur of Grenada's waterfalls that make them so special. It is quite simply that they are nature at her best – idyllically beautiful spots in the rainforest, with pools of clear mountain water to swim and dive in, all set in a rugged environment of mountain slopes that sweep steeply down, through wild backwoods, plantations of sweetly scented spice trees and carpets of wild lilies, to deserted coral beaches. There are more than a dozen waterfalls scattered over this 34-km (21-mile) 'Isle of Spice' – each magnificent in its own way. There is a special kind of silence to be found in the rainforest, and then an indescribable thrill when you first hear the sound of a waterfall, followed by the irresistible urge to plunge into the clear forest pools and watch the mesmerizing torrent of water as it endlessly splashes down over the rocks – as close to paradise as it gets.

SHARK WATCHING

Bahamas

The Bahamas is one of the few places in the world that still provides a benign habitat for sharks. The sparklingly clean waters of the Bahama Banks have precipitous drops and calm shallows, coral reefs and sandy shores, warmed by the Gulf Stream currents, all of which creates a fabulous fish metropolis – and a superbly well-stocked snack bar for the sharks. Meanwhile, the coastal inlets, mangrove swamps and lagoons are perfect breeding grounds, providing a safe nursery environment for newborn sharks. More than 40 species of shark can be found here, the Caribbean reef shark being the most common. The sight of a dozen or so miraculously appearing, seemingly out of nowhere, may well be the most exhilarating underwater experience of your life. The tourist interest has proved a mixed blessing. It has raised awareness of the need for conservation, but it inevitably leads to coastal development and pollution. The sharks are part of a delicate ecosystem. There is a very real danger in the Bahamas that human interference will unbalance the marine environment as well as the coastal mangrove swamps, which are vital for the continued survival of the shark.

HOW TO GET THERE:
International airports of Nassau and Freeport with connecting flights from major US cities.
WHEN TO GO:
November to April. The wet season lasts from May to October.
NEAREST TOWNS:
New Providence: Cable Beach; Nassau: Paradise Island; Grand Bahama: Freeport and Lucaya.

EXUMA CAYS

Bahamas

HOW TO GET THERE:
Fly from US or Nassau, or ferry from Nassau to Georgetown.
WHEN TO GO:
December to May, to avoid the hurricane season.
NEAREST TOWN:
Georgetown.

The Exuma Cays are a 150-km (90-mile) chain of more than 360 cays and islands. Starting at Beacon Cay, 40km (25 miles) southeast of Nassau, they stretch southwards to the two main islands of the archipelago, Great Exuma and Little Exuma. They are bounded on the west by the shallow waters and treacherous shifting sands of the Great Bahama Bank and on the east by the deep, emerald-green water of Exuma Sound, an undersea chasm whose sheer reef wall plummets hundreds of metres, with huge caverns and tunnels sheltering fish of all sorts and sizes. The Cays can only be explored by boat, which gives them a wonderful aura of remoteness and isolation even though they are only hours from civilization. They are sparsely populated, mainly by conch fishermen; the only sizeable settlement is Georgetown, on Great Exuma. The Cays vary enormously in both size and terrain, and narrow channels of water, teeming with corals and tropical fish, run between them. The water visibility and abundant marine life make them an outstanding place for diving and underwater photography.

PILLORY BEACH, GRAND TURK

Turks and Caicos

History has it that Christopher Columbus landed on Pillory Beach during his first Atlantic trip of 1492. Today, amazingly, the beach is still a completely unspoilt stretch of clean, white sand bordering on a translucent turquoise sea. Pillory Beach runs along the western shore of the island of Grand Turk, the administrative capital of the Turks and Caicos. Only eight of this group of 40 relatively undeveloped Caribbean islands are inhabited. They are encircled by the third-largest coral-reef system in the world, 100km (65 miles) across and over 300km (200 miles) long. Some of the most impressive walls of coral in the Caribbean are to be found here, and the Turks and Caicos are well deserving of their reputation as superb diving territory. But Pillory Beach is considered by many to be the best spot of all. One of the world's greatest wall dives, the 'Grand Canyon of the Caribbean' is a mere 300m (1,000ft) offshore and there are 15 dive sites within a ten-minute swim. From the shallow waters of the beach, the reef shelf suddenly plunges 2,000m (7,000ft) into the Columbus trench, a huge undersea passage that separates the Turks from the Caicos. The walls of this chasm are punctured with water chutes, caverns, ledges and tunnels, and the passage itself is crowded with a glorious assortment of brilliantly coloured marine life meandering through delicately tinted coral gardens. Apart from diving, sailing, snorkelling and deep-sea fishing, Pillory Beach is an idyllic place in which to unwind and watch for dolphins, or even an occasional humpbacked whale.

HOW TO GET THERE:
Direct international flights to Providenciales (Turks and Caicos). Daily flights from there to Grand Turk.
WHEN TO GO:
January to April, if you want to see the migration of the entire herd of 2,500 humpback whales. High season is December to June.
NEAREST TOWN:
Cockburn Town 2km (1¼ miles).

YOU SHOULD KNOW
The beach is part of a conservation area, the Columbus Landfall National Marine Park.

PICO TURQUINO

Cuba

At 1,974m (6475ft), Pico Turquino is the highest peak in Cuba. It towers over the western edge of the Pico Turquino National Park, an isolated area of some 170 sq km (66 sq miles) in the Sierra Maestra. This wildly rugged and remote mountain chain runs along the south coast of Cuba only a little way inland from the sea, near the charming secluded beach resort of Marea del Portillo. Some of the most pristine mountain scenery in the entire Caribbean is here – rivers, forests, peaks and valleys of overwhelming beauty. The area was virtually inaccessible until a road was built 20 years ago, and only a few indigenous subsistence farmers live here, as they always have done, in close harmony with nature. A huge variety of endemic plant life flourishes in the park as well as around 600 species of fauna. Pico Turquino is just as important historically as it is ecologically. On the climb to its summit, you can visit La Comandancia de la Plata – the headquarters of the revolutionary movement, where Fidel Castro and his followers based themselves in 1956. This national monument is in an extraordinarily beautiful spot, deep in the forest. The cleverly concealed wooden structures of La Comandancia, which can only be reached on foot, are completely integrated into the surrounding landscape.

HOW TO GET THERE:
Fly to Santiago de Cuba. Bus via Bayamo to Buey Arriba (about 3 hours).
WHEN TO GO:
Not advisable in June to October when weather conditions can be adverse.
NEAREST TOWN:
Bartolomé Masó, 35km (22 miles).

DESEMBARCO DEL GRANMA NATIONAL PARK

Cuba

HOW TO GET THERE:
Fly to Manzanillo or Santiago de Cuba then bus to Niquero.
WHEN TO GO:
Dry season: November to April. September/October is the hurricane season.
NEAREST TOWN:
Niquero 15km (10 miles) from Los Colorados.

Desembarco del Granma National Park is a land and sea conservation area of more than 325 sq km (125 sq miles), 64 sq km (25 sq miles) of it underwater. Here, on the southwest tip of Cuba, where Castro landed his forces to start the Revolution, are the spectacular *Escalera de los Gigantes* ('Giants' Stair') – the largest and best-preserved marine limestone terrace system in the world. Vertical cliffs descend dramatically, from a height of 360m (1,180ft) to a depth of 180m (590ft) under the sea, in a series of 20 steps – eight of them on land, 12 in the water. The deep-sea currents ensure that the water is immaculately clean, which makes for superb diving among the pristine coralline reefs and underwater caverns. The rolling forested hills and ancient caves of the park are equally unspoilt – a profusion of ferns and orchids grow in a practically virgin forest that teems with butterflies and birds. The park was designated a World Heritage Site in 1999 on the basis of its global significance.

VIÑALES VALLEY

Cuba

It is hard to believe that the surreally beautiful World Heritage Site of Viñales Valley, an area of 132 sq km (50 sq miles) in northwest Cuba, was once a high plateau – completely flat. Today, huge, sheer-sided, jungle-covered hummocks – *mogotes* – randomly sprout from the red-earth fields of the valley floor like giant green haystacks. The incredible prehistoric-looking topography of the valley is the result of karst – an extraordinary geological phenomenon, occurring over hundreds of millions of years,

created by the gradual dissolving of limestone bedrock by underground water. Eventually, rock hillocks, dramatically pitted with deep caverns and shafts, are all that remain of the original land surface. The rest of it has simply been dissolved away. Apart from similar scenery in Vietnam, there is nowhere in the world with such a fine example of mature karst scenery as Viñales. The individual micro-environment of each *mogote* is unique so that different fauna and flora thrive from hillock to hillock, many of them endemic. Amongst an abundance of pine, fern and palm species, there is one small patch where the 'living fossil' *palma corcho* (cork palm – *Microcycas calocoma*), estimated to be more than 250 million years old, still grows. The unique charm of the Viñales Valley also lies in its traditional rural culture. Little has changed here in hundreds of years either in farming methods or in living habits. The main crop is tobacco and the *campesinos* (peasant farmers) still use time-honoured agricultural techniques for growing and curing it. Their picturesque villages are in striking contrast to the *fin-de-siècle* colonial style of most Cuban architecture. The diverse ethnic mix of the people living here is representative of the whole of Cuban culture and the region has preserved its own rich traditions.

HOW TO GET THERE:
Fly to Havana. Bus/taxi from
Havana 180km (112 miles).
WHEN TO GO:
Dry season:
November to April.
NEAREST TOWN:
Pinar del Rio 40km (25 miles).

YOU SHOULD KNOW
Don't attempt to hike around
here on your own; people have
been known to disappear.
The scenery is deceptive and
it is all too easy to get lost and
run out of water.

SOUTHERN REEFS

Curaçao

Curaçao is a savannah island, outside the hurricane belt, off the coast of Venezuela. The largest of the Netherlands Antilles islands, it is renowned for spectacular reef diving as well as World Heritage colonial architecture and vibrant multi-culturalism. The island is completely encircled by a fringe of coral reef, millions of years old. The northern coast is rocky with few beaches and strong ocean currents but the waters on the leeward (southern) side are wonderfully still. This 54-km (40-mile) stretch of coastline, with its sheltered inlets and small, sandy beaches nestling in rocky coves, has more than 80 superb diving sites, six of which are ranked among the best in the world. Along the reef, known locally as the 'blue edge', the seafloor drops within exceptionally close range of the shore – less than 100m (330ft) away – making the southern reef one of the best places for shore diving in the whole of the Caribbean. Gentle slopes lead to dazzling coral walls, old shipwrecks and marine life in calm, clear water with a visibility of over 30m (100ft). Massive outcrops of coral, teeming with tropical fish, extend to depths below 40m (130ft), which also makes for some fantastic wall and cave diving. The Curaçao Underwater Park was established in 1983.

HOW TO GET THERE:
Direct flights from US and Amsterdam to Hato International Airport, 12km (7 miles) northwest of Willemstad.
WHEN TO GO:
Any time. October to December are rainy months, but showers only moderate.
NEAREST TOWN:
Willemstad.

MORNE TROIS PITONS NATIONAL PARK

Dominica

The island of Dominica has the wildest and most diverse scenery of the entire Caribbean. In particular, the Morne Trois Pitons National Park, in the south of the island, has a truly astounding, uniquely varied landscape. The dramatic volcanic terrain of precipitous ridges and steeply inclined valleys is blanketed in a vibrant jungle of mature, montane and elfin rainforest and is pitted with craters, fumaroles, hot-water springs, waterfalls, lakes and the world's second-largest 'boiling lake' – all in an area of less than 7 sq km (3 sq miles). Morne Trois Pitons, the 'mountain of three peaks', is a relatively young 1,342-m (4,402-ft) volcanic pile. An eruption in the 1880s left the Valley of Desolation in its wake – a deeply cratered, barren landscape of sulphurous vents, mud pots and hot springs, in contrast to the verdant rainforest surrounding it.

HOW TO GET THERE:
There are no international flights to Roseau, the capital of Dominica. Fly from nearby Caribbean islands to Canefield airport near Roseau.
WHEN TO GO:
Best between February and May. Avoid the hurricane season July to November.
NEAREST TOWN:
Laudat, a 20-minute drive from Roseau.

HUMMINGBIRDS

Trinidad

HOW TO GET THERE:
International flights and from
other Caribbean islands to
Piarco International Airport.
WHEN TO GO:
Equable temperature all year.
December to May are the
driest months, June to August
the wettest. Outside the
hurricane belt so generally
doesn't experience severe
weather.
NEAREST TOWNS:
Arima 11km (7 miles) or
Port-of-Spain 38km (24 miles).

The native Carib Indians called Trinidad the 'Land of the Hummingbirds', and there is no better place to observe these tiny, feisty creatures. Their names alone – blue-tailed emerald, ruby-topaz, black-throated mango, purple honeycreeper, blue-chinned sapphire – are irresistible. As you watch them darting around like living jewels, you cannot help being captivated. Hummingbirds can fly incredibly fast (up to 40kph/25mph) and in any direction – sideways, backwards and even upside-down – as well as hover in midair, their wings beating up to 80 times a second. One of the best places to observe and photograph them is the Asa Wright Nature Centre – an 80-hectare (198-acre) nature reserve. It is not even necessary to walk anywhere – you can just sit and be seduced from the comfort of a balcony.

PITCH LAKE

Trinidad

A perverse joke of nature can be found in southwest Trinidad. Here, in the middle of an idyllic tropical scene, where kingfishers and hummingbirds flit around the wild fruit trees and herons calmly wander among the water lilies, there is a foul stench. It comes from a travesty of a lake – 40 hectares (99 acres) of sulphurous, hissing and occasionally fire-spitting asphalt. Nobody can really explain how it was formed. Scientists think that large oil deposits must have seeped into an area of muddy clay and somehow been compressed into an emulsion of oil, clay and water, from which the volatile parts of the oil evaporated, leaving a tarry residue. Narrow streams of it still seep out from underground, damaging nearby roads and buildings. But it is also a valuable resource – the asphalt is mined, refined and exported. Pitch Lake is mostly sound enough to walk on, except for a small area in the middle, where what looks like solid surface could swallow you up. People regularly bathe here, believing that the sulphur water eases their rheumatism.

HOW TO GET THERE:
International flights, and local
flights from other Caribbean
islands, to Piarco International
Airport.
WHEN TO GO:
Year-round.
NEAREST TOWN:
La Brea, 88km (55 miles)
from Port-of-Spain.

YOU SHOULD KNOW

Pitch Lake is thought to be about 75m (245ft) deep and is one of only three natural asphalt lakes in the world – the others being in California and Venezuela.

PICO DUARTE

Dominican Republic

The 60-million-year-old Cordillera Central is a huge mountain range on the island of Hispaniola. The mountains rise in Haiti and cut across the border deep into the Dominican Republic. They are the highest and most beautiful mountains of the Caribbean. And Pico Duarte is the tallest peak of them all, although its exact height is a matter of continuing debate. It is usually recorded as being 3,175m (10,414ft) but recent measurements have reduced it to 3,087m (10,125ft). Still, it is an impressive size. Pico Duarte straddles the boundary between the Armando Bermudez and José del Carmen Ramirez National Parks, a protected area of 795 sq km (306 sq miles). Pico Duarte's peak is only a few metres taller than that of her sister mountain, La Pelona. These twin peaks are separated only by a beautiful high meadow pass of tussock grass, the Valle de Lilis, which, in the early mornings, glistens with a thin layer of frost. The 23-km (14-mile) trek up the mountain is packed with adventure: fording clear mountain rivers and hacking your way through dense rainforest of palms, ferns, wild avocado, banana and banyan trees, full of small animals, as well as the occasional wild boar, and surrounded by exotic birds. At higher levels you emerge from the rainforest to find yourself in the heady scented air of a Hispaniolan pine wood as you approach Aguita Fria, the headwaters of the two longest rivers in the Dominican Republic – Yaque del Norte and Yaque del Sur. From here, there are breathtaking views of Quisqueya (the 'mother of all lands' in Taino Indian).

HOW TO GET THERE:
Santa Domingo, Santiago and Puerto Plata all have international airports.
WHEN TO GO:
December to March is the drier time so best for climbing.
NEAREST TOWNS:
Santa Domingo, then bus to Jaracoboa – about 35km (22 miles) from trailhead.

YOU SHOULD KNOW
Park permits are required and you are not allowed to go without a guide. Camping is allowed but campers are asked to use pre-existing campsites and fire-rings and, of course, to clear up their litter.

BARRIER REEFS

Belize

As you approach Belize from the air, you will see an unbroken line of white surf. A gigantic breakwater cleaves a 250-km (156-mile) path through the sea, splitting the clear, turquoise coastal waters from a dazzling royal blue ocean. This is the longest barrier reef in the western hemisphere. It is also one of the most diverse reef formations in the world. Apart from the barrier reef itself, there are fringing reefs along the coast and three atoll reefs, as well as sea-grass beds and mangroves in the coastal wetlands, altogether creating diverse ecosystems for an abundance of wildlife. Divers will witness a fabulous array of marine life – rainbow-tinged tropical fish, sea fans, mauve and purple sponges and golden-red coral gardens. Around the atolls and outside the reef, where the seabed drops sharply to depths of 3,000m (10,000ft), there are numerous big fish – stingrays, nurse and whale sharks, tuna, marlin – and dolphins. The most popular diving area is off the Ambergris Caye, the largest of some 200 cayes that dot the coastline of Belize. The reef here is less than 2km (1 mile) offshore and part of it is a conservation area with nesting grounds for three endangered species of sea turtle. The Belize reef is particularly species-rich as it is one of the last places in the world with extensive areas of almost pristine reef, much of it as yet unexplored. The reef was designated a World Heritage Site in 1996.

HOW TO GET THERE:
Fly to Belize City. Local flight or a 90-minute water taxi journey from Belize City to Ambergris Caye.
WHEN TO GO:
Best time of year is December to March. Rainy, hurricane season is May to November.
NEAREST TOWN:
San Pedro 58km (36 miles) north of Belize City.

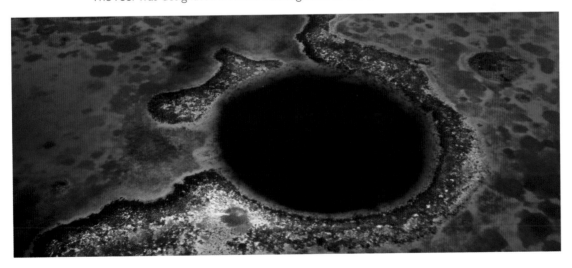

MOSQUITIA

Honduras

The Mosquitia is a wilderness in the remote eastern corner of Honduras. Bounded by the mountains of Río Plátano to the west and Río Coco to the south, it is a vast region, about a fifth of the total area of Honduras, covering 84,000 sq km (32,000 sq miles) of incredible ecological diversity – coastal swamp, lagoons, tropical rainforest, rapids and mountain savannah. Only the adventurous traveller should set out to explore the Mosquitia; you really are off the beaten track. There are no roads into the region, and only extremely basic accommodation and food. You go everywhere by river in traditional dugout canoes or on rafts, and walk along narrow jungle trails. Every bend in the river brings some astounding new impression, and travelling here is an overwhelming sensory experience of vivid colours, strange sounds and tropical scents. The area around the Río Plátano, an extensive swathe of almost pristine tropical rainforest, is a World Heritage Biosphere Reserve. It was listed as endangered in 1996 in an attempt to keep intact one of the most valuable tracts of tropical forest left in Central America.

HOW TO GET THERE:
International flights to La Ceiba or Tegucigalpa and then connecting flight to Puerto Lempira or Palacios.
WHEN TO GO:
December to April and August to September are the dry seasons and the best time to visit. Hurricane season is June to November.
NEAREST TOWNS:
The regional capital is Puerto Lempira. You can access the Biosphere Reserve from Palacios and Brus Laguna.

COCOS ISLAND

Costa Rica

Cocos is an uninhabited treasure island of 24 sq km (9 sq miles) in the eastern Pacific Ocean, 550km (344 miles) off the coast of Costa Rica and the inspiration for the film *Jurassic Park*. The island is composed of volcanic rock, draped in misty primeval rainforest and scored with ravines and waterfalls. Treacherous 600-m (1,970-ft) cliffs, whose sheer walls plunge deep underwater, are riddled with secret caves. The coastline is so precipitous that the only safe landing places are two small bays. The island was discovered in 1526 and soon became legendary as a pirate stash for stolen gold. Over the years at least 300 expeditions have been mounted in search of lost pirate bounty, and even now people have not given up hope of stumbling across a hoard of bullion in one of the innumerable coastal caves or jungle ravines.

HOW TO GET THERE:
Fly to San José, Costa Rica, then go by pre-arranged tour boat for a ten-day trip.
WHEN TO GO:
Hot and humid year-round. Diving is best between March and December.

YOU SHOULD KNOW
You can only go on an organized seasonal diving trip and with the permission of the island rangers. You are not permitted to camp or sleep on the island.

DARIÉN NATIONAL PARK

Panama

HOW TO GET THERE:
Fly to Tocumen International Airport, Panama City. Fly (or by road and boat via Yaviza) to El Réal de Santa Maria 325km (203 miles) from Panama City).
WHEN TO GO:
Year-round.
NEAREST TOWN:
El Réal de Santa Maria (30 minutes by boat from Yaviza).

As you drive south from Panama City, the road comes to an abrupt halt 100km (60 miles) from the Colombian border. You have reached the Darién Gap – a hiccup in the Pan-American Highway, the only missing bit in the 25,000km (16,000 miles) of road that connects Alaska with Argentina. This impenetrable rainforest frontier is one of the most beautiful yet dangerous regions in the world – a haven for renegades, guerrillas, adventurers and drug traffickers. Darién National Park, a UNESCO Biosphere Reserve, is a vast expanse of wilderness stretching the length of Panama's border. It is the largest tract of undeveloped land in Central America, encompassing diverse terrain. The park's strategic geographical position, bridging North and South America, makes it a melting pot for plants and wildlife of both continents.

EL YUNQUE

Puerto Rico

HOW TO GET THERE:
Scheduled international flights to San Juan.
WHEN TO GO:
Year-round. High season: December to April. Hurricane season: May to November (especially intense August to October).
NEAREST TOWN:
San Juan 40km (25 miles).

The Caribbean National Forest is the oldest nature reserve in the western hemisphere and is renowned for its primeval atmosphere and remarkable biodiversity. Known as El Yunque, after the most important mountain in the Sierra de Luquillo, southeast of San Juan, it is a relatively small subtropical rainforest, covering an area of 1,125 sq km (434 sq miles). The land was originally given protected status by King Alfonso XII of Spain in 1876, to prevent his enemies taking wood from the forest for building boats. El Yunque is composed of four distinct vegetation types according to altitude: *tabonuco*, *palo colorado*, *palma sierra* and finally, at heights above 750m (2,460ft), the extraordinary dwarf or 'cloud forest' in which distorted trees, twisted into strange shapes by the wind, are shrouded in permanent mist. A wide variety of plants thrive in the warm, wet environment. In a year, the equivalent of 100 billion gallons of water flows down the mountainsides in cascading rivers and waterfalls. This abundance of water creates a benign habitat for over 240 tree and plant species, 26 of which are unique.

DON'T MISS
El Portal
Rainforest Centre;
Luquillo Beach.

ANGEL FALLS

Venezuela

HOW TO GET THERE:
Fly to Caracas or Ciudad Bolivar. Daily flights via Puerto Ordaz to Canaima. From here go by plane or boat.

WHEN TO GO:
Best in the wet season, June to October. In the dry season the river level can become low, reducing the waterfall to a dribble.

NEAREST TOWN:
Canaima 50km (31 miles).

DON'T MISS
Mirador Laime viewpoint is the best spot to take photographs.

Salto Ángel, on the Rio Churun, is the world's highest waterfall, 16 times the height of Niagara. It is the most famous feature in the 30,000 sq km (11,580 sq mile) Canaima National Park, in the Gran Sabana of southeast Venezuela. The waterfall plummets 979m (3,211ft) from the top of Auyan Tepui ('Roaring Mountain'), freefalling 807m (2,648ft) into the impenetrable jungle of the Cañon del Diablo ('Devil's Canyon') below. Canaima National Park is in an extraordinary savanna region of huge primeval, sandstone *tepuis* (flat-topped mountains, or mesas) formed billions of years ago, crossed by broad rivers with their sides swathed in rainforest. The top of Auyan Tepui is an intricate maze of jagged sandstone, weathered into weird rock formations that are inundated with holes and caves. Giant monoliths of rock lie across each other at crazed, gravity-defying angles, and below, in the Cañon del Diablo, is a dense rainforest full of wildlife, including monkeys, pumas, giant anteaters and porcupines. There are no land trails through the forest; to reach Angel Falls, you must take a canoe upriver, negotiating rocks and rapids, and then hike for an hour up the mountain to a rocky outcrop. From here, you get a magnificent view of Río Churun taking off from the mountain top, straight over a precipice in an incredible cascade of water as it crashes down into the canyon in a swirling mist of spray. Angel Falls gets its name from an American adventurer – Jimmy Angel – who crash-landed his plane here in 1937. Before his discovery of the falls, the local inhabitants, the Pemón Indians, called them Kerapukaimeru, 'Fall of the Deepest Place'. They believed that evil, soul-stealing spirits lurked in the mysterious water-vapour mists that swirl around the top of the *tepui*.

RORAIMA

Venezuela

A trip to Roraima, the highest of the extraordinary Venezuelan table mountains, or *tepuis*, is a truly memorable experience. You will find yourself transported to a surreal primeval world full of rare endemic species, in which all sense of time and scale is distorted. Roraima's ancient Precambrian sandstone rock towers 2,810m (9,220ft) high, rising abruptly out of the jungle at the furthest tip of Canaima National Park, marking the point where the boundaries of Venezuela, Brazil and Guyana meet. It is part of a World Heritage Site, treasured not only for its breathtaking scenery but also its unique plant and animal life. A trek up Roraima starts in a long stretch of savanna meadowland alive with brightly coloured birds by day, and hundreds of fireflies at night. You ford one or two rivers and then make your way up through jungle-covered misty slopes, always under the awe-inspiring shadow of Roraima's sheer walls. Finally, you reach a spectacular 400-m (1,312-ft) cliff of quartzite and find yourself in a cloud forest of ferns and prehistoric-looking vegetation. You really could be on another planet. This is a world of strange valleys, the ground under your feet carpeted in quartz crystals, gorges with fissures tens of metres deep, swirling mists that suddenly clear to reveal incredible views, bizarre rock amphitheatres clothed with strange lichens and mosses, apparently stark rock outcrops suddenly revealing amazing lush meadows, bathing pools with fairy gardens of strange flora and fauna, caverns, rivers and waterfalls.

HOW TO GET THERE:
There are no flights direct from Caracas. Fly to Ciudad Bolivar and then fly to Santa Elena de Uairén, or go by road across Gran Sabana from Puerto Ordaz.

WHEN TO GO:
Climbing is easier in the dry season between December and April. However, the weather is always changeable and, if you are intending to visit Angel Falls as well, the waterfall is far more spectacular in the rainy months of June to October.

NEAREST TOWN:
Santa Elena de Uairén (2 hours from Paraitepui, where you start your climb).

ISLA DE MALPELO

Colombia

The Isla de Malpelo is a 350-hectare (865-acre) lump of sheer basalt rock that sticks incongruously out of the Pacific Ocean like some giant, prehistoric monolith. It is the highest peak of a 'hot spot' in the oceanic crust, some 500km (314 miles) off Colombia's Pacific coast. Malpelo is tall enough, at 376m (1,233ft), to create its own weather system and in the mornings, however clear the sky, it is often mysteriously wreathed in cloud. The unpolluted waters of Malpelo and its surrounding rocks are amazingly clear, and drift diving here is one of the most memorable experiences you are ever likely to have. A small garrison of the Colombian army is stationed on Malpelo to guard an area of the ocean – a World Heritage Site and the largest no-fishing zone in the eastern tropical Pacific.

SANGAY NATIONAL PARK

Ecuador

Sangay is over 5,000 sq km (1,930 sq miles) of contrasts and extremes – valleys and mountains; volcanoes and lagoons; forest and plains. It ranges in altitude from low-lying Amazon basin valleys to towering, snowcapped volcano peaks of over 5,000m (16,400ft). Here you will find the entire spectrum of ecosystems. At least nine life zones have been identified, from subarctic to tropical lowland forest. Sangay is extraordinary in that it sustains an incredible biodiversity at the same time as a high proportion of endemism (species unique to the area). It is an area of outstanding natural beauty, with 324 lagoons set in a rugged volcanic landscape, and three of the country's highest peaks. Sangay itself is one of the world's most active volcanoes. A peculiar event takes place in the lagoons of Osogoche and Atillo – every so often, for no known reason, hundreds of birds hurl themselves into the water to drown.

GALÁPAGOS ISLANDS
Ecuador

Ecuador's Galápagos Islands, a small archipelago straddling the Equator 965km (600 miles) west of South America, are best known for being the site where Charles Darwin made the observations that led him to develop his theory of evolution through natural selection. The group contains 13 main islands, six isles and 107 smaller rocks and islets. Land iguana and giant tortoises are a big draw, and birds that nest here include masked, blue- and red-footed boobies, albatrosses, Galápagos flamingos, magnificent frigatebirds and the buntings commonly called Darwin's finches. As well as an abundance of fish, the marine animals here include Galápagos sea lions, otters and marine iguanas. The government of Ecuador has imposed strict controls on tourist access in order to prevent too many visitors destroying the very islands and wildlife that they come to see – a tour guide certified by the national park authority must accompany each group. These spectacular but fragile islands, each with its own character, are a world treasure.

DON'T MISS
The colonies of nesting birds.

HOW TO GET THERE:
By air from Quito or Guayaquil
WHEN TO GO:
Any time of year.
NEAREST TOWN:
Guayalquil 1,000km (620 miles).

HOW TO GET THERE:
Fly to Quito, then take a train or drive 60km (38 miles) south via Aloag, to Lasso.
WHEN TO GO:
The best climbing months are December and January followed by August and September.
NEAREST TOWN:
Lasso 5km (3 miles).

COTOPAXÍ
Ecuador

The colossal, snowcapped cone of the Cotopaxí volcano is an image that is etched into the Ecuadorian national psyche. It is revered as the world's highest active volcano and was once worshipped as a god by the native Andean Indians. It has a history of more than 50 eruptions in the last 300 years. The most famous was in 1877, when mudflows swept as far as the Pacific coast, 100km (63 miles) away. Cotopaxí rises out of a grassland and forest plateau (*páramo*) to a peak of nearly 5,900m (19,350ft). Apart from being an active volcano, often spouting steam from its summit, it has one of the few equatorial glaciers in the world. The Cotopaxi National Park is more than 330 sq km (127 sq miles) of *páramo* landscape that sustains over 2,000 species of flora and fauna. It has magnificently varied scenery with panoramic views and the chance to see wild horses, deer, llamas, Andean foxes, and even the rare Andean spectacled bears. The spectacular birdlife includes condors, eagles, falcons and exquisite hummingbirds.

CHAPADA DOS VEADEIROS

Brazil

The Chapada dos Veadeiros National Park is a spectacular 655-sq-km (252-sq-mile) area in the Cerrado – the vast tropical savanna region of central Brazil. The park is a World Heritage Site of outstanding natural beauty, famous for the spectacular quality of its seasonal landscapes. Beneath a panorama of huge, changing skies, parched and yellow winter prairies are magically transformed by the summer rains into lush green meadows bursting with flowers.

HOW TO GET THERE:
By road from Brasilia via São Gabriel to Alto Paraiso 250km (156 miles), then along unpaved road to park entrance in the village of São Jorge.
WHEN TO GO:
Year-round, though the scenery is at its best between April and September.
NEAREST TOWN:
Alto Paraiso 37km (23 miles).

The high plains at 1,200m (3,940ft) above sea level are incised with deep, rocky canyons, with some of the oldest rock formations on the planet, formed some 1.8 billion years ago. Viewed from space, the region emits a strange, luminous glow due to the quantity of quartz crystals in the soil. The Cerrado is one of the world's oldest and most diverse tropical ecosystems and is the richest savanna area on Earth – with an estimated 10,000 species of plants, nearly half of which are endemic, it ranks with the Amazon in importance. Its 'bushy savanna' is characterized by grassland plateaux with peculiar gnarled trees and cut by networks of thickly forested river valleys and depressions. It is a habitat for more than 900 bird species and around 300 mammals, including several endangered species: vultures, toucans, the giant anteater, deer, maned wolves, cerrado fox, tapirs and jaguars. The Rio Preto flows through the park from the northwest, with several beautiful waterfalls and riverside forests of palm, cork, jacaranda and pepper trees. You can immerse yourself in nature as you walk, cycle, or climb through the breathtaking scenery.

YOU SHOULD KNOW

The luminosity of the landscape has attracted New Age acolytes. It is known as 'The Capital of the Third Millennium' and is one of the ten most-visited parks in Brazil.

MOUTHS OF THE AMAZON & AMAZON BORE

Brazil

HOW TO GET THERE:
Fly to Belém or Macapá.
WHEN TO GO:
The *pororoca* occurs during
February and March.
NEAREST TOWN:
São Domingos do Capim.

The Amazon estuary is so vast it is known as the 'River Sea'. It is a complex network of rivers and channels that crisscross each other in a watery maze. The river mouth is 330km (206 miles) wide and, with water up to 90m (295ft) deep, is navigable for large ocean steamers all the way up to Manaus – 1,500km (940 miles) inland. The Amazon basin drains an area roughly 40 per cent of South America, and the outpouring of water is so vast that it dumps three million tons of sediment daily. Both the colour and salinity of the ocean are affected for a distance of about 320km (200 miles) out to sea, and early explorers were amazed to find that they could drink the seawater long before they could see land. The Amazon does not have a river delta. A belt of half-submerged islands and shallow sandbanks follows the coast for 160km (100 miles) around the mouth, built up from the silt washed back by the Atlantic tides. Here the alarming seasonal phenomenon of the tidal bore, or *pororoca*, occurs. A wall of water, up to 4m (13ft) high, rolls upriver a distance of around 13km (8 miles). It gradually gathers a speed of up to 25kph (16mph), attracting surfers from all over the world – where a normal sea wave lasts for only about 15 seconds, a skilled surfer can ride the *pororoca* for up to 30 minutes. It is a particularly dangerous experience, as the wave rakes the riverbanks and drags trees, debris, snakes and alligators in its wake.

HOW TO GET THERE:
Daily flights or boat
from Natal or Recife on
Brazilian mainland.
WHEN TO GO:
Year-round.
NEAREST TOWN:
Vila dos Remédios.

ATLANTIC ISLANDS (ATOL DAS ROCAS)

Brazil

The remote archipelago of Fernando de Noronha and the Atol das Rocas are peaks of the South Atlantic submarine volcanic ridge sticking up above the surface of the ocean. These islands and the surrounding waters are a World Heritage Marine Conservation Site containing colonies of endangered turtles and dolphins as well as an abundance of fish and marine birds. Rocas, 100km (60 miles) to the west of Noronha, is the only atoll in the South Atlantic. Its surface is covered in grasses, a few palm trees and a lighthouse. At low tide the bare reef is transformed into a fantastic aquarium – the lagoon and tidal pools brimming with the brilliant colours of thousands of tropical fish. It is one of the most remarkable and remote places in the world – do not be put off by the travel obstacles in your way.

DON'T MISS
The Baia de Golfinhos dolphins, at their liveliest in the early mornings.

FERNANDO DE NORONHA

Brazil

HOW TO GET THERE:
By air from Recife or Natal on the mainland or on a cruise.

WHEN TO GO:
The dry season is from September to March, with the height of the tourist season in December and January.

NEAREST TOWN:
Natal 360km (220 miles).

YOU SHOULD KNOW
A permit is needed to visit the other islands in the group.

Declared a UNESCO World Heritage Site – along with the Atol dos Rocas – in 2001, the Fernando de Noronha archipelago is a group of 21 volcanic islands and rocks in the Atlantic Ocean just south of the Equator. The largest island, after which the group is named, is the only inhabited one and visitor numbers are strictly limited in order to minimize the impact of tourism. These islands are the remnants of part of the volcanic southern Atlantic submarine ridge and provide a vital stopping- and feeding-point for animals such as sharks and turtles as they migrate to and fro across the southern Atlantic. Most of the area around these isolated islands was declared a National Marine Reserve in 1988 in order to give protection to the abundant marine wildlife, and today most visitors to these islands come for the superb diving: manta rays, lemon sharks and many types of other fish including tuna and billfish can be seen in the warm waters. From above the water, one of the main spectacles to watch is the daily gathering of hundreds of playful spinner dolphins in the Bay of Dolphins, while in season many of the wide, sandy beaches are used as nesting grounds by marine turtles, especially the rare hawksbill turtle.

SUGARLOAF MOUNTAIN

Brazil

YOU SHOULD KNOW
The climb up the Sugarloaf is
extremely rugged and much
harder than it looks. It should
not be undertaken without
pre-planning. Getting down
is even more difficult than
getting to the top.

The Sugarloaf (*Pāu do Açúcar*) is the icon of Rio de Janeiro. This unearthly, green monolith soars straight up 396m (1,299ft) into the sky from the end of a peninsula, which juts into the Atlantic from Guanabara Bay. It is said to derive its name from the fact that it is in the traditional shape of a piece of refined loaf sugar, but it is just as likely that the name actually comes from the indigenous Tamoioa Indian language Pau-nh-Acuqua, which translates as 'high hill'. The mountain is the most famous of several 600-million-year-old monolithic granite and quartz *morros* that rise straight from the edge of the sea near Rio de Janeiro. Because of its position, it was used as a landmark by sailors crossing the Atlantic to guide them in the direction of Rio. A cablecar, first built in 1912, regularly travels a 1,400-m (4,265-ft) route, connecting its peak with that of Morro da Urca. The ride is not only an incredible experience in itself but you are rewarded with staggering panoramic views of the city, mountains and Atlantic beaches as well as another half-dozen of these extraordinary *morros* sticking up from the water's edge. It is well worth timing your expedition to coincide with sunset, when the surroundings are truly magical. The intrepid climber can also trek to the top.

CENTRAL AMAZON

Brazil

HOW TO GET THERE:
International or domestic
flights to Manaus.
WHEN TO GO:
Any time – hot and
rainy all year.
NEAREST TOWN:
Manaus 16km (10 miles) from
Encontra Das Aguas.

The Amazon is the largest tropical rainforest in the world, a region of unparalleled diversity with more than 150,000 species of plants, 75,000 types of tree and 2,000 birds and mammals. Much of it is still unexplored – amazingly, we know less about the rainforest than we do about the ocean depths. 'The Lungs of the Planet' stretch across several nations and, in Brazil, 22,000 sq km (8,490 sq miles) has been set aside as the Jau National Park. The usual route is by boat up the Rio Negro, whose black-coloured water is caused by decomposed organic matter and iron. It is the largest river in the world, apart from the Amazon itself. The rivers join at the *Encontra Das Aguas* ('Meeting of the Waters'). Here the pale waters of the Amazon and the dark ones of Rio Negro flow side by side in two distinct channels. As you glide along this wide, slow river, you cannot help being overwhelmed by a sense of the primitive forces that have shaped evolution. A trip into the Amazon rainforest is a truly life-transforming experience.

PATOS LAGOON

Brazil

YOU SHOULD KNOW
This is *gaucho* and *churrasco* country. The cities have a rich heritage, and there are many historical and cultural things to see and do in the vicinity.

Five rivers converge at the city of Porto Alegre to form the Lagoa Dos Patos, a tidal lagoon in extreme southeastern Brazil. It is the second-largest lagoon in South America, 280km (174 miles) long and 70km (44 miles) wide. The 'Lagoon of the Ducks' gets its name from some wily 16th-century Jesuit colonialists, who asked the king of Spain to grant them land to start a duck-breeding colony. He soon revoked it when he discovered he had just handed over one of the largest lagoon systems in the world. The lagoon is the remains of an ancient depression, closed off from the sea by the combined action of wind and water currents building up the sandbank. It has several islands in it, the largest being the Ilha dos Marinheiros, inhabited by people labelled 'outcasts' because they scratch a living by picking over the refuse from Porto Alegre. A plume of sediment flows into the sea from an opening at the extreme south end of Patos, which led explorers to believe that it was the mouth of a huge river, hence the name Rio Grande.

HOW TO GET THERE:
Fly to Porto Alegre, Pelotas
or Rio Grande.
WHEN TO GO:
October, November, April
and May are the best months.
December to March is very hot,
and there is a distinct winter
between June and September.
NEAREST TOWNS:
Porto Alegre, Pelotas.

EMAS NATIONAL PARK

Brazil

HOW TO GET THERE:
By road from Brasilia 700km
(440 miles) or Goiânia
500km (312 miles) to
Chapadao do Céu.
WHEN TO GO:
April to October, to avoid
scorching heat.
NEAREST TOWN:
Chapadeu do Céu
26km (16 miles).

The remote Parc Nacional das Emas is a spectacular savanna plain (cerrado) of more than 1,300 sq km (500 sq miles) in central Brazil. Combined with the protected cerrado of Chapada dos Veadeiros further north, it is a UNESCO Biosphere Reserve. The granite plateau, ranging in altitude from 400–1,000m (1,310–3,280ft), is a magnificent cerrado landscape – a vista of vast, changing skies above rolling, open-wooded grasslands. The plains are dotted with innumerable red-earth termite mounds, scored with dramatic canyons and crisscrossed by rivers and clear rushing streams, with high waterfalls and black-water drop pools. The park is part of the great, dividing cerrado plateau between the Amazon and Paraná river basins and is the site of the headwaters of the Araguaia, Formosa and Taquari rivers and their tributaries, which diverge across the plains making their separate ways to the Atlantic. This is the place for hardcore nature lovers. Large mammals roam freely here on a scale comparable with the savannas of east Africa, 87 species in all. It is also a bird-watcher's paradise, with more than 350 sorts of bird.

THE ATLANTIC FORESTS

Brazil

HOW TO GET THERE:
Fly to Rio de Janeiro or
São Paulo.
WHEN TO GO:
Always warm, dependent
on altitude. January to
September is drier.
NEAREST TOWN:
São Paulo 100km (63 miles).

In terms of biodiversity, the glorious Mata Atlântica is the richest in the world. Cut off from the rest of South America by the Cerrado savannas, the complex ecosystem of the Atlantic Forest has evolved separately, which explains the incredibly high degree of endemism here: 40 per cent of the 20,000 plant species are unique. However, the forest that once stretched north to south along Brazil's coast is now less than 10 per cent of its former size, surviving only in fragmented patches. Over the past 500 years the forest has been gradually plundered for wood and cleared of trees to make way for cattle ranches, sugar and coffee plantations and urban development. Still, there is a great deal of hope for what remains: 23,800 sq km (9,190 sq miles) has now been protected in 224 separate areas, with 4,700 sq km (1,814 sq miles) under the auspices of UNESCO, as an irreplaceable part of the Earth's heritage.

THE PANTANAL WETLANDS

Brazil

The cattle-ranching country of the Pantanal is the largest wetland area in the world. The diversity and abundance of vegetation and wildlife here is comparable to the Amazon and it is one of the most important ecosystems on the planet. The Pantanal is a bowl-shaped depression covering a vast area of 250,000 sq km (96,500 sq miles) in central west Brazil, with two major river systems flowing through – Río Paraguay and Río Cuiabá. In effect, the region is a massive inland delta. In the rainy season the rivers burst their banks, flooding 80 per cent of the surrounding alluvial plain, providing nourishment for the world's largest collection of aquatic plants. These form floating islands of vegetation, *camalotes*, on which animals and birds take refuge. The region is habitat for 75 mammal species, among them the maned wolf, giant anteater and the world's largest rodent, the capybara, as well as five species of howler monkey and the occasional jaguar. There are over 300 species of fish, and caimans loll brazenly on the grassy riverbanks. You will also see plenty of chameleons, land turtles, boa constrictors and anacondas.

It is a matter of great concern to conservationists that such a vital ecological region is largely unprotected, privately owned land used for ranching and ecotourism. You can stay on one of these ranches and explore the marshes of the Pantanal by canoe or on horseback to catch superb sights of the wildlife, bird-watch or go fishing.

HOW TO GET THERE:
Fly to Campo Grande
or Cuiabá
WHEN TO GO:
Waters start to recede in April.
Best from June to August.
NEAREST TOWNS:
Porto Jofre, Corumbá.

YOU SHOULD KNOW
The novel *The Testament*, by John Grisham, is largely set in the Pantanal.

LAKE TITICACA

Peru/Bolivia

YOU SHOULD KNOW

The people of Lake Titicaca
have preserved their
culture against the odds. You
should try to be sensitive
to what might appear a
'hard-sell' approach.

High in the altiplano between Peru and Bolivia, the limpid cobalt-blue waters of Lake Titicaca are central to Incan mythology and history: the origin of the world was here, the sun, moon and stars emerged from its waters, and powerful spirits as well as Spanish gold are in its depths. Lake Titicaca is the highest commercially navigable lake in the world, at 3,812m (12,503ft). It is 176km (110 miles) long and 50km (31 miles) wide with water up to 281m (922ft) deep. More than 25 rivers and glaciers flow down from the sierras into the altiplano to feed this huge stretch of water. The lake drains into Rio Desagaudero, but most of its water simply evaporates in the fierce winds and burning sun of the altiplano. There are 41 islands in the lake, inhabited by Quechuan Indians who have largely preserved their traditional culture. They eke out a living from terrace farming, fishing and making ethnic garments for the tourist trade. The extraordinary *islas flotantes* are a major tourist attraction. These reed islands, which need constant repairs to stop them rotting, were originally built by the Uro Indians to avoid the harassment of Spanish colonists but are now settled by Aymara Indians who have built reed houses and even a church. Despite the pressures of mass tourism, Titicaca is an amazing sight. It seems to stretch forever under the huge skies of the altiplano, the snowcapped peaks of the Sierra Cordillera just visible in the distance.

YOU SHOULD KNOW
To ascend Huascarán takes
six to seven days.

HUASCARÁN NATIONAL PARK

Peru

The Cordillera Blanca, in the Huascarán National Park, is one of the highest mountain ranges in the world. There are more than 50 glaciated peaks, 15 of which are more than 6,000m (20,000ft). Here is some of the most spectacular mountain scenery you will ever see. You will be overwhelmed with views of startlingly blue glacial lakes, dramatic gorges, torrential cascades and sparkling, icy streams, set in a vast, white landscape. Numerous trails will take you though welcoming Andean communities and pre-Incan ruins. You will wander through meadows full of strange endemic plants, scramble along deep ravines lined with red-barked queñua and medicinal quísuar trees, find yourself surrounded by glaciers and be amazed by the hundreds of aquamarine and turquoise lakes and the staggering views of the sheer rock and ice walls of the northern peaks of the Cordillera Blanca.

ANDES CORDILLERA

Peru

The Andes Cordillera is the longest continuous mountain chain on Earth and the highest outside Asia. It extends more than 7,000km (4,000 miles), running through seven South American countries from Tierra del Fuego to Venezuela. At its widest, the range is 500km (300 miles) across with an average height of 4,000m (13,000ft). The central Andes runs down the whole length of Peru, home to some of the most spectacular mountains in the world – steep, granite peaks rise above icy ridges with huge glaciers snaking down the valleys. The Peruvian Andes are divided into five sub-ranges: Cordilleras Blanca and Huayhuash in the north, and Central, Occidental and Oriental Cordilleras. Cordillera Blanca is by far the most accessible, with the highest mountain in Peru, Nevada Huaracán.

YOU SHOULD KNOW
It takes time to acclimatize
to the altitudes here so you
should make your travel
plans accordingly.

HOW TO GET THERE: Fly to Lima or Cuzco.
WHEN TO GO: Year-round, but June to August is best because it is
the dry season in the highlands.
NEAREST TOWNS: Hundreds, down the length of the Andes.

ANDES CLOUD FORESTS

Peru

The mysterious cloud forests of Peru occur only at altitudes of 2,000–3,500m (6,500–11,500ft) on high mountains where the annual rainfall is 50–1,000cm (20–400in). The twisted, stunted trees with epiphytes and lichens trailing eerily from their branches are shrouded in perpetual mist. This is a unique ecosystem for thousands of species, 80 per cent of which are still undocumented. There are more than 1,000 species of orchid alone. The forest is also a vital source of pure water. The leaves of the trees and ferns drip water into the sodden, peaty ground at a constant rate, contributing a regular, controlled water supply to rivers lower down the mountains. It is threatened by both climate change and man's encroachment, with potentially disastrous consequences for water supplies and loss of habitats. The huge 150,000-sq-km (58,000-sq-mile) World Heritage Site of Manú National Park was established to protect the remaining Peruvian cloud forest. This unique, romantic and fragile world makes up a mere 2.5 per cent of the tropical rainforest but its ecological significance is immeasurable.

HOW TO GET THERE:
Fly to Lima then domestic flight or road to Cusco. 7 hours drive from Cusco to Paucartambo.
WHEN TO GO:
Any time, but June to September is driest.
NEAREST TOWN:
Paucartambo 35km (22 miles) from Ajunaco Pass, entrance to Manú park.

NOEL KEMPFF MERCADO NATIONAL PARK

Bolivia

HOW TO GET THERE:
Fly to Santa Cruz. Fly or drive 600km (375 miles) from Santa Cruz to Flor de Oro or Los Fierros Park lodges.
WHEN TO GO:
The ideal season is October to December.
NEAREST TOWNS:
Florida, Hacienda Chirapas, El Porvenir, Piso Firme.

This exceptional biological reserve, named after a renowned Bolivian biologist, is a truly awe-inspiring region of more than 15,000 sq km (5,790 sq miles) of remote wilderness in northeast Bolivia. It is one of the least-disturbed expanses of land in the Amazon basin, and one of the most biologically diverse areas in the world. The scenery is breathtaking – extraordinary landscapes, vast rivers and stunning waterfalls. A visit to the park is a fantastic eco-adventure. The sheer scale of the wilderness *cerrado* (the largest remaining virgin tract of this rich savanna land in the world) is staggering – broad rivers cut through the savanna, their banks lined with strangely contorted trees, and great cascades of water thunder down into the streams and creeks of the rainforest. The terrain is a refuge for wildlife that has largely disappeared from the rest of the Amazon. Nowhere else in South America can you see such a wide variety of species and habitats with so little effort.

GRAN SALAR DE UYUNI

Bolivia

At 10,582 sq km (4,086 sq miles), the Gran Salar de Uyuni is the world's largest salt flat. It is 3,656m (11,995ft) above sea level and located near Potosí in southwest Bolivia, near the crest of the Andes. It was formed as a result of transformations between several prehistoric lakes, leaving it covered by several metres of salt crust that has an extraordinary flatness. The large area, clear skies and the exceptional flatness of the surface make the Salar an ideal object for calibrating the altimeters of Earth observation satellites. The crust serves as a source of salt and covers a pool of brine. This brine contains 50 to 70 per cent of the world's lithium reserves, which is in the process of being extracted. The Salar serves as the major transport route across the Bolivian altiplano and is a major breeding ground for several species of pink flamingos. A number of hotels have been built in the area to cater for tourists, but due to lack of conventional construction materials, many of them are almost entirely built from salt blocks cut from the Salar, including walls, roof and even furniture.

HOW TO GET THERE:
By road.
WHEN TO GO:
Year-round.
NEAREST TOWNS:
Potosi 200km (124 miles),
La Paz 533km (330 miles).

CAPE HORN

Chile

HOW TO GET THERE:
Fly to Ushuaia (or from Santiago to Punta Arenas). Take boat or plane to Puerto Williams then boat to Cabo de Hornos (Cape Horn) through the Beagle Channel.
WHEN TO GO:
January to March and October to December.
NEAREST TOWN:
Puerto Williams.

The continent of South America ends at a treeless granite promontory. This is Cape Horn – the southern headland of Isla Hornos, part of the Chilean Hermite islands of Tierra del Fuego. The most southerly of all the great capes, Cape Horn juts out into Drake Passage, the strait between South America and Antarctica, marking the dividing line between the Pacific and Atlantic oceans. The perilous seas of Cape Horn are a sailing legend. Gale-force winds and fearsome currents combine to stir up lashing great waves more than 20m (65ft) high, which, together with the threat of icebergs, make it one of the most hazardous sea routes in the world. Despite the danger, the route was in frequent use until the Panama Canal was built in 1914, particularly in the years of the California gold rush when adventurers considered it marginally less risky than attempting to cross the great North American prairies by land. Hundreds of ships have been wrecked here, and sailors who successfully rounded the Horn westwards were treated as a special breed – they were entitled to wear a gold ring in their left ear or nipple as a mark of their authority. The Cape Horn archipelago is one of the most pristine island ecosystems in the world and has been designated a UNESCO Biosphere Reserve. It covers a remote area inhabited by indigenous Yagán Chileans, a nomadic fishing culture that is threatened by economic development and tourism.

THE ATACAMA DESERT

Chile

At its centre, the Atacama desert is the driest place on Earth – 50 times drier than California's Death Valley. The average annual rainfall is a mere 1mm (0.004in) a year and some parts never see any rain at all.

The desert is at an altitude of over 2,000m (6,560ft), on a narrow plateau only 150km (94 miles) wide, which extends 1,000km (625 miles) from the border with Peru into northern Chile. The rain shadow cast by the Andes on one side and the Pacific coastal mountains on the other has created an extraordinary landscape of alluvial saltpans. Incredibly, about a million people manage to scratch a living out of the Atacama, inhabiting the few oases and the Pacific fringes of the desert where coastal mists supply just enough moisture to sustain algae, mosses and the odd cactus. The terrain is 15 million years old and there is a wealth of remains from a Paleo-Indian civilization. Incan artifacts and mummies have been found perfectly preserved, desiccated in the sterile desert soil. The desert landscape is visually superb – a weird, lunar scenery straight out of the imagination of Salvador Dali, where the amazing shapes and extraordinary tones of the earth contrast with reflections from the sky in the salt lagoons. The main oasis is the village of San Pedro, from where there are views of the vast peaks of the Andes to the east, and the Salt Mountains, moulded by erosion into giant mineral sculptures, to the west.

HOW TO GET THERE:
International flight to Santiago. Domestic flight to Calama 100km (62 miles) away then a shuttle flight/ road to San Pedro.

WHEN TO GO:
It is a high-altitude desert climate with extreme temperature changes. Avoid September to November when winds reach up to 100kph (62mph).

NEAREST TOWN:
San Pedro.

EL TATIO GEYSER FIELD

Chile

Situated in the Atacama desert in the altiplano of northern Chile at an altitude of 4,200m (13,775ft), El Tatio ('The Grandpa') is the third-largest geyser field in the world. There are more than 80 active geysers, 30 of which are perpetual spouters, as well as hot springs and five mud pots. The combined activity of the geysers, mud pots, colourful pools reflecting the light and cinder terraces makes the field a really awe-inspiring place. If you sit quietly and look around you, you will start to notice the wildlife. There are several species of small bird as well as foxes, chinchillas and a flamingo family, and you may even find yourself approached by friendly Andean camels. El Tatio is best visited in the early morning when, apart from the wonderful light, for some reason the geysers are at their most active. As you wander around the field you must tread extremely carefully – the cauldron crusts are thinner than they look. More than one person has been very badly burned when apparently stable rock has suddenly given way and tipped them into a cauldron of boiling water.

HOW TO GET THERE:
International airport Santiago, then fly to Calama and bus to San Pedro.
WHEN TO GO:
It is a high-altitude desert climate with sharp temperature drops at night. Avoid September to November when there are high winds.
NEAREST TOWN:
San Pedro 82km (51 miles).

PENÍNSULA VALDÉS

Argentina

HOW TO GET THERE:
Fly to Trelew International Airport, 60km (40 miles) from Puerto Madryn. Take a tour from Puerto Madryn or bus to Puerto Pirámides.
WHEN TO GO:
June to December to watch the whales. All year for seals and sea lions.
NEAREST TOWN:
Puerto Madryn 105km (65 miles).

The Valdés Peninsula, on Patagonia's arid Atlantic coast, is one of the most important marine mammal habitats in the world. Colonies of southern elephant seals, fur seals, southern sea lions, penguins, dolphins and orcas congregate on and around its shore. But, above all, Valdés is famous for its right whales. The southern right whale was once hunted almost to extinction but thanks to conservation efforts, up to 2,000 of them now migrate here to breed. Valdés is a stark, axe-shaped promontory that juts 100km (63 miles) into the Atlantic, connected to the mainland by a 25-km (16-mile) isthmus. The sheer numbers of marine mammals that the peninsula harbours is overwhelming, and you can spend many peaceful hours watching these charming creatures playing, mating and breeding in their natural habitat.

DON'T MISS
Perito Moreno glacier.

PATAGONIA

Argentina

HOW TO GET THERE:
Fly to Buenos Aires then by road or take a domestic flight to Comodoro Rivadavia.
WHEN TO GO:
November to April.

The southernmost part of Argentina and Chile, Patagonia is a beautiful, untamed land of fjords, rugged mountains, enormous glaciers, windswept plateaux, petrified forests and flat grasslands. Dominated in the west by the heights of the Andes, Patagonia is home to some of the most beautiful landscapes in the world and covers an area of over 900,000 sq km (347,000 sq miles). The Northern Lakes area of Argentina's Lake District has a number of national parks in the foothills of the Andes, and a trek through these will reveal a beautiful landscape of wildflower meadows, lakes and rugged peaks. The Southern Lakes are perhaps even more spectacular and adjoin the Los Glaciares National Park. This area has hundreds of glaciers, remnants of an ancient ice sheet, perhaps the most famous of which is Perito Moreno. This glacier, with its nose stretching 5km (3 miles) across, periodically advances across the Lago Argentino and blocks it until the mass of water held behind this frozen dam becomes too great and it ruptures, crashing into pieces as the water surges through. Further south still lie the Straits of Magellan, Tierra del Fuego and Cape Horn. The range of different habitats in Patagonia, from high volcanoes to pampa and beaches, mean that it has a huge variety of wildlife, from condors that soar effortlessly in thermals to engaging emperor penguins, rheas, hummingbirds, flamingos, steamer ducks, upland geese and long-tailed parakeets. Mammals on land include the Brazilian fox, guanacos and cougars, while in the oceans there are southern right whales, orcas and elephant seals. This remote land offers both awe-inspiring spectacle and tranquillity for any visitor.

LOS GLACIARES

Argentina

The World Heritage site of Los Glaciares National Park is a region of awe-inspiring beauty in the southern Patagonian ice field – the third-largest continental icecap in the world after Antarctica and Greenland. Los Glaciares extends 170km (106 miles) along the Chilean border, more than a third of it covered in ice. It is 4,450 sq km (1,720 sq miles) of arid steppe, wondrous, coloured beech forests, glacial lakes and the towering mountains of the Andean icecap. The icecap is the direct source of 47 large glaciers and there are around 200 smaller unconnected ones. Glaciers normally occur at altitudes of 2,500m (8,200ft) or more. Here, uniquely, they are only 1,500m (4,920ft) above sea level, so are easily accessible. The park has two huge lakes – Lake Argentino in the south, which is 160km (100 miles) long, and Lake Viedma in the north – around which you can explore some of the most extreme scenery in the world. Lake Viedma is dominated by the awesome granite spikes of the FitzRoy Massif, great jagged walls of rock towering up out of the forest. Otherwise known as Cerro Chaltén ('Smoking Mountain') because of the ring of cloud around its peak, Mount FitzRoy has the reputation of being 'ultimate', not because it is particularly high at 3,375m (11,070ft) but because of its sheer granite sides. At one end of Lake Argentino is the incredible spectacle of continual icefalls. It is the junction of three glaciers – the Onelli, the Upsala and Spegazzini. Together with the immense 5-km (3-mile) Perito Moreno glacier, they make their inexorable descent from the icecap, eroding the mountain in their path, to disgorge colossal icebergs into the milky waters of the lake in an overwhelming display of nature's power.

HOW TO GET THERE:
Fly to El Calafate International airport or by road from Río Gallegos.
WHEN TO GO:
October to April. High season January and February.
NEAREST TOWN:
El Calafate 40km (25 miles).

SIERRA PAMPEANAS

Argentina

HOW TO GET THERE:
International flights to San Juan then bus 250km (156 miles) to San Agustín de Valle Fértil.
WHEN TO GO:
Any time.
NEAREST TOWNS:
San Agustín de Valle Fértil 80km (50 miles) from Ischigualasto, 190km (119 miles) from Talampaya.

In the parched hills and pure air of Sierra Pampeanas in northwest Argentina, there is a World Heritage Site that reveals the story of evolution. The unique geological formations in the Ischigualasto and Talampaya National Parks contain the most complete known fossil record of plants, dinosaurs and mammalian ancestors. The desert here is a testament to the evolution of vertebrate life in the Triassic period. No other place on Earth has remotely comparable fossil traces. Ischigualasto, or Valle de la Luna, is a valley with surreal landscapes of grey-green rocks and petrified trees. Talampaya is a sandstone desert of rainbow-coloured rock, sculpted by the elements into dramatic Gothic formations. The Puno Indian inhabitants continue to live traditionally in their beautiful land of intense earth colours and desert mountain air.

TIERRA DEL FUEGO

Argentina

HOW TO GET THERE:
Fly from Buenos Aires or El Calafate to Ushuaia.
WHEN TO GO:
Year-round.
NEAREST TOWN:
Ushuaia 9km (6 miles).

Tierra del Fuego is known to its inhabitants as El fin del Mundo ('the end of the world'). It is a remote archipelago of islands at the tip of South America, ending at Cape Horn. The largest island is separated from the mainland by the Magellan Strait, which was the fastest and safest route between the Atlantic and Pacific Oceans until the Panama Canal was built. The island is divided between Chile and Argentina while the remaining islands of the archipelago, including Cape Horn, are mainly Chilean territory. On the Argentine side of the main island is 'the southernmost city in the world', Ushuaia, and a national park stretching 60km (37 miles) northwards from the Beagle Channel along the Chilean border. The Pan-American Highway, running all the way from Alaska, comes to an end here, at Lapataia Bay – an exquisite, remote stretch of coast where the Beagle Channel meets the Pacific Ocean. There are colonies of sea lions as well as penguins and thousands of other birds, including rare species such as the albatross, oyster catchers, steamer ducks and petrels. The park is 630 sq km (243 sq miles) of superb mountain scenery, with isolated glacial valleys, lakes and forest. It is situated around Lake Roca whose waters flow into the turbulent Lapataia river and out into the bay.

NAHUEL HUAPÍ NATIONAL PARK

Argentina

Known as the Argentine Lake District, the Nahuel Huapí is a picture-postcard region of deep blue glacial lakes and snowy mountain peaks, with wooded river valleys, meadows and countless streams. The park covers more than 7,000 sq km (2,700 sq miles) of the Andes foothills. Nahuel Huapí is the largest of the many breathtaking lakes, and the terrain ranges in altitude from 700–3,000m (2,300–9,840ft), with rainfall varying from 30cm (12in) in the eastern grasslands to 400cm (156in) in the western forests. These extremes support diverse ecosystems. In the sparse vegetation of the high mountains there are condors, pumas and the endangered huemul (Andean deer). On the lower slopes, the native beech and evergreen woods are full of flowers, which during spring are a blaze of colour. The luxuriant Valdivian forest is dense jungle of ferns, orchids and liana creepers. And the unique Bosque Los Arrayanes is a wood of 300-year-old trees with twisted trunks and strange cinnamon bark, cold and soft to the touch. In the east, the semi-arid plateau, scored with dramatic canyons and carpeted with yellow- and orange-hued grasses, is a habitat for foxes, guanacos, and birds of prey. The natural diversity of Nahuel Huapí makes it an outstandingly popular year-round resort for everything from skiing to bird-watching in an idyllic setting.

ACONCAGUA

Argentina

Cerro Aconcagua is the highest mountain in the Americas, at 6,962m (22,835ft), and is one of the 'Seven Summits' – the highest mountains on each of the seven continents. Its snowbound peak towers over the dramatic scenery of the Uspallata Pass – the border-crossing between Argentina and Chile. Edward Fitzgerald, an English mountaineer, became the first person in 1897 to scale Aconcagua. In 1985, the mummified corpse of an Incan, preserved by the cold, was discovered at an altitude of 5,300m (17,380ft), proving that pre-Columbian civilizations explored these heights. It is not a technically difficult mountain to climb, and for that reason, it is all too often underestimated. Aconcagua has one of the highest death tolls for any mountain in the world. Extreme and unpredictable weather in the form of high winds, blizzards and electrical storms as well as the effects of altitude can make it a daunting prospect and climbers are frequently beaten back by the weather or altitude sickness.

IGUAZÚ FALLS

Argentina

On the border between Brazil and Argentina, the Iguazú Falls (Iguaçu on the Brazilian side) are a massive complex of almost 300 cascades set in a lush jungle. The total span is 2.7km (1.7 miles) and the falls themselves average up to 70m (230ft) in height, far taller than Niagara and more than twice as wide. The first European to see the falls was Alvar Núñez Cabeza de Vaca in 1541, but they had been known of by local inhabitants for more than 10,000 years and their name derives from the local Guaraní term *y guasu*, meaning 'big water', although when confronted by the sheer volume thundering over the edge of an ancient lava flow, that seems like an understatement. Both nations have created national parks around the falls, and the wildlife in each is spectacular.

PENGUINS

South Georgia

South Georgia is an Antarctic island sanctuary about 2,000km (1,250 miles) east of Tierra del Fuego in the South Atlantic Ocean. It is a hauntingly still, 170-km (106-mile) glacier landscape of ice-capped mountains, with steep cliffs and bays. The surrounding rocks and islets provide shelter for the birds and marine mammals that inhabit this desolate region of chill winds, freezing waters and icebergs. The largest penguin colonies anywhere on Earth congregate here. There are around 400,000 breeding pairs of king penguins as well as a phenomenal two million pairs of the smaller macaroni penguin and sizeable colonies of four other species. These charming, vulnerable creatures display an extraordinary life force in overcoming the extreme conditions in which they live and breed. Captain Cook called the island 'Cape Disappointment' when he realized that he had not landed on the Antarctic continent in 1775, but he took note of the huge seal and whale populations. Two hundred years later both had been hunted nearly to extinction. Today numerous whales have returned to feed in the island's plentiful waters.

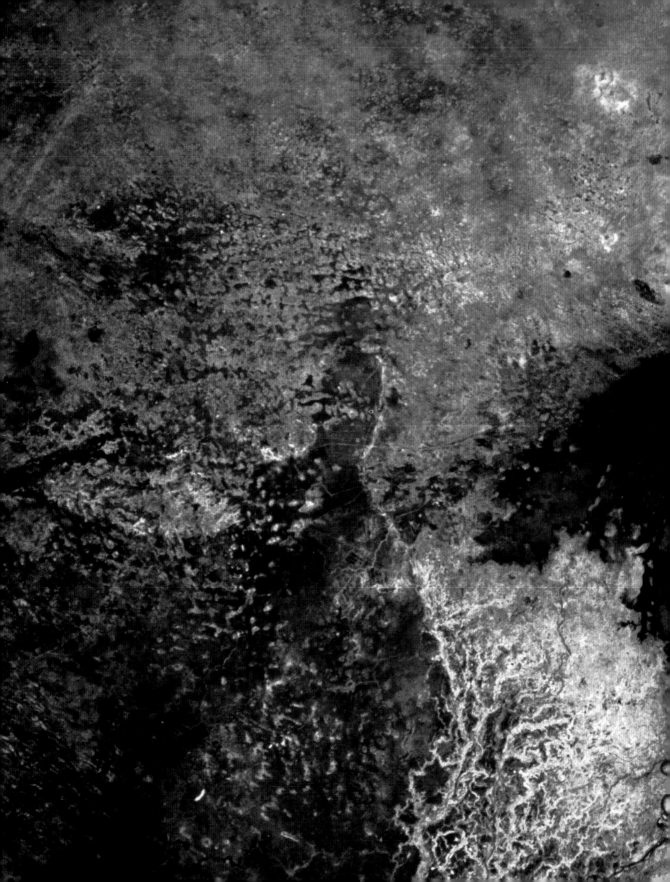

AFRICA

THE ATLAS MOUNTAINS

Morocco

The Atlas Mountains extend through Morocco, Algeria and Tunisia in a series of separate ranges that continue for about 2,400km (1,500 miles). Within Morocco, they are divided north to south into the Middle Atlas, High Atlas and Anti-Atlas, rising at the Atlantic coast and stretching east to Algeria. They effectively separate the more moderate, Mediterranean climate to the north from the drier, harsher, Saharan climate of the south. The Middle Atlas, the most westerly of the ranges, rises to the south of Fes. Its lovely oak-, cork- and cedar-covered mountains hold waterfalls and plateaux studded with volcanic lakes. This region is not much visited, and to explore it properly you will need a car. Travelling south you will reach Midelt, beyond which rise the dramatic peaks of the High Atlas. Further west, the High Atlas is usually approached via Marrakech. This is the best region for trekking holidays. Innumerable trails wind through lush, summertime valleys and mountainsides dotted with small Berber villages. One of the most popular routes includes Djebel Toubkal, at 4,167m (13,668ft), the highest mountain in Morocco. Two dramatic passes, the Tizi n'Test and the Tizi n'Tichka, have been carved through these peaks, both affording spectacular views from their narrow, hairpin bends. The High Atlas is snow-covered in winter and the skiing at Oukaimeden is thought to be the best in the country. The Anti-Atlas extends from the Atlantic northeast to Ouarzarzate. These are starkly beautiful mountains reaching a maximum height of 2,531m (8,302ft). A particularly scenic journey can be made from Taroudant to Tafraoute, a gorgeous small town on the slopes of the Ameln Valley.

TASSILI N'AJJER

Algeria

Designated a UNESCO World Heritage Site in 1982, Tassili N'Ajjer is a massive mountain plateau extending for nearly 500km (300 miles) across the Sahara desert of southeastern Algeria. The soft sandstone has been carved by the wind and sand grains that howl across the desert into fantastic landforms, with sheer cliffs and sudden, unexpected, deep chasms and more than 300 rock arches. Because of its isolation, this beautiful landscape remains relatively undisturbed.

During the last ice age this area used to be far wetter than it is today, and the sandstone has managed to retain some of the ancient moisture, allowing the growth of sparse woodland including the Saharan myrtle and Saharan cypress. The wildlife was also much richer thousands of years ago, as can be seen from the cave paintings that dot the area and show such animals as antelope and crocodiles as well as cattle, indicating that there must have been land for grazing and pasture and waterholes for the crocodiles. There are also vivid depictions of the life of the people who lived here.

In order to protect the rock paintings from further damage, visitors can only enter the central area with an official guide or accredited tour group.

GRAND ERG OCCIDENTAL

Algeria

YOU SHOULD KNOW
Go with an organized
group, who will help to
arrange permits, and an
authorized guide.

Algeria, on Africa's Mediterranean coast, possesses some of the starkest but most beautiful landscapes on Earth. Dominated in the north and south by mountain ranges and plateaux, and crossed by the Sahara desert, it also has several of the largest inland sand-dune systems in the world, including the Grand Erg Occidental and Grand Erg Oriental: the Great Western and Eastern sand seas. In lowland basins, they are thought to be the remnants of ancient shallow seas or lakes. Unlike most of the Sahara, whose ground is a mixture of stones and pebbles, the ergs are the epitome of everyone's romantic image of deserts, with seemingly endless ranks of golden, knife-edged dunes marching into the distance. There are no oases, so no-one can settle here, and there are no roads or villages. A road skirts around the southern side of the erg, affording magnificent, if distant, views of the dunes, and it is possible to travel a short way into the area from the beautiful oasis towns around its edge, such as El Goléa, Beni Abbès and Tarhit. Even a brief walk into this surreal landscape leaves visitors in awe of the scale of these giant natural sculptures and with a readjusted sense of their own importance.

HURGHADA'S UNDERWATER GARDENS
Egypt

HOW TO GET THERE:
By air to Hurghada.
WHEN TO GO:
Year-round, but the water is warmest from May to October.
NEAREST TOWN:
Hurghada is on the beach.

DON'T MISS
The Roman remains at Gabal Abu Durkan.

The Red Sea coast stretches south from the Suez Canal for some 800km (500 miles). Hurghada, until fairly recently just a small, quiet fishing village, is now an internationally known diving and snorkelling centre, and the gateway to many vibrantly coloured underwater 'gardens'. The joy of Hurghada is that there are fabulous reefs teeming with multicoloured fish within 10m (33ft) of the beach, enabling everyone to enjoy this underwater world. Even if you can't swim, you can take a trip in a glass-bottomed boat from which you can gaze through the brilliantly clear waters to the reefs below. There are many well-known sites here, each with its speciality. Altogether there are 400 types of coral, 1,500 species of fish, plus turtles and dolphins. The marine environment here is protected, and the small daily fee that is charged goes towards conservation initiatives and marine park rangers.

SIWA OASIS

Egypt

HOW TO GET THERE:
Overland from Cairo via Mersa Matruh or by air from Cairo to the airport in Al-Alamein.
WHEN TO GO:
Spring or autumn.
NEAREST TOWN:
Siwa.

YOU SHOULD KNOW
Women should cover up and alcohol is forbidden.

This remote oasis in the Western desert, on the edge of the Great Sand Sea, only a few miles from the Libyan border and 550km (342 miles) west of Cairo, has provided a place of refuge for many thousands of years. It is set in a depression 82km (52 miles) long and 9–28km (5.5–17 miles) wide. More than 1,000 slightly saline springs bring water through the sandstone rock to the surface here, and there are three major saltwater lakes. The slightly saline water allows the area's inhabitants to grow olives and dates, and lush, dense groves of these occupy the floor of the depression. Several of the springs can be bathed in, and their mineral waters are reputed to have medicinal qualities. A favourite is the Cleopatra Bath, where the water bubbles up from the ground into a deep pool. However, bathing in the lake belonging to the Oracle, which was famously visited by Alexander the Great, is regarded as sacrilegious. The mountains and hills that lie within the oasis have caves in which people have lived or buried their dead and these may be reached via numerous tracks that wind through the landscape, offering views over this beautiful, peaceful landscape.

THE BANDIAGARA ESCARPMENT

Mali

HOW TO GET THERE:
By plane to Bandiagara,
then by road.
WHEN TO GO:
October to February,
best during November
to December.
NEAREST TOWN:
Bandiagara 44km (27 miles).

YOU SHOULD KNOW
The best way to see the
area is with a Dogon guide.

Listed as a UNESCO World Heritage Site in 1989, the stunning Bandiagara Escarpment lies in the south of Mali and has flora and fauna unique in the region. Eroded from rocks that are more than 400 million years old, the escarpment separates the sandstone plateau of the same name from the plaine du Séno. The stunning cliff runs northeast to southwest for roughly 150km (90 miles) and ranges from 100m (330ft) in the south to 500m (1,650ft) in the north. The region's high seasonal rainfall escapes underground through fissures and caves and re-emerges in springs along the bottom of the escarpment, allowing the local Dogon to cultivate crops. Fissures in the rocks, ravines known as thalwags, rock pools and the areas around the springs have a unique microclimate and support a wide range of plants missing from the surrounding region, which is too dry or has been ravaged by fire. In turn, these support a variety of migrant and resident wildlife. Mammals that can be seen here include porcupines, rock hyrax, jackals and pale foxes, with which the Dogon have a spiritual relationship.

W NATIONAL PARK

Niger

Niger's only national park, which also extends deep into the neighbouring countries of Benin and Burkina Faso, acquired its name because of the giant 'W' shape of the double bend in the Niger river that forms its northern border. Covering a total area of 10,000 sq km (3,860 sq miles), of which some 2,200 sq km (850 sq miles) is in Niger, it was officially designated in 1954 and, in 1996, was included on the UNESCO World Heritage list. Because of its wetlands and the rich variety of birds that they attract, the park has also been designated a Wetland of International Importance under the Ramsar Convention. Occupying a transition zone between savannah and forest, the park is known for its many large mammals, including elephants, buffalos, antelopes, hippos, spotted hyenas, baboons and warthogs, as well as the cat carnivores – lion, leopard, cheetah and serval. Numerous waterholes have been constructed throughout the park to attract wildlife. There are thought to be at least 500 different plant species present in the park, along with some 350 species of resident and aquatic migratory bird. The W Park has managed to avoid the worst of the catastrophic consequences of unchecked poaching that has been seen in other West African parks. Yet now it is subject to another potential threat: plans for phosphate mining and the construction of a hydroelectric dam on its southern border, both of which could have long-term serious ecological consequences for the park's wellbeing.

YOU SHOULD KNOW

You will need a registered park guide and a four-wheel-drive vehicle in the park.

HOW TO GET THERE:
By road from Niamey, Niger's capital.
WHEN TO GO:
December to April (the park is closed July to November).
NEAREST TOWN:
Niamey 152km (95 miles).

LAKE CHAD

Chad

Fifty years ago Lake Chad was the fourth-largest lake in Africa and covered an area in excess of 25,000 sq km (9,650 sq miles), mostly in the far west of Chad but also extending into Niger, Nigeria and Cameroon. Believed to be a remnant of a former inland sea, at its largest around 4,000BC it measured some 400,000 sq km (154,000 sq miles). Today, however, as a result of reduced rainfall and desertification combined with increased demand for the lake's water, the area of the lake has been dramatically reduced to less than 1,000 sq km (386 sq miles) and it is now entirely within the borders of Chad. The lake, which has an average depth of only 1.5m (5ft) and is a mere 7m (23ft) at its deepest, has many islands and mudflats within it and is home to a wide variety of wildlife, including fish, crocodiles, waterfowl and shore birds. It is surrounded by swampy vegetation mostly made up of reeds and papyrus, which is used to make canoes. Some of the islands are inhabited and used as bases for fishing, though the annual fish catch from the lake is about 20 per cent of what it was 40 years ago. The lake is a vital resource for the ten million people living in the area, yet while there are various ambitious schemes to divert river water into the lake, it is by no means impossible that Lake Chad will have completely dried up by the end of this century.

HOW TO GET THERE:
By road (four-wheel drive recommended) from N'Djamena.
WHEN TO GO:
November to March.
NEAREST TOWN:
N'Djamena 100km (62 miles) from the lake's southern end.

NIOKOLO-KOBA NATIONAL PARK

Senegal

One of the largest national parks in west Africa, Niokolo-Koba National Park is situated in the southeast of Senegal and is famous for its diverse wildlife. The park, which covers an area of over 9,000 sq km (3,474 sq miles), is home to over 80 different mammal species, including lions, leopards, elephants, buffalos, hippos and hyenas, as well as some 30 types of reptile and over 300 different bird species. The landscape throughout the park is generally flat; the varied vegetation includes savannah, forests, lakes and marshes. The park is well watered as the Gambia river, along with its tributaries, the Niokolo-Koba and the Koulountou, runs though it. Included on the UNESCO list of World Heritage Sites in 1981, the park is also an international biosphere reserve. Potential visitors may need to be reminded that, as in many wildlife reserves, sightings of lions or elephants are by no means guaranteed.

HOW TO GET THERE:
By road from Tambacounda.
WHEN TO GO:
March to May
(closed June to November).
NEAREST TOWN:
Tambacounda 140km
(90 miles).

DON'T MISS
The chimpanzees
in the area of
Mount Assirik.

WAZA NATIONAL PARK

Cameroon

HOW TO GET THERE:
Four-wheel drive from Maroua.
WHEN TO GO:
Mid-November to mid-June,
but April/May is the optimum
time to see lions.
NEAREST TOWN:
Mokolo 160km (100 miles).

Waza National Park is a vast, remote area in the far north province of Cameroon. Situated on the edge of the Sahel, between Chad and Nigeria, these flat acacia plains lie to the south of Lake Chad's floodplain, and are only accessible from mid-November to mid-June due to summertime flooding. The park was listed as a UNESCO Biosphere Reserve in 1982. It consists of a forested area and huge expanses of feathery grasslands and seasonal marshes, making it home both to forest and savannah animals, as well as permanent and migrating birds. This is probably the best place in central Africa to observe wildlife, and in late spring, when only a few waterholes remain, a constant parade of fabulous animals arrive in search of water and shade, finding moments of much-needed relief from the blistering sun. The plains are teeming with animals – giraffe, antelope, hyena, cheetah, serval, warthog, elephants and lions.

SIMIEN NATIONAL PARK

Ethiopia

The Simien National Park lies in one of the most spectacular landscapes on Earth. Over millennia, the Ethiopian plateau has been eroded to create a lunar vista of flat areas and peaks separated by dramatic, steep-sided gorges that run down to broad valleys and grasslands. At 4,620m (15,157ft), Ras Dejen is the fourth-highest peak in Africa and snow often falls in the highest areas of the park, even though it is only about 13 degrees north of the equator, and temperatures can fall below 0°C (32°F) at almost any time of the year. The park's specialities include several very rare animals, including the walia ibex, which lives only here and is the reason for the park being set up, gelada baboons, simien fox and small numbers of Ethiopian wolves. This breathtaking landscape is perfect for trekking: from the lower slopes where farmers grow crops and graze animals, through the alpine forests and up to the high grasslands, where spectacular plants include giant lobelia and kniphofia. Mountain tracks between villages allow for easy access to most areas.

YOU SHOULD KNOW
A guide and an armed guard
are mandatory.

HOW TO GET THERE: By road from Gondar.
WHEN TO GO: September to November is best.
NEAREST TOWN: Gondar 101km (60 miles).

THE DANAKIL DEPRESSION

Ethiopia

This geological depression is situated in the northeast of Ethiopia and extends into neighbouring Eritrea and Djibouti, the area commonly known as the Horn of Africa. It is probably the most inhospitable place on the planet and is deserving of its nickname, the 'Devil's Kitchen'. Part of Africa's Great Rift Valley, it is one of the hottest areas on Earth and one of the driest, with only a few inches of rain falling each year. Apart from the narrow green strip along the banks of the Awash river, the landscape is a mixture of desert scrub, rocky outcrops and mountains. About 1,200 sq km (463 sq miles) of the depression is covered in salt, and salt mining is still the principal source of income for many of the nomadic Afar tribespeople who inhabit this hostile environment. The base of the depression is composed of basalt lava, and the whole area is a great source of interest to geologists and volcanologists. Hundreds of small earthquakes shake the area every year, and volcanic cones and deep cracks in the earth are common sights.

HOW TO GET THERE:
By road (four-wheel drive) from Mekele.
WHEN TO GO:
September to March.
NEAREST TOWN:
Mekele.

YOU SHOULD KNOW
A special permit to travel is required. Daytime temperatures can reach 50°C (145°F).

HOW TO GET THERE:
By road to Bahir Dar.
WHEN TO GO:
December to April.
NEAREST TOWN:
Bahir Dar, one of Ethiopia's largest towns, lies on the lakeshore.

LAKE TANA

Ethiopia

Situated in the northern highlands of Ethiopia, Lake Tana is not only the country's largest lake, it is also the source of the Blue Nile, which flows for a distance of some 1,500km (938 miles) to Khartoum in Sudan. There it joins the White Nile to become the famous Nile river, flowing through the entire length of Egypt until it reaches the Nile Delta and the Mediterranean. Thus Lake Tana is important both as a source of food and water, as well as hydroelectric power for Ethiopia. Fed by four perennial rivers and numerous seasonal streams, the lake has an average depth of only 8m (26ft), which can vary by as much as 2m (7ft) between the wet and dry seasons. The surface area of the lake similarly varies from 3,000–3,500 sq km (1,160–1,350 sq miles) dependent on the season. Lake Tana contains a wealth of fish, and there is an extraordinary variety of birds along the shores and on its islands. There are 37 islands in the lake upon which stand some 20 monasteries and churches. Some of these date as far back as the 13th century and many of them contain paintings, frescoes and various historical religious artifacts.

DON'T MISS
The view from the
top of Mount Muhavura.

MGAHINGA GORILLA NATIONAL PARK
Uganda

Despite being the smallest of Uganda's national parks, Mgahinga, at 33.7 sq km (13 sq miles), is still one of the most important. It adjoins both Rwanda's Volcano National Park and the Democratic Republic of Congo's Virunga National Park. The Virunga mountains are a series of both active and extinct volcanoes that straddle the border of these three countries, three of which (all extinct) can be climbed in Mgahinga. Mgahinga is famous for its tiny population of endangered mountain gorillas, including one family consisting

of nine animals (including two silverbacks and three adult females) that are familiarized with tracking. This family often moves across the border into Rwanda, and therefore gorilla-tracking safaris can only be confirmed a short time in advance. Groups from the neighbouring countries sometimes visit the area for a month or two. The tropical rainforest that covers the lower slopes has been somewhat depleted for farmland, but higher up there are abundant bamboo and alpine forests. Largely vegetarian, male mountain gorillas weigh as much as 194kg (430lbs) and can eat up to 34kg (75lbs) of vegetation each day. Gallium vines form a large part of their diet but they also love bamboo shoots. They will also climb up to subalpine regions in order to eat another delicacy, the soft centre of the giant senecio tree. Mountain gorillas are almost extinct. There are thought to be between 650 and 700 animals left in the world, shared between these three countries. One of two subspecies of gorilla, they have longer, darker hair than other gorillas, enabling them to live at higher, colder altitudes. These fascinating creatures are endangered by habitat loss, poaching and human diseases such as colds and flu, to which they have no immunity.

HOW TO GET THERE:
By road from Kampala,
or fly to Kisoro and then
go by road.
WHEN TO GO:
June, July, August or January.
NEAREST TOWN:
Kisoro 10km (6 miles).

YOU SHOULD KNOW
Gorilla-tracking permits are
in high demand, so organize
your trip and permit several
months in advance.

BWINDI IMPENETRABLE NATIONAL PARK

Uganda

DON'T MISS

The many spectacular birds and butterflies.

HOW TO GET THERE:
By road from Kampala via Kabale.
WHEN TO GO:
December to February and May to August.
NEAREST TOWN:
Kabale 29km (18 miles).

YOU SHOULD KNOW

In many places the forest is indeed impenetrable; only 12 visitor permits are issued per day.

Bwindi Impenetrable National Park is, at 331 sq km (128 sq miles), one of the largest areas of tropical rainforest in east Africa. Situated in a landscape of steep, rugged hills and deep, narrow valleys along the border with the Democratic Republic of Congo, it warrants its name. This is a prime example of the jungle of our imagination – vast trees, draped with creepers, mistletoe and orchids, struggle to reach the sunlight, while beneath them the dense undergrowth of twisting vines and ferns occasionally gives way to thickets of bamboo, swamps, marshes, rivers and grassland. Where the sun breaks through the leafy canopy, exotic and colourful plants such as heliconia add sudden splashes of colour. The flora and fauna in Bwindi are incredibly impressive, with over 200 types of tree and 100 species of fern. At least 120 mammal species live here, and the area is rich with primates – colobus monkeys leap between branches, families of chimpanzees search for fruit and vervets and baboons chatter and hoot, adding a subtext to the twittering and screeching of some 350 different species of bird. Amongst Bwindi's populations of endangered species are some 23 families of mountain gorilla. Living at a lower altitude than those in the Virunga mountains, it is thought that these may be a distinct subspecies, with shorter hair and longer limbs.

RWENZORI MOUNTAINS NATIONAL PARK
Uganda

The Rwenzori National Park lies on the border between Uganda and the Democratic Republic of Congo. It consists of six massifs, which, unlike many of the other mountains in the Great Rift Valley, are not volcanic. The highest mountain is Mount Stanley, named after the British explorer who was the first European to see it, in 1887. At 5,109m (16,762ft), it is the third-highest mountain in Africa. The other five massifs are Mount Speke, Mount Baker, Mount Emin, Mount Gessi and Mount Luigi di Savoia. They are separated by deep gorges with lush vegetation, which ranges from tropical rainforest, through giant, moss-covered heathers, alpine meadows and bogs, up to the snowcapped peaks. The rainforest's cushiony canopy shades begonias, aram lilies and hibiscus, which fill the air with heady aromas. In common with Kilimanjaro and Mount Kenya, the Rwenzoris are losing their ice cover, with more than half of their glaciers disappearing in less than a century. The effect that this loss will have on the range's ecosystem is not yet known.

LAKE VICTORIA
Uganda

As well as being Africa's largest lake, Lake Victoria is the largest tropical lake in the world. It covers a vast area of some 68,800 sq km (26,560 sq miles) – about the same size as Ireland. This is one of the most densely populated regions in Africa, and the lake plays a vital part in supporting millions of people. Fishing, particularly for Nile perch and tilapia, provides a living for many along the lakeside; fish from Lake Victoria are exported all over the world, as well as being sold locally. There are 200 species of fish to be found in the lake, though the introduction of the Nile perch in the 1950s led to the extinction of some 300 species of fish that had survived there for hundreds of years. As a result, Lake Victoria could unenviably lay claim to having experienced the greatest mass extinction of vertebrates in modern times. Hippos and crocodiles were once numerous in the lake, too, but their numbers are now much reduced as a result of pollution and over-population by humans. There are over 3,000 islands in the lake, many of which are inhabited; the 62 islands that form the Sese archipelago are famous for their fishing both by locals and foreign tourists. The lake is also important for its transport – there are many passenger boats and cargo vessels that ply between the trading towns and villages lining the lake's shores.

MASAI MARA NATIONAL RESERVE

Kenya

Left: Wildebeest crossing the Mara river during their migration.

Set in the southwest of Kenya, the Masai Mara National Reserve is one of the best wildlife sites in the world. Its plains and acacia scrub are home to lions and cheetahs, baboons, zebras, hyenas, waterbuck, giraffes, buffalo, white rhino, gazelles and impala. Elephant herds roam the bush, while the Mara river itself provides pools for hippos and cover for leopards and crocodiles. The Masai is also the site of one of nature's great spectacles: the annual migration of 1,200,000 wildebeest, more than 350,000 Thomson's gazelles and more than 190,000 zebra. In May and June, these animals leave the neighbouring Serengeti and head north, beginning their return journey in October following the fresh pasture that springs up after seasonal rains. A visit to this vast, rich landscape is not an experience that anyone will easily forget.

MOUNT KENYA

Kenya

An extinct stratovolcano of extreme beauty, Mount Kenya is the second-highest mountain in Africa, at 5,119m (17,058ft). Despite being not far south of the equator, it has for thousands of years been capped with glaciers, although these are now retreating at an alarming rate. The national park was created in 1949 and it became a UNESCO World Heritage Site in 1997. The high peaks, above the beautiful U-shaped glacial Makinder valley and emerald-green tarns, are a draw for climbers, but the lower slopes hold a fantastic array of wildlife in their beautiful and varied habitats. During the dry periods, large mammals, such as eland, elephant, buffalo and zebra, move upwards to the high, open moorland, and have been seen as high up as 4,000m (13,120ft). Below the moorland is an area of high-altitude heath and shrubs, then a layer of upper forest with small trees and mosses, then a dense forest of bamboo followed by a montane forest with podocarpus, juniper and cedar, and finally a dry upland forest. These varied habitats support a vast variety of wildlife. There are many climbing routes within the park, with huts to stay in overnight, suitable for different levels of fitness and ability. Although there are enough beautiful landscapes and amazing animals lower down, it is only by getting to the higher reaches of the mountain that you can appreciate this spectacular place.

THE GREAT RIFT VALLEY

Kenya

HOW TO GET THERE:
By road from Nairobi.
WHEN TO GO:
July to September and
December to February.
NEAREST TOWN:
Nairobi 60km (37 miles).

The Great Rift Valley is probably the greatest natural wonder in the world. This amazing fissure in the Earth's crust was formed some 30 million years ago when the shifting and separating of several tectonic plates uplifted volcanoes and caused parts of the Earth's crust to sink between parallel fault lines. It runs for about 6,000km (3,750 miles) from Lebanon to Mozambique, and its most dramatic section divides Kenya in two. The Western Rift is edged by some of Africa's highest mountain ranges. Mounts Kilimanjaro, Kenya, Meru and other volcanoes can be found here, as can some of the world's deepest and largest lakes. Boiling-hot springs provide evidence of the continuing volcanic activity of the region. A series of lakes runs along the Rift Valley. Some, like Lake Naivasha, are freshwater lakes, irrigating fertile orchards, vegetable crops and flowers, many of which are exported to Europe. Others, such as Lake Bogoria, are soda lakes, their waters full of sodium carbonate upon which blooms of blue-green algae form, producing a habitat for tilapia and other fish, thus drawing vast flocks of birds. Lake Nakuru lies at the narrowest point of the Rift Valley, between the Mau escarpment and the Aberdare mountains. Coming from Nairobi, the road climbs gently up through the highlands, arriving abruptly at the edge of the rift. The valley is at its deepest here, dropping dramatically by some 1,800m (5,904ft) to the floor below and providing visitors with an awe-inspiring view. The national parks and game reserves of the Rift Valley are home to hundreds of thousands of exotic animals that graze and hunt on the golden grasslands. There is no more extraordinary place on Earth.

LAKE NAKURU

Kenya

HOW TO GET THERE:
By air and/or road from
Nairobi via Nakuru.
WHEN TO GO:
July to February.
NEAREST TOWN:
Nakuru 5km (3 miles).

Less than 160km (100 miles) from Nairobi, Kenya's capital city, Lake Nakuru is world-famous for the huge number of flamingos that inhabit its shores. The extraordinary sight of the continually shifting mass of pink created by often more than a million flamingos on the lake is truly breathtaking. The flamingos are attracted by the algae that thrive in the shallow, warm and strongly alkaline waters of the lake. Scientists estimate that the flamingos consume as much as 250,000kg (551,200lbs) of algae per hectare per year. In the dry season the lake's area reduces to little more than 5 sq km (2 sq miles) but the rains increase it to about 45 sq km (17 sq miles), and the flamingo population on the lake varies accordingly. Pelicans and cormorants are also common, and there are thought to be over 400 resident bird species on the lake and in the surrounding park. In recent years the flamingo population has decreased alarmingly, partly as a result of intensive crop production in the surrounding area and the increased water usage in nearby Nakuru, which is Kenya's fourth-largest city.

LAKE TURKANA

Kenya

HOW TO GET THERE:
By three-day road trip
from Nairobi.
WHEN TO GO:
October to April for the birds,
April to May for the
crocodile hatch.
NEAREST TOWN:
Lodwar 75km (47 miles).

Lake Turkana lies within a mainly arid landscape. It is fed by three rivers but has no outflow, so water levels fluctuate during the year, creating an ever-changing landscape. Set in the eastern part of the Great Rift Valley in northern Kenya, this UNESCO World Heritage Site is a rich haven for wildlife. The surrounding land is littered with extinct volcanoes and old basalt lava flows, and one of the volcanic islands in the lake, Central Island, is still active. Europeans first discovered the lake in 1888, but it is obvious that it had been inhabited for far longer than that: the palaeontologist Richard Leakey discovered human remains here dating from some three million years ago. Visitors today come to see the wildlife: mammals here include zebras, gazelles and reticulated giraffes, as well as their predators, lions and cheetahs. Like many of the Rift Valley lakes, Lake Turkana is a hotspot for migrating birds, the most spectacular of which are the flocks of pink flamingos. However, Turkana's best-known wildlife attraction is its 22,000 Nile crocodiles, which colonized the lake long ago when its waters were higher and they could reach it from the White Nile.

YOU SHOULD KNOW
Ranger-led tours are a
must: much of the wildlife
is dangerous.

MOUNT ELGON NATIONAL PARK

Kenya

The extinct volcano of Mount Elgon lies at the heart of the spectacular national park that bears its name. It is an area with a rich variety of wildlife, including spotted hyenas, rock hyraxes and leopards, but it is for its herd of elephants that it has, rightly, become famous. The sparse vegetation that many herbivores in Africa eat does not give them sufficient minerals in their diet, including sodium, so they have to find sources elsewhere, such as natural salt licks, where salt has been leached from the rocks and deposited by water. These sites are sometimes found near the water holes that the animals use. However, in Mount Elgon National Park the elephants have taken things a step further. There are several caves here that contain deposits of salt, and over many centuries, the largest of them, Kitum, has been carved 200m (660ft) into the mountainside by the elephants so that they can exploit the salt. Each night, led by one of the herd elders, they wend their way to the cave and through its twisting passages to the salt deposit, gouging the rock surface with their tusks before licking the salt off. It is an eerie spectacle to watch, as 100 or more of these large mammals approach the cave through the night, finding their way blindly along a route memorized by previous generations of elephants over hundreds of years.

HOW TO GET THERE:
By road via Kitale.
WHEN TO GO:
June to August or
December to March.
NEAREST TOWN:
Mbale 24km (15 miles).

YOU SHOULD KNOW
The caves also harbour bats.

SERENGETI NATIONAL PARK

Tanzania

The Serengeti covers 60,000 sq km (23,000 sq miles) of Tanzania and Kenya, of which 14,763 sq km (5,700 sq miles) make up the former's Serengeti National Park, which was established in 1951 to protect the millions of animals that live here. The three African big cats – lion, cheetah and leopard – can all be seen here, as can their prey: zebra, gazelle, wildebeest and antelope. *Serengeti* means 'endless plains' in Masai, and it is the openness of the landscape here that makes it such a popular place for safaris. Twice a year, the Serengeti witnesses the mass migration and return of millions of wildebeest, zebra and Thomson's gazelles from here to the plains of the Masai Mara to the north. Seeing, and hearing, seemingly endless herds of animals thundering across the plains is an experience no one will ever forget.

NGORONGORO CONSERVATION AREA

Tanzania

Centred around the collapsed crater of an ancient volcano in the southern part of the Great Rift Valley, the Ngorongoro Conservation Area is a stunningly beautiful landscape that holds a fantastic range of wildlife. Twice a year, millions of migrants pass through on their way to and from the Serengeti, following the rains that bring fresh pasture. More than 550 species of bird have been seen in the park, with the flamingos of Lake Magadi being perhaps the most special. The huge crater formed some two million years ago when the volcano erupted violently and its magma chamber collapsed, creating the largest unbroken volcanic caldera in the world. In the wider park, there are more mountains, including several active volcanoes, forests, lakes and wide plains. In the north are the Olduvai Gorge, where some of the earliest remains of modern man and early man were discovered, and the soda lake, Lake Natron, where thousands of pink flamingos breed on little mud mounds. A visit to this remote park, with its awe-inspiring landscapes and plentiful wildlife, is a must-see for any wildlife lover.

OLDUVAI GORGE

Tanzania

One of the most significant prehistoric sites in the world, the Olduvai Gorge is located in northern Tanzania, at the border of the Ngorongoro Conservation Area and the Serengeti National Park. The steep-sided gorge is about 48km (30 miles) long and is situated on a series of fault lines, which, thanks to centuries of erosion, have yielded an unequalled treasure-trove of fossilized bones, teeth, tools, flora and fauna. The land is now semi-desert, but thousands of years ago it was covered with lush forest, fed by streams flowing into the Olduvai Lake. Successive layers of volcanic ash and stones covered the area, but exposed fossil deposits show seven distinct layers, covering a time span from about 2.1 million to 15,000 years ago. Louis and Mary Leakey began excavations here in the 1950s, and work continues to this day. The earliest discoveries showed that primitive hominids lived here in small camps, hunting for food and using stone tools made of flakes of basalt and quartz. These tools were named Oldowan, as this is the first site in which they were ever found. The skeletal remains of various early hominids have been found here, up to and including one complete skeleton of *Homo sapiens* dated to 17,000 years ago. Possibly the greatest discovery of all was made by Mary Leakey, when she found fossilized footprints dating to 3.75 million years ago, proving that our pre-human ancestors walked in an upright position.

SELOUS GAME RESERVE

Tanzania

Selous Game Reserve is an absolutely enormous area of some 50,000 sq km (19,300 sq miles). Large enough to be a country in its own right, it occupies 5 per cent of Tanzania and is larger than Switzerland. Inscribed as a UNESCO World Heritage Site in 1982, constant additions to its boundaries have made it one of the largest game reserves in the world. Selous has various safari camps and lodges, mainly situated around the Gorge area, but is otherwise uninhabited. Roads are impassable during the rainy season, but camps can be reached by plane. Safaris by boat are increasingly popular, and it is one of the only African reserves that allow safaris on foot, accompanied by an armed ranger. Few visitors come here, but those who do enter an untamed wilderness and gain a life-enhancing experience.

LAKE TANGANYIKA

Tanzania

Lake Tanganyika, which is situated within the Western Rift, is one of the most ancient lakes in the world. Largely surrounded by mountains, the side walls of the Great Rift Valley rise sharply to a height of 2,000m (6,600ft) from its western shore. The longest lake in the world, at 673km (421 miles), it is also the second-largest freshwater lake by volume, as well as the second-deepest, and its health is vitally important to an estimated ten million people. Two large and many smaller rivers flow into Lake Tanganyika, which has one major outflow, the Lukuga river. The extraordinary depth of the lake, at its maximum 1,470m (4,850ft), prevents 'turnover' of the water, resulting in much of the lower depths lacking oxygen. However, this is a lake that is teeming with life, much of it endemic, which has evolved through millennia. This is wonderful territory for researchers, anglers, divers and snorkellers – the visibility around the rocky shoreline is superb, often more than 20m (66ft). However, don't allow yourself to be totally dazzled as the lake is also home to the slender-snouted crocodile.

YOU SHOULD KNOW

The historic meeting between Livingstone and Stanley took place just south of Kigoma. Che Guevara trained his guerrilla forces on the western shores of the lake.

HOW TO GET THERE:
Train from Tanzania's capital, Dar es-Salaam, to Kigoma (27 hours) or by air to Bujumbura.
WHEN TO GO:
June to September.
NEAREST TOWNS:
Kigoma (Tanzania), Bujumbura (Burundi) and Kalemie (Congo) are all on the lake's shores.

MOUNT KILIMANJARO

Tanzania

Set in the national park of the same name in northeastern Tanzania, Mount Kilimanjaro, a dormant stratovolcano, is the highest mountain in Africa. Gases still rise from fumaroles in Kibo crater and scientists estimate that there is a pool of magma only 400m (1,300ft) below the crater. At 5,895m (19,340ft), Kibo is the youngest and highest of the three volcanic cones. Despite its position near the equator and the residual warmth from the last eruption, Kibo is so high that its peak, Uhuru, remains covered in snow all year, although the glaciers are retreating rapidly. There are various climbing routes up to the three peaks: Kibo has several that may be attempted by novices, while Mawenzi should not be attempted by anyone without rock-climbing and ice-climbing skills. Groups climb the mountain accompanied by guides and porters, stopping at mountain huts overnight. Kibo hut on the Marangu route is at 4,720m (15,500ft) and most people who make it this far opt to make the final 1,175-m (3,840-ft) ascent in the dark because the scree slope is less slippery and because they get the reward of watching the sunrise before continuing to the top. The journey up the mountain takes climbers through a variety of beautiful habitats, from rainforest to bush, sparse woodland draped with eerie hanging mosses, moorland and alpine desert, bare rock and ice. On the lower slopes the mountain looms over the landscape, only to be hidden in the dense rainforest and then burst into spectacular view again as the climbers emerge. The views across the landscapes of northern Tanzania and southern Kenya make even this challenging climb well worth every effort.

HOW TO GET THERE:
By air to Kilimanjaro international airport, then by road.

WHEN TO GO:
December to January is the most popular time. Avoid April, May and November, when it is wet.

NEAREST TOWN:
Moshi 15km (9 miles).

YOU SHOULD KNOW
You will need clothing for almost every type of weather.

DON'T MISS
A plane ride
over the falls.

VICTORIA FALLS
Zambia

Known to the people of the Kololo tribe who lived in the area in the 19th century as *Mosi-oa-Tunya* – 'the Smoke that Thunders' – Victoria Falls is one of nature's greatest spectacles. The spray above it can be seen from almost 65km (40 miles) away. The Zambezi river flows through a shallow valley across a flat, basalt plateau for miles, but in some places, cracks in the basalt exposed the weaker sandstone below and the water was able to force a way through and begin to erode it. The 8km (5 miles) of steep-sided gorges the Zambezi cuts through here represent hundreds of thousands of years of erosion.

HOW TO GET THERE:
By air to Livingstone or Victoria Falls, by road or rail from Lusaka or by rail from South Africa, then by car.
WHEN TO GO:
Winter, when the flood is not at its peak but the falls are not obscured in spray.
NEAREST TOWN:
Livingstone 10km (6 miles).

Victoria Falls is neither the highest nor the broadest waterfall on Earth, but with a single drop of 108m (360ft) and a width of 1.7km (1 mile), it is claimed to be the single-largest falling sheet of water. At the peak of the rainy season, more than 11.3 million litres (2.5 million gallons) spill over the falls per minute. Because the gorge is so narrow, it is simple for visitors to get a spectacular view of the thundering waters from as little as 60m (200ft) away, if they are prepared both to brave the path along the opposite edge and to get very, very wet. The Knife-Edge Bridge affords views of the main falls, the Boiling Pot and the Eastern Cataract, while the Lookout Tree and Victoria Falls Bridge give panoramic views of the falls and gorge. At the height of the river's spate in March to May, a plane ride along the gorge and above the falls makes an exhilarating experience and an amazing way to see one of nature's most spectacular sights.

LAKE MALAWI

Malawi

HOW TO GET THERE:
By air to Lilongwe,
then overland.
WHEN TO GO:
April to October.
NEAREST TOWN:
Salima 20km (12 miles).

YOU SHOULD KNOW

The lake is divided between
Malawi, Mozambique
and Tanzania.

Lake Malawi is the southernmost lake in Africa's Great Rift Valley. Formed about 40,000 years ago, it is 580km (360 miles) long and 75km (47 miles) across at its widest point, making it Africa's third-largest lake. Its crystal-clear blue waters are set amidst a stunning landscape of rocky outcrops and lush, wooded slopes, swamps, lagoons and reedbeds. Formerly known as Lake Nyasa, Lake Malawi has an abundance of wildlife, including chachma baboons and vervet monkeys, hippos and bush pigs, leopards, crocodiles and water monitors. Birdlife in the area includes white-breasted cormorants, which nest on several of the lake's islands. However, it is the lake's fish that justify its inclusion on the World Heritage list. It is home to a greater variety of freshwater tropical fish than anywhere else in the world, including almost 500 species of a group called the cichlids. These species constitute almost one-third of all the species in the group and make the lake an important place for biologists to study the evolutionary processes that have occurred in an enclosed environment. But it is not just scientists who can appreciate the riches of Lake Malawi: away from the settlements by the shore, it is a serene wildlife-watcher's paradise.

TSINGY OF BEMARAHA

Madagascar

Located some 80km (50 miles) inland from Madagascar's west coast, much of this reserve is a mass of sharp-ridged limestone pinnacles – *tsingy* in the Malagasy language – some rising up to heights of 50m (160ft) and cut through with canyons and gorges. Declared a nature reserve in 1927, this extraordinary mineral 'forest' was recognized as a UNESCO World Heritage Site in 1990 and opened, in part, to the public in 1998. These peculiar rock formations, which are unique to Madagascar, were created by erosion as the acidity of rainwater over the centuries gradually dissolved the stone of the chalky plateau. The pinnacles are so close together as to make the area virtually impenetrable by humans, yet there are many species of lemur here whose agility is entirely unaffected by the razor-sharp stone. Madagascar is famous for its unique diversity of wildlife – nearly 90 per cent of the species to be found on this beautiful island, the world's fourth-largest, can only be found here – and the Tsingy of Bemaraha reserve itself is the only known location for a number of rare plants and animals, some of which are endangered.

HOW TO GET THERE:
Flights from Antananarivo to Antsalova, then by road (four-wheel drive).
WHEN TO GO:
July to October.
NEAREST TOWN:
Morondava 225km (140 miles).

YOU SHOULD KNOW

There are no facilities within the reserve. The nearest hotel is 150km (94 miles) away. Road travel is slow and arduous.

RAINFORESTS

Madagascar

Madagascar lies in splendid isolation some 480km (300 miles) off the southeast coast of Africa. Its separation occurred between 150–180 million years ago, and produced the extraordinarily high levels of endemic species of flora and fauna for which the island is famed. Much of Madagascar's forest cover has been destroyed during the last hundred years, but its remaining rainforests contain a biological treasure-trove of endemic plants and animals. Almost all of Madagascar's mammals are found here, including the island's star turn, 15 species and subspecies of lemur. These remarkable, attractive creatures were evolving when the island floated free from Africa. Monkeys, which had not yet appeared, were never able to reach Madagascar, and lemurs were never able to live anywhere else. The diversity of Madagascar's plant life is bewildering – botanists are still classifying flora and discovering new species. The world needs Madagascar: Vinscristine, the drug that changed the survival rates in childhood leukaemia from 20 to 90 per cent, is just one of the drugs that came from the Madagascar rosy periwinkle, now extinct. We can only imagine what we could be losing each time a piece of this rainforest is lost.

GORGES OF THE BRAS DE CAVERNE

Réunion

The French island of Réunion lies some 650km (406 miles) off Madagascar's east coast, close to Mauritius. It is a popular destination for adventurous tourists who are attracted by the prospect of exploring and trekking in the spectacular mountainous region in the centre of the island. The gorges created from volcanic fractures have in the past made access to this region difficult and, as a result, the tropical forests of giant heathers, ferns and lichens have been preserved. One of the biggest and most spectacular of the gorges is the Trou de Fer ('Iron Hole'). Over a distance of about 3.5km (2 miles) the Bras de Caverne river plunges down almost 930m (3,050ft) over three dramatic waterfalls and then winds its way down a narrow canyon till it joins the Rivière du Mât on its way to the Indian Ocean. Only discovered in 1989, it has become something of a 'destination' for canyoning – albeit a very challenging one.

PITON DE LA FOURNAISE

Réunion

Along with Mount Erebus in Antarctica and Kilauea in the Hawaiian islands, Piton de la Fournaise ('Peak of the Furnace') is one of the most active volcanoes on Earth. It is situated in the southeast corner of the French island of Réunion, which lies in the Indian Ocean between Madagascar and Mauritius. Thought to be over 500,000 years old, it is known to the locals simply as *Le Volcan* ('The Volcano'). There have been more than 150 eruptions recorded since the 17th century and in the space of a year it erupted on three separate occasions. When the caldera is breached on the eastern side, the erupting lava sometimes reaches the sea with spectacular results. It is quite easy to walk to the top of the mountain but really the view from below is the most spectacular. Piton de la Fournaise spews out lava day and night, and the evening pyrotechnics are better than any fireworks display.

HOW TO GET THERE:
By road from St Joseph,
then by foot.
WHEN TO GO:
May to November.
NEAREST TOWN:
St Joseph 24km (15 miles).

VALLÉE DE MAI NATURE RESERVE, PRASLIN ISLAND

Seychelles

HOW TO GET THERE:
By air or ferry boat from
Victoria, on Mahé Island.
WHEN TO GO:
From May to September.
NEAREST TOWN:
Victoria 50km (31 miles).

The beautiful island of Praslin lies 50km (31 miles) northeast of Mahé, the main island of the Seychelles, and amidst the hills at its heart lies one of the smallest, most perfect of the World Heritage nature reserves, itself surrounded by the Praslin National Park. This is the tropical island of one's dreams, surrounded by shimmering white-sand beaches and turquoise seas. Its interior hosts a wealth of flora and fauna, much of which is endemic. The climate remains steady throughout the year as it lies tranquilly outside the cyclone belt. The Vallée de Mai covers only 18 hectares (44 acres) but it is unique, containing the remains of the palm forest that once covered the entire island in virtually its original state. All six of the endemic Seychelles palm species thrive here, in particular some 6,000 coco de mer palms, one of the wonders of the botanical world. These extraordinary trees are the stuff of legend, with huge fruits each weighing up to 20kg (44lbs) – the largest seeds on Earth. Germinating and growing very slowly, coco de mer palms live for hundreds of years – the oldest specimens here are over 800 years old. The valley's forest is also home to a mass of animal life. Chameleons, geckos and snakes rustle through the undergrowth, and the two streams originating in the valley are home to endemic freshwater crabs, large freshwater prawns and the only endemic freshwater fish in the Seychelles.

ALDABRA ATOLL

Seychelles

Lying in isolation in the western part of the Indian Ocean, Aldabra is the second-largest atoll in the world. Despite being little-known to outsiders, Aldabra is considered to be a natural wonder of the world by the scientific community, and was given World Heritage status in 1982. Lying mainly within the lagoon itself are 40 smaller rocks and islands, providing nesting areas for thousands of frigate birds and red-footed boobies. Many other birds come here, too, the most unusual being the Aldabra flightless rail, the only flightless bird found on any Indian Ocean island. Aldabra's remoteness has led to high levels of endemism, but its most famous inhabitant is the giant tortoise, of which there are some 100,000 individuals – ten times the number on Galápagos. For almost 100 years scientists have been studying the atoll, which is uninhabited other than by those working at the small research station here. The terrain is inhospitable to humans as the limestone has been eroded into many sharp spikes and water-filled pits.

HOW TO GET THERE:
Virtually the only way is to join a cruise ship, embarking at Victoria, on Mahé Island.
WHEN TO GO:
May to November.
NEAREST TOWN:
Victoria, on Mahé Island – but it's a long way at around 1,200km (750 miles).

YOU SHOULD KNOW
Aldabra Atoll is uninhabited and very isolated. Astove Atoll, part of the Aldabra Atoll, was occupied by African slaves who escaped from a Portuguese ship in 1760.

BLACK RIVER GORGES NATIONAL PARK

Mauritius

HOW TO GET THERE:
By air to Mauritius, then by road to the park.
WHEN TO GO:
May to December.
NEAREST TOWN:
Curepipe 6km (4 miles).

The small island of Mauritius lies in the Indian Ocean to the east of Madagascar, and its isolation has produced a quantity of endemic species of flora and fauna. The Black River Gorges National Park was established in 1994, and listed as a UNESCO World Heritage Site in 2006 in order to protect the last remaining indigenous forests of the island and the endangered species within them. Sadly, human activity, loss of habitat and natural disasters such as cyclones have caused the extinction of many of these species. The park consists of cliffs and gorges carved by water over millions of years – this was once a region of active volcanoes, now long extinct. Today there is marshy heathland, dwarf upland forest, creeks, waterfalls and fantastic panoramic views over the gorges and down to the sea. There are splendid indigenous trees here, but amongst the 163 endemic flora, the most famous is the trochetia, the country's national flower. Mauritius has only 28 of its endemic bird species remaining, but the park provides habitats for them all. There are 60km (37 miles) of marked trails that wind through the park, leading visitors to viewing points for amazing panoramic vistas.

THE SKELETON COAST

Namibia

Namibia's Skeleton Coast Park is a desolate strip of dunes, leading inland to multicoloured mountains and canyons. It is thought to be named for the skeletons of the numerous ships that have been wrecked on its shores and for the men who did not make it back to civilization. It receives less than 10mm (0.4in) of rain a year, but some life is able to survive here because of the frequent fogs caused by the interaction of the cold Benguela current and sea breezes offshore and the hot dry air of the desert. Desert plants and some small animals trap the fogs' moisture, while others, such as the oryx, are adapted to get water from the plants that they eat and to go for weeks without water. When rain does fall, the desert temporarily bursts into bloom as plants such as lithops, which normally resemble stones, flower briefly before subsiding to wait for next year's rains. Other animals in this remote landscape, which stretches 500km (310 miles) south from the Kunene river, include desert elephants, which live on plants fed by rare underground springs. The lucky visitor might also catch a glimpse of black rhino, porcupine, brown hyena, lion, ostrich, gemsbok and springbok. A wide variety of seabirds and waders can be seen along the coast. Temperatures vary wildly between day and night and between the coast, where it is always chilly, and the interior, where mornings are warm but afternoons cooler. Visitors to this otherworldly landscape are always struck by its stark beauty and desolate isolation.

ETOSHA NATIONAL PARK

Namibia

Etosha National Park in Namibia is one of the best places in which to view big game in southern Africa. Covering more than 20, 725 sq km (8,000 sq miles), it is dominated by the Etosha Pan, a vast, flat, saltpan surrounded by grassland and thorny savannah. Millions of years ago this was a lake, but today it only holds water briefly during the rainy season, attracting thousands of flamingos and white pelicans that fly in to breed. Its eerie, silvery-white surface is so huge it can be seen from space, and at ground level mirages formed by reflected heat are common. To the south are many permanent waterholes, and it is these that provide visitors with the most wonderful opportunities to see wildlife, including elephants, lions, giraffes, zebras and even the highly endangered black rhino. A car is needed to visit Etosha, which has a network of well-maintained tracks leading from the three camps within the park to various waterholes at which the animals congregate. Each camp has its own waterhole, floodlit to facilitate night viewing.

HOW TO GET THERE:
By air to Windhoek and Ondangwa, then by road.
WHEN TO GO:
May to September for game, November to March for birds.
NEAREST TOWNS:
Outjo and Tsumeb 100km (62.5 miles).

DON'T MISS
The Haunted Forest; Charitsaub/Salvadora/ Sueda waterhole cluster.

THE NAMIB DESERT

Namibia

HOW TO GET THERE:
By light aircraft or overland from Windhoek.
WHEN TO GO:
October to March.
NEAREST TOWN:
Windhoek 480km (300 miles).

YOU SHOULD KNOW
It gets cold at night.

Right: The Namib Desert.

The oldest desert on Earth, the Namib stretches for some 1,600km (1,000 miles) along the Atlantic coast of southern Africa, within the Namib Naukluft National Park. It receives less than 10mm (0.4in) of rain per year and is one of the driest places on Earth. Its massive red and grey dunes form at right angles to the prevailing wind and seem to march in unending ranks as far as the eye can see. Dune 7, at more than 380m (1,250ft), is the highest sand dune on the planet. The interaction between the dry air of the desert and moisture-laden air over the sea causes immense fogs to form. For many of the animals in the desert, the moisture in this fog is a lifeline. From the top of the dunes, sunrise and sunset are spectacular events as the dunes are 'painted' in different colours with the changing light.

KALAHARI DESERT AND OKAVANGO DELTA

Botswana

The Kalahari desert, which spreads over 930,000 sq km (360,000 sq miles) of Botswana, South Africa and Namibia, is a semi-arid land subject to summer rainfall that provides grazing. The only permanent river in this red-brown, dusty land is the Okavango, which runs southeast from the highlands of Angola and drains into the Okavango Delta in the northwest of the Kalahari, creating an area full of spectacular wildlife. The highlight is the Moremi Wildlife Reserve. Seasonal rainfall in the Angolan highlands leads the delta to flood in the north in mid-summer (November to December) and in the south in mid-winter (May to June), giving rise to a constantly changing landscape. Animals that inhabit the reserves in the Kalahari include several species of antelope, brown hyenas, lions, African wild dogs, cheetahs and meerkats. Among the spectacles of this arid region are the massive communal nests of weaver birds, which drape the acacia trees. The delta itself is home to elephants, buffalo, hippos and black and white rhinos. Giraffes, blue wildebeest, zebras, warthogs and chacma baboons are also here, as well as several species of antelope. Predators and scavengers include lions, leopards, cheetahs, hyenas and wild dogs, and the waters harbour Nile crocodiles and water monitors. A visit to this beautiful, lush landscape, set within the surrounding desert, is an experience that will not easily be forgotten.

GREAT LIMPOPO TRANSFRONTIER PARK

South Africa/Mozambique/Zimbabwe

The Great Limpopo Transfrontier Park is set to become the jewel in Africa's wildlife crown. When complete, it will become the largest game park in the world, combining the Kruger National Park and MalaMala Reserve of South Africa with the Limpopo National Park of Mozambique and the Gonarezhou National Park, Manjinji Pan Sanctuary and the Malipati Safari Area of Zimbabwe. This will create a protected area of some 35,000 sq km (13,500 sq miles) – roughly the size of Belgium. Such a park will offer visitors some of the best wildlife safaris available anywhere in Africa. It goes without saying that the 'big five' – lion, leopard, rhino, buffalo and elephant – are all here. But so great is the range of wildlife on offer that visitors are really spoilt for choice. Access is via numerous park gates, but the Giriyondo gate, which is just 100km (62 miles) from Phalaborwa airport, offers arguably the best entry point. Once inside, visitors will be free to move between the three countries without further restriction.

DON'T MISS
Zulu cultural centres
at Eshowe, Empangeni
and Ulundi.

GREATER ST LUCIA WETLAND PARK

South Africa

The Greater St Lucia Wetland Park on the east coast of KwaZulu-Natal is arguably the finest nature reserve in a country that boasts some of the richest and most exciting wildlife in the world. What makes South Africa's third-largest protected area such a living treasure is that within its boundaries lies a unique combination of ecosystems, ranging from open sea to estuary, sand dunes to swamps – and all surrounding the shimmering waters of Lake St Lucia. The Indian Ocean acts as the park's eastern border. Humpback whales and great white sharks swim here, as do coelacanths, living relics from 400 millions years ago. Nearer the shore you will find the underwater splendour of Africa's most southerly coral reefs, then moving inland over the sandy beaches, where leatherback and loggerhead turtles come to lay their eggs, there is the tallest forested coastal dune system in the world. Further west lie the park's shimmering lakes, translucent blue jewels splashed with the pink and white of flamingos and pelicans. No wonder that in 1999 it was declared a World Heritage Site.

THE SWARTBERG MOUNTAINS

South Africa

The Swartberg Mountains are a chiefly sandstone massif of considerable rugged beauty that runs roughly east–west across the Western Cape. An absolute paradise for anyone who loves the great outdoors, there are numerous popular day hikes and, for the more adventurous, the five-day Swartberg Hiking Trail. The Swartberg Mountains span some 5,000 sq km (2,000 sq miles), making them manageable enough to explore but large enough to harbour hidden surprises. There are several passes through the range, but the most famous and spectacular is the eponymous Swartberg Pass. Built by Thomas Bain in the late 19th century, it somewhat tortuously links the towns of Oudtshoorn in the south with Prince Albert in the north. It's 27km (17 miles) of winding switchbacks with jaw-dropping views at every turn. At the top, some 1,583m (5,200ft) above sea level, travellers are rewarded with quite spectacular views over the Little Karoo to the south and the Great Karoo to the north.

HERMANUS AND WALKER BAY

South Africa

HOW TO GET THERE:
By road or train from Cape Town.
WHEN TO GO:
Early autumn, March to April, offers the best weather. April to October is best for whale-watching.
NEAREST TOWN:
Cape Town 90km (56 miles).

Nestled at the heart of Walker Bay, Hermanus is a jewel of a resort. One of South Africa's oldest, it was founded by Hermanus Pieters in the early 19th century. Its popularity grew steadily, and today it is one of the most attractive destinations along South Africa's self-styled Riviera. With the blue waters of the Atlantic before it, the inspiring Overberg Mountains behind and golden beaches stretching north and south, Hermanus is breathtakingly beautiful. But if that were not enough to draw the crowds, it can also lay claim to being the 'whale capital of the world' – offering the best land-based viewing of these awesome animals anywhere in the world. In fact, Hermanus is the only town in the world with an official 'whale crier' who can be seen wandering the streets and advertising the arrival of the town's most welcome visitors with a blast of his horn. The whale-watching season typically runs from April to October, when these giant denizens of the deep sojourn in the shallow warm waters of Walker Bay to breed. At times almost 100 females and their calves congregate in the bay. A 12-km (9-mile) cliff path stretches from one side of town to the other and provides numerous vantage points. Frequently the whales come within just a few metres of the cliffs, offering spectacular views and irresistible photo opportunities.

THE CAPE FLORAL REGION

South Africa

HOW TO GET THERE:
By air to Cape Town, then by road along the N2.
WHEN TO GO:
Flowers bloom all year, but the season peaks between August and October.
NEAREST TOWNS:
The region includes many towns, including Cape Town to the west.

YOU SHOULD KNOW
Flowering begins in the Springbok area of the Northern Cape and spreads southwards as the weather becomes warmer.

The Cape Floral Region (CFR) in southwestern South Africa is a botanical Garden of Eden, blessed with an unsurpassed wealth of plant life, including a multitude of species found nowhere else in the world. The CFR comprises the smallest and the richest of the world's six floral kingdoms – and is the only one to be contained within a single country. So rich in diversity is this region that it has been declared one of South Africa's seven World Heritage Sites by UNESCO. With around 9,000 different species, 70 per cent of which are unique, this thin coastal strip of southern Africa boasts the highest density of plant species found anywhere in the world. What enables this tiny corner of Africa to host such an abundance of plant life is its incredible variety of habitats. These range from coastal dunes to rugged mountains, fertile plains to semi-arid shrublands. It is a truly remarkable area.

THE DRAKENSBERG MOUNTAINS

South Africa

DON'T MISS
The rock art of
the San people.

Listed as a UNESCO World Heritage Site in 2000, the Drakensberg (the 'Dragon's Mountain') is a bluish, spiky escarpment of rock that in part forms a natural boundary between South Africa and the kingdom of Lesotho. The highest range in southern Africa, the Drakensberg separate the coastal lowlands of KwaZulu-Natal from the high interior. Several of the peaks tower above 3,000m (9,843ft) and the highest – Thabana Ntlenyana – reaches 3,482m (11,422ft). This steep land is cut through by streams and rivers, creating a spectacular landscape of gorges and river valleys. Among the most popular attractions is the Tugela Falls in the Royal Natal National Park. These five falls make up the second-highest waterfall on the planet, dropping 947m (3,110ft) into the 'amphitheatre'. While the higher mountain areas are a paradise for hikers, there are several game reserves and wildlife parks within the area covered by the Ukhahlamba-Drakensberg World Heritage Site, offering protection to a wide variety of animals in a range of landscapes, including nearly 300 bird species, several of which are extremely rare, and 48 species of mammal, as well as more than 2,150 species of plants.

HOW TO GET THERE:
By road from Pretoria for the north, from Durban for the south.
WHEN TO GO:
November to March.
NEAREST TOWN:
Ladysmith 70km (48 miles).

YOU SHOULD KNOW
It can get very cold in winter.

THE CANGO CAVES

South Africa

DON'T MISS
The many ostrich
show farms in the area.

The Cango Caves contain some of the most stunning subterranean scenery to be found anywhere in the world. Situated along South Africa's famous Garden Route, the caverns formed over millions of years as water percolated through a narrow ridge of Precambrian limestone that runs parallel to the Swartberg Mountains. They form an interlinked system that stretches for over 5km (3 miles). The largest of the caverns measures an echoey 107m (350ft) across and 16m (52ft) high. Impressive though this is, it is not the caves' size but their remarkable contents that people come to see. For the Cango Caves contain a truly wondrous showcase of natural art, created by the limestone-laden water that has seeped and dripped its way through these voids over the millennia. There are impressive collections of stalactites and stalagmites, some joined to form mighty stone columns, and more unusual helictites – twiggy, stone formations that grow in all directions. More impressive still are the subtly coloured flowstones that resemble frozen rivers, and the almost unbelievable stone curtains that hang before your eyes like petrified waterfalls. Visitors can choose between an hour-long exploration of eight chambers or a 90-minute adventure tour that involves some steep climbs and a good deal of wriggling though narrow passages. Whichever tour you chose, however, the Cango Caves will not fail to amaze, and for summer visitors their more or less constant 18°C (64°F) will come as a welcome respite from the burning heat above.

HOW TO GET THERE:
By road from Oudtshoorn.
WHEN TO GO:
The caves are open to the public from 9am to 4pm every day except 25 December. Booking is essential.
NEAREST TOWN:
Oudtshoorn, 29km (18 miles).

DUIKER ISLAND

South Africa

Duiker Island is a small, rocky protuberance that lies just a short boat ride away from the popular fishing settlement of Hout Bay, in the Western Cape. Despite the island's name, visitors to this rocky refuge won't find any small antelope here. Instead, they will come face to face with a huge colony of Cape fur seals, a species of sea lion. The sea that churns around the island may look blue and inviting, but it is often disappointingly chilly, due to the Benguela current that carries icy water north from the Antarctic. This cold water, however, provides plenty of fish for the seals to hunt. What is in short supply, however, are safe refuges where the seals can clamber onto dry land. And it is for this reason that Duiker Island becomes so overpopulated. Although it is the seals that steal the show, visitors to Duiker Island may also be rewarded with views of numerous seabirds – including the rare bank cormorant.

THE SUDWALA CAVES

South Africa

The Sudwala Caves are believed to be the oldest caves in the world. Geologists estimate that they began forming about 240 million years ago, after stress fractures cracked the mountains' 3,800-million-year-old Precambrian dolomite. Water soon found its way through the fractures, corroding the dolomite and creating the great caverns that today house a breathtaking subterranean tableau of stalactites, stalagmites, flowstones and dripstones. A welcome refuge since prehistoric times, in 1914 the caves were first exploited commercially when the bat guano they contained was dug out and sold for fertilizer. It wasn't until 1966, however, that they were opened to the public. The main caverns are large, airy and unusually dry. This is due in part to the refreshing breeze that blows through the caves – the source of which remains one of the caves' secrets. The main cave is a truly cavernous 70m (230ft) across and is the largest dolomite chamber in the world.

THE WITWATERSRAND

South Africa

From the air, the Witwatersrand is easily overlooked. A small and quite unremarkable range of sedimentary hills, it forms the watershed between the Vaal and Olifants rivers in what is now the province of Gauteng. But the Witwatersrand isn't renowned for its scenery, or even its wildlife. A clue to its claim to fame lies in its name. Often shortened simply to 'the Rand', this region gave its name to South Africa's currency – and for good reason. For there is gold in these Witwatersrand hills – lots of it. In fact, around 40 per cent of all the gold ever mined has come from this small area. Witwatersrand translates literally to 'white-water reef'. The gold here occurs in thin bands, called reefs, mined at depths of around 3,000m (10,000ft). Mining began here in earnest in 1886, with the discovery of the 120-km (75-mile) Main Reef that runs from Boksburg to Randfontein. Although many of the older mines are close to exhaustion, this area still produces most of South Africa's gold. No visit to the Rand would be complete without a visit to a gold mine. Gold Reef City, just 6km (4 miles) south of Johannesburg, has both a museum, where you can learn about the history of gold and the special geology of this area, and an original mineshaft that has been kept in working order. Tours run several times a day

HOW TO GET THERE:
By road from Johannesburg.
WHEN TO GO:
There is plenty to see all year.
NEAREST TOWN:
Johannesburg.

HOW TO GET THERE:
A short walk or drive from Simon's Town.
WHEN TO GO:
The penguins are there all year, but Simon's Town has an annual 'penguin festival' one weekend in September, and the birds breed March to May.
NEAREST TOWN:
Simon's Town.

DON'T MISS
The Cape Point Nature Reserve.

BOULDERS BEACH PENGUINS

South Africa

Nestled on the shores of False Bay, on the east coast of the Cape Peninsular, lies Simon's Town, a historic settlement of great character and charm. South Africa undoubtedly offers some of the best wildlife experiences in the world, but here you can get up close and personal with perhaps the last creature in the world you would expect: African penguins. Wide, wooden boardwalks provide easy, if sometimes crowded, access to the site. With around 2,500 of these birds residing here, you are certain to get some marvellous close encounters. The first penguins began breeding here as recently as the 1980s, and since then the colony has grown incredibly quickly. Most of the birds are concentrated on Foxy Beach at Boulders. But there are always some along the neighbouring beaches, and Boulders is more or less the only place in the world where you can swim with penguins – even if the water is sometimes a little chilly.

LAPALALA WILDERNESS

South Africa

The lyrically named Lapalala Wilderness lies within the UNESCO Waterberg Biosphere Reserve, in Limpopo Province, just a three-and-a-half-hours' drive from Johannesburg. Despite its name, Lapalala is actually a privately owned nature reserve, created from the consolidation of 19 farms between 1981 and 1999. Currently some 360 sq km (140 sq miles) in extent, there are plans to extend the reserve still further. The Lapalala Wilderness is characterized by endless vistas of upland plains and rugged

hills, dissected by craggy ravines. The predominant vegetation here is so-called bushveld – grassland, punctuated by dense clusters of trees and tall shrubs. Bringing the whole area to life are the 90km (56 miles) or so of rivers and streams that course through it, chief of which is the Palala river with its clear pools and noisy rapids. Within this largely unspoiled landscape, visitors can encounter the wildlife both from the seat of a truck or by foot on guided walks. There are buffalo, hippo, crocodile, zebra, leopard, baboons and many kinds of antelope here, as well as over 280 species of bird. But Lapalala's 'A-list' is without doubt its black and white rhino. These are easy to tell apart – but not for the reason suggested by their names. Black rhino are the smaller species and have a hooked upper lip, which they use to grasp the leaves and shoots that they eat. White rhino, by contrast, have very wide mouths, which they use to tear off great mouthfuls of grass. It was a corruption of the word 'wide', which in Afrikaans sounds like 'white', that led to them being called white rhino, when in reality they are much the same colour as black rhino. To be able to have a close encounter with both these species in a single day leaves visitors with memories to last a lifetime and makes Lapalala a truly special place.

HOW TO GET THERE:
By road or bus from Johannesburg.
WHEN TO GO:
There is plenty to see all year.
NEAREST TOWN:
Vaalwater 50km (30 miles) to the southwest.

DON'T MISS
The Waterberg Environmental Centre, Melkrivier.

TABLE MOUNTAIN
South Africa

Almost at the southern tip of Africa, Table Mountain provides a stunning backdrop to the city of Cape Town, which nestles around it. Its level plateau is roughly 3km (2 miles) across, with the Lion's Head to the west and Devil's Peak to the east. The name derives from the mists that form suddenly, spill over the edge and slide down the mountain like a tablecloth. The mountain is part of the larger Table Mountain National Park. Most visitors take the cable car up to the western end of the plateau, although there are also many walking trails and climbing routes. The highest point of the mountain, at 1,086m (3,563ft), is Mclear's Beacon, at the eastern end. Numerous boardwalks and designated paths allow exploration of this beautiful wilderness without damaging it. The views over the city are magnificent.

HOW TO GET THERE:
On foot or by cable car from Cape Town.
WHEN TO GO:
Clear days in summer.
NEAREST TOWN:
Cape Town.

Left: Table Mountain

LITTLE NAMAQUALAND
South Africa

Little Namaqualand is a sunburned, semi-arid region of some 60,000 sq km (23,000 sq miles) that lies south of the Orange river, in South Africa's Northern Cape Province. Along its rugged western shores the cold Atlantic breakers pound and sea mists frequently roll in, gripping the region in a clammy embrace. Alluvial diamonds have been found on this coast, but these crystalline beauties are no match for the true gems of Namaqualand – its flowers. For although this region is dry and almost lifeless for nine months of the year, with the spring comes a transformation that is as beautiful as it is remarkable. Late winter rains awake the life that is lying just beneath the surface, and all at once the land is awash in a sea of colour. Flowers of every hue imaginable burst into bloom almost simultaneously, creating a wonderful spectacle. Most of the flowers are various species of daisy, but home to some 3,000 species – nearly half of which are found nowhere else – Namaqualand is truly a plant-lover's paradise. For those visitors who arrive in Namaqualand 'out of season', this unique landscape still has much to offer. Aside from the uncountable succulents, the desert itself also possesses a special beauty.

HOW TO GET THERE: By road up the N7 from Cape Town.
WHEN TO GO: July to October.
NEAREST TOWN: Springbok is the region's main town.

CAPE CROSS SEAL RESERVE

South Africa

There are nine species of mammals known as fur seals, which are, in reality, a species of sea lion. The Cape fur seal is the largest species and Cape Cross (Kaapkruis) Seal Reserve is its main stronghold and the largest of the 24 breeding colonies along this coastline. At its height, Cape Cross Seal Reserve supports between 80,000 and 100,000 seals, but in years when food is scarce, the number of seals is often lower. Each summer, the reserve is home to the spectacle of the seals' breeding season. The bull seals are first to arrive, usually in October, and they will fight for and establish breeding territories. The pregnant cows arrive in November or December and join a bull in his territory. Within a week of giving birth, the females are fertile again. The pups will continue to suckle for almost a year, until their mother leaves them to return to the beach to give birth to the next year's pup. Whether you witness the enormous bull seals fighting or the thousands of appealing pups, the sheer number of seals here is almost overwhelming.

HOW TO GET THERE:
By road from Hentiesbaai on the C34.
WHEN TO GO:
November to January.
NEAREST TOWN:
Hentiesbaai 70km (45 miles).

YOU SHOULD KNOW
Do not walk among the seals: the males are aggressive and the females become so if they see you as a threat.

HOW TO GET THERE:
By road from Krugersdorp.
WHEN TO GO:
Open Mon–Fri 8am to 5pm, Sat, Sun 8am to 6pm.
NEAREST TOWNS:
Krugersdorp 10km (6 miles), Johannesburg 50km (30 miles).

THE WONDER CAVE

South Africa

The Wonder Cave in Kromdraai, Gauteng, is the third-largest cavern in South Africa and an attraction that easily lives up to its name. Thought to be around two million years old, it was discovered in the late 19th century by miners excavating limestone to make cement. The cave itself comprises a single, vertigo-inducing void. There is a 90-step metal stairway followed by a short lift ride to the cave floor. Despite its size, the Wonder Cave still has a slightly damp, musty smell, and on summer days the cave's ambient 16°C (60°F) can feel suddenly chilly. Formed by the erosion of limestone by underground water, the cave contains a dazzling display of beautifully presented dripstone formations. The scale of everything here is astonishing – there are 14 or so stalagmite and stalactite formations all over 15m (50ft) high, most of which are still growing. There are also a huge number of imaginatively named flowstone formations that are lit for maximum effect. Some, such as the figure of the praying Madonna, are so realistic that it seems impossible that they can be the purely accidental creations of limestone-laden water.

THE MALAMALA RESERVE

South Africa

The MalaMala Game Reserve is a 160-sq-km (62-sq-mile) wildlife sanctuary located in Mpumalanga Province. Established in 1927, MalaMala lays claim to being the oldest game reserve in South Africa. At one time it was a hunter's paradise for those seeking to bag the 'Big Five', but since 1964, the only shooting that has been done here has been done by cameras. Much of MalaMala is textbook African savannah, replete with an impressive inventory of wildlife species – the richest anywhere on the continent. If that were not enough, MalaMala holds further aces that make it one of the premier game-viewing destinations in the world. First is its sheer size, guaranteeing visitors a rich and varied habitat. Second is the fact that it fortuitously shares a 19-km (12-mile) unfenced border with the Kruger National Park. This simple accident of geography benefits the reserve enormously. Thirdly, MalaMala is blessed with the life-giving waters of the Sand river. Some 20km (13 miles) of this perennial river flows north–south through the reserve, drawing huge herds of grazing animals to its banks – not to mention the numerous predators that hunt them. To allow the animals approaching from the Kruger National Park free access to the river, all the MalaMala camps are on the western bank, and throughout the reserve, human density and impact on the land is kept to an absolute minimum. The results of this single-minded management are writ large in the reserve's viewing statistics. Typically, lion, leopard, elephant, rhino and buffalo make an appearance here 335 days every year. So for visitors on a once-in-a-lifetime trip, MalaMala is unlikely to disappoint.

HOW TO GET THERE:
By air from Johannesburg to MalaMala Airfield, or by road from Johannesburg.

WHEN TO GO:
There is plenty to see all year. September to March can be very hot.

NEAREST TOWN:
Newington 19km (12 miles).

EUROPE & THE MIDDLE EAST

SVALBARD ARCHIPELAGO

Arctic Circle

The remote archipelago of Svalbard is in the Arctic Circle, at the point where the Gulf Stream current sinks. The islands are a frozen white wonderland of barren mountains, glaciers, fjords and ice caves, inhabited by as many polar bears as humans (about 2,500 of each). Svalbard is the northernmost part of the kingdom of Norway, 565km (353 miles) to the north of the mainland, about halfway to the North Pole. A trip to Svalbard is a uniquely rewarding experience. You can test your stamina on a wilderness camping expedition, try your hand at dog sledging and explore the ice caves beneath the glaciers, as well as snowmobiling, skiing, horse-riding and kayaking. You cannot fail to encounter several polar bears, which roam around freely here, even occasionally wandering into the settlements.

HOW TO GET THERE:
Fly from Oslo or Tromsø to Longyearbyen, or go on an organized cruise through a tour operator.
WHEN TO GO:
Tours take place all year but for maximum daylight, April to August.
NEAREST TOWN:
Longyearbyen.

THE MAELSTROM

Norway

HOW TO GET THERE:
Fly to Oslo, then domestic flight to Svolvær or Leknes. Or, take the coastal boat that runs between Bergen and Kirkenes. Or, road, rail or air to Bodø, then take ferry to Moskenes or express passenger boat to Svolvær.
WHEN TO GO:
September to April to catch the Northern Lights. May to July for the Midnight Sun.
NEAREST TOWNS:
Svolvær, Sørvågen, Leknes.

The Maelstrom is the most ferocious of several powerful tidal currents in the waters around the Lofoten Islands in northern Norway. The rugged Lofoten archipelago sticks straight out into the Atlantic Ocean, separated from the mainland by the Vestfjord. Twice a day, the tides cause the waters of the Vestfjord to run back against the main stream, stirring up the Maelstrom (known as the *Moskstraumen* to the locals) – great whirlpools that swirl at speeds of up to six knots. The *Moskstraumen* is one of the most forceful eddies in the world, an amazing sight that fascinates and terrifies in equal measure. 'Those who sail at the wrong time are suddenly snatched down into spiralling abysses,' wrote Olaus Magnus, a 16th-century Swedish mapmaker. The local people tend to play down dramatized accounts – they are grateful for its existence and treat it with the utmost respect. For, even though it has taken its toll of the islanders' lives, it also washes in the great shoals of fish on which their livelihoods depend. The Lofoten Islands are one of the most scenically beautiful parts of Norway, in range of both the Northern Lights and the Midnight Sun.

DON'T MISS
Hiking Kjerag mountain, close to the bottom of the Lysefjord.

PULPIT ROCK

Norway

HOW TO GET THERE:
RV13 road from Stavenger.
then ferry from Tau.
WHEN TO GO:
April to October are
the best months.
NEAREST TOWN:
Stavanger 25km (16 miles).

Pulpit Rock, or Preikestolen, is a steep cliff that rises 604m (1,981ft) above Lysefjorden, opposite the Kjerag plateau, with an almost flat top of approximately 25 sq m (82 sq ft). The cliff was formed during the last ice age when the edges of the glacier reached the cliff. The water from the glacier froze in the crevices of the mountain and eventually broke off large angular blocks, which were later carried away with the glacier. Along the plateau itself remains a deep crack – the plateau will eventually fall down, but geological investigations assure us that this will not happen in the foreseeable future. Still, with no safety railings, this is no place for vertigo sufferers. From the designated car park, it's a 3.8-km (2.4-mile) hike to the viewpoint, a surprisingly steep walk in places as the path climbs and descends various ridges. One of the most visited natural tourist attractions in Norway, the path to the site has recently been enlarged to improve access. The walk is not recommended in winter and spring when there is snow and ice, and the track may be slippery – the best season to hike the trail is from April to October. A convenient alternative is to take a tourist ferry from Lauvvik to Lysebotn. Available from mid-June to mid-August, the route passes right beneath Pulpit Rock. Booking well in advance is recommended, as this is a very popular route.

YOU SHOULD KNOW
Sturdy shoes and rain gear are recommended for the hike to Pulpit Rock.

JOSTEDALSBREEN GLACIER FIELD

Norway

HOW TO GET THERE:
From Oslo or Bergen, fly to Sogndal airport, then take the Jostedal bus; or car/bus/train plus ferry to Sogndal. The easiest way to get to Jostedal is to use the 'glacier buses', which run frequent connecting services from all the towns in the region to Jostedal.
WHEN TO GO:
End of May to mid-September.
NEAREST TOWN:
Sogndal.

Jostedalsbreen is the largest glacier in Europe, a massive ice plateau of over 480 sq km (185 sq miles), more than 60km (37 miles) long, with ice up to 600m (1,970ft) thick. The ice field covers almost half of the Josdtedal National Park, a beautiful wilderness area on Norway's west coast between Sognefjord and Nordfjord – two of the longest fjords in the world. Here you will find some of the world's most awe-inspiring scenery, carved out of the terrain by thousands of years of constant glacial activity. The ice field is an incredible labyrinth of deep, icy crevasses and outcrops. There are 22 valley branches (or 'arms') running down from the ice plateau as well as some smaller separate glaciers. The most accessible of the arms are Briksdalsbreen, Kjenndalsbreen and Nigardsbreen – the experience of walking along the blue-ice crevasses of these dynamic wonderlands, sheer ice walls towering above you, is a thrill quite unlike any other. Glaciers are an awesome natural phenomenon – a constantly moving mass of ice sliding remorselessly down from the ice field, shifting the rock and sediment in its path as it scoops out an ever-deepening valley, an endless stream of water flowing out from beneath it into the eerily still, milky-green glacial lake at its end. Jostedal contains an astounding variety of scenery as well as the ice field, ranging from tranquil, wooded valleys of alder and birch trees to bleak mountain peaks, and a barren moraine plain of shifting sands – the Fåbergstølsgrandane 'sandur' – composed of sediment deposited by rivers flowing from one of the glacier's arms. As you trek along the ancient cattle tracks, once used by herdsmen, you feel as though you are roaming through different countries and changing seasons. And when you reach the ice field, you step onto an entirely different planet.

DON'T MISS
The cliffs of Runde –
an island sanctuary
for half a million sea birds.

GEIRANGERFJORD

Norway

The Geirangerfjord is considered the archetype of fjords – the most scenically beautiful fjord of all in a fairy-tale region of sublime natural beauty. Geiranger is part of the intricate Norwegian fjord system that stretches 500km (300 miles) northwards from Stavanger along the western coast. The terrain here has been shaped by glaciation to create some of the most outstanding scenery in the world. Geirangerfjord is a 15-km (9-mile) stretch of deep blue water, branching off from the Storfjord in a narrow, winding ravine of hairpin bends. A series of spectacular waterfalls cascade down the sides of the ravine. The most famous are the Seven Sisters and the Suitor, facing each other on opposite sides of the fjord, and the Bride's Veil, so called because, when backlit by the sun, it gives the impression of a thin veil trailing over the rocks. The surrounding scenery is breathtaking – a landscape of rugged, ice-capped mountains, glacial lakes and forests traversed by rivers. Along the sides of the fjord, you will see many abandoned smallholdings – traces of the way people scratched a living from the soil before the days of mass tourism. These ramshackle dwellings are in isolated shelves of land along the escarpments; some of them are surrounded by such steep slopes that they can only be accessed by ladder from a boat. When the farmers wanted to avoid the taxman, they simply drew up their ladders.

HOW TO GET THERE:
Fly to Ålesund. Drive along
the Ørneveien to Geiranger.
WHEN TO GO:
May to September.
NEAREST TOWN:
Geiranger.

LOFOTEN ISLANDS

Norway

West of mainland Norway, the Lofoten Islands lie more than 67° north of the Equator, within the Arctic Circle. Despite this, they have a relatively mild climate because of the warm waters of the Gulf Stream. There are five main islands – Austvågøy, Gimsøya, Vestvågøy, Flakstadøya and Moskenesøya – and three smaller ones – Vaerøy, Røst and the tiny islet of Vedøy. They are mountainous, with wooded hillsides, and are fringed with pretty bays and beautiful white sandy beaches. The islands are surrounded by rich waters that support vast colonies of breeding seabirds and in summer sperm whales can be found offshore, with orca following in early autumn. One of the biggest deepwater coral reefs, the 40-km (25-mile) Røst Reef is just west of Austuagoy. The spectacular ruggedness of these islands makes them popular with climbers and hikers, and the coastline is a favourite destination for cyclists. In midsummer it is even more magical, as for more than seven weeks the sun remains above the horizon.

HOW TO GET THERE: By ferry or air from Bodø, ferry from Narvik or by road via Narvik.
WHEN TO GO: Late May to early July for the Midnight Sun; the best weather is from April to September.
NEAREST TOWN: Narvik 140km (90 miles).

YOU SHOULD KNOW
The sun does not rise for weeks in mid-winter.

FOLGEFONNI (FOLGEFONNA) GLACIER

Norway

HOW TO GET THERE: Fly to Bergen. Three-hour drive to Odda.
WHEN TO GO: Year-round skiing. May to September for hiking.
NEAREST TOWN: Odda 3km (under 2 miles).

The Folgefonn peninsula is a captivating region of dramatic mountains, forests and lakes between the Hardanger and Sor fjords about 150km (95 miles) southeast from Bergen on the west coast. The area has been designated a national park to protect the Folgefonni ice cap – the third-largest ice cap in Norway. The ice cap is composed of three adjoining glaciers, which blanket 203 sq km (78 sq miles) of the peninsula in a layer of ice up to 145m (476ft) thick. A film of water between the ice and the rock collects sediment and clay; in the summer, melting ice mixed with this watery sediment flows into the fjords, giving them their unique green tint. The largest of the three glaciers, and the only plateau glacier, is Sønde ('South') Folgefonni, which contains the highest point of the region at 1,662m (5,451ft). It is the safest of all the glacier plateaus with its gentle slopes, so it is the ideal place to practise glacier walking and cross-country skiing. Summer or winter, the stunning purity of Folgefonni's glacier landscape cannot fail to thrill even the most jaded senses and restore a sense of wonder in the power of nature.

FROZEN SEA AT LULEÅ

Sweden

HOW TO GET THERE:
Several daily flights from
Stockholm, or by car 900km
(558 miles).
WHEN TO GO:
December to February for
the frozen sea; the rest of the
year for non-snow-
related pursuits.
NEAREST TOWN:
Luleå.

A beautiful city on the coast of northern Sweden, Luleå is delightful during the summer months, when you can sail around the archipelago or hop on one of the ferries plying between the islands. However, Luleå's secret is in its subarctic climate that borders on a continental climate – meaning short, mild summers and long, cold, snowy winters when the sea freezes over and a whole new raft of cold-weather activities becomes possible. This isn't the only place in the world where the sea freezes over, but the town's location – jutting out into the sea – makes the frozen water a welcome extension of the town's streets in the depths of winter. From December to February, locals skate, snow-trek and sled across the bay, while some roads – across the sea – are passable only in winter. Signs advise you to remove your seatbelt for a quicker exit should your car come across thin ice, but if you're feeling brave, it's a thrilling experience.

SWEDEN'S LAKELAND

Sweden

HOW TO GET THERE:
By road from Stockholm
or Göthenburg.
WHEN TO GO:
Spring to autumn offers the
best weather.
NEAREST TOWN:
Göthenburg is 50km (30
miles) south of Lake Vänern.

YOU SHOULD KNOW

The Göta Canal is
open from May through
to September.

Sweden's Lakeland region covers a vast area blessed with beautiful countryside, picture-perfect villages and vibrant metropolitan areas. But above all, the lakes take centre stage. More like a small inland sea, Vänern, Sweden's largest lake and the third-largest in Europe, is a freshwater paradise for anyone who enjoys any kind of watersport, from sailing and swimming to waterskiing and windsurfing. A short drive east lies Lake Vättern, Sweden's second-largest lake and one whose water is so clean the locals claim you can drink it. The lake is also home to some of the best salmon and char fishing in Europe. The area around the lake is home to hot-air ballooning festivals and there is also an annual 300-km (186-mile) cycling race around the shoreline in June called the Vätternrundan. From the castle of Läckö, constructed in 1298 on Lake Vänern, to the island of Sollerön in Lake Siljan where there are Viking graves, Swedes think of this area as their 'cradle of culture'. Truly there is so much to see and do in this vast area that it is difficult to know where to begin. But one of the best ways to explore the watery theme of Swedish Lakeland is to take a trip along the amazing Göta canal that links Lake Vänern to the Baltic. It takes about eight days to cruise from Mem in the east to Sjötorp in the west. During that time you'll navigate some 240km (150 miles) of canal and pass through 58 locks, and you'll also have savoured one of the delights of the region.

REINDEER MIGRATION

Finland

HOW TO GET THERE:
By air to Ivalo, then by road.
WHEN TO GO:
October to April.
NEAREST TOWN:
Utsjoki, Finland.

Reindeer are the domesticated cousins of the caribou of North America. Throughout the Arctic the lives of many native peoples are closely entwined with these hardy animals. In Scandinavia the Sámi people have herded reindeer for centuries, relying on their meat for food and their skins for clothing and shelter. During the summer months the reindeer live on the coast, where the grass is rich and the herd fatten up for the hard winter ahead. As autumn approaches the migration inland begins. The reindeer have traditional breeding grounds where the annual rut takes place and usually they will return to the same rut area each year. Winter lasts from October to April, of which around eight weeks are passed in total darkness. Exactly where the reindeer spend these harsh months will depend on snowfall and the availability of their winter food – lichen. When at last spring returns, the herds move back towards the summer pastures where the females will give birth to their calves.

THE MIDNIGHT SUN

Finland

Paradoxically, the 'land of the Midnight Sun' is to be found in the chilly polar regions. It's a phenomenon that occurs both north of the Arctic Circle and south of the Antarctic Circle, but as there are no permanent settlements south of the Antarctic Circle, most Midnight-Sun-seekers head north. For six months of the year, the Earth's North Pole is tilted towards the sun. Close to the summer solstice – 21 June – this inclination is at its maximum, and the sun shines directly on the North Pole and down to a latitude of 66°34' – the Arctic Circle. More than a quarter of Finland lies above the Arctic Circle, making it a perfect place to experience this magical phenomenon. In fact, at Finland's northernmost town, Utjoki, the sun does not set for a period of 73 days during summer. Many visitors can find it difficult to sleep but the locals seem to revel in the experience, and an almost festive spirit breaks out throughout Finland. This reaches a climax with the midsummer celebrations, a time of great celebration and euphoria. When you have had enough of partying, a walk beside a beautiful lake at midnight will provide an experience never to be forgotten.

HOW TO GET THERE: To reach Utjoki, Finland's most northerly town, fly to Ivalo and then travel by road on the E75.
WHEN TO GO: 16 May to 27 July at Utjoki.
NEAREST TOWN: Utjoki 165km (102 miles) north of Ivalo on the E75.

ÅLAND ISLANDS

Finland

The Åland Islands comprise some 6,500 emerald shards, scattered in the blue waters of the Baltic at the mouth of the Gulf of Bothnia. Although part of Finland, the islands have retained a unique degree of independence and autonomy. Åland has its own flag, its own stamps and its own vehicle licence plates, even its own internet domain. Another curious idiosyncrasy is that the language spoken here is Swedish. The archipelago is home to some 26,700 souls, spread among 65 of the islands. Just under half of the population live in and around Mariehamn, the islands' only town. Founded in 1861, this is the centre of the shipping and tourist industries and is home to the *Landskapsregering* – the local seat of government. For many visitors, the islands provide an invitingly peaceful retreat to a world where time is measured by the tides and seasons. It's a place of tranquil beauty where every sunrise and sunset over the archipelago provides a photo opportunity not to be missed. What the islands lack in drama they more than make up for in their gentle beauty and the ease with which they can be explored. Hire a rowing boat and you'll soon find a beach all to yourself – perhaps even a whole island. From May to August Åland captures more sunshine than any of its Nordic neighbours, making it a popular holiday destination. But for hardier types a winter visit here is rewarded with the opportunity to experience long-distance skating or ice-boating through the ice sheets that form around the smaller islands and skerries. At any time of the year visitors can enjoy the medieval castle of Kastelholm, the Jan Karlsgården farm museum, or the maritime museum complete with the *Pommern*, a historic sailing ship built in Glasgow at the beginning of the last century.

DON'T MISS
The Inari
Sámi Museum.

LAKE INARI
Finland

Situated on the 69th parallel, deep inside the Arctic Circle, lies Finland's third-largest lake – Lake Inari. The sixth-largest in Europe, Lake Inari is actually more like a small sea. Measuring around 1,000 sq km (386 sq miles), by the time you have sailed out to its often choppy centre, the shore will have long disappeared. Almost completely frozen for more than half the year, the last of the winter ice usually melts away by the second week of June. But even on the warmest days the water temperature only just makes it into double figures. The Finnish name for Finland, *Suomi*, means 'land of lakes' – Lake Inari is, by contrast, a 'lake of lands' with over 3,000 islands peppering its surface and providing a fascinating waterborne tableau for visitors to explore. Cruises are a popular way to enjoy the lake – although for the more adventurous all manner of watercraft are available for hire. Around the lake's 2,776-km (1,725-mile) rocky and rugged shoreline there are numerous discoveries to make. At Ukonkivi there is an old sacrificial site that the Sámi people used to ensure good fishing. And when their catches were good they would store the surplus in ice caves such as the one on Iso-Maura that stays frozen all year. Fish remain one of the lake's more abundant resources, with whitefish, trout and Arctic char the most common species. Visitors in summer can enjoy the delights of Lake Inari by day or night, as from May to the end of July the sun never completely sets. The temperature at this time can reach a warmish 13°C (55°F). But it doesn't last long, and when the ice freezes in November, the lake is plunged into the one-and-a-half-month-long *Kaamos*, or dark season.

HOW TO GET THERE:
The nearest airport is in Ivalo. Inari is over 15 hours by bus from Helsinki.
WHEN TO GO:
May to July for the Midnight Sun. The lake is frozen from November to June.
NEAREST TOWN:
Ivalo, 45km (28 miles).

MAELIFELL

Iceland

HOW TO GET THERE:
The bus to
Kirkjubaejarklaustur from
Reykjavik takes five hours.
WHEN TO GO:
Spring to autumn.
NEAREST TOWN:
Kirkjubaejarklaustur.

YOU SHOULD KNOW
Maelifell can only be
reached either on foot or
by four-wheel drive.

In a country full of remarkable volcanic creations, one of the more unusual is Maelifell. It's an unnaturally uniform cone that rises from a barren desert of laval ash. It was created by an eruption under the Myrdalsjökull glacier in southern Iceland. Its cone is made up of 'tuff', a mixture of solidified ash and other volcanic debris, and rises some 200m (650ft) above the plain. About 10,000 years ago Myrdalsjökull, Iceland's most southerly, and fourth-largest, glacier, finally loosened its icy grip on Maelifell, exposing this pointy little peak to the Icelandic sun. As a consequence, this mysterious cone became clothed in a soft coat of moss. The moss, grimmia, is one of the 500 kinds of moss that make up a large percentage of Iceland's rather uninspiring 1,300 plant species. Grimmia thrives on laval soils, but what is most remarkable about it is its colour. Where the soil is dry it grows a somewhat inconspicuous silver-grey colour. But where the soils are moist, as they are on Maelifell, grimmia turns a bright, almost luminous green. Surrounded by the dusty Maelifellsandur desert, Maelifell's feet are washed by the numerous braided rivers and streams that flow from Myrdalsjökull. It's a quite otherworldly landscape presided over by the silent, green cone of Maelifell.

VATNAJÖKULL

Iceland

HOW TO GET THERE:
By road from Hofn. Hofn has
an airport and is an eight-
hour bus ride from Reykjavik.
WHEN TO GO:
The months May to August
offer the most benign weather.
NEAREST TOWN:
Hofn lies a few kilometres to
the east of the glacier.

One of the most eye-catching features of almost any map of Iceland is the huge, white mass covering the southeast of the country. This is Vatnajökull. Covering more than 8 per cent of the country, and measuring 8,100 sq km (3,100 sq miles), it is not simply the largest glacier in Iceland, it is the largest in Europe. With an average thickness of 400m (1,300ft) – but in places extending to 1,000m (3,200ft) – Vatnajökull contains a mind-boggling 3,300 cubic km (791 cubic miles) of ice. Beneath the glacier's uniformly white surface lies an undulating plateau of valleys and gorges, and like most of Iceland, it's an area of high volcanic activity. Beneath the ice, the Grímsvötn lakes sit above a huge magma chamber that erupted as recently as 2004, sending up plumes of ash and sulphur dioxide that were detected as far away as Norway. When eruptions occur beneath the glacier, they can actually lift the ice like a fluffy white blanket, allowing huge quantities of water to rapidly escape. The ensuing floods that followed an eruption in 1996 actually washed away part of Iceland's ring road. And because of the potentially devastating consequences of such glacial 'runs', Vatnajökull is monitored very closely. It has also been receiving more attention of late as scientists have been examining it for signs of global warming. Vatnajökull lies within the Skaftafell National Park and every year thousands of visitors come to hike, ski, sled and skidoo over its surface. Nearby are the equally enticing Jökulsarlon lagoon, with its flotillas of icebergs, and Öraefajökull, at 2,110m (7,000ft), Iceland's highest mountain.

BLUE LAGOON, REYKJANES PENINSULA

Iceland

Unless arriving by boat, most visitors to Iceland touch down at Keflavik, 70km (43 miles) southwest of the capital Reykjavik. Keflavik perches right at the tip of the Reykanes peninsula, a rugged, rocky finger of land that curls upwards, as if beckoning visitors to its shores. From the air the lunar-like landscape appears dark and moody, but set right in this heart of darkness shines a sapphire gem – the Blue Lagoon. Iceland is often referred to as the land of ice and fire, and with good reason. Geothermal activity is everywhere, from bubbling lava to gushing geysers. One of the more benign benefits of all this volcanism is the Blue Lagoon, a huge pool of mineral-rich seawater, heated geothermally to a comfortable 36–39°C (97–102°F). Privately owned, the site has been tastefully developed into a luxury spa, a giant geothermal hot-tub, where visitors can soak away their cares in a uniquely Icelandic way. The milky blue waters are suffused with silica and other minerals, which are claimed to benefit the skin in numerous ways. In particular the waters are said to be particularly efficacious for sufferers of psoriasis, and attached to the spa is a clinic where various treatments are available.

HOW TO GET THERE:
By road 40km (25 miles) from Reykjavik or 22km (14 miles) from Keflavik. Many tour operators offer tours to the site.
WHEN TO GO:
The Blue Lagoon is open all year. From 1 June to 31 August it opens 7.30am to 9pm, and you can stay in the water until 9.45pm.
NEAREST TOWN:
Keflavik 23km (14 miles).

LAKI

Iceland

HOW TO GET THERE:
A bus service from Kirkjubaejarklaustur that takes approximately three hours.
WHEN TO GO:
Spring to autumn.
NEAREST TOWN:
Kirkjubaejarklaustur.

YOU SHOULD KNOW
There are no facilities at Laki.

Laki, or Lakagígar, which means 'the craters of Laki', is a huge volcanic fissure some 25km (16 miles) long running through a desolate, otherworldly landscape. In a country not short of volcanic spectacle, Laki is memorable. In 1783 this fissure erupted with incredible ferocity, creating the largest lava field ever produced by a single eruption. A lethal mixture of fluorine and sulphur dioxide then killed over 50 per cent of the livestock on Iceland. A terrible famine followed, in which around 10,000 Icelanders starved – around a fifth of the population. The tragedy was of such proportions that the Danish government, which at the time administered Iceland, planned the evacuation of the remaining population. Due to its isolated location and the nature of the terrain, any visit to Laki needs to be well planned. The lava fields are, however, relatively easy to traverse on foot, while the more ambitious can go by horse or mountain bike. Whatever your mode of transport, the trip will reward you with some outstanding scenery and a special sense of unity both with the creative forces of our planet and the history of the Icelandic people.

THE GREAT GEYSIR

Iceland

Iceland may not have bequeathed many words to the world, but one that surely springs to mind is 'geyser'. Throughout the world, geyser is used to describe any hot spring that periodically ejects a column of steaming water into the air. In Iceland, however, it refers to just one: the Great Geysir. The first record of the Great Geysir dates back to 1294. After a powerful earthquake had shaken the western lowlands in the Haukadalur valley, hot springs formed, some of which began to spout. Over the centuries, more earthquakes shook the valley, and the power of one of its spouting springs – the Great Geysir – became legend. Sadly, in recent times the Great Geysir's power has waned. There was hope that it might reawaken when, on Iceland's national holiday, 17 June 2000, a quake that measured 6.5 on the Richter scale hit the area. But it was not to be. For centuries the cause of the Great Geysir's steamy outbursts was thought to be supernatural. And although today the science is well understood, it is difficult to watch a geyser erupt without feeling a connection with a power that is as old as Earth itself. At Geysir there is a water-filled natural 'pipe' that runs over 20m (65ft) underground. At this depth, pressure from above allows the water to reach 120°C (248°F) without boiling. Higher up the pipe, however, the pressure is less, so the water can boil more easily. As it turns to steam, it forces the water above it out of the pipe. This then causes a chain reaction. The rapid reduction in pressure on the super-heated water below results in it explosively turning into steam, sending the water above it up into the air. The expelled water then slowly trickles back into the pipe and the process begins again.

HOW TO GET THERE:
By road from Reykjavik.
WHEN TO GO:
All year – but winters can be cold.
NEAREST TOWN:
Reykjavik 75km (46 miles) to the southwest.

DON'T MISS
The impressive waterfall at Gulfoss.

AURORA BOREALIS

Iceland

*Left: Horses are unfazed by
the aurora borealis.*

The aurora borealis is Nature's very own lightshow, a shimmering stream of coloured light that suffuses the night sky. Visually stunning, part of an aurora's beauty lies in its ephemeral nature. Sometimes an aurora can be a disappointingly monochrome, diaphanous cloud; at others a pulsating, psychedelic curtain of colours. It occurs when electrically charged particles, travelling at speeds of up to 1,200km (750 miles) per second on the solar wind, are captured by the Earth's magnetic field. As these particles are drawn down towards the poles, they hit the ionosphere and collide with the gases in the atmosphere. These collisions produce photons – light particles – and the result is a shimmering sky show known as the aurora australis in the southern hemisphere and the aurora borealis, or northern lights, in the north.

PINGVELLIR

Iceland

Pingvellir, pronounced 'Thingvellir', is one of the so-called 'Golden Circle' attractions of Iceland, a collection of natural wonders and historical sites located within striking distance of Reykjavic. Pingvellir is, however, a collection of attractions itself, comprising the Parliamentary Plains, a rift valley and Lake Pingvallavatn, all encompassed by the oldest national park in Iceland. The Parliamentary Plains were home to the Althing, the oldest parliament in the world. Established in 930AD, it met annually until 1789, when an earthquake caused the plain to slip by a metre (3ft) and proceedings were moved to the current capital, Reykjavik. To the south lies Lake Pingvallavatn, Iceland's largest natural lake. As well as its natural beauty, the lake's clean, cool waters are popular with anglers as they are home to good numbers of char and brown trout. As well as being historically significant, Pingvellir is very beautiful. With rugged hills, some snowcapped, framing the valley, through which rivers and streams wind in and out, it is easy to appreciate why it was chosen as Iceland's first national park in 1928. Its value was further recognized in 2004 when it also became a UNESCO World Heritage Site.

THE GREENLAND ICE SHEET

Greenland

HOW TO GET THERE:
Fly to Nuuk – the capital
of Greenland.
WHEN TO GO:
Summer season.
NEAREST TOWN:
Nuuk.

DON'T MISS
The Jakobshavn
Isbræ outlet glacier.

The Greenland Ice Sheet is a vast body of ice covering roughly 80 per cent of the surface of Greenland. It consists of layers of compressed snow that date back to more than 100,000 years. It is 2,400km (1,500 miles) long from north to south, 1,100km (690 miles) wide at its greatest width and 2–3km (1–2 miles) thick. There are other ice masses in Greenland covering almost 100,000 sq km (38,600 sq miles) around the periphery. The ice in the current ice sheet is 110,000 years old. Scientists believe that if global warming continues at the current rate, the entire sheet will melt in a few hundred years. If all 2.85 million cubic km (684,000 cubic miles) of ice melts, global sea levels will rise by 7.2m (24ft). This would swamp most coastal cities in the world and drown several small island countries, as well as low-lying countries such as Bangladesh and the Netherlands. The massive weight of the ice has depressed the central area of Greenland; the bedrock surface is near sea level over most of the interior, but mountains occur around the periphery, with two north–south elongated domes that reach a height of 3,290m (10,800ft). The ice margin just reaches the sea near Melville Bay, southeast of Thule. Outlet glaciers, which are like the tongues of the ice sheet, move through valleys around the periphery of Greenland to calve off into the ocean and produce the icebergs that occur in the North Atlantic shipping lanes. In winter, the ice sheet takes on a strikingly clear blue-green colour. In summer, the top layer melts, leaving pockets of air in the ice that make it appear to be bright white. When the meltwater seeps down through cracks in the sheet, it accelerates the melting and allows the ice to slide more easily over the bedrock below, speeding its run to the sea. If the ice were to disappear, Greenland would appear as an archipelago.

ILULISSAT ICEFJORD

Greenland

Located on the west coast of Greenland, 250km (156 miles) north of the Arctic Circle, Greenland's Ilulissat Icefjord is the sea mouth of Sermeq Kujalleq, one of the few glaciers through which the Greenland ice cap reaches the sea. It is also one of the fastest-moving – 19m (62ft) per day – and most active glaciers in the world. Annually it calves over 35 cubic km (8.4 cubic miles) of ice, 10 per cent of the production of all Greenland calf ice and more than any other glacier outside Antarctica. It is an outstanding example of a stage in the Earth's history: the last ice age of the quaternary period. The combination of a huge ice sheet and a fast-moving glacial ice stream calving into a fjord covered by icebergs is a phenomenon only seen in Greenland and Antarctica. Ilulissat offers scientists and visitors easy access for close viewing of the calving glacier front as it cascades down from the ice sheet and into the ice-choked fjord. The wild and highly scenic combination of rock, ice and sea, along with the dramatic sounds produced by the moving ice, is an astonishing natural spectacle and, combined with the northern lights (aurora borealis), makes Ilulissat a 'must-visit' destination. The aurora borealis is a celestial display of greens, yellows and reds that leave you spellbound by their extraordinary beauty as they shimmer against the inky backdrop of a starry night sky. In summer you can take a midnight cruise to the ice fjord and see the Midnight Sun with the warm, red colours reflecting in the gigantic icebergs.

HOW TO GET THERE:
From Copenhagen fly to Kangerlussuaq; from there fly on to Ilulissat.
WHEN TO GO:
April to August.
NEAREST TOWN:
Ilulissat.

YOU SHOULD KNOW
The glacier has been studied for 250 years and has recently been instrumental in helping our understanding of climate change.

DON'T MISS
The aurora borealis, a mesmerizing display of lights in the Arctic night sky.

THE YORKSHIRE DALES

England

HOW TO GET THERE:
From Leeds go to Otley,
take A65 to Skipton, where
the B6265 will lead you
into the Dales.
WHEN TO GO:
Springtime, with primroses,
trees leafing and lambs
gambolling.
NEAREST TOWN:
Hawes is the largest town
within the Dales.

The Yorkshire Dales, located in the north of England, straddle the central Pennines in the counties of North Yorkshire and Cumbria. This is a landscape of dark fells, steep-sided green valleys crisscrossed with dry-stone walls, the countryside scattered with solid stone farmhouses and field barns. Modest hills look like majestic peaks, especially when clothed in snow, and after heavy rain small streams have the power of mighty rivers. The area was designated a national park in 1954 and ten million visitors come each year to marvel at the verdant landscape and to enjoy Yorkshire's famous hospitality. There are four large dales within the 1,760 sq km (680 sq miles) of the park, with a host of smaller dales meandering off into rocky gorges below the fells. Wensleydale, carving a path through the middle of the Dales, is broad and wooded, known for its castles and waterfalls and the famous cheese made at the Wensleydale creamery near the village of Gayle. Swaledale to the north is narrow and steep-sided, a wild and desolate valley topped by sweeping moorlands. Wharfedale in the heart of the dales is long and winding, its valley floor studded with pretty villages. To the west, Ribblesdale is a valley of rolling countryside, limestone gorges and towering peaks. From the summit of Ingleborough Hill, on a clear day, you will see as far as the Isle of Man to the southwest.

DUNGENESS

England

HOW TO GET THERE:
From Lydd in the northwest or from New Romney via Littlestone on Sea, along the coast.
WHEN TO GO:
The bleak otherworldliness of Dungeness makes it unusually beautiful throughout the seasons.
NEAREST TOWN:
New Romney 12km (8 miles).

Denge Marsh in Kent reaches the sea in a remote, flat, shingle headland. This is Dungeness – a vast shingle landscape, dominated by a nuclear power station built in the 1960s. The stones reach to the horizon, studded in springtime with clumps of sea kale and wild spinach, then later in the year by white-bladder campion and yellow-horned poppies. Wooden habitations, some no bigger than shacks, are scattered around, many concocted from old boats. It is quite magical in a stark, Kafkaesque way. Two lighthouses stand within view of each other – one took over active duty from the 1904 'old lighthouse', which is privately owned and open for visits. For 50 years its huge, one-million-candle-power light shone out over the English Channel, but when the nuclear power station came on stream in the early '60s, it was made redundant and auctioned off. Chipped masonry shows the Germans used the lighthouse for machine-gun target practice.

THE SEVEN SISTERS

England

These cliffs are formed on the south coast of England, where the south coast plain ends abruptly at the sea. This plain is a chalky landscape of rolling arable fields and dry valleys, with close-cropped grassland on scarps sparsely settled with small hamlets and farmsteads built of flint and brick. Roman and ancient drove roads are common, and there are many prehistoric remains with Neolithic and Bronze Age barrows and Iron Age hill forts. The spectacular white-chalk cliffs are composed of the limey skeletons of small marine organisms, which were laid down in sedimentary layers, with silica laid down in nodules within the chalk to form flint. All these layers have been contorted and lifted by the movement of the continental drifts and then corroded by the sea to form cliffs. One of the most famous cliffs here is called Beachy Head – supposedly from the French *beau chef* or 'lovely head'. From there to Cuckmere Haven the elements have carved out the bright white Seven Sisters. This whole area is popular with cyclists, walkers and hang gliders, with both challenging walks or more leisurely strolls to enjoy.

HOW TO GET THERE: The A21 from junction five of the M25 to Tonbridge – then the A26 to Uckfield and the A22 to Eastbourne.
WHEN TO GO: Good for walking all year.
NEAREST TOWN: Eastbourne 3km (2 miles).

THE LAKE DISTRICT

England

Lying in the northwest of England, the Lake District is one of the best-loved landscapes in the country and has been celebrated in poetry and literature down the ages – from Wordsworth's *Daffodils* to Arthur Ransome's *Swallows and Amazons* and Beatrix Potter's *Peter Rabbit* tales. It is the highest area in England, and its fells are wonderful hiking territory. The U-shaped valleys that radiate out from the centre of the area were carved out of the rock by glaciers during the last ice age. The higher fells, like Scafell Pike, Helvellyn, Skiddaw and Great Gable, are challenging hikes and not for the beginner, but there are much more gentle walks as well, along with a huge variety of watersports and every sort of outdoor pursuit you can imagine. Windermere is the largest lake in England, and Wast Water the deepest. Windermere, Derwentwater and Coniston Water are popular for boating and can get busy, but the more remote lakes are far more peaceful. The Lake District is not large, only 56km (35 miles) across at its widest, but its sheer variety of scenery and the continually changing light as clouds rush across the landscape make this area dramatic and incredibly beautiful.

HOW TO GET THERE:
By road, or by rail to Windermere.
WHEN TO GO:
Any time.
NEAREST TOWN:
Kendal 10km (6 miles).

YOU SHOULD KNOW
The weather in the high fells is often worse than at lower levels.

DARTMOOR

England

HOW TO GET THERE:
From London it is a 281-km (174-mile) journey west to Exeter.
WHEN TO GO:
Any time is good, but November to February is especially atmospheric.
NEAREST TOWN:
Tavistock is the largest of Dartmoor's towns.

DON'T MISS
The cream teas offered in the moor's idyllic villages.

Sprawling across Devon in southwest England, Dartmoor is as starkly beautiful as it is historically fascinating. Occupying 4,700 hectares (11,610 acres) of desolate wilderness – heather-strewn moors, barren bog land and mile upon mile of raw granite – this is the place to come for a sense of nature at her most stoical. At its centre is Dartmoor Forest where you can find the famous wild ponies, ancient weather-chiselled tors (flat granite hilltops), and, if you catch the right weather, you will see the mist coming down, imbuing this desolate terrain with a bleak and magical beauty. But be warned, it is easy to lose your way, and bottomless bogs and stinking mires are never far away. Dartmoor was once home to many Bronze Age settlers whose artefacts can be viewed all over the area, particularly to the east at Grimspound.

WOOKEY HOLE

England

DON'T MISS
Wells Cathedral
and Glastonbury Tor.

The caves and caverns of Wookey Hole on the edge of the Mendip Hills are an exciting and folklore-filled area. The ancient river Axe carved these caves over many thousands of years into the limestone escarpment of the Mendips. The caves are thought to have been inhabited for at least 70,000 years, as they were safe, dry and easy to defend. They first gave shelter to Stone Age man, and much later to the Celts, who farmed the fertile valley floors. The action of the river on the limestone has carved out more than 25 chambers and pools, linked by the subterranean river Axe, all discovered during the 20th century by a series of diving expeditions – and there is still more exploration pending. Nearby are Cheddar Gorge and Ebbor Gorge, a Site of Special Scientific Interest and a quieter spot than Wookey.

THE PEAK DISTRICT

England

The Peak District stretches from the beautiful town of Ashbourne in the south to the craggy and remote High Peak District west of Sheffield. This, the first-established of the national parks, reaches deep into six English counties – Derbyshire, Cheshire, Staffordshire, South

HOW TO GET THERE: The M1 motorway runs to the east and north of the park. From junction 33, the A57 runs through the city of Sheffield and into the north of the park, which is also crossed by several major roads.
WHEN TO GO: All year round.
NEAREST TOWN: Ashbourne 10km (6 miles) from Dovedale in the south Peak district.

Yorkshire, West Yorkshire and Greater Manchester, but to most people the Peaks mean Derbyshire. Rock dominates the landscape, in its pinnacles and spires and airy limestone crags that overhang the deep dales, whose greenness is counterpaned with grey-white dry-stone walls and wandering, threadlike rivers. The central core is the White Peak, limestone country, scarred everywhere by the green gorges of the dales. Surrounding this is an area of shale and thin sandstone through which rivers such as the Derwent and the Goyt have carved their wider, flatter valleys, and embracing all is the Dark Peak, sombre and forbidding, the gritstone rock rising to a moorland plateau. Wild, desolate and stunning.

THE JURASSIC COAST

England

This, the first British World Heritage Site, is 152km (95 miles) of coast, recording 185 million years of ancient history through the Triassic, Jurassic and Cretaceous geological periods that comprise the Mesozoic Era. It stretches from the Orcombe Rocks in east Devon through to Studland Bay and Poole in west Dorset. The cliff exposures along this coast provide an almost continuous sequence of rock formations spanning the Mesozoic Era. The area's important fossil sites and classic coastal geomorphologic features have greatly contributed to the study of Earth sciences for over 300 years. The Triassic period is seen from Exmouth to Lyme Regis, then the Jurassic from Lyme Regis to Swanage, and finally the Cretaceous period through to Studland Bay and into Poole harbour.

This area is also rich in wildlife, with large populations of avocet, dark-bellied brent goose, Slavonian grebe and the little tern at Chesil Beach. The Lulworth skipper butterfly can be spotted amongst the early spider orchid, gentian, wild cabbage and the Nottingham catchfly. There is a long history of mining for shale, and local stone from Portland, Beer and Purbeck have been used throughout the UK for building work.

The Jurassic coast, and in particular Lyme Regis and Charmouth, with their clay-based, old tropical seas with soft, muddy and often stagnant lower levels, was perfect for preserving shells, bones and even the soft tissue of long-dead prehistoric creatures. Imagine the excitement of discovering green ammonites and 197-million-year-old Belamnite Marl alongside other vertebrate and invertebrate marine and terrestrial fossils, and even ancient fossilized footprints.

SNOWDON AND SNOWDONIA

Wales

HOW TO GET THERE:
By road from Caernarfon or
rail from Llanberis.
WHEN TO GO:
April to October.
NEAREST TOWN:
Llanberis 5km (3 miles).

YOU SHOULD KNOW
It takes about five hours
to get to the top of the
mountain on foot.

At 1,085m (3,560ft), Snowdon is the highest mountain in Wales and the fourth-highest in the British Isles. The Snowdonia National Park was formed in 1951 to protect an area 56 by 80km (35 by 50 miles), which covers most of northwest Wales. Snowdon itself is one of the most popular mountains in Britain for climbers, but the less energetic can get to the summit by catching the Snowdon Mountain Railway from Llanberis in the west. There are half a dozen routes up the mountain, so pick one that suits your ability. There are also walking, hiking, pony, mountain-biking and cycling trails lower down the mountain and throughout the park. The views from the top of the mountain are unbelievable, but there is also stunning scenery lower down, from woodland to secluded valleys with gushing waterfalls. The weather can often be worse up in the high peaks, so if the forecast is not good, other activities such as white-water rafting, sailing and pony trekking are on offer. There are 37km (23 miles) of sandy beaches to enjoy on the Lleyn peninsula. The park is home to a wide variety of wildlife, including otters in the lower rivers, a good range of butterflies in the wildflower meadows, important populations of the minute lesser-horseshoe bat, buzzards, peregrine falcons and many smaller species of birds, plus the feral goats that have roamed the area for at least 10,000 years.

FINGAL'S CAVE

Scotland

Fingal's Cave is on the tiny island of Staffa, which is just west of the Isle of Mull in the Inner Hebrides, off the west coast of Scotland. Approached over the water, Staffa looks as if a giant hand has reached into the Atlantic, pulling it upwards and outwards, stretching it like black rubber. The dark and elegant symmetry of the hexagonal columns that surround the island, flanking the entrance and interior of Fingal's Cave, defies description and caused the famous naturalist Sir Joseph Banks, when he 'discovered' the cave in 1772, to exclaim 'compared to this, what are the cathedrals and palaces built by men!' The cave is 20m (66ft) high and 69m (226ft) deep. Six-sided black basalt formations create a spectacular forest of columns, some 11m (36ft) tall, and the eerie sounds of the waves rising and falling against the glossy dark pillars give the place the atmosphere of a natural concert hall. The columns were created after a mass of hot lava from an ancient lava flow cooled, forming hexagonal patterns as it cracked and shrank (in a similar way to drying mud) and slowly forming the pillars subsequently exposed by erosion. The cave is named after Finn MacCool, a hero of Celtic folklore who is supposed to have built the Giant's Causeway – a collection of some 40,000 basalt columns on the northeast coast of Antrim, Northern Ireland, which was once joined to Fingal's Cave. Only sheep live on Staffa. It is a speck in the ocean, but the stark and lonely beauty of the place and the wondrous sight of the 'Cathedral of the Sea' attract visitors from around the world.

HOW TO GET THERE:
Car ferries from Oban and Lochaline on the Scottish mainland to Mull, then by boat from Ulva Ferry Pier on the west side of Mull.
WHEN TO GO:
Spring, when the clifftops are a mass of wildflowers.
NEAREST TOWN:
Tobermory 32km (20 miles) from Ulva Ferry.

LOCH FYNE

Scotland

Loch Fyne, on the west coast of Argyll and Bute, is Scotland's longest sea loch – 64km (40 miles) long. It carves its way north into the heart of the western Highlands where the hills, the sea and the sky, together with the pellucid light, make it one of the most beautiful places in the world. Dolphins visit these waters, seals laze around on the rocks, otters live here year-round and even basking sharks sometimes frequent the lower stretches of the loch during the summer months. The loch is heaven for divers. The marine life is superb, with squat lobster, scallops, large whelks and edible crabs. Feather starfish and brittle starfish are everywhere. Near Kenmore Point is Stallion Rock, a vertical overhanging rock that rises from the seabed 30m (98ft) below. Here are found sea squirts, anemones and large, brilliantly coloured sponges. The pretty little 18th-century town of Inveraray lies on the west side of the loch, with its famous castle, which has been the residence through the centuries of the Dukes of Argyll.

HOW TO GET THERE:
From Glasgow A82 to Arrochar, then A83 to the head of the loch.
WHEN TO GO:
Avoid the midges in July and August.
NEAREST TOWN:
Inveraray, beside the northwest shore of the Loch.

YOU SHOULD KNOW
During the Second World War, over half a million troops were trained in amphibious landing techniques on the shores of Loch Fyne prior to the D-day landings.

THE HIGHLANDS

Scotland

HOW TO GET THERE:
Fly or drive to Glasgow or Edinburgh and head north.
WHEN TO GO:
August for the purple, heather-clad hills.
NEAREST TOWNS:
Inverness, over 100 miles from any other Scottish settlement, is the only 'city' in the Highlands.

The Highland Line in Scotland, the divide between the smooth Lowlands and the sudden lifting of the mountains, runs from the south end of Loch Lomond towards Aberdeen and around to Inverness. Cross this line going north and you are in what many people think of as the 'real' Scotland. Here, a dramatically stark beauty characterizes one of Europe's last great wilderness areas, where solitude, space and silence can be found in abundance. Narrow roads twist through mountain passes and run beside the lochs, with cloud-shrouded summits rearing overhead. Ruins of old dwellings remain, testimony to the times before the Highland Clearances, when the landlords drove the people from the land in favour of more profitable sheep farming. The northwestern Highlands is a wild and lonely place and, for many, the finest part of Scotland. Serrated by fjord-like sea lochs, the coastline is scattered with windswept, white-sand beaches and rugged mountains sweeping up from the shoreline.

THE CAIRNGORMS

Scotland

The Cairngorm Mountains lie in the Cairngorms National Park, which is often described as having some of the most spectacular landscapes in Britain, from the wild tundra of the high mountaintops to the seclusion of ancient pinewoods and heather. Here, too, is moorland, vivid with summer colour, and grand glens and rivers all scarred by glacial action. There is little population due to the harsh climate, but the wildlife is wonderful. A funicular railway has recently been opened to the Ptarmigan centre, 150m (490ft) from the summit of Cairngorm, giving easy access to hillwalkers, winter-sports enthusiasts, climbers, bird-watchers and deerstalkers. Flyfishing and hang-gliding are amongst other pursuits, but it must be remembered that the Highlands can be a dangerous and hazardous place with unpredictable weather.

LOCH NESS

Scotland

Loch Ness is a deep freshwater loch in the Scottish Highlands, forming the northeastern end of a geological fault called the Great Glen that runs from Inverness to Fort William. The loch is best known for the alleged sightings of the Loch Ness Monster, fondly nicknamed 'Nessie', but is itself a true spectacle, being the largest body of water in the Great Glen and the second-deepest loch in Scotland, some 230m (754ft) at its deepest. However, the water is murky as a result of the high peat content of the surrounding soil, making sightings of Nessie difficult. The Great Glen, which effectively divides the Highlands in half, is one of Britain's major geographical features, containing its highest mountain as well as its greatest lake by volume. When the last ice age retreated some 10,000 years ago, the land, no longer weighed down by the ice sheet, rose to form the basin of this magnificent loch. Apart from enabling a thriving tourist industry, the loch also acts as a reservoir for hydroelectric power. At the southern end, its only island, called Cherry, is thought to be a 'Crannog', an Iron Age, man-made island for protection purposes.

SMOO CAVE

Scotland

HOW TO GET THERE:
Flights to Inverness, then by road to Durness. Coaches run between Inverness and Smoo Cave daily.
WHEN TO GO:
Year-round.
NEAREST TOWN:
Durness 3km (2 miles).

Smoo Cave is east of the village of Durness on Scotland's north coast, sheltered from the Atlantic by the Cape Wrath peninsula. Reminiscent of the Shetlands, it is set into dramatic limestone cliffs with swirling seabirds diving for food, puffins nesting in their burrows and seals in the crashing waves below. Smoo Cave itself lies at the inner end of a narrow inlet eroded into the limestone, and contains a record of human occupation during several periods of historic and prehistoric time. Access to the cave is down a steep path, where you will find signs of an old midden (refuse-heap) just inside the entrance. Passing through from the main cave to a smaller cave, the river Allt Smoo noisily pours in and falls 24m (80ft). Cross the river again and climb up to a ledge, from which you get good views of the waterfall – in the enclosed space, the noise is quite deafening. There are other, smaller caves thought to be side caves of Smoo Cave, called Glassknapper's and Antlers, and there are yet more adjacent sites and collapsed caves to be investigated. A delightful way to approach Smoo Cave is to drive past Balnakiel craft village to the west of Durness and park beside the beach – walk over the golden sands on one side and the sea on the other, and a well-defined path takes you up over the cliffs, viewing the wildlife, on a circular route to Durness village and the caves.

BEN NEVIS

Scotland

HOW TO GET THERE:
By rail or road (A82) from Glasgow to Fort William.
WHEN TO GO:
Avoid the midge season – July and August.
NEAREST TOWN:
Fort William 1km (0.5 miles).

DON'T MISS
The Ben Nevis Race, held annually on the first Saturday in September.

The massive bulk of Ben Nevis looms above the town of Fort William, its 1,343-m (4,406-ft) top often obscured by clouds. It is known simply as 'The Ben' to the 75,000 hikers and climbers who come each year to walk the track to the summit or to conquer the vertiginous cliffs of the north face, riven with buttresses, ridges and pinnacles. The pony track or tourist path that leads to the summit begins in Glen Nevis at Achintee on the south side of the mountain The dappled woodland of pine, oak and birch opens out to heather moorland, tufted hair grass and peaty bogs, climbing steeply and then zigzagging up the rounded dome of the upper mountain through deer grass and weather-shattered scree. On a clear day the views from the top are magical – to the east Aonach Mor, beyond, to the south, the rocky ridge of the Mamores and still further, the mountains of Glen Coe.

THE GIANT'S CAUSEWAY

Northern Ireland

HOW TO GET THERE:
By road or along the
Causeway Coastal Cliff Path.
WHEN TO GO:
Spring or summer.
NEAREST TOWN:
Bushmills 3km (2 miles).

YOU SHOULD KNOW
Sensible footwear is a must.

The Giant's Causeway was formed about 60 million years ago when a massive volcanic eruption poured out almost unimaginable amounts of molten rock. As this magma cooled, it shrank, cracking into the mostly hexagonal pillars of basalt we see today. Some 37,000 of the columns remain. In places, the solidified lava flow is 28m (92ft) deep and the tallest columns are 12m (36ft) high. The tiny Hebridean Isle of Staffa to the north has similar formations, which are part of the same massive lava flow – legend has it that the causeway was built by the giant warrior, Finn MacCool, so he could reach his lover there. The only UNESCO World Heritage Site in Northern Ireland, the causeway is set in a lovely landscape of seabird cliffs, sea caves and sandy bays. These rocks have been eroding almost since they were formed, ground down by ice, wind and waves into a variety of shapes, including the Giant's Boot and the Pipe Organ. As you scramble about, look out to sea where they would once have stretched, and imagine the scene when that expanse of water was a sea of flowing, molten magma.

LOUGH NEAGH

Northern Ireland

A shallow lake with a maximum depth of 25m (82ft) but averaging only 9m (30ft), Lough Neagh, in the centre of Northern Ireland is the largest lake by area in the British Isles. Five of the six counties of Northern Ireland border its shores. Ancient deposits in Toome Bay, on its northwestern shore, have yielded the oldest-recorded human artefacts in Ireland. Mesolithic humans are believed to have first appeared in Ireland (c. 6,000BC) near the lake, and Neolithic remains have also been found locally. Bird-watchers are attracted to Lough Neagh due to the number and variety of birds that winter and summer in the boglands and shores around the lough. The traditional working boats on Lough Neagh were wide-beamed, clinker-built and sprit-rigged. Old barges called 'lighters' were used up to the 1940s to transport coal over the lough, and adjacent canals and log boats (coití) were the main means of transport until the 17th century. Few traditional boats are left now, but on the southern shore, a series of working boats are being rebuilt by the Lough Neagh Boating Heritage Association.

HOW TO GET THERE:
Flights and ferries to Belfast, then take the M2 and A26 to Antrim.
WHEN TO GO:
The wildlife is of interest especially in migration times.
NEAREST TOWN:
Antrim is on the northeast shore of the lake.

DON'T MISS
The beautiful northeast coast of Ireland.

THE MOUNTAINS OF MOURNE

Northern Ireland

HOW TO GET THERE:
Flights or car ferries to Belfast, then drive south on the A1 to Newry, east of the Mourne Mountains.
WHEN TO GO:
Has interest for enthusiasts at most times of year.
NEAREST TOWN:
Newry.

The granite slopes of the Mourne Mountains of County Down in the southeast of Northern Ireland are situated in an area of outstanding natural beauty. The highest peak is Slieve Donard, at 849m (2,285ft). *Slieve* is an Irish word derived from *sliahb*, meaning 'mountain'. Slieve Donard's grey, rocky slopes rise up from the largest Irish dune heath and beach, edging the southern and eastern sides of the Mourlough National Nature Reserve. The raw beauty of this mountain was the inspiration for the song by Percy French, whose line – 'Where the Mountains O'Mourne sweep down to the sea' – makes it the most famous mountain in Ireland. Another interesting feature of this mountain range is the Mourne Wall, a 35-km (22-mile) dry-stone wall that crosses the 12 summits of Mourne.

THE DINGLE PENINSULA

Ireland

The northernmost of the five peninsulas that project out into the Atlantic like fingers at the southwest tip of Ireland, the Dingle Peninsula (Corca Dhuibhne) is the westernmost point of mainland Ireland. It lies on a sandstone ridge that also forms the Slieve Mish mountains in the east of the peninsula and Mount Brandon, Ireland's second-highest mountain, at 953m (3,127ft). Often beset by the weather that the North Atlantic throws at it, this wild landscape is known for its spectacular scenery, with stunning views of the Great Blasket Island, Dingle Bay and across Castlemaine Harbour to MacGillicuddy Reeks. Described by many as one of the most beautiful landscapes on Earth, it has rocky outcrops and rugged cliffs, soft, rounded hills with forests, beautiful alpine flora higher up and wide, sandy beaches. There is a magnificent view around almost every corner. Off the beaten track, there are many side roads and paths that allow visitors to explore this breathtaking countryside at their leisure. In spring and early summer, seabirds such as gannets nest on the cliffs, while Fungie the dolphin has lived in the harbour since 1984. Popular activities include walking, boat trips out to the Great Blasket Island, swimming, surfing, walking or horse-riding through the edge of the surf. There are also hundreds of archaeological sites to visit.

HOW TO GET THERE:
By road.
WHEN TO GO:
Summer but pack a raincoat!
NEAREST TOWN:
Dingle.

THE CLIFFS OF MOHER

Ireland

HOW TO GET THERE:
By road on the N85.
The closest airport is
Shannon International.
WHEN TO GO:
Year-round.
NEAREST TOWNS:
Doolin 3km (2 miles), Galway
80km (50 miles).

South of the village of Doolin in County Clare in the west of Ireland, the Cliffs of Moher are Ireland's most visited natural attraction, with up to a million visitors every year. Standing 214m (702ft) at their highest point, they stretch for 8km (5 miles) along the Atlantic coast. On a clear day you can see the Aran Islands and Galway Bay, as well as the Twelve Pins and the Maum Turk mountains in Connemara, Loop Head to the south and the Dingle Peninsula and Blasket Islands in Kerry. O'Brien's Tower stands near the highest point and has served as a viewing point for visitors for hundreds of years.

The cliffs are home to Atlantic puffins, razorbills and other wild birds – bird-watchers are advised to bring binoculars. At the southern end of the Cliffs of Moher stands Hags Head, a natural rocky promontory that resembles a seated woman when viewed from the north. A visitor centre is located almost midway along these spectacular cliffs, which include 800m (2,624ft) of protected cliffside pathways and viewing areas to revel in the vista.

YOU SHOULD KNOW
There is a €6 charge per person that also gives you access to the visitor centre. Children are free.

DON'T MISS
Spectacular views of the Aran Islands, Galway Bay and the Burren.

DON'T MISS
The Poulnabrone Dolmen on the way to the cave.

AILLWEE CAVE
Ireland

In sight of Galway Bay, the north coast of County Clare is a scarred limestone plateau called the Burren. It's bleak, flat and inhospitable even to sheep. Only the occasional tuft of greenery breaks the 50 shades of lichen-stained grey that spreads for miles of cracked rifts and deep fissures. The weird landscape is unique on Earth (US astronauts trained here until they discovered it wasn't really like the moon at all), but it hides something more extraordinary. Aillwee Cave is the sole entrance to a vast

underground complex from which you can explore the Burren from below. Aillwee leads through a tunnel into a succession of caverns, carved by rain and torrential streams seeping through the surface rock over millions of years. Raging water created cathedrals like Midsummer Cavern, pillared with 5,000-year-old stalagmites, tube-like passages, galleries of bare rock, and chambers like Mud Hall, whose knobbly stalagmites took 8,000 years to reach their present enormity. You walk over bridged caverns and under waterfalls, past shallow excavations hollowed out by bears as hibernation pits before they became extinct in Ireland 1,000 years ago. Bear Haven marks the recent discovery of fossil bear bones in situ. Throughout the system – at present, over 1.3km (0.8 miles) are lit and monitored for visitors' safety – one of the strangest features is the roof. You look up to see the roots of many rare plants hidden in the fissures of the Burren above. In the open air, the biting Atlantic winds inhibit everything but the hardiest alpine flora, but deep in protected fissures are colonies of plants, mosses and lichens that properly belong in a Mediterranean climate, including some very rare orchids. The geological oddities of Aillwee enable you to get up close and personal.

HOW TO GET THERE:
Take the Corkscrew Road from Ballyvaughan; after 2km (1.25 miles) turn left on R480 south towards Lisdoonvarna. Aillwee Cave is off to the right after 3km (2 miles).
WHEN TO GO:
January to November. Try to avoid summer crowds.
NEAREST TOWN:
Ballyvaughan 5km (3 miles).

YOU SHOULD KNOW
If you find an orchid, don't touch it and never reveal its exact position.

DONEGAL BAY

Ireland

Donegal Bay is Ireland's largest bay, a half-moon with the highest cliffs in Europe. Its beaches and coves are among the world's cleanest, and perfect for surfing. It is ringed with small towns and villages where Ireland's most traditional crafts still flourish. Above all, it is washed by the luminous immensity of sky and water. If there is majesty in nature, this is it.

Donegal Bay lies in northwest Ireland and funnels the predominant westerly winds of the Atlantic Ocean onto Rossnowlagh and Bundoran, two beaches on its southern side renowned for the championship consistency of their waves. Bundoran Town is a popular resort, but from here the 'Rougey Walk' leads you on a typically spectacular combination of clifftop and cove, past the Fairy Bridges – cliff arches carved by pounding waves – and Wishing Chair rock to the vista of Tullan Strand, a flawless arc of white sand below the cliffs. Just past the bustle of Killybegs on the northern side is Kilcar, the gateway to the Donegal Gaeltacht, one of the few regions where Gaelic is freely spoken. From nearby Teelin a path leads to Bunglass Point and epic views across the Bay to Sligo. The path continues along One Man's Pass, a 3-km (2-mile) ridge of rock and peat bog that rises and narrows until both sides fall sheer into the waves crashing into fingerstacks of rock at the foot of Slieve League, a precipitous 598-m (1,961-ft) drop. You can see clouds literally forming below you, and marvel as they coalesce and sweep up and over your head into the forested clefts and peat bogs on the way to the megalithic complex at Malin More, Donegal's most westerly headland. It is a huge and mystic beauty to behold.

HOW TO GET THERE:
By car/bus to Donegal City or any other town lining the Bay.
WHEN TO GO:
Year-round.
NEAREST TOWNS:
Best bases are Bundoran (south) and Killybegs (north).

YOU SHOULD KNOW
Peat is 4,000-year-old, bog-preserved moss.

GARAJONAY NATIONAL PARK

La Gomera, Spain

This national park and UNESCO World Heritage Site in the middle of La Gomera forms a marked contrast to anywhere else in the Canary Islands. Set on the volcanic peaks of the same name, it is a lush escape from the nightlife of the other islands. About 70 per cent of its 40 sq km (15.4 sq miles) is covered in laurisilva (with laurel-like leaves) forest, sustained by numerous springs, streams and the humid fog that frequently visits the heights of La Gomera. This forest is a remnant of the subtropical rainforest that covered large swathes of southern Europe millions of years ago but died out during the ice ages. There are also cedar woods and Azores laurel, Canary holly and Canary willow. The evergreen trees are cloaked in moss, and often shrouded in the fog brought by the Atlantic trade winds.

As you explore the park, you will climb up and down hillsides and cross streams on little wooden bridges. It is necessary to keep an eye on where you are putting your feet, but don't forget to look around you at the woodlands and the occasional glimpses of more distant views. As you near the top, you will see the area of Los Roques and eventually will see Teide, on neighbouring Tenerife, in the distance. This unusual and beautiful park is well worth a day trip from the other islands in the group.

HOW TO GET THERE:
By plane to La Gomera airport or ferry, then by road and on foot.
WHEN TO GO:
Any time of year.
NEAREST TOWN:
San Sebastian de la Gomera 12km (7.5 miles).

YOU SHOULD KNOW
The road up to the park is vertiginous.

ORDESA Y MONTE PERDIDO NATIONAL PARK

Spain

HOW TO GET THERE:
By road from Zaragoza.
WHEN TO GO:
Summer.
NEAREST TOWN:
Sabiñánigo 40km (25 miles).

YOU SHOULD KNOW
Don't stray over the border into France without your passport.

At the very top of the Pyrenees lies the massif of the Three Sisters (Tres Sorores), whose highest crests form the border with France. From these heights, glacial valleys radiate out between crests, and gradually the bare heights give way to rough meadows with typical wildflowers including edelweiss, then black-pine woodlands, then beech, oak, ash, birch and fir in the valley bottoms far below. The park adjoins the Parc National des Pyrenées across the border, and together they form a UNESCO World Heritage Site.

The limestone landscape is full of gorges and caves hewn out of the rock by water, while in the heights glacial cirques are reminders of the forces that created this landscape. The glacier in the north side of Monte Perdido is retreating rapidly, and those on the south have long since disappeared. Although the Pyrenean ibex is thought to have become extinct in the area recently, several other species are still to be found, including marmots, otters, the rebecco, wild boar and a species of water mole called the Pyrenean desman.

There is plenty for the bird-watcher: the walls of gorges are good places to look for the lovely pink of the wallcreeper, while dipper should be common on rocks in mountain streams. Larger birds seen in the area at various times include short-toed, golden and booted eagles and honey buzzards, as well as lammergeier and griffon vultures that soar up over the high peaks.

DOÑANA NATIONAL PARK

Spain

HOW TO GET THERE:
By road from Seville
via El Rocio.
WHEN TO GO:
Almost any time of year.
NEAREST TOWN:
Almonte 15km (9 miles).

The Parque Nacional de Doñana is a vast, coastal marshland southwest of Seville. It was formerly the delta of the Guadalquivir river before it was gradually blocked off by the growth of a sandbar. Its three habitats – the marshland (or *marismas*), the Mediterranean scrublands and the mobile coastal dunes and beaches – form one of the most important conservation sites in Europe. In winter the reserve floods, attracting wildfowl to its lagoons, and then partly dries out in summer making it suitable for storks, egrets, vultures, lanner falcons, oxpeckers and partridges, various waders and terns, as well as the critically endangered Spanish imperial eagle. In spring and late summer, the park is alive with migrants on their way to or from Africa. Although the core of the reserve is out of bounds except on guided tours, paths from the visitor centres lead to bird hides from where visitors can watch birds to their hearts' content.

TEIDE

Tenerife, Spain

Away from the towns of Tenerife, the largest of the Canary Islands, it is difficult to escape the sight of the island's central volcano. As you travel round the base of it through lush green plantations, it is always there, in the corner of your eye. At 3,718m (11,823ft), it is the tallest mountain in Spain and the tallest volcano in Europe. It is a stratovolcano, sitting on a hotspot in the eastern Atlantic, and the last eruption, from one of the side vents, occurred only in 1909. Fumaroles at the top emit hot gases such as sulphur dioxide, so visitors are not allowed in the crater. Some 150,000 years ago, a far larger eruption caused the collapse of the previous cone, leaving a caldera 10 by 15km (6 by 9 miles) across and up to 600m (1,970ft) deep. The current peak derives from a later eruption. The floor of the caldera has strange rock formations that stick up like thumbs and result from later erosion. The views from the cable-car station across the lunar landscape of the caldera are breathtaking: two short paths allow visitors to access viewpoints but you must have a permit to climb the last 200m (660ft) to the peak.

HOW TO GET THERE:
By road from Santa Cruz
de Tenerife or via the
cable car to La Rambleta.
WHEN TO GO:
Spring to autumn.
NEAREST TOWN:
Granadilla de Abona
20km (12 miles).

YOU SHOULD KNOW

You need a permit to climb to the peak itself, and entry to the crater is strictly forbidden.

CANTABRIAN COAST

Spain

HOW TO GET THERE:
By road from Santander.
WHEN TO GO:
Any time of year.
NEAREST TOWN:
Santander.

Perched on the southern coast of the Bay of Biscay, Cantabria offers a startling contrast of landscapes within a small area. In the north, the coastal strip of low hills drops down spectacular, sheer cliffs to the sea, while to its south the land rises rapidly through to the mountains of the Cordillera Cantabrica. The rolling lowland hills are separated from each other by river valleys that terminate in *rias* – drowned river valleys formed as the seas rose after the end of the last ice age. The sediment brought down these rivers has created some of the most beautiful beaches in Europe, such as that at Laredo. Cantabria is part of what is known as 'Green Spain', warm because of the effects of the Gulf Stream and lush because the area receives higher levels of rainfall than the arid interior. It is a beautiful place to visit at any time of year. Among the highlights is the Dunes of Liencres Natural Park, the largest continuous expanse of sand dunes in northern Spain, with a good range of typical duneland plants and full of butterflies. Part of the coast between San Vicente de la Barquera and Comillas is protected as the Oyambre Natural Park, and includes the estuary of the Ria de la Rabia, where thousands of birds breed in the wetlands in summer.

DON'T MISS
The chance to spot
brown bears.

PICOS DE EUROPA NATIONAL PARK
Spain

A massive national park located in the Cordilla Cantabrica and shared between the provinces of Cantabria, Asturias and Léon, the Picos de Europa (Peaks of Europe) is also a UNESCO Biosphere Reserve because of the importance of its wildlife. Among the rare species that live here are brown bears, wolves, capercaillies and lammergeier, while buzzards, choughs and the mountain deer known locally as *rebeccos* are more common. The limestone rocks of the area have been shaped by the action of glaciers and rivers, creating a typical limestone karst landscape with some of Spain's deepest cave systems, of which new ones are continually being discovered. The narrow gorge carved by the Cares river between two of the mountain ranges in the park is a draw for many visitors, because it can be reached via the aerial tramway between Fuente Dé and the village of Caín. The river itself has been canalized, but the pathway alongside offers views of its 1.5-km (1-mile) depths. The area is extremely popular with climbers, as the varied landscape offers pitches of different levels of difficulty. One of the most spectacular formations is the Naranjo de Bulnes in the central massif, which offers 500-m (1,550-ft), multi-pitch climbs.

HOW TO GET THERE:
By road from Santander
or Oviedo.
WHEN TO GO:
Spring to autumn.
NEAREST TOWN:
San Vicente de la Barquers
20km (12 miles).

SIERRA NEVADA NATIONAL PARK

Spain

In southern Andalucia, within just a few kilometres of the Costa del Sol, lies the second-highest mountain range in Europe, the Sierra Nevada. Two of Spain's highest mountains – Mulhacén at 3,482m (11,420ft) and La Veleta at 3,394m (11,140ft) – are to be found here. Surprisingly for somewhere this far south, the mountains can be snow-covered and the weather icy cold from November to April. High in the mountains, visitors will find glacial lakes, alpine meadows and scree slopes, which give way lower down to pine forests cut by waterfalls and deep gorges, woodlands of oak, sweet chestnut and maple, scrub and then the fertile lands of the Alpujarras in the south. Because of the sierra's isolation from other similar high mountain ranges, a large proportion of its plants are species or subspecies that occur nowhere else. The area is a draw for bird-watchers: birds that breed here include Bonelli and golden eagles, peregrine falcons and griffon vultures. Mulhacén itself takes a couple of days to scale, but lower down a network of footpaths and tracks crisscrosses the area, allowing access for the walkers, trekkers, horse-riders and mountain bikers who are drawn to explore this beautiful area.

HOW TO GET THERE:
By road from Granada or Almería.
WHEN TO GO:
Any time of year.
NEAREST TOWN:
Orjiva 3km (2 miles).

DON'T MISS
The O Sel Ling Tibetan Monastery.

FUERTEVENTURA'S INTERIOR

Fuerteventura, Spain

HOW TO GET THERE:
By plane or ferry to Puerto del Rosario.
WHEN TO GO:
Any time of year.
NEAREST TOWN:
Puerto del Rosario.

YOU SHOULD KNOW
Fuerteventura means 'strong wind'.

Like the other islands in the Canary group, Fuerteventura is volcanic. However, it is so old – perhaps 30 to 35 million years – that its volcanic rocks have been weathered smooth over much of the island, exposing the sedimentary rocks on which the volcano was built. Away from the resorts, the island is peaceful and can be explored by the paths that run round the coast, or by four-wheel drive to reach the interior or the wild areas in the south. While many volcanoes are quickly colonized by plants, Fuerteventura's interior is so dry that there is little plant life except lichens, and there are few animals. The landscape is a mixture of eroded pumice, rocky grounds and lava flows. Hiking across it reveals a strange, lunar landscape of rocks that look as if they have been sandpapered. The highest point is Jandia's Pico de la Zarza at 807m (2,647ft). The climb gives rewarding views, but it is tough going because of the wind that almost always blows across the island.

HOW TO GET THERE:
By road from Córdoba.
WHEN TO GO:
Spring to autumn.
NEAREST TOWN:
Puertollano 20km (12 miles).

SIERRA MADRONA AND THE VALLE DE ALCUDIA

Spain

Part of the Sierra Morena, the mountain range that divides Andalucía from the Castilian plateau, the Sierra Madrona is an important refuge for the Iberian lynx and wolves. The slopes are covered with unspoiled forests of oak, holm oak and cork oak – with some large specimens thought to be at least 100 years old – punctuated by deep gullies and waterfalls. There are also numerous strawberry trees, which the range is named after, and olive groves. The valley to the north, the Valle de Alcudia, is the landscape through which Miguel de Cervantes' hero, Don Quixote, journied. A huge forest carpets the valley's sides, while in early summer the floor is covered with fields of scarlet poppies. This landscape, widely acknowledged to be among the most beautiful of this part of inland Spain, offers plenty of trails for walkers, long-distance hikers, horse-riders and mountain bikers, as well as climbing in the mountains themselves. The region's rivers and lakes are popular for kayaking, and the area is also known for its thermal springs. This area has been inhabited for thousands of years and among the attractions here are palaeolithic remains at the lovely Retamar Lake.

MONFRAGÜE NATIONAL PARK

Spain

HOW TO GET THERE:
By road from Salamanca.
WHEN TO GO:
April to October.
NEAREST TOWN:
Plasencia 20km (12 miles).

Not far from the Portuguese border, Monfragüe is a lovely area of woodland, pastures and scattered cork and holm oaks – this landscape is known locally as *dehesa* – and higher, craggy peaks, set around a vast reservoir, the Embalse de Torregon. It covers some 170 sq km (65 sq miles) and is one of the natural highlights of Spain. As well as being an area of outstanding beauty, it is a UNESCO Biosphere Reserve. Mammals here include wild cats, Iberian lynx, wild boar, otters and red, roe and fallow deer. But it is the birds of prey that make Monfragüe

DON'T MISS
The birds of prey, including the extremely rare black vultures.

special. Not only does it have the largest breeding colony of the extremely rare black vultures, with upwards of 200 pairs, but it has ten pairs of Spanish imperial eagles. Two other species of vulture, four other species of eagles and three kites also breed here. Large numbers of wildfowl also nest here by the rivers and the reservoir. The rarest bird in the park, however, is the black stork, which constructs its nest high in the crown of trees. The best spot to see the nesting vultures and storks is the canyon near the Pena Falcon cliff. Even those who are not natural bird-watchers cannot fail to be enthralled by this beautiful park.

THE ROCK OF GIBRALTAR

Gibralter

HOW TO GET THERE:
By air, sea or road
from Spain.
WHEN TO GO:
The climate is pleasant
throughout the year.
NEAREST TOWN:
Gibraltar, on the Rock itself.

YOU SHOULD KNOW
The interior of the Rock is
an enormous labyrinth of
fortified tunnels, built
to defend the Rock
against invaders.

Probably the most famous rock in the world, the Rock of Gibraltar rises 426m (1,396ft) from sea level to tower over the narrow body of water that separates Europe from North Africa, namely the Strait of Gibraltar. In mythology, Hercules pulled Spain and Africa apart, and from time immemorial, the two mountains on either side of the strait, the Rock and Djebel Moussa, have been known as the Pillars of Hercules. In reality, the Rock is a monolithic limestone promontory, linked to Spain by a narrow, sandy isthmus. Formed by the collision of European and African tectonic plates, a subsequent shift enabled the Atlantic Ocean to break through, creating the Mediterranean Sea. The location of the Rock is of extreme strategic importance: transferred to Britain by the Treaty of Utrecht in 1713, it has, since then, played a major part in the protection of the Mediterranean seaways during times of war. Covering some 6.5 sq km (2.5 sq miles), the eastern side is formed by almost sheer cliffs, with sandy beaches at the base. The western side is a much more gentle slope, the lower half being the city, while the upper half is a nature reserve, home to some 250 Barbary macaques (more often known as apes) that are the only wild monkeys in Europe. The range of flora and fauna on the Rock is surprisingly rich and includes endemic species such as Gibraltar thyme, candytuft and chickweed. Sea mammals such as dolphins, pilot whales, orcas and even sperm whales can be seen here, too – for such a tiny, infertile territory, Gibraltar is of considerable interest.

THE AVEN-ARMAND CAVE

France

HOW TO GET THERE:
By road from Nimes.
WHEN TO GO:
Any time except December
to February, when it is shut.
NEAREST TOWN:
Meyreuils 8km (5 miles).

Home to the largest-known stalagmite in the world, the cave of Aven-Armand was discovered in 1897 by Louis Armand, a local blacksmith. Located within the Cévennes National Park, this limestone karst cave is reached by two deep chimneys. It is vast: 45m (150ft) high, 60m (200ft) wide and 110m (360ft) long. Its collection of hundreds of stalagmites is known as the Virgin Forest. At least 400 of the stalagmites are more than 1m (3ft) high, many of them top 20m (66ft) and the tallest is over 30m (100ft) from base to tip. Many of the stalagmites are of a particular shape, known as plate-stack or palmtrunc, with broader tops, reminiscent of the trunk of a palm tree. They form in this way because the height of the cave allows drops of water to accelerate so they hit the top of the stalagmite with a splash. A visit to this eerie place, where stalagmites loom at you and the background drip of water reminds you that they are still being formed, is an experience not to be forgotten.

THE GARLABAN MASSIF

France

Looming over Aubagne, and easily visible from much of southern Provence, the blue-white limestone rock of the Garlaban towers into the skies above the Plan d'Aigle. It was used in ancient times as a landmark by Greek and Roman sailors approaching Marseille. The slopes were heavily forested until the 20th century, but a series of forest fires means that the lower slopes are now chiefly covered in the rough scrub known locally as *garrigue*, scenting the air in summer with such herbs as rosemary, wild thyme, lavender and artemisia. The bare, higher reaches of the massif loom starkly over the secluded valleys below. The Garlaban itself is 714m (2,343ft), although the peak of the range is the Butte des Pinsots at 729m (2,392ft). Other well-known peaks are Tête Rouge, which resembles a head and is red because of the bauxite in its soils, and Taoumé. The author Marcel Pagnol was born in nearby Aubagne in 1895, and he returned to the beautiful, wild landscape that he loved again and again in his books.

HOW TO GET THERE: From the N96 between Aubagne and Roquevaire.
WHEN TO GO: Late spring, early summer or early autumn, as the height of summer is extremely hot.
NEAREST TOWN: Aubagne 5km (3 miles).

GORGES DU TARN

France

Left: White limestone cliffs enclose the Tarn river in the Gorges du Tarn, in the Languedoc region of southern France.

The Gorges du Tarn have long been considered one of the most beautiful sights in France. Over millions of years, the Tarn river has found itself a route through the limestone of the Grands Causses, slowly eroding away the soft stone, forming steep cliffs and spectacular scenery. Starting at Mont Lozère in the Cévennes, the river runs some 370km (230 miles) to Moissac before joining the Garonne, but it is the section through the Grands Causses, particularly the Causse du Larzac, for which it is best known. This 60-km (37-mile) stretch is truly breathtaking, especially from the roads that switch back and forth as they climb up the high walls of the valley. The aptly named Point Sublime is one of the best places to stop to catch the views, and perhaps to catch your breath.

CÔTE D'ALABÂTRE

France

The Côte d'Alabâtre, or Alabaster Coast is, in fact, a line of chalk cliffs on the coast of Normandy. They are part of the same formation of Cretaceous chalk that makes up the Seven Sisters and the White Cliffs of Dover on the other side of the English Channel. They were formed more than 65 million years ago from billions of fossil skeletons of creatures that lived in shallow, warm seas. Once they covered most of Britain, but still extend as far north as Yorkshire and as far south as the Paris Basin. The principal towns on the coast are Fécamp and Etretat, where the most spectacular cliff formations are to be found. The western cliff, the Falais d'Aval, has been scoured into an arch, called the Porte d'Aval, by the waves. From its clifftop, visitors can see more rock formations, including *l'aiguille*, the needle, a soaring seastack. At low tide visitors can walk through the arches. In summer it is still bustling with tourists, but in winter it is a spectacular, lonely place to watch the waves crashing into the cliffs.

YOU SHOULD KNOW
The cliffs are crumbly and rock falls are a hazard.

DON'T MISS
Walking through the Porte d'Aval.

THE CAVES OF THE DORDOGNE

France

The limestone plateau that the Dordogne river flows through is riddled with caves. As well as those with prehistoric paintings, for which it is rightly famous, many of them have spectacular stalactite formations. Padirac, in the Causse de Gramat, is an immense group of caverns, accessed via two lifts that descend to the bottom of the 100-m (330-ft) chasm, then a vertiginous walkway, followed by a boat down the low-roofed river and across the underground lake. Lacave is a less well known but equally fascinating cave nearby. To the west, the river Vézère's gorge is another hot spot for caves. The Grand Roc is riddled with a network of caves, full of spectacular stalactites. Geologists have estimated that the caves must have been formed about 60 million years ago and that the stalactites have taken many hundreds of thousands of years to form. A short distance to the northwest is Carpe Diem, whose 200-m (660-ft) length is crammed with stalactites and stalagmites. The sites where our ancestors painted the animals they hunted are justifiably popular, but these caves where nature's work is evident are also definitely worth a visit.

HOW TO GET THERE:
By road from Bergerac.
WHEN TO GO:
Summer.
NEAREST TOWNS:
Rocamadour for Padirac 9km (5.5 miles) and Lacave 3km (8 miles), Les Eyzies for the Grand Roc 1km (0.5 miles) and Carpe Diem 2.5km (1.5 miles).

HOW TO GET THERE:
By road from Lyon.
WHEN TO GO:
Any time of year.
NEAREST TOWN:
Clermont-Ferrand 10km (6 miles).

DON'T MISS
The cable-car ride and walk to the top of the Mont Dore.

THE MOUNTAINS OF THE AUVERGNE

France

The Auvergne is well known for the beauty of its wooded slopes and rocky peaks, particularly those of the Monts Dômes (also known as the Chaine des Puys) and the Monts Dore. What many do not realize, however, is that this stunning landscape in the Massif Central is a result of relatively recent volcanic activity. The youngest, and highest, volcano in the Monts Dômes is the Puy-de-Dôme, which last erupted less than 8,000 years ago. This stunning mountain, with its double crater, is one of the most popular sights in France. A steep road spirals most of the way up the mountain, but the original Roman zigzag track to the top of this 1,464-m (4,803-ft) peak is popular with hikers. From the edge of the inner crater, the views north and south over the lava domes and cinder cones of the rest of the chain are stunning. To the southwest, the Monts Dorés are also volcanic. There are three main volcanoes – the Puy de Sancy, the Puy de l'Aiguiller and the Banne d'Ordanche – that dominate a landscape of woodland, lakes, rivers and waterfalls. This beautiful landscape is popular for hiking, canoeing and sailing in summer, and skiing and snowboarding in winter.

MEUSE VALLEY AND THE ARDENNES FOREST

France

HOW TO GET THERE:
By road from Charleroix
or Reims.
WHEN TO GO:
Summer.
NEAREST TOWN:
Monthermé.

Although in its lower reaches nearer the North Sea the Meuse is industrialized, in its higher reaches it runs through beautiful landscapes on the border between France and Belgium. The Ardennes, whose name comes from the Celtic for 'deep forest', is a wild land of dramatic valleys and hills carpeted with deciduous forests. The Meuse makes sweeping double meanders in the area around Monthermé and Revin, and this is generally thought to be the most spectacular part of the river valley. The steep valley sides generally mean that agriculture is difficult and the river cannot be navigated by boats of any great size, so the area remains sparsely populated and it is very easy to escape the few other people there are. The area abounds in wildlife, such as boar and deer, although they are not easy to spot. There is also a wide variety of forest birds. There are numerous hiking trails that lead up into the hills, and up to viewpoints like Mont Malgré-Tout above Revin. The warped and twisted granite rock formations that line the gorges of the area – including the rather obviously named Roche à Sept Heures – appeal to climbers of all abilities. The lack of commercial traffic on the rivers makes the Meuse popular with canoeists.

CIRQUE DE GAVARNIE

France

HOW TO GET THERE:
By car on the scenic D921
to the village of Gavarnie,
then by mule or on foot.
WHEN TO GO:
Early summer for the
wildflowers, early to mid-
September for the birds.
NEAREST TOWN:
Luz-St-Sauveur 20km
(12 miles).

YOU SHOULD KNOW

The ground at the base
of the cirque can be
treacherously soggy when
the waterfall is in full spate.

In the high Pyrenees, and within
the Parc National des Pyrenées,
just below the French–Spanish
border, the Cirque de Gavarnie
is a spectacular, natural, horseshoe-
shaped amphitheatre that boasts
Europe's tallest waterfall, at
422m (1,384ft).

Gouged out of the rocks of the
Pyrenees by an ancient glacier,
the 800-m (2,625-ft) base of the
cirque is littered with terminal
moraine. The floor of the valley
was carved out by the glacier and
the river is strewn with larger
rocks, some house-sized, left high
and dry as the glacier retreated.
As you get nearer the base of the
waterfall, the woodland gives way
to allow you to gaze up at the
towering cliffs around you.

Eleven of the peaks around the cirque soar to over 3,000m (10,000ft)
and lead up to the sharp crests that separate France and Spain.
Gavarnie used to be on one of the pilgrimage routes from France
to Santiago de Compostella, and there are several good walking and
hiking trails in and around the valley, offering spectacular vistas and
glimpses of wildlife such as isards (the Pyrenean version of chamoix),
the comical whistling marmots and birds such as golden eagles,
lammergeiers, griffon vultures, honey buzzards, alpine accentors, water
and rock pipits, alpine choughs and ravens. In the river valley, dippers
and wallcreepers may be seen and little owls and black woodpeckers
heard. There are also spectacular butterflies in summer.

GORGES DE L'ARDÈCHE
France

HOW TO GET THERE:
By road from Orange
or Avignon.
WHEN TO GO:
Spring to autumn, but the
best time for kayaking down
the river is from May to June.
NEAREST TOWN:
Vallon-Pont-d'Arc 5km
(3 miles).

Rising in the Ardèche mountains in the department of the same name, this short river flows roughly southeastwards until it flows into the Rhône a few kilometres from Pont St-Esprit. The most scenic section is between here and Vallon-Pont-d'Arc, where it flows rapidly through the Gorges de l'Ardèche. This area has one of the most rugged landscapes in France, with cliffs that reach 300m (1,000ft) in places. In some stretches the sides of the gorge are a brilliant white, while in others they are in shades of ochre. One of the most famous features is the Pont d'Arc near the head of the gorge, a 60-m (200-ft) arch spanning the river, evidence that thousands of years ago the river flowed through underground caverns here, before erosion weakened their roofs and they collapsed. One day, this final, remaining arch will fall into the river that created it. The best way to see the gorge is from the road that parallels the top of the cliffs for most of the gorge's length and offers frequent viewpoints, such as the Belvédère de Gournier.

THE CAMARGUE
France

HOW TO GET THERE:
By road from Arles.
WHEN TO GO:
Late spring to early autumn.
NEAREST TOWN:
Arles 5km (3 miles).

A vast, beautiful expanse of wild marshland and lagoons on the Mediterranean's Golfe du Lion, the Camargue is a protected area full of wildlife. It is formed by silt deposited by the Grande and Petit Rhône rivers as they reach the sea and is continually encroaching into the Mediterranean. The northern part and the edges were turned over to agriculture, primarily red Camarguais rice, in the middle of the 20th century, but the central part, sheltered from the sea by sandbars, remains

DON'T MISS
The flamingos on the
Étang Fangassier.

as a haven for wildlife. The Étang de Vaccarès was declared a regional park in 1927 and was incorporated into the Parc Régional de Camargue in 1972. The briny lagoons (*étangs*) and reed marshes are home to thousands of birds and also provide a haven for migrants, with a total of more than 400 species of birds having been recorded here. The symbol of the area is the greater flamingo, of which some 13,000 breed on the Étang Fangassier. Mammals in the area include badgers, beavers and wild boar. The other animals for which the area is famous are the white horses and the black bulls. The bulls roam free, guarded by *gardiens*, who ride tamed Camarguais horses. It is possible to explore by canoe or you can hire a horse.

THE DORDOGNE RIVER

France

At almost 300km (200 miles) in length, the Dordogne is not France's longest river, but it does flow through some of the most spectacular and varied landscapes in the country. Among the most beautiful, and popular, stretches of the river is the Vallée de la Dordogne, west of Souillac. The surrounding land is some of the most unspoiled in France, even though it has been inhabited for many thousands of years, as can be seen from the amazing number of caves in the region with prehistoric paintings. Over hundreds of thousands of years, the Dordogne and its tributaries have carved their way through the soft stone plateaus, and the sheer cliff walls tower over the river below, only to give way to picturesque farmland before sharply rising again to rocky outcrops often topped by a small château. Some of the roads that loosely follow the river are frankly terrifying, and a gentler alternative is to kayak downstream on one of the easier stretches or, in summer, go on a trip on a *gabarre*, a type of boat typical of the region.

DON'T MISS
The prehistoric cave paintings.

HOW TO GET THERE:
By road from Clermont Ferrand or Toulouse.
WHEN TO GO:
Spring to autumn.
NEAREST TOWN:
Martel 5km (3 miles).

HOW TO GET THERE:
By road.
WHEN TO GO:
Summer.
NEAREST TOWNS:
St-Guilhem-le-Désert for the Grotte de Clamouse 3km (2 miles), Courniou for the Grotte des Devèze 0.5km (0.3 miles), Ganges for the Grotte des Demoiselles 4km (2.5 miles), Limousis for the grotto of the same name 1km (0.6 miles), Mialet for the Grotte de Trabuc 1km (0.6 miles) and Fontrabiouse for its namesake 1km (0.6 miles).

THE CAVES OF LANGUEDOC-ROUSSILLON

France

The limestone hills of this region of southwestern France are rich in spectacular caves. Many have been known about for centuries, but some for only a few years, such as the Grotte de Clamouse, which was discovered in 1945 and has yet to be fully explored. There are dozens of them, so a few will serve to show their variety. In the west, Fontrabiouse has spectacular coloured formations that shimmer in the light, while in the east, the Grotte de Trabuc is the largest cave in the Cévennes. In Aude, the Grotte de Limousis has eight halls with rock and crystal formations. Perhaps the best-known caves in the region lie in Hérault. The Grotte de la Devèze is renowned for its smooth, delicate limestone formations, the Grotte des Demoiselles is known as the fairies' cave, and to the east is the Grotte de Clamouse, a vast complex.

LES CASCADES DU HÉRISSON

France

Set at the edge of the Parc Naturel des Haut Jura near the Swiss border is one of France's hidden beauties, the Cascades du Hérisson, a group of 31 waterfalls that drop the waters of the lakes above them 600m (1,960ft) in just 3.5km (2.2 miles). The two largest cascades are l'Eventail ('the fan') and le Grand Saut ('the great leap'), which are 65m and 60m (213ft and 196ft) respectively. The name *Hérisson* comes from the Greek for 'sacred' and the Celtic for 'water.' The path along the river valley from Doucier takes you through beautiful woodland scenery, accompanied by the constant gurgle of water. As you approach the falls, the gurgle grows to an overwhelming roar. The lowest fall, the Cascade Girard, is 35m (115ft) of tumbling water, rushing over the rocks. The path leads up from one waterfall to the next, each one more beautiful than the last until you finally reach the Cascade de l'Eventail at the top. The river is fed by waters from the lakes high in the mountains here – and various trails lead to them, and further up to the Pic d'Aigle for an amazing panoramic view over this beautiful region. In the Grand Saut, the water drops into a deep pot and it is possible to walk behind the curtain of water, while the Gour Bleu is a limpid blue pool where the water temporarily halts in its mad rush down the mountainside. Farther back down the valley is a cave set in the side of the cliff, the Grotte Lacuzon, which can be reached with care.

HOW TO GET THERE:
By road from Besançon to the hamlet of Doucier, then on foot or on the GR 559 long-distance footpath.
WHEN TO GO:
Late spring is best.
NEAREST TOWN:
Champagnole 25km (16 miles).

MONT BLANC

France

Set high in the Alps on the border between France and Switzerland, at 4,807m (15,771ft), Mont Blanc is Europe's highest mountain. Sometimes called *la Dame Blanche*, 'the White Lady', by the French, it is, naturally, popular with serious climbers. The scenery around the mountain is beautiful, with alpine meadows, gorges, waterfalls and glaciers, including the Mer de Glace, the second-largest glacier in the Alps. To the northwest of the mountain, the waterfalls of the Gorges de la Diosaz are thought by many to be the most beautiful in France. The world-famous resort of Chamonix-Mont-Blanc has long catered for skiers, but the area is now also important for summer sports and activities, including white-water rafting, hiking (there are more than 310km/195 miles of trails in the area), mountain biking, donkey trekking, skiing on the glaciers, dog trekking and paragliding. A network of cable cars allows access to the upper slopes, but the most spectacular way to see the area is by helicopter. The flora and fauna are typical, with a profusion of spring flowers in the meadows in June and marmots and chamois on the higher slopes. Whether or not you wish to tackle climbing Mont Blanc itself, this is a special place, with beautiful scenery and plenty to do and see.

HOW TO GET THERE:
On the route des Hautes Alpes to the Chamonix-Mont-Blanc resort or via the Mont Blanc tunnel from the south.
WHEN TO GO:
At any time.
NEAREST TOWN:
Megève 15km (9 miles).

LES GORGES DU VERDON

France

The second-largest canyon on Earth, after the Grand Canyon, the Gorges du Verdon are a spectacular sight in the north of Provence. Known only to the locals until 1905, the gorge was 'discovered' by the caver Edouard Alfred Martel and rapidly became a tourist attraction. Its proximity to the Provençal coast made it an ideal place to retreat during the heat of summer. Millions of years ago, this area was under a forerunner of the Mediterranean Sea, and layer upon layer of limestone and then coral were deposited over the whole area. After the region was lifted up because of the northwards movement of Africa, the land was crumpled and cracked, allowing water and ice to find their way through faults in the soft rock, creating caverns and underground rivers, whose ceilings finally collapsed, slowly etching out this deep, V-shaped valley. The gorge is only about 20km (12 miles) long, but the roads that climb the two sides of the valley are so winding that the whole circuit is more than 130km (80 miles). The most famous viewpoint is the Belvédère de la Maline, although there are other stopping points around the gorge. The roads, especially those round the southern side of the gorge, are full of switchbacks and tight turns, and a much more relaxing way to appreciate the views is to kayak along the river instead. However, this area's main draw is its rocky cliffs and sheer drop, which are also very popular with rock climbers. There are more than 1,500 different climbs in the area, most of

them far too difficult for beginners. There are also several designated hiking routes through the gorge, including the Sentier de l'Imbut, Sentier du Bastidon and that named after the valley's discoverer, the Sentier de Martel. However you choose to spend your time in this beautiful landscape, you will not forget it easily.

HOW TO GET THERE:
By road from Avignon
or Nice.
WHEN TO GO:
In good weather in summer.
NEAREST TOWN:
Castellane 12km (7.5 miles).

ARDENNES PEAKS

Belgium

The Ardennes is a rugged wilderness landscape, stretching east from France across Luxembourg and Belgium and on into Germany. The highest part, the Hautes Fagnes ('High Fens'), in the German-speaking far east of the country, is an expanse of windswept heathland popular with skiers, but the most scenic corner lies further west between Dinant, La Roche-en-Ardenne and Bouillon. Here the river valleys and deep, wooded, winding canyons reach up to high green peaks, sublimely and inspiringly beautiful. The Ardennes' cave systems are also a major attraction, carved out by underground rivers that, over the centuries, have cut through and dissolved the limestone of the hills, leaving stalagmites and stalactites in their dripping wake. The gateway to the most scenic area within the Ardennes is Namur, sited at the junction of the Sambre and Meuse rivers (known as the 'Grognons' or 'Pig's snout'), with its massive hilltop citadel, once one of the mightiest fortresses in Europe and accessible by an exhilarating cable-car ride. From Namur, the Meuse passes through a landscape of gently wooded slopes, interrupted by steep escarpments and jagged crags capped by ruined castles. This area draws rock climbers in their droves. The little town of Rochefort, some 50km (31 miles) south of Namur, is a good centre for exploring the Ardennes and an attractive base for cyclists and walkers. This is lovely countryside, with thickly wooded hills, river valleys and plenty of castles. At Han-sur-Lesse just east of Rochefort is a wild-animal reserve containing animals that have inhabited the Ardennes since prehistoric times – bison, bears, deer and wild boar.

HOW TO GET THERE:
From Brussels head southeast to Namur.
WHEN TO GO:
Spring and summertime for walking, cycling and canoeing.
NEAREST TOWN:
Namur 60km (37.5 miles).

DON'T MISS
The Tresor du Prieure d'Oignies, exquisitely beautiful gold and silver.

HOW TO GET THERE:
By road from Stuttgart
WHEN TO GO:
Spring to autumn.
NEAREST TOWN:
Freiburg im Breisgau.

THE BLACK FOREST

Germany

There are three main regions to the Black Forest, or Schwarzwald: northern, central and southern. The northern part has the gentlest landscape, with broad ridges covered in dense woodland or forest, punctuated by pretty little lakes such as the Wildsee and the Mummelsee. The central area, around Triberg, has spectacular landscapes of glacial valleys and the Triberg waterfall, which is the longest in the area. To the south, the land rises further, and the scenery becomes more dramatic. The highest mountain in the area is the Feldberg, at 1,493m (4,500ft), and the most beautiful waterfall in the region, the Hangloch, can be found just to its south. There are also two beautiful glacial lakes, the Titisee and the Schluchsee. The Rhine river runs to the west of the forest and the Danube has its source here, making the ridge below the forest part of the European continental divide, with waters that drain to the Atlantic and the Black Sea. Now the focus of a popular tourist region, the forests are no longer the terrifying places that inspired the worst of the Grimm brothers' fairy tales, but are instead a magical backdrop for walking and hiking holidays.

MIDDLE RHINE VALLEY

Germany

The Rhine is over 1,300km (807 miles) long. The Middle Rhine is what people call the 65-km (40-mile) gorge that carries the river between Bingen and Koblenz. This short stretch, where the water bullies a meandering path through unyielding slate mountains, is Germany's single-most iconic geographical feature – but for all its physical drama, it is in fact a cultural landscape. Man, not nature, fashioned the Middle Rhine valley. Castles, villages and cities punctuate the vineyard trellises that crowd the terraces on both banks. Gullies or rock inclines too steep to exploit are filled with local flora and fauna, which have adapted themselves to accommodate this extraordinary symbiosis of man and nature. Whether you see the gorge from a car, train or boat, you participate in what UNESCO cited as 'the continuous evolutionary nature of the cultural environment' of the Middle Rhine. For 2,000 years, it has been a highway for commerce and tourism. Its importance can be measured by the number of castles, ruined or restored, that command the heights.

There are hundreds of good reasons to see the Middle Rhine. Take a boat if you can, because with the right ticket you can stop off as many times as you like.

HOW TO GET THERE: Car/train/boat from Koblenz or Bingen.
WHEN TO GO: April to October.
NEAREST TOWNS: Any of the many small towns lining the gorge.

ERZGEBIRGE

Germany

Virtually unsettled and covered with dense forest, the Erzgebirge gained its name (it means 'Ore Mountains') only in the 15th century, when the discovery of silver and tin deposits brought a flood of settlers to found its towns and cities. For 130km (81 miles) along the German–Czech border you can see the recovering scars of hundreds of former quarries and mine workings. Now, with its mineral riches exhausted, the Erzgebirge's regeneration is protected by its status as a Biosphere Reserve, and one of Germany's loveliest mountain landscapes has been restored to its natural beauty. You can follow the Ridge Trail for 197km (122 miles) from Klingenthal in the Vogtland/Erzgebirge nature reserve. It is an elemental but austere landscape, its remoteness a perfect habitat for rare animals and plants. The mountains rise ever higher towards the trail's end at Altenberg to the south. The numerous peaks around Fichtelberg make this part of the Erzgebirge a magnet for winter visitors. Not only does the landscape and microclimate lend itself to the snowy magic of fairy tales, but the region is famous for its wood-carved toys, intricate fretwork and every kind of Christmas decoration. The industry began as a desperate measure by former mining communities when the silver ran out. Now every local industry depends on encouraging the Erzgebirge as a whole to recover its pristine variety of fauna and flora.

YOU SHOULD KNOW
Reifendrehen (carving toy animals from wooden hoops) is a skill unique to the Erzgebirge.

HOW TO GET THERE:
By car/bus to Seiffen or Oberweisenthal.
WHEN TO GO:
Year-round, but the region is most crowded in winter.
NEAREST TOWN:
Zwickau 20–30km (12–19 miles) from the central range.

THE BASTEI ROCKS IN THE ELBE VALLEY

Germany

Southeast of Dresden lies one of Europe's biggest sandstone canyons. Carved by the Elbe river and its tributaries over 100 million years into a bizarre assembly of soaring stone finials, mesas and buttes, its gloomy crags overhang the graceful curves of the water up to 400m (1,312ft) below. The tallest trees are dwarfed by the huge boulders on which they totter, and one spectacular vista opens into another all the way to Bad Schandau on the border with the Czech Republic. Between April and October, riverboats ply between Dresden and Bad Schandau so that visitors can enjoy nature at its most romantic and darkly majestic. This feeling is most intense at the Bastei ('Bastion') Rocks, a series of needle-like sandstone spires 170m (558ft) high standing sentinel along the ravines and gorges hacked out of the canyon's walls. You can cross the rocky pinnacles on graceful stone bridges built in the mid-19th century, or the river itself on the 305-m (1,000-ft) Bastei Bridge, which offers the most magnificent view of all across the Elbe valley and its extraordinary massif. Close to the bridge, a path weaves more than 700 mossy steps deep down the gorge called the Swedish Holes and into a hollow. This is the Felsenbuhne Rathen, a natural amphitheatre specializing in open-air, summer productions of operas and adventure stories as eerie and fearsome as the setting. Crossing the bridge leads you to the Konigstein Fortress, its colossal scale and severity in perfect harmony with the jagged landscape. From its heights, you can see a panorama of rolling hills, winding river, imposing peaks and table mountains. Locals call it 'Sachsische Schweiz' – Saxon Switzerland – and the region is protected as the Elbe Sandstone Massif Nature Reserve.

HOW TO GET THERE:
By car/bus/boat from Dresden or Bad Schandau.
WHEN TO GO:
Year-round – but boats only operate during summer.
NEAREST TOWN:
Rathen 1km (0.6 miles).

DON'T MISS
The panorama from the ramparts of Konigstein Fortress.

FRANKISCHE SCHWEIZ

Germany

Defined by the Regnitz and Main rivers to the west, and by the river Pegnitz to the east, the rolling vales and dolomitic outcrops of the Frankische Schweiz certainly do resemble Switzerland, but this region of northern Franconia is a distillation of a Swiss picture postcard. Green pastures follow the contours of coppiced hills, and lanes wind through the floor of a hundred steep valleys. Streams bite deep in the fertile loam, and then disappear in a jumble of rock into the limestone plateau below. Millennia of weathering has broken down the limestone into huge outcrops, cliffs and cathedrals of cave systems. The best of these are the Binghohle at Streitberg and the Teufelshohle ('Devil's Hole') at Pottenstein. It is the contrast of pastoral domesticity in the fields and woods and this rocky terrain breaking out in bizarre and dramatic formations that makes the region so scenic and intriguing. Such a pleasing landscape makes wonderful walking, and there are 4,000km (2,500 miles) of marked trails.

YOU SHOULD KNOW

Frankische Schweiz has the highest density of private breweries in the world (72).

HOW TO GET THERE:
By train/bus/car to Nurnberg, Bamberg or Bayreuth.
WHEN TO GO:
Year-round.
NEAREST TOWN:
Forchheim.

THE HELGOLAND CLIFFS

Germany

HOW TO GET THERE:
By boat from Cuxhaven or private air taxi.
WHEN TO GO:
March to November.
NEAREST TOWN:
Cuxhaven (2 hours).

The island of Helgoland is a geological oddity — a block of red sandstone 70km (43 miles) out in the open sea, quite unlike anything else on the whole of the continental North Sea coast. A thousand years of weathering has eroded and submerged all the dunes and marshes that used to connect it almost to the mainland. On the north, west and southwest, 50-m (164-ft) cliffs cut a rosy pink line against the blue steel of the sea. Part of this spectacular vista is the Lummenfelsen wildlife reserve, and at the beginning of June you can witness young guillemots, still unable to fly, hurling themselves off a 60-m (197-ft) cliff. What makes Helgoland so very special is its climate. It gets the full benefit of the Gulf Stream without a large landmass to retain cold. The two long beaches resemble the Caribbean, with palm trees nodding in the turquoise sea. It is the sunniest place in Germany, and with winter temperatures frequently 10°C (18°F) higher than Hamburg, warm enough to grow figs.

THURINGIAN FOREST

Germany

Known as the 'green heart' of Germany, an upland corridor of emerald forest some 20km (12.5 miles) broad stretches 60km (37.5 miles) southeast from Eisenach to Greiz. This highland plateau is the core of the greater 4,725-sq-km (1,824-sq-mile) Thuringian Forest, and it includes its most dramatic, unspoilt and beautiful natural scenery. Bounded by fault lines, its hills rise in steep scarps directly from the dense spruce and broadleaf forest; the canopy occasionally broken by brightly flowered pasture where the inhabitants of ancient hamlets still work smallholdings. Weaving along a ridge connecting the highest peaks in this pastoral idyll is part of the legendary Rennsteig Trail, which runs from Horschel to Blankenstein, 168km (105 miles) away on the upper Saal river. The Rennsteig has been relatively inaccessible until recently. As a result, its natural ecology has revived wonderfully, and the region is a wildlife haven.

BERCHTESGADEN ALPS

Germany

Berchtesgaden National Park, in the far southeast of Bavaria and on the border with Austria, is the only alpine national park in Germany. Within it lie the Watzmann massif, the third-highest mountain in the country, and the Königssee, a beautiful glacial lake. The slopes of the glacial valleys are carpeted with dense forest separated by deep gorges, while the valley bottoms make an idyllic farmland. As its name suggests, the Königssee ('King's Lake') was popular with the Bavarian royal family, and it is still a popular place for recreation today – its water is reputed to be the cleanest in Germany. Looming over the lake is the Watzmann massif, a popular challenge for experienced climbers only. The national park was declared a UNESCO Biosphere Reserve in 1990 because of its alpine landscape and its wildlife. A popular hike for many is up the 1,835-m (6,020-ft) Kehlstein. Most famous as the site of Hitler's command complex and the Eagle's Nest retreat, the top of this peak provides stunning views across the valley.

DON'T MISS
The view from the top of the Kehlstein.

BODENSEE

Germany

Better known as Lake Constance, Bodensee has been synonymous since Roman times with unsurpassed natural beauty. It's a freshwater lake 63km (39 miles) long and 14km (9 miles) at its widest, and it nestles at an elevation of 395m (1,296ft) between the mountains of Germany, Switzerland and Austria. From Bregenz in the Vorarlberg, where the nascent Rhine feeds it, to Schaffhausen in the west, where the river crashes out of the lake via the Rhine Falls, Bodensee is a magnificent panorama of snowcapped mountains reflected in the endless waterscape. East to west, it's a continual highlight. The lake was actually formed by the Rhine glacier during the last ice age, but its effortless beauty now owes nearly as much to subsequent human activity. Its shores are lined with orchards, vineyards, meadows and pastures, occasionally interrupted by the colourful roofs of ancient towns and villages, some of them on bijou islands like Lindau, a medieval town of intricate lanes and crooked towers that appears to sail on the water. At the other end of Bodensee, near Konstanz, is the 'Flower Island' of Mainau. Here, in 1827, Prince Esterhazy realized that the lake's summer microclimate (it's considerably warmer than any of its surroundings) was perfect to create the profusion of subtropical trees, fruits and plants for which Mainau is still famous. Reichenau, a haven of solitude in the Untersee, the western bowl of Bodensee, has an ancient monastery; and Meersburg, on the Baden-Wurttemberg mainland a ferry-ride from Konstanz, is a typically lovely resort town of half-timbered houses and Germany's oldest *schloss* (castle). Many, varied and lovely are all these places – but it is the lake itself that adds grandeur to their picturesque charms.

RÜGEN

Germany

It's only 51km (32 miles) long and 43km (27 miles) at its widest, but Rügen, the Baltic island close to Germany's northeast border with Poland, has an astonishing 574km (357 miles) of coastline. Inevitably, the long strands of white sand backed by ancient woodlands and gleaming lakes have made Rügen one of Germany's most popular holiday resorts for generations of visitors. Much more remarkable is that the island has preserved its greatest natural treasures intact, thanks to nature parks that protect the Baltic coastline. Biggest and most important is the Biosphere Reserve of southeast Rügen, a region of peninsulas, small islands, hooked spits and sandbars barely submerged beneath shallow inland waters. Hiddensee, a long, thin island at the other side of Rügen, shares a similar landscape, but cars are forbidden and its isolated wetlands are a habitat for some of the rarest flora and fauna in the world. One of Rügen's loveliest walks takes you through the Jasmund Reserve on the east coast. The Königsstuhl ('King's Chair') is the highest point of Germany's only pure white, chalk cliffs.

THE SPREEWALD

Germany

Just 100km (62 miles) south of Berlin is a huge nature reserve, 75km (47 miles) long and 15km (9 miles) wide. It is a lowland of water meadows and broadleaf woods intersected by 970km (606 miles) of streams and water courses and unique in central Europe. Incredibly, so close to Germany's capital, it has resisted history: its people, the Sorbs – one of only two recognized minorities with their own ancient customs, dress and still-spoken language – and its landscape have both remained intact and untouched. The Spreewald is a paradise of benign wilderness given over to thousands of very rare species of plants and animals. However you reach the Spreewald region, you need a boat to travel within it. There are thousands of waterways (called *fliesse*), and punts are the usual transport for local farmers as well as visitors. There's no public transport, and the Spreewald succeeds in being remote even in the middle of an industrialized society.

THE HARZ MOUNTAINS

Germany

For 100km (62 miles) across central Germany, the Harz Mountains divide the northern lowlands from the southern uplands. The region has benefited from 20th-century politics, which left it virtually uninhabited and provided its evergreen and broadleaf woodlands, its marshes, alpine meadows, cliff-faces, waterfalls and gorges with the ideal opportunity for regeneration. The entire mountain range is now a protected nature reserve, but its centrepiece is the Upper Harz plateau, the 65 sq km (25 sq miles) circling the rounded granite peak of the Brocken, the highest at 1,142m (3,746ft) in the Harz. Shrouded in mists 300 days a year, the Brocken's harsh appearance inspired Goethe to re-create its wild atmosphere in the nightmares of Faust. If the high moors are austere, the surrounding forests of rowan, maple and beech frame more than 100 lakes that are often linked in systems of torrent streams and thin strands of waterfalls. The force of the water has cut whole cave systems in its scramble round jagged outcrops of granite, imperturbable in the yielding limestone. The Harz and the Bodetal are stunning in every season, providing solitude and peace.

HOW TO GET THERE:
Train to Bad Harzburg, then car/bus to Torfhaus (for Goethe Trail up the Brocken).
WHEN TO GO:
Year-round.
NEAREST TOWN:
Wernigerode 10km (6 miles).

SCHWABISCHE ALB

Germany

HOW TO GET THERE:
By car/bus/train to Ulm or Reutlingen.
WHEN TO GO:
Year-round.
NEAREST TOWN:
Blaubeuren 16km (10 miles).

DON'T MISS
The Apokalypse cavern.

South and east of Stuttgart, the Schwabische Alb is a highland plateau 220km (137 miles) long and about 50km (31 miles) wide. The landscape is a combination of bizarre rock formations and gently rolling slopes. There is almost no surface water, because the region's limestone is the residue of what was once a seabed, and weathering has created an entire system of subterranean rivers and caves. Not only does the region bear easily visible witness to 200 million years of geology, it is also a paradise for rare fossils. On the western edge of the Schwabische Alb is the Albtrauf, an escarpment 180km (112 miles) long, from which you gaze towards the Black Forest. The Alb shelves gently to the east and south, where its boundary is the newborn Danube. Geologists have described the area in between as an underground barrel, supplying warm, mineral-rich water to the springs that justify the fame of the region's many thermal baths and health resorts.

BAYERISCHE WALD

Germany

The oldest of Germany's national parks, the Bayerische Wald winds around the Bavarian forest peaks of Falkenstein, Rachel and Lusen along the border with the Czech Republic. In partnership with the neighbouring Sumava National Park in the Czech Republic, it is the largest protected forest area in central Europe. Nowhere else between the Atlantic Ocean and the Ural mountains has a major forest been returned completely to nature. No human lives there, and no human intervention is allowed to shape the development of the forest in any way. With no agriculture, husbandry or commercial logging, the forest has regenerated a wide variety of habitats among its many wet valleys, streams, bogs, moors and meadows. Rare species like the lynx, black stork, eagle owl, pygmy owl, three-toed woodpecker, and Bohemian gentian have returned, among hundreds of others. In some places, huge tracts of spruce lie in rotting tumbles, shrouded in moss and undergrowth: your heart sinks, until you see the evidence of a whole new kind of forest emerging from centuries of commercial exploitation that have left it vulnerable to the ravages of the bark beetle, agent of the devastation. As the bark beetle kills off the spruce, nature is replacing them with the truly native beech, mountain ash, rowan and other deciduous species, which in turn are attracting even greater varieties of flora and fauna. You can witness this unique landscape along 300km (187 miles) of walking trails and 200km (125 miles) of cycling paths. The Hochwaldsteig takes you (via rope ladder) to the 1,373-m (4,503-ft) rock dome of the Lusen, above the tree line; the Watzlikhain, near the Zwieslerwaldhaus sanctuary, is a forest wilderness discovery path; and the Igelbus (the national park bus) will drop you at the Seelensteig, a trail of incredible beauty. When you come to Bayerische Wald for the first time, visit the information centre at Neuschonau for one-to-one advice on how best to enjoy your personal enthusiasms, and for a first-class children's discovery room.

HOW TO GET THERE:
By car/train (the 'Waldbahn') to Zwiesel, Eisenstein, Grafenau or Frauenau; then by bus (ask for the Bayerische Wald ticket).
WHEN TO GO:
Year-round.
NEAREST TOWNS:
Eisenstein/Neuschonau, Grafenau.

NORDLINGER RIES

Germany

DON'T MISS
The medieval town, church and steeple of St Georg, made of coesite.

HOW TO GET THERE:
By car/train/bus to Nordlingen.
WHEN TO GO:
Year-round.
NEAREST TOWN:
Nordlingen (about 12km/ 7.5 miles to anywhere on the rim).

YOU SHOULD KNOW

Nordlingen is twinned with Wagga Wagga, Australia.

North of the Danube, in the Donau-Ries district of Bavaria, lies the depression of Nordlinger Ries. It is the impact crater of a huge meteorite that struck the region almost 15 million years ago, circular in shape and 25km (16 miles) in diameter. The bottom of the crater is 100–150m (328–492ft) below its rim, and the city of Nordlingen, itself defined by its still-complete circular medieval wall, lies in the middle of the crater. Until 1960 the Ries was believed to be of volcanic origin, until scientists found direct evidence of the shock-metamorphic effects of a meteor strike. The high temperature of the strike caused laminations and welding in the local sandstone, creating tektites, identifiable by their glassy spatters of molten material. But the conclusive proof was the discovery of coesite, a variety of shocked quartz that occurs only when a force as powerful as a meteor causes microscopic deformations in minerals. While celebrating, they realized that the ancient town church of Nordlingen was itself made out of a huge chunk of coesite. Visitors can see details of the meteor strike and subsequent local geology at the Ries Crater Museum in Nordlingen. But you get a better idea of the colossal impact 12km (7.5 miles) south of Nordlingen, where the crater rim outside the village of Monschdeggingen rises in a steep escarpment, and even now the grass is broken by rocky outcrops containing coesite and tektites. From here you get a vision of nature that is almost too powerful for easy contemplation: it is simply awesome.

WIMBACHKLAMM

Germany

The Bavarian Alps, tucked away in Germany's southeast on the Austrian border, are the definition of a romantic landscape. Snowcapped mountains plunge into the patchwork of fields that chequers deep, green valleys. Steep rock faces thrust out of dense forest, and every rocky outcrop gives way to a fresh panorama of waterfalls, grey scree, and the serried green of larch, spruce, pine and beech. In the heart of this fairy-tale setting – itself protected for its pristine beauty in the 210-sq-km (81-sq-mile) Berchtesgarden National Park – is Wimbachklamm, a slab-sided gorge of authentically Wagnerian drama. Wimbachbrucke, where you arrive by bus or car, is one of the main entrances to the park as a whole. Inside, you pay a small fee to enter the Wimbachklamm itself, and follow the trail into and up the gorge. Almost immediately, all other sound is drowned out by the rushing torrent of the Wimbach as you take a couple of turns out of sight into wilderness. The trail becomes a wooden stairway hugging the rock face rising on either side. Jagged crags spit out mountain streams and crowd higher and closer together until what seemed a canyon is a ravine, twisting and turning upwards in exhilarating majesty. Just when the climb is becoming as exhausting as the brilliant view, the river disappears beneath a rock bed, and you must climb a further 2km (1.25 miles) before you reach a more gentle incline, and emerge into an alpine pastoral of woods and meandering stream that leads to the hut called (wittily) Wimbachschloss, and summertime refreshments. After 10km (6 miles), they will be welcome. Wimbachklamm has the dramatic intensity of the very best German poetry and opera. It is a truly classic German landscape, and truly beautiful.

HOW TO GET THERE:
Bus/car to Wimbachbrucke from Ramsau or Berchtesgarden.
WHEN TO GO:
May to September/October.
NEAREST TOWN:
Ramsau 3km (2 miles).

DON'T MISS
The rocky valley where the Wimbach runs underground.

YOU SHOULD KNOW
Take some poetry by Schiller or Goethe with you.

MØNS KLINT

Denmark

HOW TO GET THERE:
By road from Copenhagen.
WHEN TO GO:
Spring to autumn.
NEAREST TOWN:
Stege 15km (10 miles).

YOU SHOULD KNOW
As many as 100,000 visitors
flood the area in July. Experts
estimate that in 10,000 years
the entire island will have
been reclaimed by the sea.

Møns Klint are awe-inspiring chalk cliffs that stand proudly along the eastern coast of Høje Møn in the Baltic Sea. Extending for some 6km (3.7 miles), at their highest they tower 128m (420ft) above the crashing waves. The sheer majesty of these cliffs, rising white out of clear blue water, draws tourists from all over Europe to this faraway corner of Denmark. The chalk formed over 70 million years ago from the skeletons of tiny creatures that lived in the warm sea that once covered Denmark. During the Cretaceous period this sea receded and the land rose. Then during the last ice age, glaciers scraped off a thick layer of the chalk and crushed it together, creating Høje Møn. Since then the sea has been busily trying to undo the glacier's work, cutting into the island's shoreline and sculpting the cliffs we see today. Although the results have been dramatic, the sea's erosive efforts are relentless. In 1994 the highest part of Møns Klint, the Sommerspir, crumbled into the Baltic, and in 2007 an even larger slip created a 300-m (1,000-ft) peninsula of chalk debris and uprooted trees. Behind this battle zone lie the peaceful woods of Klinteskoven, and a little further off is Aborrebjerg, which at 143m (470ft) is one of the highest hills in Denmark. The chalky soil here provides the perfect conditions for many rare plants. Eighteen of Denmark's 35 species of orchid can be found here, including the tall lady orchid that flowers in early summer. Much of the cliff area is protected and there are many marked paths for walkers, riders and cyclists to explore. There is also a series of wooden stairways down which you can descend to the feet of these awesome cliffs. Since 2002 the cliffs can boast another star attraction: nesting peregrine falcons. They can often be seen hunting their prey in the skies above Møns Klint.

THE DANISH LAKE DISTRICT

Denmark

Denmark's Lake District, or Søhøjlandet, lies in eastern Jutland and covers an area of around 1,720 sq km (660 sq miles). It's an area of outstanding natural beauty and surprising variety. The landscape is one of gently rolling hills, woodlands, rivers, heath, dunes, and cultivated land, as well as many meadows, water meadows and marshes. It is, of course, the dozen or more lakes that provide much of the region's unique appeal. By far the largest is Mossø, which stretches out for some 10km (6 miles) and in places is over 2km (1.2 miles) wide. And there are few better ways to enjoy the beauty of the Danish Lake District than from a boat on its glassy waters. Just as the English Lake District is home to England's highest mountain, the Danish Lake District is also home to some of the highest peaks in Denmark, including Ejer Baunehøj, Yding Skovhøj and Himmelbjerget. Of course in this part of Denmark, 'high' is strictly relative. Himmelbjerget, for example, may enjoy the sobriquets 'Heaven Mountain' and 'Sky Mountain', yet it boasts an altitude of less than 150m (500ft). Those that do venture to its less than vertiginous summit are, however, rewarded with lovely views over the lake and surrounding countryside. From the base of the Sky Mountain, boating enthusiasts can enjoy an experience that undoubtedly is heavenly – a cruise to Silkeborg aboard one of the world's oldest and most elegant paddle steamers. The *Hjejlen*, or 'Golden Plover', was built in 1861 and has plied the lake's waters ever since, carrying over 250,000 passengers a year.

HOW TO GET THERE:
Fly to Randers, then by road.
WHEN TO GO:
All year – but the best weather is from May to August.
NEAREST TOWN:
Skanderborg is the region's most central town.

DON'T MISS
Silkeborg, home of the prehistoric, peat-bog-preserved 'Tollund Man'.

BIEBRZA NATIONAL PARK

Poland

The Biebrza marshes in Podlaskie, northeast Poland, are widely considered to be the most unspoilt and valuable expanse of peat bog in Europe. And while the words 'peat' and 'bog' may lack the pizzazz of 'piste' and 'beach', the Biebrza marshes offer a unique opportunity to step into a landscape that is both ancient and largely unchanged. Incredibly peaceful and unpopulated, the marsh and the national park that surrounds it are home to an incredible wealth of wildlife. The Biebrza National Park runs southeast to northwest from the Biebrza river's confluence with the Narew river up towards Poland's border with Belarus. In total it covers an area of nearly 600 sq km (230 sq miles) and is the largest of Poland's national parks. Often referred to as the region's 'Green Lungs', the park comprises large areas of forest and agricultural land, but it is the 255 sq km (100 sq miles) of wetland – the Biebrza marshes – that form the soggy treasure at its heart. Biebrza is a mecca for myriad bird species that flock here in spring. Over 180 species breed here, including around 20 of the 56 most threatened species in Poland. From eagles to egrets, bitterns to bearded tits, Biebrza is a veritable who's who of the bird world. As well as its incredible birdlife, and enough rare plants to bring out the botanist in anyone, the park is also home to mammals. Among the 48 species that live here are elk, wolf, beaver, otter, pine marten, roe deer and wild boar.

HOW TO GET THERE:
The marshes are a 200-km (125-mile) drive from Warsaw.
WHEN TO GO:
Spring to autumn is best. Winters can be very cold.
NEAREST TOWN:
The small town of Gugny is right in the park.

THE GREAT MASURIAN LAKES

Poland

HOW TO GET THERE:
By road from Warsaw
or Gdansk.
WHEN TO GO:
Summer.
NEAREST TOWN:
Elblag 22km (14 miles).

The Great Masurian Lakes in northeastern Poland are one of the highlights of the region. Known as the land of a thousand lakes, the area encompasses the largest stretch of fresh water in Europe, as well as beautiful forests and hills. There are 45 major lakes, which are joined by 12 canals and eight rivers, as well as many smaller lakes, in an area that stretches some 290km (180 miles). Roughly 15 per cent of its 52,000 sq km (20,000 sq miles) is water. They are rich in wildlife, and the birdlife here includes black storks, bitterns and herons. At the Lake Luknajo Reserve, the largest breeding population of mute swans, which are rare this far east, can be seen in summer. Two of the largest remnants of ancient forest – Augustow and Pisz forests – are here. Augustow has beavers, bison, boar, elk and wolves. The Pisz forest is strewn with lakes that are dotted with islands, perfect for messing about in boats and bird-watching, while on land there are many trails for walking, hiking and cycling. In this tranquil, scenic landscape, it is possible to spend hours in peace, drinking in its beauty at your own pace.

SMOCZA JARMA

Poland

HOW TO GET THERE:
Fly to Kraków. The cave
is in the heart of the city,
on Wawel Hill.
WHEN TO GO:
The cave is open 10am to
5pm from May to October.
NEAREST TOWN:
Kraków.

Set right in the heart of Kracków, Poland's ancient royal capital, lies Poland's best-known cave: Smocza Jarma – the 'Dragon's Den'. A multi-chamber limestone cavern, it draws nearly a quarter of a million tourists down into its dark, dank depths every year. Smocza Jarma's appeal, however, derives not from any special subterranean merit, but more from its links with the supernatural. For it is the cave's association with the 'Legend of the Wawel Dragon' that ensures its undying popularity. The most popular version of this legend has it that a long time ago an evil dragon took up residence in the cave on Wawel Hill. For years it caused mayhem and murder, until a local cobbler stuffed an animal skin with sulphur and threw the offering into the cave mouth. Next morning the dragon gobbled the gift and soon the sulphur was burning its throat so badly that the doomed beast began to drink the Vistula dry – until eventually its stomach exploded. Down in the cave itself there are three large limestone chambers that take about 20 minutes to explore.

YOU SHOULD KNOW
In summer it's best to go early
to avoid lengthy queues.

THE CURONIAN SPIT

Lithuania

HOW TO GET THERE:
Fly to Vilnius, then bus
to Klaipéda and ferry
across to Smiltyné.
WHEN TO GO:
Sea climate with a late spring
and long autumn.
NEAREST TOWN:
Nida.

According to Baltic legend, the girl giant Neringa took pity on the fishermen, who were being bullied by the god of storms; she flung an apronful of sand out to sea to create the Curonian Spit and the sheltered fishing waters of the Curonian Lagoon. This extraordinary 98-km (61-mile) spit, lined with woods and dotted with fishing villages, is at least 5,000 years old, with the highest shifting sand dunes in Europe – up to 60m (200ft) tall. It heads northward from Russia's Sambian peninsula, the first 46km (29 miles) being Russian territory. The remainder is the Lithuanian municipality of Neringa, which meets the mainland port of Klaipéda at its northern tip, separated only by a narrow strait – the exit for the waters of the Curonian Lagoon. The width of the spit varies from just 400m (0.25 miles) to nearly 4km (2.5 miles). A single road runs along it, passing through nine small fishing communities with traditional blue- and brown-painted timbered and tile houses. Both Russian and Lithuanian parts are national parks, and the entire spit is a World Heritage Site. Towards the end of the 19th century, Neringa was discovered by artists, writers and bohemians. Gradually they have taken over from fishermen as mainstays of the communities, renovating the old houses and protecting the landscapes and wildlife. The Curonian Spit is one of the most curious and charming places in Europe, where you really do feel in harmony with nature.

BIALOWIEZA FOREST

Belarus

This enchanting place, the last remnant of the primeval forest which once cloaked Europe from the Atlantic coast to Russia, survives in one of the world's most polluted countries, Belarus, and continues into Poland. Bialowieza shelters hundreds of native bison, a once plentiful species that provided food for prehistoric Europeans, as well as subject matter for primitive cave paintings. The European bison – or wisent – became extinct in the wild 100 years ago, having been hunted almost to extinction by famished soldiers in the First World War. With careful reintroduction they are now flourishing with a population figure of over 1,800. Elk, wild tarpan horses and hundreds of varieties of flora and fauna are to be found in this forest. It is situated 100km (62 miles) southeast of Bialystok, with the Belarus–Poland border running through it. For centuries Bialowieza was a private hunting ground for Polish kings, Russian tsars and Belarussian princes, but in the 1920s the Polish government turned large sections of it into a national park, accessible only on foot or by horse-drawn carriage, in order to protect the wildlife. The forest's endless depths seem serene and peaceful but the atmosphere will suddenly change as huge trunks of hornbeam, spruce and oak loom up and swell into a dark canopy, pierced here and there by slivers of sunlight. There is a famous thicket of huge oaks, 40m (131ft) high, very different from the smaller oaks of England.

HOW TO GET THERE:
Two-hour bus ride from Bialystok in Poland.
WHEN TO GO:
Spring, summer or autumn.
NEAREST TOWNS:
Hajnvka in Poland 2km (1.25 miles) or Brest in Belarus 70km (44 miles).

THE BOHEMIAN FOREST

Czech Republic

The Bohemian Forest is a low mountain range in central Europe, extending from the Czech Republic on one side to Germany and Austria on the other, thus creating a natural border between the countries. This heavily forested range, with its unforgiving climate, is one of the oldest in Europe and is the divide of the watershed between the North Sea and the Black Sea. The peaks have been eroded by the climate into rounded forms with few rocky parts, and have peat bogs and high plateaux. The highest peak in the range is Grober Arber, reaching 1,456m (4,775ft). The origins of this forest go back to about 400BC, when it was inhabited by the Boii people. These were ancient Celts from Gaul, northern Italy, Bohemia, Moravia and Slovakia. The name *Bohemia* comes from the Latin for 'the home of the Boii'. Today the Bohemian Forest is a popular holiday destination for its hiking and biking and skiing in the winter. The region is also known for its glassmaking and schnapps production.

HOW TO GET THERE:
Czech Republic – fly to Prague, take the E50 to Plzen, then the E53 to Klatovy. Germany – fly to Nuremburg, take the E56 to Regensburg, then the E53.

WHEN TO GO:
At any time but best in summer for hiking and all outdoor sports; in winter for skiing.

NEAREST TOWNS:
In the Czech Republic, Klatovy 20km (12.5 miles); in Germany, Regensburg 18km (11 miles).

MACOCHA GORGE

Czech Republic

HOW TO GET THERE:
Flights, trains, buses to Bratislava or Brno, then take the E461 to Lipuvka, the 374 to Blansko and on to Vilemovice, which is in the Moravian Karst.

WHEN TO GO:
May to September.

NEAREST TOWN:
Brno 40km (25 miles).

DON'T MISS
Balcarka Cave.

This is a wonderful area of Moravian Karst with a multitude of caves, underground streams and dead-end valleys. The karst's best-known features are the Punkva Cave and the Macocha Gorge, located north of the city of Brno, in the Drahanska Highlands. The Macocha Gorge is also known as the Macocha Abyss, and part of its beauty is that it was formed following the roof collapse of an underground cave, creating a 'light hole' that filters light down into the abyss below. The gorge is a 'doline', or sinkhole, 139m (455ft) deep, the deepest of this type in central Europe. This area forms part of the Punkva Natural Reserve and is not open to traffic, but tourists and hikers can see the interiors and the beautiful stalagmites and stalactites of the Punkva caves on the Punkva river, which leads to the bottom of the Macocha gorge.

BALCARKA CAVE

Czech Republic

The Balcarka Cave is in the northern part of the Moravian Karst, which is 100 sq km (62 sq miles) of beautiful, heavily wooded, hilly terrain to the north of Brno, honeycombed with more than a thousand caves. Discovered in the 1920s, this is a two-storey cave, a maze of rambling corridors connected by chimneys and high domes with extraordinarily colourful stalagmites and stalactites. The spectacular effects have been created by the drip of acidic rainwater through limestone, slowly dissolving it. The natural entry portal is an important archaeological site. Bones of Pleistocene animals and tools made of flint and bone from the late Stone Age were found here, but for the visitors who flock to this place the big draw is nature's subterranean decorations on the walls and ceilings. Unlike the other, better-known caves around here, you do not need to buy your ticket in advance for Balcarka. There is a guide to take you through the 'Halls'. The entry hall leads through an artificial tunnel to a circular gorge 10m (33ft) high and covered with sparkling sinter cascades. This leads into the biggest hall of the labyrinth, Large Foch's Hall, where the ceiling is decorated with transparent stalactites and sinter curtains. The most beautiful chambers, the Gallery and the Natural Hall, follow on from here; the stalactite decorations on the walls and ceilings are very rich and clear. From here, continue into the Destruction Hall, created by the ceiling collapsing and containing the Madonna Cactus stalactite waterfall, to finally reach the Hall of Discoveries, where the walls are covered in 'nickaminek', a calcic pulpy substance.

THE RHÔNE GLACIER

Switzerland

HOW TO GET THERE:
By road via the Furkapass
or Grimselpass.
WHEN TO GO:
Spring to autumn.
NEAREST TOWN:
Andermatt 26km (16 miles).

YOU SHOULD KNOW
The roads are very steep
and twisting.

The once mighty Rhône glacier, high in the Dammastock mountains, is not only one of the best-known glaciers in the world, but one of the most endangered, too. Seen from a distance, the grey wedge in the side of the valley above the Gletsch is still impressive, yet only 150 years ago it reached the edge of the village. Between 1996 and 2006, it shrank by 50m (165ft) and in the last 150 years has receded 2.5km (1 mile) and is 450m (1,476ft) higher up the valley. It is estimated that the last 9.5km (6 miles) may be gone before the end of the 21st century as the process speeds up. Access to the glacier is via the Belvedere Hotel, just west of the switchback Furkapass. As you get nearer to it, its colour changes from grey to a pale, sky blue. A trail and wooden steps lead to the face of the glacier and to the 'ice cave', an artificial tunnel carved deep into the glacier. Some 30–40m (98–131ft) of tunnel have to be cut each year to compensate for the glacier's movement down its valley. Inside, the light is a startling deep blue-green and the air is cool but still. Despite the creaks of the ice as it shifts and the occasional cracking sounds, and the knowledge that this mammoth glacier may not be here much longer, there is a sense of serenity and calm.

THE MATTERHORN

Switzerland

Lying on the border between Switzerland and Italy, the iconic 4,478-m (14,693-ft) Matterhorn (Monte Cervino in Italian) is perhaps the most widely recognized mountain in Europe. Its four faces – facing north, south, east and west – remain almost snowless because they are so steep. The snow instead feeds the glaciers that lie at the foot of each face. It was first climbed in 1865, by the route that is most commonly used today, the Hörnli ridge above the Swiss village of Zermatt. Although about 3,000 people a year attempt the climb, many have to turn back because it requires a great deal of strength and stamina. The other major route is from the Italian side. Renowned as a winter skiing area, the lower slopes of the mountain are also excellent for hiking in summer, with stunning views, larch forests, alpine meadows and mountain tarns. One of the most amazing views on offer is that from the Gorner Grat ridge across the Gorner glacier, with the backdrop of the Monte Rosa, the Dom, the Breithorn and the Matterhorn behind. The ridge can be reached on foot or by the railway. The Schwarzsee, or Black Lake, to the north of the mountain is a worthwhile destination in itself, and also offers closer views of the mountain and spectacular views across the valley, too. The high meadows have lovely alpine flora in spring and are home to marmots and a range of alpine birds.

HOW TO GET THERE:
By road to Tasch, then by train to Zermatt, and on foot or by ski lift from there.
WHEN TO GO:
The best time for climbing and hiking is July to September.
NEAREST TOWN:
Visp 40km (25 miles).

GIMMELWALD

Switzerland

The landscape surrounding the tiny hamlet of Gimmelwald is breathtaking. Perched high up on the Schilthorn, it looks east across the Lauterbrunnen valley towards the Jungfrau, Münch and Eiger. In both summer and winter, it is picture-postcard Switzerland. It is a traffic-free, television-free paradise: the only access is via the Luftseilbahn Stechelberg-Mürren-Schilthorn cable car or on foot. The walk from Stechelberg or Mürren takes about an hour and a half: from the former it is uphill and from the latter downhill. From the top of the 2,970-m (9,744-ft) Schilthorn, the panoramic views encompass the Jungfrau range, Titlis, the Juras and the Black Forest. On clear days, Mont Blanc, some 110km (70 miles) away, can just be seen. The cable car goes to the mountaintop, but the Schilthorn hike takes you through a range of scenery that is almost unimaginable – steep, narrow gorges, waterfalls, huge boulders left lying by glaciers, alpine meadows, scree slopes, pinewoods, craggy peaks, U-shaped valleys, rounded ridges in which you can see the scars left by the ice and always, the snow-tipped mountains filling the view.

HOW TO GET THERE:
By road to Stechelberg or train to Mürren, then on foot or by cable car.
WHEN TO GO:
At any time.
NEAREST TOWN:
Interlaken 14km (8 miles).

YOU SHOULD KNOW
The trail up to the village is sometimes closed in winter because of the risk of avalanches.

THE REICHENBACH FALLS

Switzerland

HOW TO GET THERE:
By funicular railway from Willingen.
WHEN TO GO:
The funicular operates only from mid-May to the beginning of October. May to July is the best time to see the falls.
NEAREST TOWN:
Meiringen 2km (1 mile).

The five cascades that make up the Reichenbach Falls have a total drop of some 250m (820ft), and the upper falls are one of the longest individual cascades in the Alps. The train ride to reach them is a must, as it crisscrosses the rushing waters below. In seven minutes, it whisks you up 244m (800ft). From the mountain rescue hut, a trail leads round to good viewing spots. The falls are a wonderful sight in late spring and early summer, as the waters tumble into the gorge and clouds of spray rise like smoke. However, the falls are as well known for their literary connection: on the other side of the falls, accessed via a little footbridge, is a white star marking the place where, in Conan Doyle's *The Adventure of the Final Problem*, Sherlock Holmes and Professor Moriarty grappled before falling together into the 'boiling pit'.

LAKE LUCERNE

Switzerland

Lake Lucerne (in German, Vierwaldstättersee) and its surroundings form the image that most people picture when they think of Switzerland. Surrounded by mountains and beautiful lakeshores, it is also one of the most important places in the country's history: the Rütli meadow, where the people of the area first swore the oath that began the Swiss Confederation and its defiance of the Hapsburgs, is near its shores.

Three iconic mountains around the lake are Mount Pilatus, where according to legend Pontius Pilate is buried; the Bürgenstock; and the Rigi, which so fascinated Turner that he painted it in its different moods and at different times of day. At sunset, it can appear a brilliant red.

Although it is possible to drive around most of the lake's shore, by far the most popular way to get from place to place is to take one of the many steamers that crisscross the lake. The most popular way to get up Pilatus is via the world's steepest cogwheel railway, which operates when the route is free of snow, and there are aerial gondolas and cableways that operate all year. The views northeast across the lake from the top are spectacular: as well as the lake, there are mountain pastures, spruce forests and the Rigi. The latter has many hiking trails, and the top can be accessed by cable car or rack railway. Sunrise over the Zugspitz, as the light floods across mountains and sneaks into valleys, is a stupendous sight.

HOW TO GET THERE:
By road or rail
from Zürich.
WHEN TO GO:
Summer.
NEAREST TOWN:
Lucerne, on the lake's edge.

DON'T MISS
The views from
Mount Pilatus.

THE JUNGFRAU

Switzerland

The Jungfrau may not be the most difficult mountain to climb in this range in the Bernese Oberland, but it is the highest at 4,158m (13,642ft) and, flanked by the Eiger and Mönch mountains, dominates the landscape. However, there has been no need to climb this particular mountain for years as visitors can get to within 600m (2,000ft) of the top by train and lift. From either Lauterbrunnen or Grindelwald, the Wengenalpbahn (WAB) takes you to Kleine Scheidegg, at the foot of the north wall of the Eiger, the notorious Eigerwand that has claimed the lives of so many climbers. The cogwheel railway is the longest in the world and has been operating since 1893. From here, at a height of 2,029m (6,762ft), you can see the Eigerwand, the Mönch and the Jungfrau itself. The next stage of the journey is the Jungfraubahn (the JB), an electric railway that climbs up through the three mountains until it reaches the Jungfraujoch terminus. On the way, there are two short stops where holes have been cut into the mountainside to allow visitors a glimpse of the ice below and the peaks above. From the rail terminus, a lift whisks you to the Sphinx Terraces, which lie between the Jungfrau and Mönch and offer views of the Aletsch Glacier, which winds its way round the mountain and which in places is moving at the astonishing rate of 180m (600ft) a year. Because the snow and ice cover are permanent up here, winter sports are on offer all year round. The views from the terraces across the heights of the Bernese Oberland are spectacular, particularly in summer when the white peaks contrast with the greens of the valleys far below.

HOW TO GET THERE:
By rail.
WHEN TO GO:
Any time of year.
NEAREST TOWN:
Interlaken 16km (10 miles).

YOU SHOULD KNOW

The trains operate all year, except in very bad weather.

GRINDELWALD VALLEY

Switzerland

HOW TO GET THERE:
By road or rail from
Interlaken.
WHEN TO GO:
Any time of year.
NEAREST TOWN:
Interlaken 20km (11 miles).

DON'T MISS
The cable-car
ride to Männlichen.

Known for its skiing in winter, this beautiful valley, surrounded by jagged mountain peaks, is the epitome of the Bernese Oberland. Dominated at the western end by the Eiger and to the south by the Mättenberg and Wetterhorn, this U-shaped glacial valley is among the most popular areas of Switzerland. The scenery is magnificent, with forests clinging to the lower slopes of the mountains, the spectacular Sandbach waterfall and, of course, the mountain peaks themselves. There are some 90km (55 miles) of hiking trails in the valley, which lead through woodland, across the valley floor and over the mountains' lower slopes. Higher routes can be accessed via the cable cars used by skiers in winter. The best way to get views over the whole valley is to take the cable car from Grindelwald village to Männlichen.

TRÜMMELBACH FALLS

Switzerland

Deep in the Lauterbrunnen valley, the Trümmelbach is carving its way through the side of the Schwarze Münch. This river carries almost all of the meltwaters from the Eiger, Münch and Jungfrau in an amazing series of twisting cascades. When the snowmelt is at its peak in early summer, up to 20,000 litres (4,400 gallons) of icy water can burst through every second. Seven of the ten cascades run through cave-like canyons, and tunnels have been bored through to allow access to visitors. The noise is deafening, and you feel the walls of the tunnels vibrate as the water pounds against them. The viewing point at the top is above where the falls enter the mountain, then the route follows steps down through the mountain where the rushing water is floodlit to emerge at another viewing point. The valley is also worth exploring: from the flat valley floor you are rewarded by sheer limestone cliffs, lushly wooded slopes, more waterfalls and spectacular views of the mountains above.

HOW TO GET THERE: By rail from Interlaken to Lauterbrunnen, then on foot or by bus.
WHEN TO GO: April to July is best. The falls are closed from November to March.
NEAREST TOWN: Interlaken 11km (7 miles).

THE EIGER

Switzerland

HOW TO GET THERE:
By train from Interlaken.
WHEN TO GO:
Any time.
NEAREST TOWN:
Interlaken 15km (9 miles).

High in the Bernese Oberland, at the eastern end of the Jungfrau range, the Eiger is one of the best-known – and most notorious – mountains in the world. Climbing its north face is still a byword for attempting the impossible, even though the feat was first achieved in 1938. The relatively easy route up the west flank was first accomplished in 1858, but even that is for serious climbers only. At 3,970m (13,025ft), it is 188m (617ft) shorter than the nearby Jungfrau.

As you approach on the train from either direction, the north face, or Eigerwand, dominates the valley below. Both routes have become more hazardous in summer over recent years: warmer temperatures and less snowfall have reduced the amount of ice, and rockfalls are more common. In 2006, some 700,000 cubic metres (24,719,800 cubic feet) sheared off the north face in one massive rock slide. The Eiger Trail runs from Wengen to Alpiglen and takes in both a walk near the base of the north wall and the Eiger glacier. To walk the full trail takes a day's strenuous effort, but the short section from the Eigergletscher station to Alpiglen takes less than three hours, according to the authorities.

HIGH ALPINE MEADOWS

Switzerland

The high meadows of the Alps remain some of the most unspoiled landscapes in Europe. They are internationally important for the unique groups of plants they contain. Among the best areas are the Parc Naziunal Svizzer – Switzerland's only national park – near Engadin in the east; around Wengen in the Bernese Oberland; and in the area around the Matterhorn in the south. Under feet of snow during winter, it is amazing that any delicate plants survive here, but in early summer, watered by the melting snow, a riot of flowers appears: blue and yellow gentians, lady's slipper orchids, the rare edelweiss and bellflowers carpet the dry meadows for a brief period. Up here, no fertilizers are used and these tiny plants grow as they have for thousands of years. Even higher up, wet meadows, small lakes with ice-cold water and bogs are fed by water from the melting glaciers. One of the most famous tarns – lakes that form in the base of glacial cirques – is the Schwarzsee below the Matterhorn. The scenery in these areas is, of course, spectacular, as they are dominated by the mountains above with views over the forests and valleys below. Wildlife that may be spotted within or from these meadows and the high slopes above includes marmots, chamois, wild goats, ibex and elk. In the national park, golden eagle and reintroduced Egyptian vulture may be seen. The flower meadows attract a wonderful array of butterflies.

HOW TO GET THERE:
By hiking in the areas below the glaciers.
WHEN TO GO:
Early summer.
NEAREST TOWNS:
There are many in the area.

THE KRIMML FALLS

Austria

One of the greatest attractions in Austria is the Krimml Falls on the western edge of the Hohe Tauern National Park. The Krimml is the biggest waterfall in Europe and ranks in the top eight great waterfalls of the world. It falls a total distance of 380m (1,246ft) in three dramatic drops, each of more than 100m (330ft), connected by twisting rapids. The incredible thunder of the water as it comes crashing down is truly awesome. Krimml flows through a narrow, wooded valley in the heart of a dramatically beautiful glaciated region of the eastern Alps – there are more than 300 mountains over 3,000m (9,850ft) high, and the tallest mountain in Austria, the Grossglockner, at 3,798m (12,460ft). A tenth of Hohe Tauern is covered in glacial ice, the mountains are permanently snowcapped, and winter here can last for up to eight months. The 4-km (2.5-mile) trail to the top of the falls, the headwaters of the Salzach river, takes you through a dazzling landscape of mountain and forest, which you view through a fine haze of water sprayed up in great clouds by the force of the Krimml. The path is extremely steep in places and it takes about one and a half hours to complete the entire route. However, it is well worth persevering to reach the viewing point at Bergerblick – you will be rewarded with an amazing sense of achievement and the most superb view. In winter, the slopes above Krimml village are a popular skiing resort, and the waterfall is frozen into a bizarre, static, ice cascade.

HOW TO GET THERE:
Fly to Salzburg or Innsbruck. Road or rail to Zell am See, 50km (30 miles) away. Steam-train trip recommended from Zell am See to Krimml.
WHEN TO GO:
At its most amazing in the spring.
NEAREST TOWN:
Krimml 4km (2.5 miles).

YOU SHOULD KNOW
The Krimml Falls is one of the most popular tourist resorts in Austria, so be prepared for plenty of company. Most people can't be bothered to climb the entire way – by the time you reach Bergerblick, you should have left most of them behind.

NORTH TYROL

Austria

HOW TO GET THERE:
Fly to Innsbruck.
WHEN TO GO:
Time of year depends on
your sports interest.
NEAREST TOWN:
Innsbruck.

The fairy-tale alpine scenery of North Tyrol is the stuff of picture books – swift mountain rivers tumbling down forested slopes, fertile pastoral valleys dotted with smallholdings and villages, ice-clad peaks and sparkling glacial lakes. This beautiful region is a sports paradise, with its panoramic landscapes, pure mountain air and sparklingly clean lakes. Wildspitze, the second-tallest mountain in Austria, is 3,374m (10,980ft) high. Its slopes are glaciated but otherwise straightforward, which makes it perfect for ice climbing. There are more than 700 other mountains over 3,000m (9,840ft), so this is great climbing territory. In winter, there is terrific downhill and cross-country skiing at world-famous resorts like Kitzbühel and St Anton am Arlberg; in the warmer months you can go white-water rafting and kayaking as well as trekking, horse-riding and mountain biking. Above all, the scenic beauty of the landscape makes the Tyrol idyllic walking country, with more than 15,000km (9,375 miles) of trails to roam. You will find walks at all levels of difficulty to match your fitness, and there are numerous mountain huts in which to shelter or spend the night.

EISRIESENWELT ICE CAVES

Austria

The Eisriesenwelt is the largest accessible ice labyrinth in the world, with more than 40km (25 miles) of explored passageways. The caverns are lined in ice 20m (65ft) thick and are elaborately ornamented with stunning ice stalactites, stalagmites, columns, domes and waterfalls. Opposing air currents keep the ice frozen all year round. In the winter, cold air blows into the cave entrance, freezing the water from the melting snow that has dripped into the labyrinth through the summer. In the warmer months, cold air from deep inside, in its attempt to flow out, prevents the ice near the entrance from melting. Opened to the public in 1920, it rapidly became one of the most popular tourist attractions in Austria.

YOU SHOULD KNOW

A tour of the cave lasts 75 minutes, so remember to wear warm clothes to protect you against the freezing temperature inside.

HOW TO GET THERE: Fly to Salzburg. Road or rail to Werfen, about 40km (25 miles) south, then a bus to Eisriesenwelt.
WHEN TO GO: Open May to October.
NEAREST TOWN: Werfen 5km (3 miles).

SALZKAMMERGUT

Austria

HOW TO GET THERE:
Fly to Salzburg or Linz. Road
or train to Vocklabrück or
Bad Ischl.
WHEN TO GO:
Year-round.
NEAREST TOWNS:
Vocklabrück, Bad Ischl.

Salzkammergut is a World Heritage Landscape, famous for its enchanting scenery of lakes, mountains and picturesque villages. It is arguably the most beautiful region in the whole of Austria, where, in the days of the Hapsburg Empire, the emperors and noble families used to take their holidays. The word *salzkammergut* means 'estate of the salt chamber'; salt has been quarried here since the Bronze Age without defacing the landscape. In fact, the salt (or 'white gold') trade has only added to the region's charm since it led to enormous wealth, reflected in the fine architecture of the historic towns here. The government had a monopoly on the trade, and Salzkammergut was banned to outsiders until the 19th century in case they were salt smugglers. The oldest salt mine in the world is here, in the village of Hallstatt. This unbelievably quaint, 17th-century toy town is squeezed precariously between the brink of the 135-m (440-ft) deep Hallstättersee (Lake Hallstaetter) and the precipitous slopes of the Dachstein mountains. The largest lake in Austria – Attersee – is one of the 76 beautiful lakes in Salzkammergut. It is famous for its pure water and easterly *rosenwind*, which wafts the scent of roses from nearby castle gardens across its waters. Perhaps the most scenically beautiful lake is Altausseersee, known as the 'ink pot' for its dark-blue water.

HOW TO GET THERE: By road or rail from
Catánia.
WHEN TO GO: Any time of year.
NEAREST TOWN: Piedimonte Etneo.

MOUNT ETNA

Italy

Mount Etna's looming presence can be felt over a large area of northeastern Sicily. It is more than 30km (19 miles) across the base, and 3,323m (10,900ft) high. There is usually some geothermal activity somewhere on the mountain, and more major events happen every few weeks or months. The structure of the volcano is complex, and eruptions are not confined to the main crater. Unlike many volcanoes, Etna produces more than one type of eruption – in some, lava flows quickly down the sides of the mountain, while in others it spits out gas and launches gobbets of magma high into the air, making particularly spectacular displays at night. Eruptions from the multiple vents on the mountain's flanks have created numerous smaller peaks and valleys, such as Monte Spagnolo and Monte Gallo: these are delightful places to hike. Protected from development, the wooded slopes can be explored along a maze of nature trails and are home to wild cats, porcupines, a variety of reptiles and golden eagles.

Right: Mount Etna towers over the town of Taormina.

VESUVIUS

Italy

HOW TO GET THERE:
By train/bus/taxi from Naples.
WHEN TO GO:
At its best between April
and June.
NEAREST TOWN:
Naples 9km (5.6 miles).

YOU SHOULD KNOW

It is estimated that, at times
during the 79AD eruption,
the ash column from the top
of Vesuvius shot 32km (20
miles) into the stratosphere
and 4 cubic km (1 cubic
mile) of lava was emitted
over a period of 19 hours.

Probably the best-known volcano in the world, Mount Vesuvius
towers over the Bay of Naples. It is most famous for the eruption of
79AD, which caused the total destruction of the towns of Pompeii and
Herculaneum. It has erupted more than 50 times since then, most
recently in 1944, and is one of the most dangerous volcanoes in the
world. Vesuvius is around 13,000 years old and countless eruptions
have given the summit a distinctive 'humpbacked' shape of a cone
within a cone. The present summit is 1,282m (4,202ft) high and is
almost completely encircled by the steep rim of a caldera. Apart from
the lava scars running down its sides, the mountain is green and fertile,
its lower slopes covered in vineyards. The surrounding area is a national
park with a network of paths, as well as a road that takes you to
within 200m (650ft) of the summit. You can explore historic Pompeii
– a town frozen in time. The buildings and inhabitants were perfectly
preserved under 10m (30ft) of lava, buried and forgotten for nearly
1,600 years. The town was uncovered again during rebuilding work
after a devastating eruption in 1631, but it was not until 1748 that
archaeologists started to excavate it systematically. Today, more than
three million people live in the immediate vicinity of Vesuvius – a cause
of great concern.

LAKE GARDA

Italy

HOW TO GET THERE:
Fly to Brescia or Verona. Bus
from Verona to Garda or train
from Verona to Desenzano
del Garda.
WHEN TO GO:
April to October.
NEAREST TOWNS:
Desenzano del Garda,
Sirmione, Riva del Garda,
Malcesine, Garda.

The Italian lakes are renowned for their sublime beauty, and Lake Garda is the star. It is the largest lake in Italy, with spectacularly blue water and landscapes full of contrast and colour. It has an exceptionally mild microclimate that supports year-round green vegetation. From its northern tip, for about two-thirds of its length, Lake Garda is a narrow fjord, enclosed by mountains. Steep limestone escarpments sweep down to the edges of the lake, and winding roads and paths snake their way through isolated villages, past castles and ancient churches. Towards the south, it feels much more Mediterranean. The lake suddenly opens out and the landscape is transformed into gently rolling hills with citrus trees, vines, oleander and bougainvillea. The ancient town of Sirmione juts out on a peninsula at the southern edge, with its quaint cobblestone streets, fairy-tale 13th-century castle and thermal springs. Lake Garda is one of the top resorts in Europe for sailing and windsurfing.

CHARYBDIS

Italy

The island of Sicily is separated from the Calabrian coast of southern Italy by the treacherous waters of the Strait of Messina – the Scylla and Charybdis of Greek legend. This 32-km (20-mile) strait connecting the Ionian Sea to the Tyrrenhian Sea is only about 90m (295ft) deep, but its turbulent water has such strong currents that they rip the seaweed off the ocean bed. Two opposing currents switch direction every six hours, creating a whirlpool of complex wave patterns – this is Charybdis, the voracious daughter of Poseidon and Gaia, who lives under a giant fig tree on a mythical rock in the strait. Four times a day, she swallows the water and spits it out again. The sea monster Scylla hides in a cave in the rugged Calabrian cliffs, making terrible howling noises. She has 12 legs and six snake-necked heads with three rows of teeth in each. The Strait is only just over 3km (1.9 miles) wide at its narrowest point so, in Odysseus's attempt to avoid both Scylla and Charybdis, he was 'caught between a rock and a hard place'.

HOW TO GET THERE:
From Italian mainland,
ferry from Villa San Giovanni
or hydrofoil from Reggio
di Calabria.
WHEN TO GO:
Southern Mediterranean
climate – most beautiful in
spring and early summer.
Scorching heat in July
and August.
NEAREST TOWN:
Messina.

YOU SHOULD KNOW
Shakespeare used Messina
as the setting for *Much Ado
About Nothing*.

THE BLUE GROTTO

Italy

The southern Italian isle of Capri, beloved of the emperors Augustus and Tiberius, lies off the Sorrentine peninsula at the south of the Bay of Naples. It is predominantly made of limestone and this soft rock has allowed the sea to carve numerous sea caves into its cliffs.

The most famous of these is the Blue Grotto, on the south coast, which the emperors supposedly used as a private bath. Once under the low entrance to the cave, visitors are surrounded by blue light that fades as the cave recedes away into the darkness. But where does the eerie blue light come from? It is, in fact, sunlight getting into the cave through another, submerged, entrance and being reflected off the white limestone and sand on the cave's floor, so lighting the water from underneath. If the entrance to the cave were higher, sunlight would get in that way, too, and drown out the magical blue glow. Depending on the height of the waves, guides on the boat trips – the only way to get into the cave – may ask visitors to lie down in the boat to avoid bumping their heads. If you shut your eyes on the way through the entrance, the effect of the blue around you as you open them is even more startling.

HOW TO GET THERE:
By boat from Naples or Sorrento to Capri's Marina Grande, then a local boat trip.
WHEN TO GO:
Summer.
NEAREST TOWNS:
Capri town 3km (2 miles).

YOU SHOULD KNOW
The guides sometimes sing in the caves.

DON'T MISS
A guided trip to the crater, at sunset, if possible.

STROMBOLI

Italy

Stromboli is the summit of a volcanic mountain sticking 926m (2,950ft) out of the Tyrrhenian Sea. The rest of it is submerged to a depth of 1,500m (5,000ft). It is the most remote of the Aeolian Islands, a volcanic archipelago off the northern coast of Sicily, about 50km (30 miles) from the Italian mainland. 'The Lighthouse of the Mediterranean' is one of the most active volcanoes on the planet – it has been in a state of more or less constant eruption for the past 2,000 years. The volcano stands alone in the middle of the sea, emitting a constant plume of steam from its cone. At night, there is the awesome spectacle of its flame shooting into the sky, like a giant firework. Constant minor explosions throw incandescent blobs of lava over the crater rim several times an hour, and the term 'Strombolian eruption' is used to describe this sort of volcanic activity anywhere. Amazingly, this tiny island, only 12.6 sq km (5 sq miles), is inhabited by about 500 people, who live philosophically in the shadow of the volcano in two villages and several tiny hamlets perched on its slopes. The views from the upper slopes are stunning – rugged cliffs tower above the black-sand beaches and you gaze across a clear blue sea dotted with islands. Throughout Stromboli's long history, large eruptions and lava flows have been rare. There was one in 2002 for the first time in 17 years, which created the Sciara di Fuoco ('Slope of Fire'), a horseshoe-shaped crater, and caused two landslides and several tsunami waves up to 10m (33ft) high. The most recent major eruption was in April 2009. Since then, Stromboli has been under extra surveillance.

HOW TO GET THERE:
Fly to Catania in Sicily, then bus/train to Milazzo or Messina and ferry/hydrofoil to Lipari; or, from mainland Italy, ferry/hydrofoil from Reggio di Calabria or Naples to Lipari. Boat from Lipari to Stromboli.

WHEN TO GO:
April to mid-June to see the island at its most beautiful.

NEAREST TOWN:
Lipari town, island of Lipari 34km (21 miles).

MARMOLADA

Italy

DON'T MISS
A trip to
Lake Misurina.

HOW TO GET THERE:
Fly to Bolzano, Verona,
Venice, Milan. Rail/road to
Bolzano or Ora 37km
(23 miles) or 45km (28 miles)
from Val di Fassa.

WHEN TO GO:
Time of year depends on
your interests.

NEAREST TOWNS:
Canezei (and villages Alba
and Penìa) in Val di Fassa.

The massive ridge of Marmolada dominates the Val di Fassa, a fairy-tale land of flower-filled meadows, lakes and spiked mountain peaks in the eastern Alps of northern Italy. 'The Queen of the Dolomites' rises up from the Fedaia Pass to its summit of 3,344m (10,972ft) at Punta Penìa, towering over its neighbours, which themselves are some of the region's most impressive mountains. Marmolada runs east to west with five separate peaks and the only large glacier in the Dolomites — the most extensive ice formation in the whole of the eastern Alps. In both winter and summer, it is a superb natural playground for sports enthusiasts. Along its south face, there is a wall of sheer cliffs several kilometers long — an irresistible challenge for climbers. The gentle, glaciated slope of the north side, still snow-covered long after it has melted elsewhere, is famous for the freedom of off-piste skiing. The countless ridges and passes are ideal terrain for mountain biking, and the outstandingly beautiful countryside and sublime landscape views make it a joy for paragliders and hill walkers. Geologically complex, the dolomite rock, from which the mountains get their name, is interspersed with volcanic lava ridges. The black rock of the lava stands out in striking contrast to the white dolomite and the bluish sheen of the glacier to create a uniquely fascinating landscape.

SKOCJAN CAVES

Slovenia

The Skocjan caves are the most famous site in the world for the study of karst phenomena. The Reka river runs through the limestone terrain of Kras, in southwest Slovenia, disappearing underground for 34km (21 miles). Over thousands of years, the river has dissolved the surrounding rock to create a magical subterranean world of thundering waterfalls, still lakes and turbulent rivers in a fantastical setting of multicoloured stalactites, stone curtains, dramatic sinkholes, collapsed dolines (valleys) and natural bridges. The sheer scale of the Skocjan caves is overwhelming. The incredible variety of the formations have been documented since ancient times and are a constant source of fascination for geologists – the karst here is known as 'original' or 'classical' and is the paradigm for karst phenomena everywhere. Skocjan is a true wonder of the world.

MOUNT TRIGLAV AND THE JULIAN ALPS

Slovenia

This little-known region of northwest Slovenia, named after the Julian dynasty of Roman emperors, is a fairy-tale land of romantic castles and medieval villages set in a spectacular landscape of soaring peaks and deep gorges, with thundering waterfalls, clear rivers and mountain lakes. The rugged white limestone mountains rise up out of thick forests and wildflower meadows that, in winter, are transformed into a snowbound wonderland. The Julian Alps create a natural land barrier between Italy and Slovenia. The colossal Mount Triglav stands between the rivers Soca and Sava in the middle of Triglav National Park. It has the highest summit in the Julian Alps at 2,864m (9,394ft), with panoramic views over the exquisite alpine valleys that spread out like a fan below. Just below the summit is the Triglav glacier, where there is a chasm of ice more than 280m (920ft) deep. The north face is a difficult and dangerous climb for experienced mountaineers, but there are also trekking routes to the summit for the amateur. From the top, you can see all the way from Austria to the Adriatic Sea.

THE PLITVICE LAKES

Croatia

In the heart of the forbidding forests of Croatia's Dinaric mountains – marked on old maps as 'The Devil's Garden' – there is an enchanting valley. Here is one of the most outstanding natural wonders in Europe – the Plitvice Lakes. These are 16 interconnected, naturally terraced lakes. At each terrace, water gushes out through hundreds of holes in the porous wall as well as spilling over the lip, cascading into the lake below in never-ending streams of sparkling clear water. The exquisite colours of the lakes – azures, blues and greens – are constantly changing according to the sunlight and the quantity of mineral deposits in the water. The terraces are made from travertine – a weird, rock-like substance composed of limestone sediment (deposited by the mountain streams) mixed with algae and mosses. The travertine builds up in layers around the vegetation, petrifying it and creating bizarre shapes as it hardens. At Plitvice, the travertine has built up so thickly that it has formed natural dams, which have led to the creation of the lakes. The lakes are in two separate clusters, extending over 8km (5 miles). The upper part of the valley contains 12 lakes, ending in Veliki Slap ('Big Waterfall'), which spills over a sharp drop into a sheer canyon 70m (230ft) below.

THE BLUE CAVE

Croatia

Bisevo is one of the thousands of limestone islands that are strewn the length of Croatia's Dalmatian coastline. It is a tiny, rocky outcrop that supports a small population. Like many other islands in the area, it has sea caves that can be visited by boat. The most famous of these is the Blue Cave (*Modra spilja*) in Balun Cove. Originally, the only way to enter the cave was by diving through the undersea entrance, but more than 100 years ago an artificial entrance was added to allow boats to enter. The light is at its best in early July and early September, between 11am and noon. Bright, sunny, calm days are the best; the colour will not be so intense under overcast skies or when the water is rough. The effect is created by sunlight entering the cave through an underwater entrance and being reflected by the white floor up through the 20m (66ft) of water and creating a glorious blue colour. It is magical and well worth a trip.

Right: Visitors enter the famous Blue Cave.

DALMATIAN COAST

Croatia

HOW TO GET THERE:
Fly to Zagreb. Domestic
flight to Split or Dubrovnik,
or high-speed train to Split.
Jadrolinija coastal ferry
plies the waters between
Dubrovnik and Rijeka.
WHEN TO GO:
April to October.
NEAREST TOWNS:
Rijeka, Zadar, Split, Dubrovnik.

The rugged Dalmatian coastline is an exquisite stretch of more than 1,780km (1,100 miles) of intricate coves, channels and inlets, fringed by a complex network of more than a thousand islands. It runs along the eastern shores of the Adriatic Sea, from the island of Rab in the northwest to the Gulf of Kotor in the southeast, with a hinterland that is only 50km (30 miles) at its widest point. There are hundreds of glorious, unspoilt beaches, seven national parks and some of the most beautiful medieval towns and villages in Europe. From space, the Adriatic is the bluest patch of sea on the planet. Each island has a unique charm of its own. The stark white karst (limestone) cliffs of the barren Kornati islands stand out in spectacular contrast to the cobalt blue seas. Krapanj, famous for its sponges, is a peaceful haven for a secluded holiday. Hvar is the place for celebrity-spotting, and the beach of Brac is renowned among surfers. The green hilly island of Korkula was Marco Polo's birthplace, and the beautiful forests of Mljet are a national park. Named 'Destination of the Year' by *National Geographic* magazine, the Dalmatian coast has a growing reputation as the 'new Riviera'. With its balmy, Mediterranean climate, magical beauty and fascinating history, one can see why.

HOW TO GET THERE:
From Belgrade 360km
(225 miles). From Skopje
65km (41 miles).
WHEN TO GO:
April to October (closed
outside these months).
NEAREST TOWN:
Pristina 20km (12 miles).

MARBLE CAVE

Republic of Kosovo

When you enter the Mermerna Pecina ('Marble Cave'), you will encounter an incredibly rare and beautiful phenomenon – the metamorphosis of limestone to marble. Fluctuations in underground temperature and pressure transform the basic structure of the limestone. Its crystals are forced into different arrangements, changing into aragonite, and eventually, marble. This process is happening in front of your eyes in the Marble Cave. You are in a magical realm of coloured marble, bizarre aragonite crystals and speleothems ('cave ornaments' – such as stalactites and stalagmites). The entrance to the cave was discovered in 1966 by Ahmet Diti while he was building an extension to his house in the village of Donje Gadimlje. It was full of silt and was not opened to the public for another ten years. Much of it remains unexplored and there are entire passages, still choked up with mud and gravel, waiting to be discovered. So far, a total length of 1,260m (4,130ft) has been uncovered, and 440m (1,440ft) is open to the public.

DON'T MISS
The World Heritage
Site of Kotor on the
Boka Kotorska fjord.

DURMITOR NATIONAL PARK & TARA CANYON
Montenegro

The Tara river flows through a spectacular canyon 1,300m (4,260ft) deep – the second-deepest in the world after the Grand Canyon of Arizona. The river current is unbelievably fast and there are 21 rapids, some of them dangerous. The canyon cuts a path 80km (50 miles) long through the scenic meadows and forests of Durmitor National Park in northwest Montenegro. The park is a World Heritage Site of breathtaking beauty, shaped by the effects of glaciation. It is a rugged plateau of forests and meadows, incised with gorges and underground rivers, overlooked by permanently snowcapped mountains with lakes, streams and bubbling springs. It is bordered by canyons on three sides, with the wondrous Durmitor massif, 2,552m (8,370ft) high, towering up as though to touch the sky. The 18 glacial lakes – known as Gorske Oci ('Mountain Eyes') – are an outstanding feature of the landscape. Nowhere else in the world are there so many in such a compact area. The most famous is Crno (Black) Lake at an altitude of 1,416m (4,644ft). It is fed by mountain streams, which in summer become a waterfall, and is in fact two lakes interconnected by a narrow channel. Crno nestles in a dense conifer forest, which causes the reflection from the water to be an intense dark blue-green colour.

HOW TO GET THERE:
Fly (or train from Belgrade) to Podgorica, then by road to Zabljak.
WHEN TO GO:
December to March for skiing. May to September for summer season.
NEAREST TOWN:
Zabljak.

DOBSINÁ ICE CAVE

Slovakia

Dobsiná, a karst formation 7,000–9,000 years old, is one of the most significant ice caves in the world. It is situated in the Slovensky Raj ('Slovak Paradise') National Park, a beautiful region of eastern Slovakia. The cave was officially discovered in 1870 by Eugene Ruffini, opened to the public just one year later, and, in 1887, was the first show cave to be lit by electricity. In fact, it had been known to the locals for generations as the Studená Diera ('Cold Hole'). Dobsiná is 1,388m (4,550ft) long, with 475m (1,560ft) open to the public. Its north-facing entrance is at an altitude of 970m (3,180ft), from where the cave descends straight downwards. This ensures that the interior remains a constant 0°C to -1°C (32–30°F), whatever the external temperature – warm summer air cannot flow downwards, and in winter, the freezing north wind prevents air escaping upwards. At the entrance, you are immediately startled by a cold blast. The icy passage walls are smooth to the touch and, in the course of your descent into the cave, you pass a stunning array of frozen stalactites, stalagmites and waterfalls. The largest chamber is the Big Hall, with a ceiling 12m (40ft) high, a floor covered in ice 26.5m (87ft) thick, and walls dripping with extraordinary ice formations. In places, the floor is smooth enough to be used as a skating rink. In spring, a shimmering layer of frost crystals makes the entire ceiling sparkle like a fairy palace.

OCHTINSKÁ ARAGONITE CAVE

Slovakia

Of the thousands of caves in Slovakia, 12 of which are open to the public, the Ochtiná cave is recognized as being incomparable. It exemplifies an incredibly rare phenomenon – the creation of aragonite. Its structure is so unstable that its delicate crystals can only form, without immediately collapsing, under very precise conditions of temperature and pressure. Then, a magical chemical transformation takes place and ordinary-looking limestone sediment, instead of forming stalactites and stalagmites, metamorphoses into delicate aragonite twigs and flowers. In Ochtiná, there is a staggering amount and variety of aragonite ornamentation. The most beautiful of the many attractions is the Milky Way Hall – named after the clusters of pure white aragonite that have formed an incredible sparkling trail along the ceiling, shining like stars.

VYSOKÉ TATRY

Slovakia

HOW TO GET THERE:
Fly to Poprad or to Bratislava (four hours by car or train to Poprad).
WHEN TO GO:
All year depending on activity.
NEAREST TOWN:
Poprad 25km (16 miles).

Although they only stretch for 26km (16 miles), the Vysoké Tatry (High Tatras) rival any mountain range in Europe for their challenging terrain, stark beauty and breathtaking views – a perfect version of the Alps in miniature. They rise in the eastern part of Tatras National Park, which covers 750 sq km (290 sq miles) of the border area between Slovakia and Poland, and are the only mountains of a truly alpine character in Slovakia. They are the highest and northernmost mountains of the 1,500-km (900-mile) Carpathians that curve around central Europe from Austria to Romania. There are 11 narrow, jagged peaks of more than 2,500m (8,200ft), with Gerlachovsky Stit at 2,655m (8,710ft) being the highest point in the whole of the Carpathians. Successive glaciations over tens of thousands of years have carved out a breathtaking granite landscape of deep, rounded valleys, exquisite mountain lakes, waterfalls and dramatic cliffs 1,000m (3,280ft) tall, which soar straight up, seemingly out of nowhere, from the completely flat terrain of the Liptov plain. The climate of the Vysoké Tatry is unique. The mountains impede the movement of central European air masses, which makes for extreme temperatures ranging from -40°C (-40°F) in winter to 33°C (91°F) in summer. The weather is exceptionally volatile, with sudden dramatic changes in conditions; the possibility of sudden summer snowfalls adds an extra thrill to climbing here. There is a rich variety of flora and fauna, including bears and wolves, and there are 600km (375 miles) of well-maintained trails leading through all the valleys and to the summits of ten of the mountains. The high-mountain character of the Vysoké Tatry combined with their accessibility makes them the perfect place for skiing, hiking and climbing enthusiasts.

HORTOBÁGY NATIONAL PARK

Hungary

HOW TO GET THERE:
Fly to Debrecen.
WHEN TO GO:
The autumn months are
best for birds, as well as
temperate weather.
NEAREST TOWN:
Debrecen 38km (24 miles).

YOU SHOULD KNOW

Puszta translates as
'bleak' or 'bereft'.

Hortobágy National Park is the largest continuous stretch of grassland in Europe. It is 800 sq km (300 sq miles) of salt marsh, grassland and wetland around the Tisza river in the Puszta (steppe) of eastern Hungary – a stark, daunting land of fierce winds, extreme temperatures and haunting mirages. The landscape appears to stretch forever, a strangely varied mosaic of vegetation merging into a vast sky, without any sign of human occupation other than the occasional traditional well or shepherd's hut, which may, disconcertingly, appear to be hanging in the sky as a result of the weird visual distortions often experienced here. Ancient domesticated animals graze freely on the plain – flocks of indigenous sheep, curly-furred mangalica pigs, huge-horned Hungarian grey cattle, water buffalo and nonius horses. The nonius horse originated in the Puszta. A fecund young stallion called Nonius, captured from the French during the Napoléonic Wars, was sent here for breeding in 1816. He mated with 368 of the local Hortobágy mares and his progeny are world-famous. Hortobágy is renowned for its birdlife, including the increasingly rare great bustard. The flocks of migrating birds are an incredible sight and sound. What at first sight looks like a bare windswept plain is not only one of the most important and diverse bird habitats in Europe – with over 330 species – but also a fascinating pastoral environment. The Puszta sustained a nomadic society of herdsmen for more than two millennia, and in Hortobágy you will discover a rich cowboy folk culture with a long tradition of harmonious human and animal interaction.

LAKE BALATON

Hungary

Lake Balaton, 80km (50 miles) southwest of Budapest, is the largest lake in central Europe. Hungary is a landlocked country, and Lake Balaton, with its wonderful beaches and clean water, at a summer temperature of 25°C (77°F) , has always served as a superb 'seaside' resort. It is surrounded by lovely, varied countryside for walking, cycling and bird-watching, with towns and villages steeped in history. The southern shore is especially suitable for family holidays, since the gentle incline of the shore makes it ultra-safe for children. To the southwest there are the unique wetlands of Kis-Balaton, while the northern shore has Balaton Uplands National Park, a beautiful hilly region of gorges, forests and meadows. To the west, the quaint university town of Keszthelly has incredible views. Balaton is also a popular winter resort, when the surface of the lake freezes and the daring (or foolhardy) skate on it.

BARADLA-DOMICA CAVES

Hungary

The Baradla-Domica cave system is not only by far the largest, but also one of the most beautiful cave systems in central Europe. One of the most renowned and researched caves in the world, there is plentiful archaeological evidence that its halls were inhabited by prehistoric man. It was first written about in 1549, and the world's first-known cave map, based on a 2-km (1-mile) section of it, was made in 1794. Tourism and geological research began in earnest in Baradla in the mid-19th century, and in 1932, it was established that Baradla and Domica were separate entrances to the same cave. They contain the world's tallest stalagmite at 32.7m (107ft), a 13-m (43-ft) stalactite, an ice abyss, a lake and two underground rivers. It is also a habitat for 465 different creatures, from unicellular organisms to crabs and bats.

DON'T MISS
Other unique caves
in the area –
Vass Imre and Béke.

TRANSYLVANIAN ALPS

Romania

HOW TO GET THERE:
Fly to Bucharest.
WHEN TO GO:
May to October (unless you
are going specifically for
winter sports). Winters are
extremely cold.
NEAREST TOWNS:
Brasov, Zarnesti, Sibiu,
Petrosani.

YOU SHOULD KNOW

The word 'Transylvania' is
derived from Latin *trans silva*,
meaning 'across the forest'.

The legendary land of the vampires is surrounded by mountains, of which the highest and wildest are the Transylvanian Alps – the barrier between Transylvania and southern Romania and the most remote and impressive range of the Carpathian mountains. One of the last remaining undeveloped regions of Europe, they slope gently down in a romantic idyll of valleys and streams, overlooked by fairy-tale castles (including Brad – Count Dracula's family seat). In stark contrast, the wild, south-facing slopes are jagged, limestone escarpments, incised with ravines and covered with menacing pine forests in which bears, lynx and wolves still prowl. From the Prahova valley you can climb the weathered rocks of the Bucegi massif, where eagles soar above you and the only other people are local shepherds. The astoundingly beautiful Piatra Craiului – a razor-like limestone ridge – has a precarious 18-km (11-mile) path that leads through a dramatic landscape of pitted slopes, scarred with caves and gorges. To the west is the breathtaking landscape of Retezat National Park, where the terrain has been transformed by glaciation into massive peaks, glacial lakes, rivers and primeval forest. The joy of exploring the Transylvanian Alps is their aura of remoteness, the incredible scenic contrasts and the sensation of time-warping into the Middle Ages.

DON'T MISS
A stay in one of the
delta villages.

THE DANUBE DELTA
Romania

The Danube delta is the largest continuous marshland in Europe, a huge wilderness of utterly isolated waters with expansive skies and almost unpopulated landscapes. Shared between Romania and Ukraine, the delta formed where the waters of the Danube flow into the Black Sea.

Reeds, which create floating or fixed islands, dominate its marsh vegetation. Classified into 12 different habitats, ranging from lakes to wet meadows to forests on slightly higher ground, the area was declared a Natural World Heritage Site in 1991 and is internationally significant for birds, both breeding and migratory.

Over 300 species of birds have been recorded here, among them cormorants, pelicans, herons, storks, swans, falcons and harriers. The floating islands are also one of the last refuges of the European mink, wildcat, freshwater otter and stoat, not to mention the huge variety of freshwater fish found here, including sturgeon. Permission is needed to visit specific nature reserves, which are closed during the bird-breeding season. The scattered small villages around the delta are also fascinating and timeless microcosms in themselves. Home to a variety of peoples – Ukrainian, Russian, Lipovan, Bulgarian, Moldovan, Turkish and Gagauz – these fishing and farming communities have changed very little from former times.

HOW TO GET THERE:
Car or train to Tulcea. From Tulcea, by boat to Sulina, Sfantu Gheorghe, Crisan.
WHEN TO GO:
The weather is best in May or October.
NEAREST TOWN:
Tulcea.

YOU SHOULD KNOW
Camping is allowed in most areas of the delta.

CARPATHIAN MOUNTAINS

Ukraine

Always remote, and never touched by mass tourism, the Carpathian mountains of southwest Ukraine are a treasury of European natural resources. Between Poland, Slovakia and Romania, they form a corridor 280km (175 miles) long and roughly 100km (62 miles) across, in which one of Europe's oldest landscapes stands intact as nature intended, a sanctuary for many of its rarest species and guardian of a huge proportion of endemic flora and fauna. They are famously beautiful: the rounded peaks and wide ridges of their central spine are covered with subalpine and alpine meadows called *polonyny*, for millennia the summer grazing grounds of nomadic herders. Between and below them are the spruce and fir forests, crowding the rocky spurs of countless ravines, where mountain torrents have carved their path either side of this European watershed. Lower down, beech fills the steep valley slopes, along with extremely rare Carpathian cedars and berry yew-trees that are 4,000 years old. At every level, rarity in abundance is the hallmark of the hundreds of flower species that mark the seasons; just as the presence of lynx, wolf, bear, bison, elk, salamander and a host of rare birds, like grey herons, indicates the pristine state of this region. The Ukrainian Carpathians' tranquil joys are typified by the Chornohora massif round the small town of Yaremche, south of Ivano-Frankivsk. Between Yaremche and Mount Hoverla, at 2,061m (6,760ft) the highest in Ukraine, you can sample the very finest from top to bottom: alpine flora in the *polonyny*, the tranquility of the forests, the Prut river crashing out of the mountain into the Yaremche canyon, and the series of cascades leading to the Probiy falls. There are dozens of other equally beautiful places in the region – and dozens of astonishing cave systems, panoramas and bizarre rock formations.

HOW TO GET THERE:
By air/train to Ivano-Frankivsk or Chernovtsi; then bus/car.
WHEN TO GO:
April to October.
NEAREST TOWNS:
Kolomyia, Khust.

YOU SHOULD KNOW
'Brynza' is the very strong cheese made in the *polonyny* by the Hutsul nomad shepherds.

DON'T MISS
Narcissus Valley in the Khust massif.

THE BALKAN MOUNTAINS

Bulgaria

HOW TO GET THERE:
By road or train.
WHEN TO GO:
July, August and September.
NEAREST TOWNS:
There are many towns and
villages in these mountains.

The Balkan mountains, or Stara Planina, extend some 560km (350 miles). The highest peaks are in the central section, and include Mount Botev, at 2,376m (7,795ft). Rivers from the Balkan mountains mainly flow north to the Danube or south to the Aegean Sea, and 20 passes and several railway lines cross the range. The region is notable for its flora and fauna, and includes nine nature reserves, four of which are UNESCO Biosphere Reserves. Ancient forests cloak the slopes of the Central Balkan National Park, giving shelter to ten species and two subspecies of flora that are endemic. Edelweiss grows here, 256 species of mushroom can be found, and 166 species of medicinal plant. The mountains are full of birds – 224 different species – making the region a magnet for twitchers. There are lovely wildflower meadows, waterfalls that tumble down almost vertical rock faces, deep, mysterious canyons and exciting caves.

THE PIRIN MOUNTAINS

Bulgaria

This rugged mountain range in southwest Bulgaria is notable not only for its limestone and granite landscapes, but also for its rich and diverse flora and fauna. Most of the area is a protected national park, and was listed as a World Heritage Site in 1983. The highest peak, Vihren, is 2,914m (9,616ft), and a further 60 peaks rise above 2,500m (8,250ft). This is a wonderful alpine landscape of marble and granite mountains and spectacular glacial lakes. The largest and deepest of these is the Popova Lake, but there are about 180 others, all crystal clear. Pirin can be divided into three parts, both geographically and geologically: north, central and south; alpine, subalpine and tree line; and it is this diversity that has produced such a rich flora and fauna. There are unique stands of ancient pine and fir, and over 1,300 plant species including 18 that are endemic. The Pirin mountains have something for everyone. Trekkers and hikers enjoy the summer beauty, and in winter there are ski resorts and other sporting activities.

HOW TO GET THERE: By road.
WHEN TO GO: All year round.
NEAREST TOWNS: Many towns and villages surround the Pirin mountains, but Bansko, at the entrance to the park, has the best tourist facilities.

251

BUTRINT NATIONAL PARK

Albania

With the Ionian Sea at its western extreme and the Greek border to the south, Butrint National Park is a remarkable area in southwestern Albania. Not only does it contain a unique wetland ecosystem and a wealth of diverse habitats, but also the ruins of the ancient city of Buthrotum. Within the park's boundaries, the ancient city and part of the surrounding area of lakes, including the southern part of Lake Butrint, is a UNESCO World Heritage Site, while the surrounding wetlands are protected under the Ramsar Convention.

The landscape is outstanding and very varied. The woods consist mainly of oak, elm, ash, white poplar and laurel, and on the Ksamili Peninsula and islands there are areas of typical Mediterranean maquis. The wetlands, however, are the dominant feature, with brackish lagoons, salt and freshwater marshes, reed beds, rivers, channels and a rocky shoreline. These unspoilt habitats support large numbers of birds, some of which are threatened, and 105 species of fish for which the lagoons are an important spawning ground, nursery and migration route to the sea. Butrint is particularly known for its reptiles and amphibians, including the epirote frog and the Balkan sand lizard, and holds the highest number of species recorded on any Albanian site. The main human activities here are fishing and mussel farming, as well as some agriculture. At present, most of the tourism is concerned with the main archaeological site, which has been occupied since the 8th century BC and is elegantly situated by the placid blue waters of the Vivari channel and Lake Butrint. However, plans are afoot to develop the ecotourism potential of the wetlands, as well as to encourage wintertime twitchers.

HOW TO GET THERE:
By road, or by ferry from the Greek island of Corfu.
WHEN TO GO:
During the summer months, although winter is the best time for bird-watching.
NEAREST TOWN:
Saranda 19km (12 miles).

DON'T MISS
The archaeological site of Buthrotum.

LAKE OHRID

Albania/Macedonia

This is the oldest lake in Europe, with a natural ecosystem so rare it's often called a 'museum of living species'. Three-million-year-old Lake Ohrid is so deep – 288m (945ft) – that it survived the last ice age, along with many of the creatures in its waters. Ten of its 17 fish species exist nowhere else in the world. Its future, and the future of the lake as a World Natural Heritage Site, depends on the ability of Albania and Macedonia, who share the 88-km (55-mile) shoreline, to co-ordinate their efforts to maintain its long-term ecological stability. Lake Ohrid is a mountain lake set at 693m (2,273ft). This height, plus the microclimate driven by its exceptional depth and position close to the Mediterranean, makes its reed beds and wetland areas very special for both endemic and migratory species.

Lake Ohrid's crystal-clear water – you can see to a depth of over 20m (66ft) – rises in giant springs on the south shore. The water originates in neighbouring Lake Prespa, 153m (502ft) higher, and is purified during its underground limestone transit. But Ohrid is drained by just one river, the Drin, which empties into the Adriatic 110km (69 miles) away, and its enormous depths take 70 years to exchange. Now that precarious eco-stability is threatened – by an increase in the shoreline population; by largely uncontrolled tourism; and by the diversion, in 1963, of the Sateska river into the lake. The Sateska has dumped huge quantities of silt, and tons of rubbish and toxic waste, into the fragile ecosystem. Around Pogradec, a lovely and ancient resort on the Albanian lakeshore, you can see the signs of transborder co-operation, as Albanians and Macedonians demonstrate a willingness to work in tandem to preserve their truly precious lake.

HOW TO GET THERE:
By air to Tirana, Albania, then taxi/taxi-van/bus to Pogradec.
WHEN TO GO:
April to October.
NEAREST TOWN:
Pogradec, on the lake shore, close to some of Ohrid's most beautiful and varied scenery.

YOU SHOULD KNOW
The Albanian Adriatic is Shakespeare's Illyria, a byword for natural beauty.

SANTORINI

Greece

Rising from the blue waters of the Sea of Crete in the eastern Mediterranean, the picture-postcard multicoloured cliffs of Santorini belie their cataclysmic past. As your boat or plane approaches the island, it is a sobering thought that the circular bay was once the heart of a volcano. In around 1650BC, a massive eruption emptied the chamber below the volcano of magma with such speed and force that the entire mountain collapsed into the void left behind. It is estimated that 30 cubic km (7 cubic miles) of magma must have been thrown out to create a bay this size. The traces of previous eruptions can be seen in the coloured bands of rock on the island's cliffs: each one is a layer of compressed ash ejected in one eruption. The little island in the middle of the bay is evidence of more recent volcanic activity, where a new volcano has formed in the heart of the old one. It has long been thought that the eruption could be connected with Plato's legend of the lost island of Atlantis, even though his land was located in the Atlantic Ocean. Evidence now suggests that he may have been relating a tale, corrupted over more than 1,200 years, of the destruction of the Minoan civilization on Crete by a tsunami created when the mountain collapsed. Whether this is true or not, this is a beautiful island with spectacular scenery.

HOW TO GET THERE:
By boat from the Greek mainland or other Greek islands or by plane from Athens or Thessaloniki.
WHEN TO GO:
Spring to autumn.
NEAREST TOWN:
Heraklion, Crete 123km (76 miles).

HOW TO GET THERE:
By plane or boat to the island, then by car.
WHEN TO GO:
Between June and October for the loggerhead's reproductive season.
NEAREST TOWN:
Keri.

YOU SHOULD KNOW
Many restrictions apply to the protected areas, which include boating and water sports within the sea itself.

LOGGERHEAD TURTLES, ZAKYNTHOS

Greece

Of the eight species of sea turtle swimming the oceans today, the loggerhead is the largest. Greece is the only country within Europe where these turtles nest, and the sandy beaches of Laganas Bay, on the island of Zakynthos, host the largest nesting colony of this endangered species. At night, between June and August, the female loggerheads drag themselves up the beach to lay some 200 eggs, which they cover with warm sand. In 1999 a National Marine Park was established in southern Zakynthos to protect about 6km (4 miles) of separate, sandy beaches where about 900 turtles come to nest each year. Sadly, by 2004, many violations of the protection laws were occurring. However, as of 2010, Greek authorities do not allow planes to take off or land at night in Zakynthos in order to protect the turtles.

THE SAMARIA GORGE

Greece

The Samaria Gorge is a spectacular geological feature in western Crete that is also important in the island's history. It is Crete's only national park. This gash in the White Mountains drops 1,250m (4,100ft) in 16km (10 miles). For thousands of years, its secret tracks have provided a last hiding place, and secret base, for the locals to go when invaders strike.

Today, its well-trodden, if still tricky, path is a must-do for visitors to the island. Most people get the bus from Chania to Omalos at the top of the gorge and then pick up a boat ride at Agia Roumeli to return to Chania. The first section of the trail is a steep descent of 1,000m (3,300ft) in less than 2km (1 mile), down a feature known as the Wooden Stairs. The other 14km (9 miles) is a relatively easy descent of 250m (800ft), and it is much easier to appreciate the spectacular scenery and wildflowers. The old village of Samaria, halfway down the gorge, is also a good place to catch your breath and take in the delightful views before making the final descent towards the Iron Gates, where the sides of the gorge narrow dramatically to leave a passage a mere 3m (10ft) across. Late spring, when the wildflowers are at their best, is the ideal time to undertake this hike: the gorge is not opened until the river has stopped flowing and in the height of summer, the heat in the gorge can be stifling. For this reason, an early start is a good idea, so that you spend as little of the four to seven hours the descent takes in the heat of the day.

HOW TO GET THERE:
By bus from Chania to Omalos.
WHEN TO GO:
Late spring.
NEAREST TOWN:
Omalos.

YOU SHOULD KNOW
It is advisable to take plenty of water and a snack or two.

MOUNT OLYMPUS

Greece

Steeped in ancient history, Mount Olympus is the highest mountain in Greece. Once home to the appallingly behaved principal ancient Greek gods, this is where Zeus stood to fling thunderbolts at anyone who displeased him. The archaeological museum at Dion is where Alexander the Great made sacrifices to the Olympian gods before setting off to conquer lands as far away as India.

The lower slopes of the mountain have a rich variety of plants: more than 1,700 species have been identified here. It became Greece's first national park in 1937 and is especially rich in wildflowers in late spring. The sides of the mountain are cloaked in forests of beech, cedar, oak and pine, in which bears, lynx and wolves roam. In ancient times it was forbidden for humans to set foot on this mountain, but the restriction was lifted centuries ago.

The highest of the eight peaks, Mytikas (or 'Nose') was first reached in 1913 by the local Christos Kakalos and Swiss mountaineers Frederic Boissonas and Daniel Baud-Bovy. The hike from Litochoro at sea level up this 2,919-m (9,570-ft) giant and back takes most people two days. There are many trails up the mountain and refuges to stay at overnight, although you may need to book in summer. The climb is not difficult in itself, but the mountain can be hazardous in bad weather. The beautiful scenery and stunning views make the effort worthwhile.

HOW TO GET THERE:
By road or rail from Athens or Thessaloniki to Litochoro.
WHEN TO GO:
In good weather between June and August.
NEAREST TOWN:
Litochoro 10km (6 miles).

YOU SHOULD KNOW
Sunscreen, good hiking boots, a map, food and water, a sleeping bag and warm clothes are necessary.

DON'T MISS
The archaeological museum at Dion at the foot of the mountain.

GÖREME NATIONAL PARK

Greece

HOW TO GET THERE:
By road from Kayseri.
WHEN TO GO:
Spring to autumn.
NEAREST TOWN:
Üçhisar 3km (2 miles).

YOU SHOULD KNOW
Although the volcanoes are now extinct, earth tremors can occur.

DON'T MISS
A balloon ride over the area.

In the heart of Cappadocia, Göreme National Park has one of the strangest landscapes on Earth. Over millions of years, volcanoes in the area covered the land with thick layers of soft tuff stone, which were then covered with layers of lava that hardened and sealed the top. Eventually, water broke through and the soft rock below became subject to weathering, which has carved it into conical pillars, towers and needles of varying colours and heights of up to 40–50m (130–165ft). The volcanic plain once covered some 10,000 sq km (3,850 sq miles) of landscape and the park now protects the central 95 sq km (37 sq miles). The soft rock is also easily carved by humans, and over the centuries many of the pillars, the so-called fairy chimneys, have been turned into homes or churches. The latter are famous for their Byzantine murals. Away from the villages, the landscape is best explored on foot or by bicycle. A popular walk is the 12-km (7.5-mile) circuitous path to Üçhisar through the Uzundere valley. The valleys are dominated by the volcanoes that produced the landscape, such as Erciyas Dag and Hasan Dag. Up in the hills of this spectacular valley, wolves and beech martens can sometimes be spotted, and badgers, foxes and hares also inhabit the park. Although it is expensive, a popular way to get a grasp on the whole landscape – and to get amazing photographs – is to take one of the many balloon trips on offer. Drifting over this weird landscape on a clear, still morning is a magical experience.

MOUNT ARARAT

Turkey

Lying in the far east of Anatolia, Mount Ararat (Agri Dagi) is worth taking the trouble to visit, both for its beauty and its importance in the Bible, as it is the site where the Book of Genesis says that Noah's Ark came to rest after the great flood. The higher of this volcano's two peaks, Buyuk Agri, is the highest in Turkey, at 5,137m (16,854ft). Mount Ararat is not extinct, but merely dormant; the last eruption was in 1840. In 2004 the area around and including Mount Ararat was designated as the Kackar Mountains National Park, but access to the mountain is by permit only for foreign visitors because this is a politically sensitive area. Permits must be applied for at least two months before a proposed visit through a registered tourist agency that operates treks. However, reaching the summit of the mountain makes all the hassle worthwhile.

The views from the snow-covered peak – across to Iran and Armenia and west across the plain – are spectacular. Climbs leave from the village of Eli and normally take five to six days for the ascent and descent. The climb is strenuous and not for the inexperienced.

HOW TO GET THERE:
By air to Van, then by road.
WHEN TO GO:
The climbing season is from June to September.
NEAREST TOWN:
Doguveyazit 10km (6 miles).

YOU SHOULD KNOW

Cloud tends to gather in the afternoon, so the final summit should be attempted in the morning.

DEMIRKAZIK

Turkey

HOW TO GET THERE:
By road from Adana or Kayseri.
WHEN TO GO:
July to September.
NEAREST TOWN:
Demirkazik village.

Demirkazik, at 3,756m (12,323ft), is the highest peak in the Taurus mountains, which run along 560km (350 miles) of southern Turkey's southeast coast. This portion of the chain is known locally as Aladaglar, the crimson mountains. There are various well-known climbing routes on the mountain. The first successful ascent was made in 1927, but the dangerous north wall was not conquered until 1991. The climb to the peak is for experienced climbers only, but there are other easier routes on the lower slopes. The Taurus mountains are young, geologically speaking, and are still in the process of being raised as the African plate moves north, squeezing the Anatolian plate into the Eurasian plate in the north and grinding past it in the east. Demirkazik dominates the eastern end of the Aladaglar National Park and the valley below, and it is hard to turn your eyes away. For those who are not climbers, there is a beautiful landscape to see in the region, including the pine forests, karst rock formations, pretty waterfalls, underground streams, some of the largest caves in the country and the beautiful Yedigoller (Seven Lakes valley).

KARAPINAR CRATER LAKES

Turkey

The area around Karapinar in south-central Anatolia is an ancient volcanic landscape, dotted with cinder cones, lava fields and craters. There are numerous lakes within the craters and two of the best known are Aci Gölü ('bitter lake') and Meke Gölü ('smelling lake'). The former is beautiful, and at night sparkles with light, while the latter is blue-green and salty. In this dry area, they are both important sources of water for birds. The caldera in which Meke Gölü sits was created millions of years ago in an eruption so massive that it caused the top of the volcano to collapse, while the eruption that caused the 300-m (1,000-ft) cinder cone in the middle is much more recent, occurring about 9,000 years ago. Everywhere you go in Turkey you will see blue-glass beads called *nazar boncugu* that ward off the evil eye, and Meke Gölü is said to be the country's own version. In a geologically active land, prone to earthquakes, people have long been aware of their surroundings: a wall painting at nearby Çatalhöyük showing a volcanic eruption has been dated to about 6200BC. Although off the beaten track, these beautiful lakes are well worth a detour.

HOW TO GET THERE:
By road from Könya.
WHEN TO GO:
Summer.
NEAREST TOWN:
Karapinar 10km (6 miles).

Right: The spectacular Meke Gölü crate lake in Turkey

HOW TO GET THERE:
By air to Van, then by road or by train to Tatvan.
WHEN TO GO:
Summer.
NEAREST TOWN:
Tatvan 15km (9 miles).

NEMRUT DAGI

Turkey

Nemrut Dagi, a volcano at the western end of Lake Van, is named after Nimrod, the mighty hunter who, according to legend, ruled here in ancient times. It is now 3,050m (10,000ft) high, having lost its top 1,400m (4,600ft) in an eruption some 6,000 years ago. The lava blocked the river running around its base and led to the creation of Lake Van. Two craters, evidence of more recent, if smaller, eruptions, have lakes within them. The views from the crater rim over Lake Van are amazing. Once into the crater, you will find a different, and totally unexpected, world: in contrast to the arid slopes of the mountain, there is vegetation including juniper, aspen and beech. The crater lakes provide a stopping-off point for a variety of birds. The larger, crescent-shaped lake – Sogukgöl – is cold, except for some hot springs towards the middle of the caldera, while the waters of the smaller lake – Sicakgöl – are warm, indicating that the rocks below are still hot, although whether this is because of continuing volcanic activity deep down or residual heat is not clear. It is an ideal place for a swim after a dusty climb.

THE CHIMAERA

Turkey

DON'T MISS
The ruins of nearby Olympos and the beautiful beach.

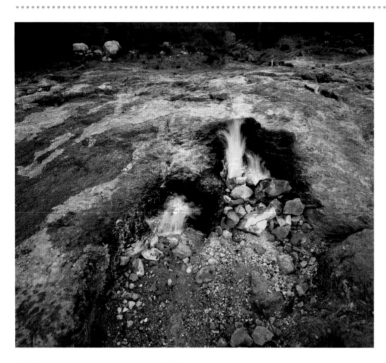

To the ancient Greeks, the Chimaera was a fire-breathing monster with the head and front paws of a lion, the body of a goat and the tail of a serpent, and this name long ago attached itself to this astonishing site, where flames spontaneously ignite as gas emerges from fissures in the bare rocks. The Chimaera is a stiff, 30-minute walk up a steep, and in places slippery, path from the car park north of the hamlet of Çirali. At its foot are the scant remains of a temple to Hephaistos, the Greek god of fire. The phenomenon is eerie during the day, but is best seen at night and a popular time to make the trip is just before sunset, although this entails a torchlight scramble back down the path. The gases are released as a result of geological processes deep in the Earth below, as the Anatolian plate is squeezed between the African and Eurasian plates. Although methane has been detected in the gas, its exact composition is unknown, and if you put out one of the flames, it will soon reignite itself. A couple of miles to the south, along the beach where loggerhead and green sea turtles nest, or along part of the inland route of the Lycian Way, is the ancient site of Olympos, with ruins from the second century BC to the 12th century AD, including an ancient theatre, church, rock-cut tombs and parts of a villa and aqueduct. Out of the high tourist season, wildlife in the stream here includes turtles, kingfishers and water rails. The surrounding landscape of the Olympos Beydaglari National Park is full of forested hillsides, secluded valleys and craggy peaks, and on some of the higher slopes red squirrels are sometimes seen.

HOW TO GET THERE:
By road, taking the road marked 'Çirali 7, Yanartas, Chimaera' off the A400 south from Antalya to Kumluca.
WHEN TO GO:
In autumn, out of the main tourist season.
NEAREST TOWN:
Kumluca 26km (16 miles).

DON'T MISS
A swim in the thermal baths.

PAMUKKALE

Turkey

HOW TO GET THERE:
By road from Denizli.
WHEN TO GO:
Any time of year.
NEAREST TOWN:
Denizli 20km (12 miles).

Visible from kilometres away, the dazzling 100-m (330-ft) white cliff of Pamukkale is one of the geological wonders of the world. Water from hot springs on the volcanic plateau above bubbles out of the ground at 35°C (95°F) and streams down the side of the cliff, depositing calcium carbonate in the form of blinding-white travertine as it cools and creates strangely shaped terraces and pools as it goes. *Pamukkale* means 'cotton fortress' and according to legend the white cliffs were created when the giant Titans left their crop of cotton out to dry. Over thousands of years, the terraces have grown out from the cliff like a magical giant staircase or solid waterfall. Everywhere you go, you are accompanied by the sound of splashing water. Because of earlier damage to the soft, porous rock, only a few terraces are open to the public, but paths lead right around the site. At the top of the cliff, it is possible to bathe in the town's thermal baths, which include the original sacred spring. As you swim about, you can see the water bubbling out of the ground beneath you. The site, and the supposedly health-giving effects of the water, have been known about for thousands of years, and the ruins of ancient Hierapolis, which grew up around the spring, dot the top of the cliff. Close to the baths is the Plutonium, a grotto sacred to the god of the underworld. From the grille that prevents entry, you can hear rushing water and the hiss of the poisonous gas that escapes from the ground here.

TROODOS MOUNTAINS

Cyprus

Directly behind the crowded beaches of western Cyprus lies a cool sanctuary of pine-scented forests, reaching up past fertile valleys to a series of high peaks, alternately snowcapped or flower-strewn according to the seasons. These are the Troodos mountains, the backbone of the island. Their centre is the small village of Troodos itself, on the east flank of Mount Olympos, the highest peak in Cyprus at 1,952m (6,402ft). From here, four distinct regions fan out, each with its own character and specialities. Solea, to the west and 56km (35 miles) from Lefkosia (Nicosia), is known as Apple valley. The picturesque mountain villages of Galata and Kakopetria are famous for their folk architecture and painted churches. The Pitsillia district covers the eastern slopes of the range, where ancient hamlets cling to steep vineyards and orchards of hazelnut and almond trees. The fertile northern valley of Marathassa produces world-beating cherries, and is the setting for the 11th-century Kykko Monastery – most important and richest of the ten Byzantine churches in the region listed as World Heritage Sites for their exquisite icons, frescoes and architecture. The Krassochoria region to the south is just as charming.

HOW TO GET THERE:
By road from Paphos.
WHEN TO GO:
Year-round; best in spring
and autumn.
NEAREST TOWNS:
Platres, Kakopetria.

MOUNT OLYMPOS

Cyprus

HOW TO GET THERE:
By road from Paphos
or Lemosos.
WHEN TO GO:
Year-round. January to March
for skiing.
NEAREST TOWN:
Lemesos 51km (32 miles).

DON'T MISS
The abandoned
Hadjipavlou
chromite mine.

At the heart of the Troodos mountains in western Cyprus stands Mount Olympos, at 1,952m (6,402ft) the island's highest peak, known locally as Chionistra. If you ignore its actual summit – crowned by a huge globe full of military tracking and communication devices, and surrounded by heavy barbed-wire – the mountain can be truly magical. Its beauty is in its precipitous valleys where highland forests give way to orchards and fields of wildflowers. Each has its own special character, evident in the ancient hamlets that cling to the hillsides and in the tiny, Byzantine masterpieces of their 11th- to 15th-century churches. The mountainside is a maze of trails where cool, leafy glades open suddenly on huge vistas, and whatever the season, the world seems reborn in the crystal air. From January to March, even when visitors are sunbathing on the coast 120km (75 miles) away, Mount Olympos has enough snow for undemanding skiing.

DON'T MISS
The monasteries
of the Qadisha valley.

FOREST OF THE CEDARS OF GOD

Lebanon

The cedars of Lebanon have been venerated throughout history. In ancient times they grew in profusion across the land, but today the trees that grow on the slopes of Mount Makmel, which towers over the Qadisha valley, are some of the last survivors of those forests. Known as Arz el-Rab or the 'Cedars of God', this precious grove of trees grows at an altitude of over 2,000m (6,562ft) and was listed as a UNESCO World Heritage Site in 1998. The cedar of Lebanon is a coniferous tree that is both very slow growing and very long lived. Although there are fewer than 500 trees protected on these slopes, 12 of them are well over 1,000 years old. They have large trunks, some reaching 14m (46ft) in circumference, and are up to 35m (115ft) high. Their shape is dependent on density – taller and straighter in higher densities, but producing spreading, horizontal branches where they have the space.

Over thousands of years these beautiful trees have been prized by every civilization, and their exploitation is the reason that relatively few remain today. The Phoenicians used the wood for ship building, the resin was used by ancient Egyptians in the mummification process, Moses commanded Jewish priests to use the bark in circumcision ceremonies, and cedar wood was also used by the Romans, Greeks, Persians, Assyrians and Babylonians.

HOW TO GET THERE:
By road.
WHEN TO GO:
It is beautiful at all times of year, particularly in winter, when the trees look superb under a covering of snow.
NEAREST TOWNS:
The village of Bqaa Kafra is close to the Forest of the Cedars of God. Or Beirut, 121km (76 miles).

MOUNT HERMON

Syria/Israel

HOW TO GET THERE:
From Syria, Israel or Lebanon.
WHEN TO GO:
All year round.
NEAREST TOWNS:
On the mountain itself are the Israeli town of Neve Ativ and the Druze town of Majdal Shams.

Uncomfortably divided between Syria and Israel, and overlooking Lebanon, Mount Hermon, known in Arabic as Jabal Ash Shaykh, is something of a political hot potato. The southern and western slopes were captured by Israel in 1967 and unilaterally annexed in 1980. Syria controls the highest peak, where they have a military observation post, and there are also plans for developing a multi-billion-dollar ski resort. Israel already has its only ski resort here, a popular getaway for thousands of Israelis who can hike in lovely countryside in the summer months and enjoy skiing and other winter sports during winter and spring. Israeli Security Forces have a heavily guarded observation post at Mitzpe Shelagim. Mount Hermon, which stands at the northern tip of the Golan Heights is, in fact, a group of mountains with three separate summits, the highest of which rises to 2,814m (9,230ft), and is in Syrian hands. The mountain is crucially important to the people who live in this most politically sensitive part of the world, not only for political reasons but also because its height traps a great deal of precipitation in an area that is otherwise extremely arid. All three of the peaks are snow-covered for much of the year, and even in the middle of summer there will be snowy areas at the highest points.

HOW TO GET THERE:
By road from Jerusalem or Amman.
WHEN TO GO:
Spring or autumn.
NEAREST TOWN:
El Ariha 10km (6 miles).

THE DEAD SEA

Israel

Any description of the Dead Sea contains superlatives: it is the deepest exposed point on the Earth's surface and it is the deepest hypersaline lake on the planet. However, contrary to popular belief, it is not the saltiest water on the planet: Lake Asai in Djibouti and Don Juan Pond in western Antarctica both have greater salinity. However, it is the salt that prevents the lake harbouring anything but extremely hardy bacteria and microbes. It lies on the border between Jordan, Israel and the West Bank in the Jordan valley. It is so salty because it has no outlet and receives minimal amounts of rain. Most of the water entering the lake is rich with minerals, including salt, and when the water evaporates, the salt remains. In recent years the flow in the Jordan has lessened while evaporation rates have stayed the same, so the lake is both shrinking and getting saltier. The southern part of the lake is drying out rapidly and giving way to salt flats. Its mineral-rich muds are thought by many to have health-giving properties, and there are spas and treatment centres dotted around the lake's edge.

THE AVSHALOM CAVE

Israel

HOW TO GET THERE:
By road from Jerusalem
or Tel Aviv.
WHEN TO GO:
All year round.
NEAREST TOWN:
Beit Shemesh 2km (1 mile).

The star attraction of the Avshalom Reserve, on the western foothills of the Judean Hills, is the Avshalom, or Soreq, Cave, the only 'show cave' in Israel. In 1968, whilst blasting was being carried out in a nearby quarry, an opening into this magnificent cave was exposed. The discovery was not made public for nine years, during which time wooden walkways were constructed and a special lighting system was installed in order to protect the living formations within. A relatively small cave, Soreq is some 83m (273ft) long, 60m (198ft) wide and 15m (50ft) high. What makes it unique is the sheer quantity, beauty and variety of its formations. Created millions of years ago by surface water penetrating and dissolving the limestone, once the cave had been hollowed out, the droplets, full of limestone sediments, began depositing this sediment on both the floor and the ceiling, and over hundreds of thousands of years these grew, and continue to grow, into slender stalactites and stalagmites in all sorts of unusual shapes, some as much as 3,000 years old. There are many different types of speleothems and flowstone walls that divide the cave into different chambers, and many of them are active formations, undergoing a process of continuous change.

WADI RUM

Jordan

Wadi Rum is quite simply one of the most astonishingly, austerely beautiful places in the world. It fulfils every romantic notion of a desert landscape, complete with sheer, dark-granite mountains, sandstone ridges rising vertically from the pink sand of the desert floor, and ancient graffiti scratched on the rocks of these vast and silent valleys. Man has inhabited this place from Neolithic times, and the presence of freshwater springs made it a natural meeting place for caravans wending their way across the desert. In the 1st century BC, the Nabataeans settled here, before decamping to the rose-coloured city of Petra. Everyone left their mark in the form of Neolithic flint axes, Iron Age pottery, cave paintings and a Nabataean temple. Jabal Rum is the highest peak here at 1,754m (5,315ft). On a clear day, rock climbers can see both the Saudi Arabian border and the Red Sea from the summit. In early spring, after the rains, the desert explodes with life. Wildflowers colour the landscape while eagles and buzzards wheel and drift in the sky above, just two of the 110 bird species recorded here. Nomadic Bedouin still graze their herds, judging when to pack up and move on. This is a protected environment: before entering Wadi Rum you will find the fort of the famous Desert Patrol, who police the area astride camels, wearing flowing robes and red-and-white headdresses, daggers at their waists and rifles across their backs. Rest under the vast, star-spangled night sky sipping a cardamon coffee, and listen to the sound of silence.

HOW TO GET THERE:
By road from Aqaba or Petra.
WHEN TO GO:
March, April, September,
October and November.
NEAREST TOWNS:
Wadi Rum village 6km
(4 miles); Rashidiya 30km
(19 miles).

TANGEH SAVASHI, ALBORZ MOUNTAINS
Iran

The Alborz mountain range is located in northern Iran, which stretches from the Armenian border and around the Caspian Sea, ending in the east at the borders of Afghanistan and Turkmenistan. Between 60km (37.5 miles) and 130km (81 miles) in width, this range contains the largest of Iran's mountains, with Mount Damavand rising to 5,670m (18,600ft). This peak is permanently snow-covered, and the whole range endures long, cold, snowy winters, during which Iranians flock to the ski resorts that have sprung up.

The northern slopes of the Alborz are covered with deciduous trees that form the largest area of vegetation in the country. These forests are home to the alborz red sheep, the orcal ram and the endemic Iranian wild ass, as well as gazelle, ibex, porcupine, badger and mongoose, and this plentiful wildlife has drawn hunters to the area for centuries. Tangeh Savashi is a narrow mountain pass within the range, gouged out by a stream that is fed by a series of lovely waterfalls further upstream. This was once the favourite hunting ground of the Qajar king, Fath Ali Shah (1797–1834), who kept a hunting lodge on the lush grassland here. Midway through the pass, which is 1km (0.6 miles) long and 4m (13ft) wide, a bas-relief can be found, depicting the king, his sons and grandsons in hunting scenes. Carved into a niche in the mountainside by order of the king, the relief is sheltered from the worst of the weather and remains well preserved. It is, however, quite difficult to access, and involves fording the stream (which can be waist-deep at times) that runs through the gorge, and clambering along a precipitous mountain path.

HOW TO GET THERE:
By road.
WHEN TO GO:
Mid-April to early June, and late September to early November.
NEAREST TOWN:
Firouzkouh 15km (9 miles).

THE CASPIAN SEA

Iran

Bordered by Russia, Turkmenistan, Azerbaijan, Kazakhstan and Iran, the Caspian Sea is classified either as the world's largest lake, or its smallest sea. Formed some 30 million years ago, it became landlocked about 5.5 million years ago and has no natural outlet, apart from evaporation, other than the Manych canal, which connects it to the Black Sea. Forming Iran's northern boundary, the lake is fed by numerous small rivers and streams. However, Iranian rivers only provide 10 per cent of the Caspian's water – 90 per cent is supplied by only five rivers, the largest of which is the Volga. Despite this, the Caspian is saline, though much less so than most oceans, and this is attributed to its origin as an ancient ocean, connected to both the Atlantic and Pacific oceans. The Caspian Sea is of major economic interest to all those who border it, but the water boundaries of the five nations have not yet been fully established. This is an energy-rich area – major oil and natural gas fields have been found here, but this is not the only difficulty: there is the problem of access to international waters, currently only possible through Russia's Volga river and canal system. Finally, there is a great deal of money to be made through fishing – 90 per cent of the world's sturgeon swim in these waters, and caviar is big business. There are about 120 species of fish in the southern part of the Caspian Sea, including seven species and subspecies of sturgeon, and Iranian caviar is renowned.

ALI SADR CAVE

Iran

The Ali Sadr Cave is one of Iran's most famous natural wonders. Situated in the Soubashi mountains to the north of the city of Hamadan, the limestone cave is highly unusual. It is a water cave; however, the water within it is more like a series of long lakes than a river. An inscription at the entrance of the man-made tunnel makes it clear that it was built during the reign of Darius 1 (521–485 BC). Formed some 70 million years ago, the cave has been used by man for 1,200 years. For years the cave acted as a reservoir for people in the nearby village, but in 1978, when the water supply diminished, a local man followed the tunnel deep into the mountain in search of more. New areas of the cave were discovered in 1994, and in 2000 a German expedition began a survey that eventually charted 11km (7 miles) of canals. On entering the tunnel, a passageway leads to a wharf. From here, the journey must be undertaken by boat.

RUB' AL KHALI

Saudi Arabia

Rub' al Khali, meaning the 'Empty Quarter', is also known as the Great Sandy Desert. This vast area, 1,000km (600 miles) long and 500km (300 miles) wide, is virtually uninhabited and, until recently, largely unexplored. Formed over two million years ago, this great sand desert occupies over 25 per cent of Saudi Arabia, and stretches into Oman, Yemen and the United Arab Emirates. Some 40,000 years ago this was a fertile area, covered with a number of lakes that were filled by monsoons that subsequently moved on to Egypt and India. Remnants of this era can still be seen in the perfectly fossilized teeth of hippopotamus and the bones of water buffalo, long-horned cattle, goats and gazelle – even freshwater shells have been discovered. Today, 24 bird species, 31 plant species, arachnids and rodents are the only things that can survive the harsh environment. Nomadic Bedouin move around the outer edges, but before 300AD, when the desertification was not as severe, caravans carrying frankincense crossed the Rub' al Khali, stopping at cities now lost in the shifting sands. At night, the temperature drops to 0°C (32°F) and frequently surpasses 55°C (131°F) at noon, and where once there was water, now there are enormous sand dunes over 250m (800ft) high. Beneath this vast, inhospitable expanse of sand lies a wealth of oil, possibly the largest reserves on the planet, and the source of Saudi Arabia's fortune.

HOW TO GET THERE:
Some tour companies offer GPS-equipped excursions into the desert.
WHEN TO GO:
Between November and February.
NEAREST TOWN:
Najran, close to the Yemeni border.

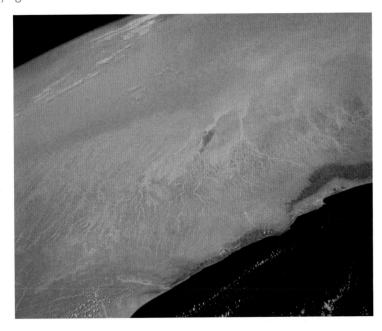

YOU SHOULD KNOW
Saudi Arabia issues only a few, restricted, expensive visas to visitors.

AUSTRALASIA & OCEANIA

THE TWELVE APOSTLES

Australia

HOW TO GET THERE:
On the Great Ocean Road.
WHEN TO GO:
Spring to autumn.
NEAREST TOWN:
Port Campbell 7km (4 miles).

Just off the coast of southern Victoria is a spectacular group of limestone sea stacks. Originally they were known as the sow and her pigs, but were renamed in the 1950s. The howling winds and high seas of the Southern Ocean are eating away at the soft limestone walls of the coast here, and these stacks are the remnants of land that has already fallen into the sea. They are under threat themselves: in the winter of 2005, one of them collapsed into the sea in a matter of seconds. The cliffs here are up to 70m (230ft) high, and the tallest of the apostles is about 45m (150ft). They are a spectacular sight from the clifftops, with the waves crashing against them. The wider area of the Twelve Apostles Marine National Park also has areas where visitors can swim, surf, kayak, snorkel or dive, if weather and wave conditions allow. Diving is permitted both on the wreck of the Lorc Ard and in the area of the underwater canyons known as the The Arches, where there are spectacular landscapes of seaweed-covered walls with sea fans, lace corals and sea mosses. Sometimes there are fur seals playing here, zipping through tunnels and underneath arches. This is rightly one of the three most popular natural attractions in Australia.

DON'T MISS
A swim in a pool
in Mossman Gorge.

THE WET TROPICS OF QUEENSLAND
Australia

In the 1980s, a battle was waged between environmentalists and the federal government on one hand and the timber industry and the state government on the other. This resulted in the addition to the World Heritage List of a 450-km (280-mile) swathe of the coastal area of northern Queensland between Townsville and Cooktown in order to prevent any more logging in the area. What remains is a unique environment, with plants that are examples of types found on the ancient supercontinent of Gondwana. But the area is not just important as a living relic of evolution: it is also beautiful, with rugged peaks, beautiful sandy beaches, dramatic gorges, dense rainforest and Australia's tallest single-drop falls, the Wallaman Falls, near Trebonne.

Lying between the coast and the Atherton Tablelands and their dry, eucalypt habitat, the forests contain eucalypts, banksias and paperbark trees. Around the rivers there are swamps, and mangroves protect the coasts. Mossman Gorge, near the town of the same name, has spectacular scenery and lovely swimming holes. This protected, pristine area is brimming with wildlife, from cassowaries and tree kangaroos to golden bowerbirds, yellow-bellied gliders and estuarine crocodiles. Its four national parks are havens for the animals that live in this tiny relic of a habitat that once occupied much of Australia.

HOW TO GET THERE:
By air to Cairns, then by road.
WHEN TO GO:
Any time except December to March when it is hot and humid and the roads are often impassable.
NEAREST TOWN:
Cairns.

GLASSHOUSE MOUNTAINS

Australia

A few miles in from Queensland's Sunshine Coast, a set of strange landforms dominate the plain around them. They are visible from the sea and were given their name by Captain Cook, who thought their shimmer in the distance was similar to that of sun on glass. They are the plugs of volcanoes active some 25–27 million years ago, left standing proud of the sandstone plateau around them, which has been eroded away to a depth of several hundred metres, leaving these structures. Much of the area around the peaks consists of national parkland, and there are trails of varying grades through eucalypt forests, plantations, scrubby gum, coastal rainforest, melaleuca swamp and casuarina groves. There is also a 22-km (14-mile) scenic Forest Drive that runs through the park and has several good lookout points. Although several of the peaks should only be attempted by climbers, others, like Mount Beerburrum, Mount Ngungun and designated tracks on Mounts Tibrogargan and Beerwah, are more accessible.

DON'T MISS
The view from the Glasshouse Mountains lookout.

HOW TO GET THERE:
By road or rail from Brisbane.
WHEN TO GO:
In good weather from spring to autumn.
NEAREST TOWN:
Caboolture 20km (12 miles).

NORFOLK ISLAND

Australia

HOW TO GET THERE:
By air from Sydney, Brisbane, Newcastle or Auckland.
WHEN TO GO:
Any time of year.
NEAREST TOWN:
Auckland 1,080km (690 miles).

Fringed by the blue waters of the Pacific Ocean, this tiny island has some of the most beautiful, and most precious, landscapes you will ever find. Hundreds of kilometres from the nearest landmass, it has its own unique plants, including the Norfolk Island pine, as well as rainforests full of giant tree ferns. A third of the island is a national park and botanic garden that protect many of the species that are unique to the island or endangered. Walking and cycling trails allow visitors to get up close to the world's tallest tree ferns and to lose themselves in this green haven. The island is also home to several extremely rare birds, including the Norfolk Island green parrot and the Norfolk Island morepork (also known as the boobook owl), which was down to one female in the late 1980s before two males of a closely related species were brought to the island. The sacred kingfisher is more common and can be seen all over the island. There are also plenty of spectacular seabirds during the breeding season. Norfolk Island's greatest jewel is, perhaps, its fringing coral reefs, which are full of brightly coloured corals and shoals of spectacular fish.

THE GREAT BARRIER REEF

Australia

The Great Barrier Reef stretches some 2,000km (1,250 miles) from near Bundaberg in the south to the Torres Strait that separates Queensland and Papua New Guinea in the north. The main part of the coral reef sits on the continental shelf off the coast, protecting lagoons, cays and islands between itself and the mainland. There are more than 2,600 individual reefs, covering an area of 350,000 sq km (135,100 sq miles). Some 400 different types of coral give the reef its amazing colours and shapes, and also provide homes for 4,000 species of mollusc, 1,500 types of fish, 350 species of starfish, sea urchins and other echinoderms and uncounted types of crabs, shrimp and other crustaceans. The most popular way to get close to the corals is by diving or snorkelling from one of the many tour boats, but glass-bottomed boats and semi-submersibles allow you to look without getting wet. Helicopter rides over the corals provide a good overview of the structure. This marvel of nature is under a number of threats: rising sea levels, the water becoming both too warm and too acidic for the corals to survive, pollution, damage from fishing nets and anchors, the threat of drilling for oil and damage from cyclones. Sport-fishing near the reef is thought by some to be partly responsible for a cyclical problem: the crown-of-thorns starfish, which preys on the corals. Get there while you can.

HOW TO GET THERE:
From any of the coastal towns offering boat trips.
WHEN TO GO:
Spring to autumn.

YOU SHOULD KNOW
Coral is sharp!

BUCHAN CAVES RESERVE

Australia

In the heart of Victoria's southern Gippsland, the Buchan Caves Reserve surrounds two of the most spectacular show caves in Australia: the Royal Cave and the Fairy Cave.

The 400-m (1,300-ft) Fairy Cave has several distinctive stalagmite and stalagmite formations, including the Jewel Chamber, the Grotto, the Wedding Cake, the Hall, the Bridal Chamber, the King's Chamber and the Queen Victoria Chamber. Different colours are caused by different minerals being deposited with the calcium carbonate from which the formations are made: copper makes green shades, while the rusts and browns are caused by iron oxide.

The Royal Cave has formations such as Niagara Falls and the Font of the Gods, a beautiful pool ringed with calcite formations. Important archaeological finds have been made at the Buchan Caves and other caves in the area, including the fossilized bones of a horse-sized wombat and an equally large kangaroo skeleton, as well as evidence of Aboriginal occupation from about 15,000BC. The surrounding reserve has a variety of animals, including koalas and kangaroos, as well as more than 40 species of birds, among them the currawong, whose fluting tones ring through the air as they call out their own name.

HOW TO GET THERE:
By road from Canberra or Melbourne.
WHEN TO GO:
Any time of year.
NEAREST TOWN:
Buchan 1km (0.5 miles).

DON'T MISS
The guided tours through the caves.

THE PAINTED DESERT

Australia

Northeast of the opal-mining town of Coober Pedy, in the northern part of South Australia, is one of the most unusual landscapes that visitors will ever encounter. Once the floor of an ancient sea, this land has been eroding for millions of years and the different soils, gravels and rocks that make up the mesas and mountains here create a colourful landscape whose hues change from minute to minute with the changing light. The rapid changes at dawn and dusk are particularly worth seeing. In the Moon Plains, to the south of the main part of the desert, fossils of ichthyosaurs (marine contemporaries of the dinosaurs) and other marine life have been found. There are areas of petrified wood, and evidence that the climate here was once markedly different in the form of large boulders left by glaciers. In the north, the road passes through plains covered with sheets of fragile gypsum. Although remote and desolate, this region is beautiful, with contrasting shades of rust-red, ochre yellow, rich brown and black and white. It is so photogenic that it has been used in many films, including the *Mad Max* series and *Priscilla, Queen of the Desert.* As you drive or hike through the area, the face of each mesa, mountain or hillock is a new delight to explore and photograph.

CAPE BYRON

Australia

Cape Byron, the most easterly point in mainland Australia, was named by Captain Cook in honour of an earlier circumnavigator of the globe. Just south of the laidback town of Byron Bay, this headland's rocky cliffs support coastal rainforest and heath, and a beautiful banksia forest. There are three trails on the headland: the clifftop path, the coastal footpath and a shady track that leads you through the bushland. Lookouts give jaw-dropping, panoramic views over the green hinterland, white sandy beaches and out over the Pacific Ocean. The headland's position makes it a great place for watching large marine wildlife from above. This area is a hotspot for the highly endangered grey nurse shark, as well as rays, turtles, dolphins, wobbegongs, octopus and lots of subtropical fish, including clownfish. Leopard and tiger sharks can be seen here in summer, and there are occasional reports of great white sharks. The corals provide refuge for the smaller fish, anemones and starfish. From July to November hundreds of humpback whales make their way up the east coast of Australia. Because of their size, the headland is the best place to see these massive creatures as they move sedately past.

THE BLUE MOUNTAINS

Australia

Right: The Three Sisters, a formation in the Blue Mountains.

Forming part of eastern Australia's Great Dividing Range, the Blue Mountains are, in fact, the edge of the great sandstone plateau that once covered the whole of this side of the continent. Over millions of years the soft rock has slowly been eroded, creating a wonderful landscape of rugged cliffs, deep gullies, steep-sided valleys, waterfalls, caves and forests. In summer the eucalypts give off the blue haze that gives this area its name. Most visitors head for the Blue Mountains town of Katoomba, which gives easy access to such well-known sights as the Three Sisters, Echo Point and Honeymoon Lookout. To the north lie Govett's Leap, on a high cliff and offering views over one of the most beautiful landscapes on the planet, Bridal Veil Falls, Perry's Lookout and Pulpit Rock.

JERVIS BAY

Australia

HOW TO GET THERE:
By road from Sydney.
WHEN TO GO:
Any time of year.
NEAREST TOWN:
Nowra 40km (25 miles).

Some 150km (90 miles) south of Sydney is one of the most unspoiled sites in eastern Australia. An almost enclosed natural harbour measuring 16 by 10km (10 by 6 miles), it was originally purchased by the government in Canberra from the New South Wales government. A large part of the area was handed over in 1998 to the local Aboriginal people and is now officially known as the Booderee National Park and Botanic Gardens, meaning 'plenty of fish' or 'bay of plenty' in the Dhurga language. Almost the entire bay is fringed with white sandy beaches and ringed with lush green bush. The floor of the bay is carpeted with seagrasses that provide a haven for fish, the prey of the whitetailed sea eagle, which is the guardian of the Wreck Bay Aboriginal settlement and symbol of the national park. The bay is home year-round to a pod of wild bottlenose dolphins, who may approach boats if the mood takes them, as well as huge jellyfish that can sometimes be seen drifting in the astonishingly clear waters. There are also colonies of New Zealand and Australian fur seals. In winter, beyond the heads and in the surrounding coastal areas are ideal places to look for migrating humpback whales, dwarf minke, false killer and southern right whales. The land around the bay has popular beauty spots such as the Hole in the Wall and Green Patch Beach, and there are trails in the lovely bushland, too.

HOW TO GET THERE:
By road from Brisbane or
the Gold Coast.
WHEN TO GO:
Spring to autumn.
NEAREST TOWN:
Coolangatta 20km (12 miles).

SOUTHEAST QUEENSLAND'S SUBTROPICAL RAINFORESTS

Australia

Inland from the lights of the Gold Coast are wide areas of relatively untouched subtropical rainforests. The McPherson Range is a paradise for walkers. In the north, Tambourine Mountain is a 600-m (2,000-ft) plateau reached by a winding road. Eucalypt forest clings to the hillside round the gorges and falls, such as Cedar Creek Falls and Witches Falls. The walking trails to the latter, and to Cameron Falls, have spectacular lookouts. Kookaburras are common, especially near picnic areas, and galahs may be seen flitting through the trees. Shyer inhabitants of the area include koalas, brush turkeys, the nocturnal tawny frogmouth and goannas. In the south of the range, the Lamigton National Park has thickly wooded valleys with subtropical rainforest. The spectacular landscape has gorges, waterfalls and pools, caves and superb views. To the east, the Springbrook plateau has temperate rainforest with eucalypt, and a network of trails that allow you to explore the cliffs, forests, gorges and waterfalls. If there has been sufficient rain, the Waringa Pool is a great spot to cool down after a strenuous walk.

LAKE EYRE

Australia

Named after Edward Eyre, the first European to spot it in 1840, Lake Eyre is sometimes Australia's largest lake. It is at the bottom of a catchment basin that covers parts of Queensland, the Northern Territory, South Australia and western New South Wales, although only a small proporation of rainfall from any distance away reaches the lake. When dry, the floor of the basin is covered by a thick layer of salt because water from the lake is lost only through evaporation, so the minerals it carries are deposited here. It is when there are heavy rains in the immediate area of the lake that it suddenly comes alive: small creatures that have adapted to droughts that last years, suddenly emerge and thousands of birds come here to feed, bathe and breed. The land around the lake also springs to life, as plants burst into flower and seeds that have lain dormant for years sprout, all in a rush to complete their life cycle before the ground dries out again.

ROTTNEST ISLAND

Australia

Rottnest was first found in 1696 by Willem de Vlamingh, a Dutch explorer who mistook the island's small marsupials (the quokka) for rats and named it Rottnest ('Rat's Nest'). The entire island is run as a reserve and the surrounding waters as a marine park. The island is best explored by bicycle – private cars are not allowed – and the 24-km (15-mile) circular route around the island runs through some of the most beautiful scenery. Offshore, the fringing reefs are among the best in Australia, with 20 species of colourful corals and 360 species of fish, as well as bottlenose dolphins and sea lions. Sea kayaking, scuba-diving, snorkelling and visiting the reef in glass-bottomed boats are all popular activities. Land animals include a small number of reptiles – the island's thousands of years of isolation from the mainland means that several have evolved into species not found on the nearby mainland – as well as three types of frog. The island's shores, salt lakes and swamps provide homes for a variety of birds. This is a lovely, relaxed place to visit, where the scenery and wildlife are amazing for such a small place.

ULURU (AYERS ROCK)

Australia

Uluru is an icon of Australia: a giant red rock standing out from the surrounding desert. Like any significant landscape feature, it is a sacred site for the Aboriginals and it is a major point in the songlines of the local people, the Anangu. The rock is an inselberg, a remnant of an eroded mountain range. The national park it stands in – the Uluru-Kata Tjuta National Park, also covers the Olgas, a group of 36 other giant red rocks a few kilometres away. When the original mountain range formed, the layers of sandstone were raised from horizontal to vertical and you can see the banding in the rock. Where water gets into cracks and fissures, it erodes away deep channels that spout waterfalls after heavy rains. Water also soaks through the sandstone, eventually to emerge again as springs around the bottom of the rock that sustain some greenery and animals, making it an invaluable source of water and food in this arid land. The rock owes its red colour to the oxidation of iron at the surface: freshly eroded rock is grey. However, it is the more short-lived colour changes of the rock as the sun goes down, when it changes from red to purple then black (and changes in the reverse order during sunrise) that many visitors come to see. The climb to the summit is not as easy as you might think, and the Anangu would prefer it if people did not try it. However, the views from the plateau at the top are amazing. The Anangu lead walking tours around the 9-km (6-mile) base, during which they tell visitors about the plants and animals here, and about their culture and dreamtime.

KAKADU NATIONAL PARK

Australia

HOW TO GET THERE:
By air or rail to Darwin,
then by road.
WHEN TO GO:
March to October.
NEAREST TOWN:
Jabiru.

The largest national park in Australia, Kakadu National Park lies about 150km (90 miles) east of the Northern Territory's capital, Darwin. This tropical landscape is home to more than 10,000 insect species, kangaroos, wallabies, water buffalo, dingoes and almost a quarter of Australia's fish species. Its varied habitats include eucalypt woodland, swamps, mangroves, rainforest and heathland, as well as drier areas to the south of the park. One of the main features here is the South Alligator river, which is home to large populations of both of Australia's crocodile species: the Johnston, or freshwater, crocodile, and the estuarine, or saltwater, crocodile. This part of Australia is not much more than 15 degrees south of the equator, and from November to February it is extremely hot, humid and wet, and the roads can be blocked by water for days, so it is best not to visit at this time. Highlights of the park include Barramundi Gorge, Jim Jim Falls and Nourlangie Rock.

GRAMPIANS NATIONAL PARK

Australia

An area of natural beauty, the Grampian mountains are almost the last part of the Great Dividing range that for years isolated the interior of Australia from the eastern coastal plain. Spread over 1,700 sq km (650 sq miles), the national park has a wide variety of landscapes, including stringybark forests, fern-filled gullies, red gums, subalpine forests, woodland, heaths, wildflower meadows and swamps. It is home to a large variety of animals, including different species of wallabies, grey kangaroos, possums, gliders, koalas and echidnas. There are many birds here, including a sizeable population of emus. There are many tracks and trails leading to lookouts. Mackenzie Falls is spectacular in spring and after rains. Mountains that can be hiked here include Mount William (also called Mount Duwill) and the aptly named Mount Abrupt, but among the most popular, if strenuous, walks is to the summit of the Pinnacle. Activities in the area include rafting, rock climbing, abseiling, cycling, canoeing and bird-watching. There are several roads through the park, while from the central area, tracks and bushwalking trails lead into the wilderness.

HOW TO GET THERE: By road from Melbourne.
WHEN TO GO: Spring to autumn.
NEAREST TOWN: Stawell 20km (12 miles).

WOLFE CREEK IMPACT CRATER

Australia

First spotted from the air in 1947, the Wolfe Creek Impact Crater, located in Western Australia, was formed some 300,000 years ago when a meteorite with a mass of about 50,000kg (125,000lb) crashed into the desert at a speed estimated at 15km (9 miles) a second. The resulting crater is 880m (2,890ft) across and was originally roughly 120m (400ft) deep, with a sharp rim that rises 25m (82ft) above the desert.

Over the millennia, sand has been blown into the bottom of the crater, reducing its depth by over half. Evidence of the heat caused by the impact can be seen in the traces of quartz and rusty coloured balls that are strewn all over the desert floor here. Fragments of the meteorite itself have been found many kilometres away. As you approach, the rim of the crater emerges – firstly as a small feature on the horizon, and then as a broad, low wall. It is only when you scramble up it and gaze down into the crater that it becomes apparent what it is. It is possible to hike around the rim of the crater, and there is a path leading to the crater floor, where you will find a surprising number of plants that can exist because the porous rocks down here can hold on to water longer than those of the desert floor above. The walls of the crater provide some rare shade in the area.

HOW TO GET THERE:
By four-wheel drive on the Tanami road, then offroad.
WHEN TO GO:
May to October.
NEAREST TOWN:
Halls Creek 145km (90 miles).

YOU SHOULD KNOW
The Djaru Aboriginals call the crater 'Kandimalal'.

BUCCANEER ARCHIPELAGO

Australia

Lying just off the northwest coast of Western Australia, the Buccaneer archipelago's 1,000 islands were once part of the mainland but have been cut off by rising seas since the last ice age. Vegetation on them is scarce, except for tiny patches of rainforest and protective mangroves. Set in the blue seas of the Indian Ocean, they are known for their beautiful, isolated, sandy beaches, extreme tidal range and the extraordinary 'horizontal waterfall' in Talbot Bay, caused by the tidal water building up in front of the two narrow gaps leading to the ocean faster than it can flow through them, causing a build-up of up to 4m (14ft) of turquoise water that rushes between the red rocks. Despite the apparent lack of habitat, more than 100 species of birds have been recorded here, as well as 11 species of snake, a variety of lizards, rock rats, marsupials called quolls and bats. There are numerous sacred sites on the islands, some of which are still in use. A popular way to explore the islands in depth is on a guided sea safari, camping on a different beach each night.

CRADLE MOUNTAIN-LAKE ST CLARE NATIONAL PARK

Australia

HOW TO GET THERE:
By road from Launceston.
WHEN TO GO:
Spring to autumn.
NEAREST TOWN:
Sheffield 50km (30 miles).

Part of Tasmania's Wilderness Area World Heritage Site, the Cradle Mountain-Lake St Clare National Park is a stunning area of craggy ridges and crests, valleys scooped out by glaciers, cirques and lakes, dropping down through alpine heathland, button grass, wildflower meadows, pine and beech woods to areas of ancient rainforest. The hike up the 1,545-m (5,068-ft) Cradle Mountain and back takes about eight hours, but there are easier walks on its lower slopes, and the three-hour walk around the beautiful Dove Lake is not to be missed. Cradle Mountain is in the north of the park, and Lake St Clare – Australia's deepest freshwater lake – in the far south. The six-day hike from one to the other – known as the Overland Track – is one of the most popular in Australia and draws walkers from all over the world. It leads through some of the wildest pristine landscapes on the island, with glacial lakes, icy streams and waterfalls and spectacular views of the mountains above. There are nine huts spaced along the 80-km (50-mile) trail, in which walkers can make overnight stops. Even in summer it can be very cold at night, and snow is not unheard of in the higher areas. Other activities on offer in the park include rafting on the Franklin river, an exhilarating ride that takes you through even more beautiful areas of pristine wilderness.

KIAMA BLOWHOLES

Australia

HOW TO GET THERE:
By road or rail from Sydney.
WHEN TO GO:
Any time of year.
NEAREST TOWN:
Kiama.

On the coast of New South Wales, south of Sydney, is what is claimed to be the world's biggest blowhole. As a wave rushes in to the hole in the cliff, the air in the lower part of the hole is compressed into an inner chamber; then, as the wave starts to fall back, the compressed air expands, forcing the water up through the upper part of the blowhole and into the air with a loud 'ooomph'. The first European to see the blowhole was a whaler, George Bass, who anchored here in 1797; the Aboriginals call the blowhole Khanterintee, and the town's name means 'where the sea makes a noise'. The hole is some 7.5–9m (25–30ft) across. There is a second, smaller, blowhole a couple of kilometres to the south. The rough seas and winds along this part of the shore have created other beautiful forms in the cliffs, such as Cathedral Rocks, Stack Island and Fry's Cave, while a little higher up the valley is the magnificent Minnamurra Rainforest Reserve, a tiny remnant of the original flora of the area, which is particularly noted for its variety of tree ferns and for the pretty Minnamurra Falls.

FRASER ISLAND

Australia

HOW TO GET THERE:
By boat from the mainland
or by air from Hervey Bay.
WHEN TO GO:
Summer, or August to
September to watch whales.
NEAREST TOWN:
Hervey Bay 15km (9 miles).

Stretching 123km (76 miles) alongside Queensland's coast, Fraser Island is one of the most beautiful places on Earth. Made almost entirely of sand, it is unique. In the lowlands, the heathlands are awash with wildflowers in spring and summer, while in the interior, ancient rainforests surround more than 100 freshwater lakes. Among the highlights of the island are the wetlands of the Great Sandy Strait, where dugongs and turtles may be seen, and Hervey Bay during the whale migration season, when more than 1,500 humpbacks pass through. Inland, the lakes are beautiful, particularly Lake Wabby and the lakes round McKenzie. The northern part of the island has been designated as a national park. If you drive up the eastern beach northward from the Pinnacles, you will pass the 25-km (15-mile) expanse of the Cathedrals – cliffs made of coloured sand – on your way to Indian Head, which is a great spot for looking for dolphins, sharks and whales. Other wildlife here includes what are probably the purest strain of dingoes (do not feed them: they are losing their fear of humans and there have been several fatal attacks), loggerhead turtles, manta rays, possums, bats, sugar gliders, wallabies and echidnas. The most noticeable of the 200 or so species of bird here are the sulphur-crested cockatoos because they make so much noise; the rainbow lorikeets are rather more colourful.

THE MORNING GLORY

Australia

HOW TO GET THERE:
By road from Cairns.
WHEN TO GO:
September to October.
NEAREST TOWN:
Burketown.

YOU SHOULD KNOW

The cloud's appearance is unpredictable, so plan to stay at least a few days.

DON'T MISS

A ride beside the cloud in a glider.

The tiny outback town of Burketown, near the southern end of the Gulf of Carpentaria, has one claim to fame: it is the best place to spot the cloud formation known as the Morning Glory. Each spring, in September and October, weather enthusiasts and glider pilots flock here to see it. No one knows exactly why this huge roll of cloud, up to 1,000km (600 miles) long, forms here at this time of year, but it has a fascination for many, especially when as dawn breaks the black smudge of cloud can be seen on the horizon, galloping towards the viewer. The local Aboriginals call it the 'yippipee' and say that it presages bad weather, while people in Burketown say that if there is a sea breeze and high humidity the day before, the Morning Glory may occur. For glider pilots, riding the Morning Glory is like surfing a giant wave. In effect it is the aerial equivalent of a tidal bore, with the roll of cloud forming under the crest of the wave. The updraught in front of it gives them lift, allowing them to stay up in the air far longer than they normally can when relying on thermals. Good pilots can fly along the length of it, avoiding – at all costs – the turbulent downdraught at the back.

LORD HOWE ISLAND

Australia

Just 11km (7 miles) long and 2km (1.2 miles) at its widest, Lord Howe Island is the remnant of an undersea volcano that was born some seven million years ago but most of which has now been eroded away. It has left just the peaks of Mount Gower at 875m (2,870ft) and Mount Lidgbird at 777m (2,550ft) in the south, a central lowland and some hills to the north, as well as a few outlying islands: Admiralty Islands, Mutton Bird Islands and Ball's Pyramid. Most of the island is covered in palm forest and subtropical forest, with trees including banyans and kentia palms, while there are also grasslands here and on the smaller islands.

The island's isolation until 1878 means that many of the species of plants here occur nowhere else. The islands are surrounded by beautiful coral reefs, with more than 80 species of coral. The lagoon between Lord Howe Island itself and the reef is a beautiful blue, protected from the ocean waves that crash against the coral. The island is, or was, until cows, sheep, goats, pigs, mice and rats were introduced, a safe place for seabirds to nest, and eradication programmes are helping to raise the numbers of birds for some species. Birds that can be found here include red-billed tropicbirds and masked boobies. This is a beautiful, isolated, quiet spot where visitors really can get away from it all.

HOW TO GET THERE:
By air from Sydney or Brisbane.
WHEN TO GO:
Any time of year.
NEAREST TOWN:
Newcastle 600km (373 miles).

DON'T MISS
Diving the coral reef.

THE BUNGLE BUNGLES

Australia

Left: A range of rounded rock towers, striped with silica and lichen.

Known to the local Aboriginals as Purnululu, and set in the national park of the same name, the Bungle Bungles are a unique range of orange, black and white landforms up to 400m (1,300ft) high. The sandstone they are made from was laid down about 350 million years ago, and over the last two million years they have been uplifted then eroded into amazing, beehive-shaped domes. From the Piccaninny Creek car park, it is a short walk to Cathedral Gorge, a giant natural amphitheatre that carries people's voices round from one side to the other. The full walk through the Piccaninny Gorge requires an overnight camp and some scrambling in places, but is worth it for the stunning views of cliffs, domes, chasms and the sight of Black Rock Pool. It takes considerable effort to get to this remote spot, but it is worth it.

SHARK BAY

Australia

Shark Bay is almost unique. It is one of only two or three sites where easily identifiable decendants of some of the earliest life forms on Earth, living marine stomatolites, exist and the only place where they can easily be seen. In the very salty waters of the Hamelin Pool Marine Nature Reserve, a group of strange columns, hillocks and mounds about 50cm (20in) high sit between the high and low tide lines. Without their ancestors, which developed some 3,500 million years ago, life on Earth as we know it would not exist. These strange cushions are made up of photosynthesizing bacteria that absorb carbon dioxide and emit oxygen. Without them, our atmosphere would be unbreathable and the ozone layer that protects us from solar radiation would not exist. Other inhabitants of the bay are the dolphins near Monkey Mia, as well as more than 10,000 dugong, who graze among the sea grasses. This is the largest and most stable population of these beautiful, gentle creatures. Here, where they are safe, these giant mammals — thought to be the inspiration for mermaids — might take notice of a boat if they feel like it but are usually happy to get on with their own lives. Sharing their world for a few minutes is a privilege that not many can boast.

THE WHITSUNDAY ISLANDS

Australia

Lying between Queensland and the outer reef of the Great Barrier Reef, the Whitsundays consists of 74 islands – forest-clad peaks of sunken mountains – fringed with spectacular coral reefs, crystal-clear waters and white sandy beaches. They were first discovered by Captain Cook in the 1770s on his fraught voyage to try to find an exit from the reef system without destroying his ship. Most of the system is a national park, although some of the islands are private and uninhabited, and away from the four main, developed islands they are still almost unspoiled wildernesses. A few of them have camping sites. Not only are the Whitsundays' reefs spectacular in their own right, the islands are ideal stopping-off points for the Great Barrier Reef itself. For those who don't want to sail themselves, there is a bewildering variety of sailing boat, catamaran and cruise trips to the islands and reefs, many to sites where visitors can scuba or snorkel among the reefs and watch the fish. Several companies also run trips in glass-bottomed boats or semi-submersibles. It is also possible to hire sailing boats and explore where you want, although the waters around the reefs can be tricky for the inexperienced. But the islands are not just worth visiting for the marine life: many have walking trails up to their peaks through lovely rainforests full of birdsong, and there are so many beaches to find a quiet place to look at the beauty surrounding you.

KANGAROO ISLAND

Australia

Just off the coast of South Australia, much of Kangaroo Island is an unspoiled wilderness. Here, animals that you see only in zoos or at a distance are close by, in their natural habitat. More than a third of the island is protected and is home to kangaroos, wallabies, possums, bandicoots, bats, goannas, little penguins, echidnas, New Zealand fur seals and Australian sea lions, as well as introduced koalas and platypuses. Protected from introduced predators, these animals thrive. The landscape of the island is varied and the dunes of Little Sahara rise unexpectedly in the middle of the island, emerging from the bush like the keel of an upturned boat. Scrambling up their steep sides and sandboarding down again is an exilharating experience. The beaches here are pristine, with Vivionne Bay's reputedly the best in Australia. There are four conservation parks on the island: Flinders Chase, Kelly Hill, Seal Bay and Cape Willoughby. Flinders Chase has the Admiral's Arch and Remarkable Rocks formations, while Kelly Hill has magnificent limestone karst caves. Seal Bay has a large colony of Australian sea lions, which visitors can walk among.

THE GREAT SANDY DESERT

Australia

Stretching from Uluru in the southeast almost to the coast near Broome in the northwest, the Great Sandy Desert covers some 280,000 sq km (110,000 sq miles) of northwest Australia. From the air, you can see that most of its landscape is made up of row upon row of parallel red sand dunes, cut in places by gullies where seasonal streams run. Even around the edge of the desert there are few settlements apart from old mining communities because it is impossible to make a living here. One route that does go across the desert is the Canning Stock Route, established between 1906 and 1920 by Alfred Canning, who explored the route and sank wells along the way to provide water for cattle. Even now, it is a hard route for four-wheel drives and requires advance planning and fuel drops. If you want to drive into Aboriginal land, you will need a permit from the Central Land Council.

PALAU ARCHIPELAGO

Palau

YOU SHOULD KNOW

The currents are very
strong in places and
care is needed.

The Palau archipelago in western Micronesia is renowned for having some of the best dive sites in the world, taking in both wildlife-rich reefs and spectacular underwater caves. Chandelier Cave is an especially interesting system that is accessed from underwater. The rear caves are above sea level and have coloured, crystal growths. Jellyfish Lake has two species of jellyfish that follow the sunlight around the lake. German Channel is renowned for its 'cleaning station' where sharks and manta rays allow cleaner wrasse to pick parasites and other bits of food off them, and even from inside their mouths. There is also a very good reef and large numbers of small fish here.

Among the more advanced dive sites, the Blue Holes are a vast system of interconnected caves, lit by diffuse sunlight that filters in through fissures. Nearby, the Blue Corner is normally kept until last – it spoils divers for other sites. It is a triangular reef, with sheer drops beside it. Strong currents bring vast quantities of plankton, providing a base for a food chain that culminates in barracuda and grey, black-tip and white-tip sharks. The quality of the fish is matched only by the drama of the site. Other well-known dive sites in these islands include Turtle Cove, Tombstones, Soft Coral Arch, Ulong Channel, Turtle Cove, Short Drop-Off, Siaes Tunnel, Peleliu Wall, Ngerchong Inside and Ngerchong Outside. Each offers a different array of species and a different challenge.

CRAB MIGRATION

Christmas Island

HOW TO GET THERE:
From Perth by air.
WHEN TO GO:
November.
NEAREST TOWN:
Bandung, Indonesia 550km
(330 miles).

Each November, at the right phase of the moon and once the rains have set in, Christmas Island is host to an amazing sight: millions of crabs emerging and heading for the coast. The island is the top of an old volcano, and its central plateau is about 300m (1,000ft) above sea level. For most of the year you would not know that these crabs even existed, but for just a few days they take over the island, compelled by their need to get down to the sea to spawn. Until they are three years old, they live in burrows in the rainforest, but in their dash downhill they clamber up steps onto people's verandahs and into their houses, cross roads with abandon and (unintentionally) terrorize pets. Although they are classed as land crabs, they still breathe through gills that must be kept moist, and the larval stage of development must take place in the sea. Early residents do not mention the crabs in diaries or correspondence, and it is possible that Maclear's rats, which also inhabited the island at this time, ate them and their population exploded only after the rats' extinction in the early 20th century.

NEW GUINEA'S BIRDS OF PARADISE

Papua New Guinea

HOW TO GET THERE:
By air from Australia.
WHEN TO GO:
Late August to early
September.
NEAREST TOWN:
Port Moresby.

There are more than 40 species of birds of paradise, many of which live on New Guinea, from the lowland forests near the coast to the rainforests inland and the high cloud forests. They are renowned both for the males' beautiful plumage and for their spectacular courtship displays. It can be a challenge to see them, because they live deep in the rainforests, but local guides know the best spots in different areas of the island. Among the best known are the yellow, white, brown and green greater and lesser birds of paradise and the King of Saxony bird of paradise, which has two bright blue eyebrow plumes that Archibold's bowerbirds appropriate for their bowers. There are two main types of display: some species, such as the lesser bird of paradise, display in groups in order to try to attract females, while others, like the magnificent bird of paradise, display singly. Most of them are polygamous and the females tend the eggs with no help from the males. Perhaps the most spectacular display is that of the superb bird of paradise: he attracts the female's attention by singing, then hops around in front of her. Then he extends a cape of velvety black feathers above his head and stretches out his irridescent, blue-green bib and dances around. Whichever species you manage to see, their attempts to attract females as they flap about, flash bright colours, dangle upside-down and generally flaunt themselves, can't help but impress.

FALEALUPO LAVA TUBES

Samoa

In the far northwest of Samoa's island of Savai'i, near the Falealupo Forest Preserve, is a rare geological phenomenon – a series of lava tubes. These form when the surface over a fast-moving lava channel cools sufficiently to crust over while lava continues to flow underneath and drain away. Eventually, the outflow from the volcano stops and the tube empties. These tubes can be kilometres in length. The whole of Savai'i is volcanic and there are extensive lava fields in places all over the island, including where villages have been destoyed by lava flows.

Here, however, the lava tubes can be of great benefit to people: on occasions in the past when cyclones have threatened, such as during the early 1990s, the tubes provide a safe refuge in an emergency. More ominously, according to local legend one of the caves on the Falealupo peninsula is one of the gateways to the underworld, through which spirits emerge at night and return before sunrise. Guides from the village take visitors about 500m (1,600ft) into the tubes, so they can see the strange texture of the walls and get the eerie feeling of being inside part of a volcano. It is unsettling to think what it must have been like when molten rock was flowing through the tube floor and the walls were glowing with the heat.

YOU SHOULD KNOW
Currents can be strong around the reef.

PALOLO DEEP MARINE RESERVE

Samoa

In this part of northern 'Upolu the reef is only a few hundred metres offshore, making this spectacular dive site – one of Samoa's best – easily reached from the access point at the secluded and pretty Vaiala Beach just east of the city harbour. Here, you can hire snorkels and goggles. Swimming over the reef and its multitude of fish at high tide, when you are less likely to step on the coral and damage it, you approach a dark circle in the water. When you reach it, you are greeted by a deep blue hole, full of bright, tropical fish and walled with colourful corals. In the hole, and on the reefs around, you will see starfish, sea cucumbers, sea slugs and clown fish. Moray eels hide out in holes among the coral, and while you will see farmed giant clams in cages, you might be lucky enough to spot wild ones as well. The coral-encrusted walls of the hole drop straight down into the depths. The reserve is also the site of a remarkable phenemonon in October and November of each year, when at the right phase of the moon, the Palolo reef worms release wriggling bundles of spawn that are a local delicacy.

ALOFAAGA BLOWHOLES

Samoa

Also known as the Taga blowholes from the village nearby, these are claimed by many to be the most spectacular of their kind on the planet. At the remote southwestern corner of Savai'i, these blowholes in the low cliffs are a must at high tide. Tubes in the lava field reach what is now the coast, and the action of waves over the years has led to the collapse of the roofs of several of them. When rough seas flood into the tubes, pressure forces the water through these holes to an astonishing height every few seconds. In really wild weather, the fountain of water can reach 60m (200ft) into the air before it comes crashing back down onto the shiny black rock.

The locals have a favourite party trick to demonstrate the power of the water: timing it just right, they throw coconuts into the blowholes so that these, too, go soaring into the air. This wild, dramatic place, where young volcanic rocks meet the Pacific Ocean and white foam surges over the lava and the blowholes create their spectacle, truly is a place forged from the ancients' four elements of earth, air, fire and water.

HOW TO GET THERE:
By air or ferry from 'Upalu, then on the coast road.
WHEN TO GO:
Any time of year, at high tide in rough weather.
NEAREST TOWN:
Taga 4km (2 miles).

YOU SHOULD KNOW
The rocks can be slippery and dangerous when wet.

TOGITOGIGA FALLS RECREATION RESERVE

Samoa

DON'T MISS
Swimming in
the pools.

HOW TO GET THERE:
On 'Upopu's main South
Coast Road.
WHEN TO GO:
Any time.
NEAREST TOWN:
Saleilua 7km (4 miles).

YOU SHOULD KNOW
The waterfalls become a
raging torrent after heavy rain.

Surrounded by lush rainforest and overhung by palms, the gentle cascades of Togitogiga are a treat. They are accessed via a 1-km (0.6-mile) track through beautiful greenery. Deep pools sit below each cascade, making wonderful places for a swim in hot weather. Getting into the middle pool requires a scramble on some steep rocks and then a leap of faith. It is possible to get to the lower pool from below, but the jump into it from the middle pool is exhilarating. Before jumping into any of the pools, check where the water is deepest and make sure there are no logs just under the surface. The falls are usually quieter during the week. A couple of hours' hard walk through the jungle leads to the Pe'ape'a cave, an old lava tube that is home to the swiftlets that give it its name. To the south lies more of the national park, through which an extremely rough road and another overgrown trail lead down to the spectacular lava coast, where a rough path leads along the cliffs for amazing views of the ocean and the weird formations in the solidified lava.

DON'T MISS
Sleeping on the
canopy platform.

FALEALUPO RAINFOREST PRESERVE

Samoa

At what could be said to be almost the most westerly point on the planet (the international date line is only a few kilometres away), the Falealupo Rainforest Preserve is an area sacred to the locals. The forest was damaged by severe cyclones in the early 1990s, but has returned to its former beauty.

HOW TO GET THERE:
By air or sea from 'Upolu, then on the coast road.
WHEN TO GO:
Any time.
NEAREST TOWN:
Asau 9km (4 miles).

A typical species of the forest is the banyan tree, two of which support one of the highlights of the area, the canopy walkway. Stairways scale 9m (30ft) up into the treetops, leading to a 24-m (80-ft) swing bridge slung between the trees. As you walk across it, you will realize that 'swing' is definitely the correct term for it. Another 20m (66ft) higher is a platform in the very top of one of the banyans: from here the views over the forest and up to the island's volcanoes are truly amazing. The platform doubles as a hotel room, where visitors can sleep under the stars if they're brave enough.

This is a land rich in legend, and a little to the west is Moso's Footprint, a large indentation in the lava said to have been left by the giant Moso when he stepped here from Fiji (where there is another footprint on Viti Levu).

TARAWA

Kiribati

YOU SHOULD KNOW
Several of the islets
have already succumbed
to rising sea levels.

This tiny atoll, perched on an extinct and eroding submarine volcano, is one of the most remote spots on Earth. Tourist development and infrastructure are minimal, so for people who really want to get away from it all, it is a must. The capital, Bairiki, is in the south and there is a small resort on Buariki in the north. The islets are sparsely inhabited and low lying. As the volcano below them erodes, the corals grow to maintain their position at just the right height below the surface, but several of them have already been submerged by rising seas and others are predicted to be lost the same way within just a few years. The reefs are topped by sandy beaches and the lagoon is edged by palm trees, making this quiet place, where the only sounds may be the surf crashing against the coral and the calls of seabirds, ideal for relaxing. The island's reefs have a wide variety of different species of coral and pretty shoals of colourful fish. Divers may see rays, snapper, clams or black-tipped shark and bonefish. If lucky, they may catch sight of a wary octopus squeezing itself into a crevice. This undeveloped and beautiful atoll is a very special place.

FRANZ JOSEF GLACIER

New Zealand

Like the Fox glacier 20km (12 miles) to the south, the Franz Josef glacier is fed by snow and rainfall high in the Southern Alps. Even more dramatically than its neighbour, it exhibits a cycle of retreat and advance caused by the tipping of the balance between how much material is added at the top and how much melts away at the bottom.

During the period between the 1940s and 1980s, it rapidly retreated several kilometres, but after that it began advancing again by an average of about 70cm (27.5in) a day and is currently 12km (7.5 miles) long and terminates 19km (11.5 miles) from the sea at an altitude of 240m (790ft) above sea level. At the peak of the last ice age it probably reached all the way to the Tasman Sea. There are various ways of getting on to the glacier. From the terminus, visitors can take a guided walk or go by themselves as far as the first icefall, but from here it is not possible to go any higher up. A popular way of doing so is to take one of the many helicopter trips on offer to the area between the first and second falls for a guided walk across the glacier and, on some walks, into the ice caves.

HOW TO GET THERE:
By road from Greymouth.
WHEN TO GO:
Spring to autumn.
NEAREST TOWN:
Franz Josef township
5km (3 miles).

YOU SHOULD KNOW
The Maori name for the glacier is *Ka Rolmata o Hinehukatere* – 'the tears of the avalanche girl'.

MOUNT ASPIRING NATIONAL PARK

New Zealand

Straddling the southern end of the Southern Alps, Mount Aspiring National Park was established in 1964. It is vast, covering 3,555 sq km (2,210 sq miles). Like much of the wilderness areas of the southwest of South Island, it is popular with walkers, climbers and hikers because of the beauty and variety of its scenery, which includes high mountains and beautiful river valleys set among a wilderness of lakes, beech forests, alpine and subalpine meadows and tussock grasslands. The most commonly used route up Mount Aspiring itself, which stands at over 3,000m (9,843ft), starts from Raspberry Flat, northwest of Wanaka by road, but the park can also be accessed from Queenstown, Haast and Glenorchy. Among the most popular walking tracks is the Routeburn Track, which partly follows an old Maori route into the area. The Maori came here to find greenstone, a dark form of jade that they used for tools and ornaments. There is plenty of wildlife to be seen here, and one bird that is difficult to miss in the alpine areas is the kea. These large green mountain parrots are very intelligent and mischievous, and like nothing better than the challenge of extracting the seals from around car doors, except perhaps unzipping people's bags in order to extract their lunch.

THE BAY OF ISLANDS

New Zealand

The 144 islands in the Bay of Islands Maritime Park are dotted around a bay with clear blue waters and a rich variety of wildlife. It is a paradise for sailors, a mecca for big-sports fishermen and heaven for wildlife-watchers. Warm, equatorial waters mean that it has an equable climate and locals claim that it doesn't have a winter. The best way to appreciate the coastline of the bay and the islands is from the water, whether from a kayak, yacht, cruiser or amphibious 'duck'. For many visitors, the highlight of a stay here is the opportunity to go dolphin- or whale-watching: sightings are almost guaranteed here. It is even possible to swim with dolphins or, rather, to go on a licensed tour, get into the water and let them decide whether to come and swim with you. Among the several good dive sites is the wreck of the Greenpeace ship, *Rainbow Warrior*, which was sunk here by the French secret services in 1985 and is slowly being colonized by marine organisms.

LAKE MATHESON

New Zealand

HOW TO GET THERE:
By road, then on foot. The lake is 6km (4 miles) from Fox glacier township along Cook Flat Road, and the walk around the lake takes about 70 minutes.

WHEN TO GO:
Spring to autumn in good weather.

NEAREST TOWNS:
Fox Glacier village/Weheka 5km (3 miles).

Carved out at the peak of the last ice age some 14,000 years ago by the Fox glacier, when it was much nearer the Tasman Sea, Lake Matheson provides one of the iconic images of New Zealand. The peaks of Aoraki/Mount Cook and Mount Tasman are reflected in its still waters, framed by the rainforest that surrounds the lake and protecting it from breezes that would disturb its perfect surface. Because the lake bed contains large amounts of dissolved sediment left there by the glacier, its waters are dark, increasing its properties as a mirror. The 40-minute stroll down to the lake from the Fox glacier village leads through beautiful temperate rainforest to the jetty, positioned to give the best possible views. You also catch glimpses of the reflection from the lake-shore path. If you can, the best times of day to come here are sunrise and sunset. As dawn breaks over the mountains in the east, eerie blue light spills over the snow-covered peaks and down into the valley below, highlighting the mist as the reflection gradually becomes clearer and brighter. At the other end of the day, the mountains take on an orange hue as the sun drops, chased up the mountainsides by ever-deepening shades as it finally drops below the horizon.

WAITOMO CAVES

New Zealand

HOW TO GET THERE:
By road from Hamilton,
71km (44 miles).
WHEN TO GO:
Spring to autumn.
NEAREST TOWN:
Te Kuiti 12km (7.5 miles).

YOU SHOULD KNOW
Gardner's Gut is for
experieced cavers only.

Set in the south of the Waikoto region of North Island, this group of caves is known for its spectacular stalagmites and stalactites. Access ranges from the very easy (Waitomo) to the very difficult (Gardner's Gut). The Waitomo cave system was first explored in 1887, although the local Maori had known of its existence for years. Chief Tane Tinorau and Englishman Fred Mace discovered the lower entrance and found the underground river, glow-worm cave and limestone formations. The chief continued to explore and eventually found the upper entrance, which is the one used today. He opened it to the public in 1889. From the entrance at the top level, visitors first go to the Catacombs, then down a vertical shaft to the Banquet Chamber. From here a short detour leads to the Pipe Organ, but this is often shut because carbon dioxide builds up here and cannot escape. The main route from the Banquet Chamber leads down to the Cathedral, a chamber about 18m (60ft) high with wonderful accoustics. Boats depart from the jetty to the Glow-Worm Grotto, a cave lit by the ethereal light of these small insects clinging to the roof, and past more spectacular features until the river emerges back out into the open.

HOW TO GET THERE:
By road from Christchurch
183km (113 miles).
WHEN TO GO:
Any time of year.
NEAREST TOWN:
Kaikoura.

WHALE-WATCHING IN KAIKOURA BAY

New Zealand

Once a whaling town, Kaikoura is now the centre of a year-round whale-watching scene because of the year-round population of sperm whales. They stay here because the underwater geology provides them with perfect feeding grounds. Two currents of water meet here, a cold, nutrient-rich one from the south and a warm one from the north that brings the nutrients up from the deep ocean to form the basis of a food chain that culminates with the whales, seals and dolphins. The other factor here is a series of extremely deep canyons offshore, in which octopus, squid and large fish lurk. The whales dive down into the canyons to feed and then re-emerge to catch their breath, spending about three-quarters of their time underwater. Boat trips out to see them use hydrophones to listen in on their clicks to locate them and estimate when and where they will surface. Kaikoura Bay is also home to Hector's dolphins, which can be seen from the waterfront. Another, even closer, encounter is the boat trip out to see – and swim with – the dusky dolphins that live a few kilometres offshore in summer.

MAYOR ISLAND/TUHUA

New Zealand

HOW TO GET THERE:
By boat from Whangamata
or Tauranga.
WHEN TO GO:
Summer.
NEAREST TOWN:
Whangamata 36km (22 miles).

The top half of a dormant shield volcano in the Bay of Plenty, Mayor Island covers an area of 13 sq km (5 sq miles), most of which is occupied by a crater blown out by the last phase of eruption about 7,000 years ago. Two small crater lakes lie within it. The Maori name for the island is their word for obsidian, black volcanic glass, which they prized highly for making cutting tools, arrow heads, etc. The Bay of Plenty still lives up to its name, and the waters near here are a mecca for game fishermen, although the waters round the island are protected, as is the island itself. The site of the old game-fishing headquarters on Sou'East Bay is on a beautiful beach, and the clear waters and rich variety of fish here make the island a popular destination for divers. There are several tracks on the island, so visitors can explore the native bush and see the birdlife. Because it is protected, the easiest way to get there is with a registered tour operator.

RAKIURA NATIONAL PARK

New Zealand

Rakiura National Park covers about 85 per cent of Stewart Island, across the Foveaux Strait from South Island. It is renowned as being the one place where you can almost guarantee to see kiwis in the wild, as there are about 25,000 of them here. Rakiura is one of the Maori names for the island, and means 'Glowing Skies', which may be a reference to either the glowing sunrises and sunsets that often occur here or to the aurora australis – the southern lights. There is a variation in the Earth's magnetic field here, which means that this area gets more than its fair share of auroras. The national park is New Zealand's most recent, having been set up in 2002. Although predators such as cats and rats have wrought havoc on the island's bird populations and introduced deer have overgrazed parts of the forest, it is in a far better state of conservation than anywhere on the mainland. The Rakiura Track, one of New Zealand's ten great tracks, leads through lush forests with giant tree ferns, ground ferns and epiphytic orchids. The track is a 36-km (22-mile), three-day walk through the bush.

HOW TO GET THERE: By ferry from Bluff or plane from Invercargill.
WHEN TO GO: Summer.
NEAREST TOWN: Oban, located on Half Moon Bay.

THE SOUTHERN ALPS

New Zealand

HOW TO GET THERE:
By road or on the the
TranzAlpine train from
Christchurch.
WHEN TO GO:
Summer.

Running down almost the entire length of South Island is the range that Captain Cook dubbed the Southern Alps, which form the character of the whole island. To the west they drop sharply almost to the sea along the line of the Alpine Fault, with only a narrow coastal plain, and this land is isolated and sparsely populated. To the east the plains are dotted with towns, villages and farms, and the major cities cling to the coast. Seventeen mountains in this 550-km (340-mile) range exceed 3,000m (10,000ft) and remain snowcapped for much or all of the year. The mountains are still actively being formed, as the Pacific plate is being pushed into the Australian plate, causing the latter to buckle and crumple. Surprisingly, although they are being pushed up, they are not growing any taller, because they are eroding at the top just as quickly. The moist winds from the west drop most of their rain and snow on the western side of the range, and whereas the glaciers to the east are retreating, several of those on the west side are currently growing. This beautiful range of mountains is a stunning sight from a distance – Captain Cook described them as 'prodigious high' when he saw them from out at sea. The mountains and valleys are popular with climbers, hikers and walkers, who enjoy the ever-changing landscape of glaciers and icy tarns, temperate rainforest, alpine meadow, lush woodland and pastures.

ABEL TASMAN NATIONAL PARK

New Zealand

The smallest of New Zealand's national parks, the 225-sq-km (89-sq-mile) Abel Tasman National Park was set up in 1942, the three-hundredth anniversary of the Dutch captain's disastrous attempt to land in Golden Bay to the north. However, he lost four of his crew in a skirmish with the local Maori and never returned.

HOW TO GET THERE:
By road from Nelson,
80km (50 miles).
WHEN TO GO:
Any time of year.
NEAREST TOWN:
Motekua 20km (12 miles).

The area had been logged since 1855, and part of the park's *raison-d'être* is to allow the plant life here to regenerate to its former beauty by removing non-native species and encouraging the local plants to recolonize. The 113km (70 miles) of beaches, which form part of a separate scenic reserve, are beautiful, and sea-kayaking and sailing along the bay are popular pastimes here, as is walking. One of New Zealand's famous Great Walks, the Abel Tasman Coastal Track, takes three to five days and features gorgeous views of the beaches, coast and blue-green waters of the bay as it climbs up ridges and then back down to the coast. The Abel Tasman Inland Track leads through the regenerating forest, where black beech lines the dry ridges and damp gullies are filled with a rich variety of plants. The landscape is beautiful, with occasional granite and limestone outcrops, streams and gorges.

MILFORD SOUND

New Zealand

Milford Sound is the best known of the fjords in the isolated area of the southwest coast of South Island known as Fiordland, and the only one accessible all the way by road. Unlike most places on New Zealand's coast, this was not named by Captain Cook, but by John Grono, captain of a seal-hunting ship, who in 1822 named it after his birthplace in Wales.

Glaciers carved out the sounds and lakes of this area between 15,000 and 20,000 years ago, but unlike farther north in the Southern Alps, the glaciers are long gone, leaving a wilderness of mountains, lakes and waterfalls, native bush and temperate rainforest, alpine meadows and the calm, still waters of the sounds themselves. Even the drive to get here from Te Anau is glorious. An even better way to get here is the Milford Track, a four-day trek that leaves from the northern end of Lake Te Anau and crosses the Mackinnon Pass before meeting up with the road again under the looming 1,412-m (4,633-ft) Mitre Peak. On the way, hikers pass through forests whose giant trees drip moisture-loving lichen, ferns, moss and vines: this area receives a startling 7.6m (300in) of rain a year.

Among the activities in the sound itself are wildlife cruises to the mouth of the sound, where you may see seals and dolphins and perhaps penguins in autumn.

FIORDLAND WORLD HERITAGE PARK

New Zealand

HOW TO GET THERE:
Across Lake Manapouri by catamaran, then by road to Deep Cove.
WHEN TO GO:
Spring to autumn.
NEAREST TOWN:
Manapouri 80km (50 miles).

Doubtful Sound is the largest sound in the area. It was originally named Doubtful Harbour by Captain Cook because he was not sure whether it was navigable. The glaciers that carved its three arms no longer fling ice into it, and it is a peaceful, if dramatic, place. In good weather its waters are flat and mirror the cliffs looming above them and the little islands that perch in the middle. This is a remote area, not as often visited as Milford Sound to the north, and access from the sea is as easy as access from the land. Boat trips explore the length of the sound, or for an even more tranquil experience, sea kayaks can be hired. The landscape is spectacular, with high cliffs and several large waterfalls, including Helen Falls, easily visible from Deep Cove and the 600-m (2,000-ft) Browne Falls. After rain, which can be very heavy, the entire side of the sound can seem to be one giant waterfall. Wildlife in the sound includes friendly bottlenose dolphins, which race to play in the bow wave of the tour boat, fur seals and both blue and Fiordland crested penguins.

LAKE TAUPO

New Zealand

HOW TO GET THERE:
By road from Auckland 180km (111 miles).
WHEN TO GO:
Spring to autumn.
NEAREST TOWN:
Taupo 5km (3 miles).

Lurking under the northern half of Lake Taupo is a giant volcano, thought to be a supervolcano. Over the last 330,000 years it has erupted on numerous occasions, although little evidence for many of these eruptions survives as many of the sites have been destroyed by subsequent events or are under the waters of Lake Taupo. The eruption that is thought to have created the caldera is the Oruanui eruption, which occurred about 26,500 years ago, although it is possible that there was an earlier lake. The most recent eruption was about 1,800 years ago, and spread ash and pumice right across North Island, in some places to a depth of about 5m (16.5ft). The volcanic nature of the area can be seen in the numerous thermal features, including hot thermal springs and the geysers and plopping mud puddles at, for example, Wairakei at the northern end of the lake. However, what this violent past has left is a beautiful landscape, where the largest freshwater lake in New Zealand is surrounded by bush-clad mountains and more distant volcanoes. The lake's crystal-clear waters are perfect for yachting and kayaking, while the countryside around is popular for walking, hiking, skiing in winter and wildlife-watching. One day the volcano may erupt again, devastating the land, but in the meantime it is a special place to contemplate the forces of nature.

MOUNT TONGARIRO

New Zealand

Mount Tongariro, a complex of peaks and craters, is at the heart of North Island's volcanic landscape. Geologists think that this massif, with a base 15 by 3km (9 by 5 miles) and a summit 8 by 3km (5 by 2 miles), used to be higher but lost its top in a series of massive eruptions, and that the craters and peaks seen today are the result of subsequent activity. The remnants of at least a dozen cones make up the mountain, and the most recent activity in the central part of the massif occurred in Red Crater, in 1926. This feature is still actively venting acrid gases and the ground here is hot to walk on.

The first authenticated ascent of the higher of the two peaks occurred in 1867. Until a year or so earlier the Maori had prevented anyone climbing the mountain because it had been made *tapu* ('taboo'). The peaks are 1,968m and 1,959m (6,457ft and 6,427ft) and are not difficult climbs, while the route from Mangatepopo hut in the south to Keleteh hut in the north, after a steep start up to the saddle, crosses the broad south crater, tops a small ridge by Red Crater, drops to the Emerald Lakes (their colour comes from minerals from Red Crater), skirts the central crater and Blue Lake (in another old crater) and drops down the slope below the north crater. The views over this harsh, volcanic landscape to the forests below, especially from near Red Crater and the Emerald Lakes, are panoramic and absolutely beautiful.

WHAKAREWAREWA'S THERMAL VALLEY AND MUD POOLS

New Zealand

HOW TO GET THERE:
By road or rail to Rotorua city.
WHEN TO GO:
Any time of year.
NEAREST TOWN:
Rotorua city.

One of the most active thermal areas in the strange landscape of Rotorua is the Whakarewarewa Thermal Valley, which hosts an eclectic selection of giant mud puddles, fumaroles and steaming hot pools, as well as the geysers of Geyser Flat. The appearance and behaviour of mud pools depends on the relative proportions of mud and water. In this valley, the mud is quite thick, and the successive bubble-bursts form concentric rings that disappear only very slowly, leaving a landscape of unearthly ridges. There are roughly 500 pools in the valley, many of which are alkaline hot springs. Their edges are encrusted with silica and steam rises over their blue waters, adding to the eeriness of the landscape. To the local Maori, this area is where the fire goddesses Te Pupu and Te Hoata first came to the surface, and the hot springs and mud pools are caused by their breath. Locals say that each of the geothermal features here has its own personality and they can tell their moods from how they sound. The land here is continually changing, and careful checks are made daily to see whether hot springs are emerging or new cracks are forming.

PAPAITONGA DUNE LAKE RESERVE

New Zealand

HOW TO GET THERE:
By road from Wellington.
WHEN TO GO:
Apring to autumn.
NEAREST TOWN:
Levin 5km (3 miles).

YOU SHOULD KNOW
Access to the islands
is forbidden.

Set in the broad, coastal Horowhena plain north of Wellington, Papaitonga Dune Lake Reserve holds a rare remnant of the flora that used to be typical of this region: coastal podocarp and broadleaf woodland. On the track that leads down to the lake, visitors will see a variety of tree ferns, tawa — once common here — phormiums and nikau palms. The lake itself is beautiful and its islands, waters and the surrounding lowland forests and wetland serve as refuges for migrating wildfowl, as well as holding resident species that have been squeezed out of other places through habitat loss. The two islands are called Motukiwi (or Papaitonga) and Motungarara (or Papawhaerangi). The latter is an artificial island, created by the Muaupoko people in the early 1820s. The recreational reserve adjoining the lake has walking trails. The area around the lake was bought in 1897 by Sir Walter Buller, author of *The History of the Birds of New Zealand*, in order to protect it; the lake was added in 1991 and the total area now covers 1.2 sq km (0.7 sq miles). The area is important to the Tangata Whenua — the descendants of the people who first inhabited this area — and they still use the lake as a source of food and material for their traditional crafts.

NORTH ISLAND'S VOLCANIC PLATEAU

New Zealand

On the southern edge of the lake-filled Rotorua caldera is a giant volcanic plateau that stretches south from Rotorua for well over 20km (12 miles). To the west of the city is Kuirau Park, normally the site of mud pools that splat, gloop and plop gently, but sometimes these pools are witness to larger events, such as in 2006 when a mud fountain, as high as 20m (66ft) and 30m (100ft) across, gushed into the air for an hour. In 1886, Mount Tarawera to the south erupted, and a 17-km (10.5-mile) rift opened in the Earth's crust, virtually splitting the mountain in half. Within a few years, Lake Rotomahana had become established in the valley, together with the largest hot spring in the country.

In the area known as Hells Gate, you will find boiling lakes, Kakahi Falls – the world's largest hot waterfall – and a bizarre mud volcano. Every six weeks or so, the top of this 1.8-m (6-ft) cone hardens and once pressure has built up, it explodes, throwing 'bombs' of hot mud flying into the air around it. The mud pool known as the sulphur bath is strongly acidic (ph 1.5) and the air is filled with the rotten-egg smell of sulphur dioxide. At Wai-o-Tapu, the Lady Knox geyser was discovered by prisoners on work duty in the early 20th century. It erupts promptly at the same time each morning, and each eruption can last for up to an hour. This area is filled with spectacular coloured pools and terraces. Set against the beauty of the lake and the green lowland forest that surrounds it, these geothermal areas seem not to belong on this planet at all.

HOW TO GET THERE:
By road from Taupo 80km (50 miles).
WHEN TO GO:
Any time.
NEAREST TOWN:
Rotorua city.

DON'T MISS
Kakahi's mud volcano and hot waterfall.

AORAKI/MOUNT COOK

New Zealand

The highest mountain in New Zealand at 3,754m (12,316ft), Aoraki/Mount Cook stands at the heart of a national park that covers 700 sq km (270 sq miles) and contains more than 140 peaks over 2,000m (6,600ft) and 72 named glaciers. It was named Mount Cook by Captain Stokes in 1851, and the name was officially changed to Aoraki/Mount Cook in 1998. The Maori name means 'cloud piercer'. On the approach to Aoraki/Mount Cook village, near the shore of Lake Pukaki and alongside the Tasman river, you gradually realize just how immense this spine of mountains is. The village sits – overwhelmed – at the termination of the Hooker and Mueller glaciers that spill off the southern side of the mountain. There are walks and climbs for people of every ability in the area, from the gruelling trip to the mountain's peaks (there are three) to tough hikes that require stamina and experience but are worth it for the views over the glaciers and tarns. There are also gentle strolls in the lowlands, through temperate rainforest, remnants of beech woods and alpine meadows that are full of wildflowers in summer. Unlike some of the glaciers on the other side of the Southern Alps, the glaciers on this side are retreating.

HOW TO GET THERE:
By road from Dunedin.
WHEN TO GO:
Summer.
NEAREST TOWN:
Mount Cook village
12km (7 miles).

YOU SHOULD KNOW
Mount Cook was 10m (33ft) higher until 1991 when 10 million cubic m (350 million cubic ft) of ice and rock crashed down from the summit.

FOX GLACIER

New Zealand

Also known as Te Moeka o Tuawe, Fox glacier is highly unusual. Not only does it terminate in a rainforest, but – unlike so many glaciers around the world – it is actually advancing, by an average of about 1m (3ft) a day. Fed by four glaciers high in the Southern Alps, Fox glacier drops 2,600m (8,530ft) on its 13-km (8-mile) journey to within 300m (1,000ft) of sea level. Unlike glaciers in the European Alps, where winter snowfall is diminishing, the catchment area (*névé*) of the Fox glacier (and the Franz Josef glacier to the north) currently receives up to 30m (100ft) of snow a year.

The 'roaring forties' winds bring moist air from the Southern Ocean which is forced up the sides of the Southern Alps, cools and drops rain and snow in large quantities. This becomes compacted, blue, glacial ice, which flows under its own weight down the glacier valleys. A layer of water underneath the glacier, and rapid melt lower down its course, allow the glacier to flow anything up to ten times faster than most glaciers. The valleys through which the Fox glacier grinds its way down is stepped, forcing the ice to stretch and break up, creating massive crevasses, pinnacles and sheer icefalls. The viewpoint at the bottom of the glacier provides spectacular vistas, but there are also guided walks onto the more stable parts of the glacier for those who dare.

YOU SHOULD KNOW
There are frequent icefalls, and the barriers at the foot of the glacier are for visitors' safety. If you want to go onto the glacier, take a guided walk.

HOW TO GET THERE:
By road from Greymouth.
WHEN TO GO:
Spring to autumn.
NEAREST TOWNS:
Fox glacier village/Weheka 5km (3 miles).

BOUNDARY STREAM MAINLAND ISLAND

New Zealand

The 'Mainland Island' is not in fact an island but some 8 sq km (3 sq miles) of land on the eastern side of the Maungaharuru Range of North Island, with a variety of habitats from lowland forest at about 300m (1,000ft) to montane forest at 1,000m (3,300ft). Its importance lies in the highly endangered bird species that are protected here. Before people arrived here, especially Europeans, there were very few predators, so several bird species, including the iconic kiwis, took to the ground. Over millennia they lost the ability to fly and nested on the ground or underground, which made them vulnerable to hunting and predation from introduced cats, rats, stoats, ferrets, weasels and hedgehogs. Some of the birds are kept within large enclosures for their own protection, and this enables visitors to see them close up, which would normally be impossible, while allowing the birds to live completely naturally. Others, such as the kokako, wander freely. Scenic walks through the area, which is being restored to provide habitat for the birds, offer panoramic views.

LAKE TE ANAU

New Zealand

For many, Lake Te Anau is the gateway to South Island's Fiordland. It is 65km (40 miles) in length and three fiords form arms on its western side. The original name was Te Ana-au, meaning 'the cave of swirling water' in Maori. To the east is mostly rolling farmland, but to the west are the ridges of the Franklyn, Stuart, Murchison and Kepler mountains. The cave after which the lake is named was lost to all but memory until, in 1948, after thee years' work, Lawson Burrows traced it by following the clues in old Maori legends. It is now chiefly known for the glow-worm colonies that live within its protective walls. It can only be visited by guided tours, because the ecosystem is too fragile to allow it to become swamped with visitors. As well as the glow-worms, these limestone caves, which are still being carved out from the mountain, are filled – as their Maori name might suggest – with whirlpools and waterfalls. Lake Te Anau is the starting point for two of New Zealand's best-loved long-distance walks: the Milford Track leaves the northernmost point of the lake for Milford Sound, while the circular Kepler Track starts and ends at the south tip of the lake beside the upper Waiau river.

TONGARIRO NATIONAL PARK

New Zealand

Centred on the three magnificent volcanoes – Tongariro, Ruapehy and Ngauruhoe – the Tongariro National Park is an outstanding area for its landscape and cultural value, and was recognized by UNESCO, who added it to the list of World Heritage Sites in 1990. The core of the land was gifted to the nation in 1887 by Te Heuheu Tukino IV, the paramount chief of the Maori Ngati Tuwharetoa iwi, in order to prevent its exploitation. More land was acquired by the government and the area was established as the first national park in New Zealand, and the fourth in the world, in 1894. More land has been added since.

The Tongariro Massif is part of North Island's volcanic plateau, which stretches almost all of the way to the Bay of Plenty in the north. The area in the immediate vicinity of the volcanoes, especially Ngauruhoe, is very sparsely vegetated because of volcanic activity, but lower down, podocarp/broadleaf rainforest and beech woodland can be found. Birds that find a refuge here include North Island brown kiwis, kakapos, bellbirds, southern boobooks and silvereyes. The only two mammals native to New Zealand – short-tailed and long-tailed bats – are also present. Hiking tracks criss-cross the park, including the Tongariro Crossing, which runs from Mount Tongariro to Mount Ngauruhoe and forms part of one of New Zealand's Great Tracks, the Tongariro Northern Circuit. Walking through this area is certainly the best way to appreciate its beauty.

HOW TO GET THERE:
By road from Auckland 330km (205 miles).
WHEN TO GO:
Any time of year.
NEAREST TOWN:
Taurewa 10km (6 miles).

DON'T MISS
Pohutu geyser
which erupts up to
15 times a day.

GEYSER FLAT, WHAKAREWAREWA

New Zealand

HOW TO GET THERE:
By road from Auckland
196km (122 miles).
WHEN TO GO:
Any time.
NEAREST TOWN:
Rotorua.

Close to the Maori village, old fortress and heritage centre of Te Puia lies a series of barren areas, where the earth is covered with light encrustations. This is the best of New Zealand's remaining geyser fields. There are more than 60 geyser vents in all, but only seven of them are currently active. The encrustations around them are called sinter, and are silica deposited here as the waters cooled. The best known of them is Pohutu geyser, which can send water shooting up to 30m (100ft) into the sky, usually once an hour. Pohutu means 'explosion' or 'big splash'. The big geysers are all situated above a buried fault line running roughly north–south. Hot water seeps up through the fault into natural reservoirs underground but can escape only through a narrow vent, which acts like the cork in a champagne bottle. The water in the reservoir gets more and more pressurized and hot, until bubbles start to form and rise through the vent. Once a bubble breaks through the water at the top of the vent, the pressure is suddenly released and hot water and gas spurt into the air. These geysers are in constant flux because of geological activity here and elsewhere and human activity nearby. The Prince of Wales Feathers geyser only came into being in June 1886 after the eruption at Mount Tarawera kilometres away. It used to spurt just before Pohutu, and used to be called the Indicator geyser, but now it is active nearly all the time. Other geysers in the area have disappeared or become dormant: the Wairoa geyser used to reach 50m (170ft) and its irregular activity could last for some two hours. However, there has been no activity for some years.

MOUNT NGAURUHOE

New Zealand

Part of the Tongariro massif, Mountt Ngaurohoe first erupted about 2,500 years ago and since then has grown to 2,291m (7,516ft), looming more than 1,000m (3,300ft) above its surroundings. It was one of the most active volcanoes on the planet during the 20th century. Its last eruption was in 1975, but in June 2006 there was a series of earthquake swarms about 4km (2.5 miles) below the crater. The mountain was first climbed in 1839 from the northwest by J.C. Bidwill, and this is still the most popular route today. From the Mangatepopo hut, the scramble to the crater is supposed to take about two hours, but in practice it can take longer as the volcanic clinker that makes up the mountain is loose and it can be hard to keep your footing. The climb gets steeper nearer the top, when you suddenly reach the narrow ridge that surrounds the crater. This gaping hole was tailor-made to star as Mount Doom in the *Lord of the Rings* films: its forbidding, dark rim is stained with patches of red reminiscent of dried blood. While the inside of the crater is no longer filled with clouds of steam, hot vents around its edge are still spewing noxious gases, so entry to the crater is not allowed. If the weather is good, the views from the crater rim are stunning.

HOW TO GET THERE:
By road, then on foot.
WHEN TO GO:
Late spring to early autumn.
NEAREST TOWN:
Taurewa 16km (10 miles).

HOW TO GET THERE:
By road from Greymouth.
WHEN TO GO:
Spring to autumn.
NEAREST TOWN:
Fox glacier village.

WESTLAND TAI POUTINI NATIONAL PARK

New Zealand

This large national park covers 1,175 sq km (450 sq miles) of spectacular scenery between the peaks of the central Southern Alps and the remote, wild beaches of the west coast of South Island. It contains glaciers, temperate rainforest, scenic lakes, grasslands and wetlands, as well as fantastic beaches. Like Lake Matheson, many of the lakes in the coastal wetlands are dark in colour because of nutrients leached out from the soil and this makes them perfect for waders, such as white heron. One of the most popular walking trails, of which there are many, is the Copland Track, which leads up from Highway 6. This 17-km (10.5-mile) hike up the beautiful Copland valley to the pass of the same name takes about seven hours. A diversion is the natural hot pools by the Welcome Flat Hut, although it is important to remember not to submerge your head: the warm water hosts bugs that cause amoebic meningitis.

Right: The forest canopy in Westland Tai Poutini National Park.

MOUNT RUAPEHU

New Zealand

One of the world's most active volcanoes, Mount Ruapehu has suffered 60 eruptions of various sizes since 1945. It first erupted some 250,000 years ago and now has three peaks – Tahurangi, Te Heuheu and Paretetaitonga – that surround the crater. The last major eruption was in 1995, but there were also minor eruptions in 1996 and 2006. Because Ruapehu is so active, its crater is so hot that snow melts and a warm, acidic lake occupies the crater between major eruptions. Held in only by a thin dam of solidified volcanic ash called tephra, the lake fills year by year until the wall finally breaks and a mudslide – a lahar – bursts down the side of the mountain. In March 2007, a lahar swept 1,400,000 cubic m (50,000,000 cubic ft) of water, rock and mud down the eastern side of the mountain. The release of pressure at the top of the crater led to concern that a new eruption might occur, but over the following few months activity did not increase markedly. There are two public ski fields on the volcano's slopes, and hiking and walking trails on the lower slopes. The route to the top is not technical, but it can be dangerous because the weather on the mountain can close in suddenly.

LAKE MANAPOURI

New Zealand

The deepest of South Island's southern glacial lakes, Lake Manapouri is a quiet haven. Surrounded on three sides by high mountains, which remain snowcapped for a large part of the year, this beautiful lake and its surroundings are popular with wilderness-lovers from all over the country. There are several walking and hiking trails that pass by or close to the lake, of which the 67-km (42-mile) Kepler Track and the Circle Track are the best known. These lead through native bush and require a degree of fitness. In winter and spring, the higher parts of the routes will be closed because of snow. The lake saw the beginning of the early green movement in New Zealand when in the early 1960s conservationists fought, and won against, the proposal to raise the water levels 30m (100ft) to enlarge the reservoir for the Manapouri power station, which would have drowned most of the 33 islands dotted within the lake. The power station was built, but the water levels are maintained as close to natural fluctuation levels as possible.

DON'T MISS
The wonderful
diving.

BORA BORA

French Polynesia

HOW TO GET THERE:
By air from Tahiti or by boat.
WHEN TO GO:
May to October.
NEAREST TOWN:
Papeete, Tahiti 230km
(140 miles).

One of the Society Islands in French Polynesia, Bora Bora consists of the tip of a submerged volcano almost completely surrounded by a near-rectangular reef. It is simply beautiful. The beaches on the reef have the white sand of ground-up coral, and the lagoon is the exact shade of blue that all lagoons should be. The lagoon and reefs have a bewildering array of fish, crabs, clams and eels, but the best spots to see marine life are in the open ocean beyond, where barracuda, tuna, red snapper, jackfish and several species of ray are to be seen, as well as black-tipped, grey and lemon sharks and turtles. Between August and October, humpback whales may also be seen on migration. Every sort of watersport ever dreamed of is available in the lagoon or the ocean nearby, but for the less active, the reefs, with their huts on stilts and palm trees, are the ideal place to relax. Glass-bottomed boats show off the wildlife in the lagoon, while among the most popular excursions are the ray- and shark-feeding trips. On the main island, the best way to get around is by bicycle. Other activities on offer include horse-riding and tours up to the twin volcanic peaks for lovely views over the idyllic lagoon.

ASIA

KAMCHATKA PENINSULA

Russian Federation

A wilderness peninsula jutting from the mainland of Russia's far east between the Sea of Okhotsk and the Bering Sea, Kamchatka is a naturalist's paradise, a cultural stronghold of the Itelmen, Koryak, Even and Chukchi peoples, and the most active volcanic region on the planet. A full 27 per cent (3.7 million hectares/9.1 million acres) of Kamchatka is occupied by six linked nature reserves that provide the most comprehensive view anywhere of volcanic diversity. In the northern Klyuchevskoy Reserve you can see the world being born. It's a world of fire and ice where you can see the lava glowing red on the glaciers, and the lunar landscape is younger than many visitors. As you travel south, there are fewer active volcanoes but more geysers and geothermal springs bubbling red or translucent turquoise. These landscapes bear witness to the evolution of a volcanic ecosystem over millions of years to the present. Nalychevo Park is a microcosm of Kamchatka's magnificence and natural abundance. Better still is the Kronotsky Reserve in the peninsula's centre, which will amaze even the most experienced traveller. Among the steaming cones and deep-blue crater lakes lie the Valley of Geysers, the boiling mud pits of the Burlyaschy volcano, and the Uzon caldera where large numbers of Kamchatka brown bears (Eurasia's biggest) peacefully gather berries and fish for salmon. None of the reserves are accessible by road, so there are no quick exits should you encounter one unexpectedly. There are 10,000 of them, and it's advisable to know how to behave in their territory.

HOW TO GET THERE:
By air to Petropavlovsk-Kamchatsky, then by road or helicopter.
WHEN TO GO:
June to October.
NEAREST TOWN:
Petropavlovsk-Kamchatsky is the hub for all six reserves.

THE GOLDEN MOUNTAINS OF ALTAI

Russian Federation

Wild and majestic, the Altai range marks the junction of central Asia and Siberia, and of Russia with China, Mongolia and Kazakhstan. It's the heartland of Russia's most ancient cultures, but the standing stones and sacred sites of the Altai and Scythian peoples have all but been reclaimed by wilderness. Colossal tracts have now been set aside as reserves to protect the mosaic of ecosystems that underwrites the region's grandeur and variety. Just one of them, the Altaisky Nature Reserve, has a core area of 881,200 hectares (2.2 million acres) that includes every permutation of steppe, taiga, alpine meadow, highland forest, glacial lake, mountain tundra and snowcapped peak, and at every level the richest diversity of appropriate fauna and flora, and some of the rarest. The Altaisky also contains the 'Jewel of Western Siberia', Lake Teletskoye. It is a sky-blue ribbon snaking between cragged peaks and imperial stands of Siberian cedar forest. Fed by 70 rivers and 150 meltwater cascades, its crystal water is among the purest on Earth.

SIKHOTE-ALIN MOUNTAINS

Russian Federation

The south-central section of the Sikhote-Alin range looks like an ocean of dense forest, set between the Ussuri river and Russia's far eastern coast on the Sea of Japan. Ridge succeeds ridge as far as the eye can see, divided only by fissures and canyons carved by torrent streams. It's a vast wilderness, almost completely untouched by humans, and it is a sanctuary for the world's biggest and rarest cat, the Amur (Siberian) tiger. The World Heritage Reserve that protects this magnificent creature is established where the taiga meets the subtropics, so that southern species like the Amur tiger and Himalayan bear live alongside northern species like the brown bear, lynx and ermine. In fact, dual species of every kind abound here – of mammals, insects, plants and birds – and include the rarest of each. The distinctive flora and fauna of each level is unmatched in Russia or the world for variety and rarity. Despite its remoteness, the Sikhote-Alin Reserve is accessible and well worth a visit.

LAKE BAIKAL

Russian Federation

HOW TO GET THERE:
By air or Trans-Siberian
railway to Irkutsk, then
by road or ferry.
WHEN TO GO:
Summer.
NEAREST TOWN:
Listvyanka 1km (0.6 miles).

The Russian Federation's Lake Baikal lies in an active continental rift at a height of 456m (1,496ft). The rift is widening by some 2cm (¾in) each year. Its surface area is 31,500 sq km (12,159 sq miles) and it is 1,700m (5,557ft) deep, making it the deepest lake in the world. The rift itself is 8–9km (5–5.5 miles) below the surface, covered in kilometres of silt. Lake Baikal contains 20 per cent of the Earth's unfrozen fresh water, more than all of America's Great Lakes together. The lake is renowned for its clear waters and for its wildlife, much of which occurs nowhere else in the world, including the nerpa (Baikal seal). These animals have evolved in isolation, and the lake has been dubbed the 'Galápagos of Russia'. It is also, more poetically, known as the 'Blue Eye of Siberia'. Baikal's catchment area is vast: no fewer than 336 rivers drain into it, while it has only one outlet, the Angara river, which exits the lake near its western end and flows north. It is not just its size that makes Lake Baikal a must-see. Much of its coastline and its islands are stunningly beautiful. It is surrounded by forested mountains, with an area of taiga on the north shore. Listed as a World Heritage Site by UNESCO in 1996 because of its importance for the study of evolution and climate, and for the wildlife in the lake and surrounding areas, Lake Baikal is one of the world's most special places.

HOW TO GET THERE:
From Anchorage (Alaska)
via Provideniya (Russia)
on an organized tour.
WHEN TO GO:
July and August.

WRANGEL ISLAND

Russian Federation

North of the Arctic Circle, straddling the 180° meridian where east meets west, lies one of the most treasured wildlife habitats in the world – a bleak, rocky island with only one human settlement. The island's coastline is varied – high cliffs, swamp, coastal lagoons and shingle or rock beaches. A place that for humans is one of the least hospitable on Earth – freezing cold, howling winds, snow-covered for eight months of the year and in complete blackout from November to January – is a wildlife paradise. Wrangel has the highest density of polar bear dens and the largest population of Pacific walruses in the world – up to 100,000 congregate here. It is also the only breeding ground for Asia's last remaining snow goose population. In winter, Wrangel is dark, still, and eerily silent apart from the constant howl of the Arctic wind. But come spring, the island suddenly bursts into life: tens of thousands of birds arrive to nest in the rocky cliffs, polar bears emerge from their dens with newborn cubs in tow, and walruses loll around on the ice floes and rocky spits. The island has an ephemeral, magical quality that will remain etched in your memory.

DON'T MISS

The Skete of St Nicolas
on Nicolski I – the most
beautiful of all.

VALAAM ARCHIPELAGO
AND LAKE LADOGA

Russian Federation

Vast, pale-blue skies merge with the endlessly bright water, splintering their mutual reflection in a wash of gold. Strokes of spring green or autumnal russet meld into the horizon, where islands stand seasonal vigil against the northern immensity. This is Lake Ladoga, at 17,700 sq km (6,830 sq miles) the largest lake in Europe, and emblem of the soul of Russia. And Valaam is its pearl, the biggest of 660 islands.

Most visitors take a boat or hydrofoil 215km (134 miles) from St Petersburg, or a shorter ferry from the Karelian towns of Sortavala and Pitkyaranta.

Coasting the bays, cliffs and skerries where spruce and pine forests cling to every rocky ledge, and bathed in the luminous enormity of a huge sky, it's easy to feel a growing sense of the spiritual seclusion that defines the region. For here the cultural landscapes are as important as the natural: Ladoga and Valaam reflect 1,000 years of Russia's ancient and modern history. Long before the Second World War, when the frozen lake became known as the 'Road of Life' by providing the only access to besieged Leningrad (St Petersburg), Valaam was the oldest monastic community. Then and now endemic ringed seals lounge on the rocks beside the complex of chapels, churches, alleys, orchards and bridges linking the many hermitages and sketes, where monks pursue the specialist rites of antiquity. The magnificent icons and reliquaries of the Cathedral of the Transfiguration and its satellite monasteries match those of Mount Athos in Greece – and when you see how seamlessly the domes and cupolas blend into nature, and hear the wind-borne Znameny chant in all the divine glory of its ancient harmonies, you begin to understand Valaam's matchless spiritual significance.

HOW TO GET THERE:
By boat/hydrofoil from
St Petersburg, Sortavala
or Pitkyaranta.
WHEN TO GO:
Year-round.
NEAREST TOWN:
Sortavala 43km (27 miles).

YOU SHOULD KNOW
America's first saint,
St Herman of Alaska,
came from Valaam.

VIRGIN KOMI FORESTS

Russian Federation

The Virgin Komi forests cover 3.28 million hectares (8.1 million acres) of tundra and mountain tundra in the northern Urals, the most extensive area of virgin boreal forest remaining in Europe. Almost completely undisturbed by economic activities, the region is a real treasure-trove of taiga biodiversity. It accounts for over 40 species of mammal, 204 species of bird and valuable fish. The Virgin Komi Biosphere unites two major sites: the Pechoro-Ilychsky Nature Preserve and the enormous Yugyd-Va National Park. Their combined territory stretches for 300km (188 miles) along the western slope of the Polar and Northern Urals, marking the transition of mid- and northern taiga to forest and mountain tundra, and the northwestern limit of the Siberian cedar's habitat. Their position is important to the entire regional ecosystem: the humid western slopes contribute to the great Pechora river basin where European plant species abruptly replace the Siberian flora of the eastern Urals. Among the Pechora piedmont of spruce, pine and fir forests are both pine and moss swamps, and the Gusinoe Bolota ('Goose Swamp') is a peat bog over 5m (16ft) deep, near which a small research establishment is still conducting experiments in domesticating moose.

HOW TO GET THERE:
By air, rail or bus to Pechora; by road to Troitsko-Pechorsk.
WHEN TO GO:
May to September.
NEAREST TOWNS:
Pechora or Troitsko-Pechorsk.

MOUNT ELBRUS

Russian Federation

HOW TO GET THERE:
By plane to Mineralnye Vody; then bus to Terskol.
WHEN TO GO:
April to October.
NEAREST TOWN:
Nalchik 129km (81 miles).

DON'T MISS
The tribal villages of the Baksan Valley.

The main range of the Caucasus mountains marks the border between the Russian Federation and Georgia, and the southern boundary of Europe with Asia. About 10km (6 miles) north of the main range stands Mount Elbrus, the highest point at 5,643m (18,340ft), which is wholly in Russia and in Europe. The outstanding natural beauty of Mount Elbrus attracts as many visitors as does its mountaineering status. Both walkers and serious climbers need to spend time acclimatizing in nearby valleys – but be aware that most of these are subject to stringent access rules because of their proximity to national borders. It takes a lot of vital paperwork to get near Elbrus as well as on to or up it, so to avoid problems it's best to approach the mountain only from the Russian side. Standing so tall between north and south, Elbrus suffers temperature extremes and weather that often changes dramatically in minutes, so go prepared.

WESTERN CAUCASUS

Russian Federation

Where the foothills of the Great Caucasus plunge into the Black Sea lies the only large mountain area in Europe undisturbed by significant human impact. Incredibly, only 50km (31 miles) northeast of Sochi, for years the centre of Russia's busiest Black Sea beach resorts, is a truly pristine wilderness where endangered, rare, endemic and relic plant and animal species are concentrated. Nowhere else are subtropical, lowland, alpine and high mountain landscapes located so closely to one another. It's a place of rushing torrents and crystal waterfalls, mountain lakes and towering firs more than 70m (227ft) high, of forests of beech, chestnut and oak, flower-strewn meadows and wetlands noisy with 126 species of bird life. Ancient and modern glaciers have cut the limestone massifs into a complex underground system of rivers and lakes. Vorontsov's caves is one of the largest cavern systems in Russia, reaching 1,600m (5,200ft) deep and 16km (10 miles) long. Other spectacular highlights include the Orekhovsky waterfall, Khostinsky canyon, the Pseuapse river valley and the Dolmen site, one of over 100 Paleolithic, and later, monuments in the region. The natural and wildlife miracle of the Western Caucasus is likely to endure now that the smaller national parks of the region have been brought within the greater Biosphere Reserve. It's Europe's single richest eco-reserve, of global importance, and utterly breathtaking.

HOW TO GET THERE:
From Sochi or any of its neighbouring towns on the Black Sea.
WHEN TO GO:
Year-round.
NEAREST TOWN:
Sochi 50km (31 miles).

YOU SHOULD KNOW
The European mountain bison's real name is the wild wisent.

DON'T MISS
Vorontsov's caves.

KAINDY GORGE AND LAKE

Kazakhstan

Some 320km (200 miles) east of Almaty and a bit beyond the crowded Kolsay Lakes region is a peaceful, if eerie, scene. Within the last century, a massive landslide in the Kaindy Gorge dammed the flow of the waters through it and created a basin that gradually filled to form this beautiful lake. In geological terms, the event happened so recently that the Schrenk's spruces that were submerged by the lake have not yet had time to decay in the cold water, and their trunks emerge from the water like a strange work of art.

The way up to this remote spot offers views over the landscape of the western Tien Shan, in particular the valley of the river Chilik, the Saty Gorge and the rugged, crumbly limestone walls of Kaindy Gorge itself. The lake is 400m (1,300ft) long and up to 30m (100ft) deep in places. Although the water can be very cold in spring, later in the year it is possible to swim out and explore the semi-submerged trees. The timber forests around the gorge are beautiful and are full of birds, and the region is noted for its rich wildlife, particularly during the spring and autumn bird-migration seasons.

HOW TO GET THERE:
By road from Almaty.
WHEN TO GO:
Spring or autumn.
NEAREST TOWN:
Zhalanash 70km (45 miles).

THE SINGING BARKHAN

Kazakhstan

HOW TO GET THERE:
By road and off-road from Almaty.
WHEN TO GO:
Spring, late summer or early autumn.
NEAREST TOWN:
Almaty 180km (120 miles).

In the valley of the Ili river, just a short distance from its right bank and some 50km (30 miles) off the road from Almaty, is a desert landscape that includes one of the strangest phenomena in nature: a 3.2-km-long (2-mile-long), 150-m-high (400-ft-high) sand dune that makes an eerie noise as you walk on it and cause the sands to move beneath your feet and roll down the slope as you walk across it. The sound has been described as being like a riverboat siren, loud singing or an aeroplane. This crescent-shaped, shifting dune and its companions are in the west of the Altyn Emel National Park, which extends eastwards into the Aqtau mountains. Its variety of scenery and habitats, from the desert by the river to wooded slopes and mountains, makes it both beautiful and an excellent place for wildlife-spotting. Because of its remoteness, this well-protected park is a peaceful place to visit and well worth the effort.

LAKE BALKHASH

Kazakhstan

HOW TO GET THERE:
By road from Almaty.
WHEN TO GO:
Spring or autum.
NEAREST TOWN:
Balkhash.

The vast, scimitar-shaped Lake Balkhash is the second-largest lake in area in central Asia. Strangely, it is salty in the east and freshwater in the west, and is deeper in the eastern arm. Its maximum depth is only about 27m (90ft) and its surface is usually frozen solid from November to March. It is an endorheic lake, which means that it loses water by evaporation as it has no outflow. The two halves of the lake are separated by a sandbar and the main inflow is from the Ili river. Lake Balkhash is a vital stopping point for birds during the migrating seasons, and the area is becoming increasingly popular with Western bird-watchers.

The reedbeds of the Ili delta are thought to be among the best places to see various rarities, including Dalmatian and white pelicans, several species of terns, spoonbills, night herons, feruginous duck and white-tailed eagle, although there are also other spots on the lake from where many of these can be seen. There has been concern in recent years that water extraction upstream and the damming of the Ili are causing the lake to dry out, but concerted efforts are now being made to prevent this happening as far as is possible.

CHARYN CANYON

Kazakhstan

HOW TO GET THERE:
By road from Almaty.
WHEN TO GO:
Spring or autumn.
NEAREST TOWN:
Chilik.

DON'T MISS
The Valley of
the Castles.

In the east of Kazakhstan, near the border with China, is a site that many people say rivals America's Grand Canyon, for spectacle if not size. The most popular part, the Valley of the Castles (Dolina Zamkov), has fantastic, different-coloured rock formations showing the history of the landscape. At the bottom are volcanic rocks and above are red gravels and grey rocks formed of ash and stones from later eruptions. Apart from the salt marsh through which you approach the canyon and the river itself, hidden from view until you are almost upon it, this whole region is an arid desert, and the river creates an oasis for plants and a few animals that would otherwise not survive. It is possible for experienced drivers to get to the base of the canyon in a four-wheel drive, but there is an easy hiking trail from the camp site at the end of the Valley of the Castles. From the trail into the floor of the canyon, the rock formations reach up between 90 and 300m (300 and 1,000ft), and the weird and wonderful shapes really do resemble fortifications. In some places, visitors can see fossils in the canyon walls. In summer, it is possible to cross the river in a basket, or on a wire, but at this time of year it is very hot.

TIEN SHAN

Kazakhstan

HOW TO GET THERE:
By road from Almaty.
WHEN TO GO:
Summer.
NEAREST TOWNS:
There are many.

YOU SHOULD KNOW

There are 30–40 small earthquakes in the Tien Shan each year, and snowmelt in spring can cause mudslides.

The Tien Shan mountain range stretches for more than 2,400km (1,500 miles), forming the border between northwest China and Kazakhstan and Kyrgyzstan. The highest peak is the Pobeda at 7,439m (24,406ft), also known as the Jengish Chokusu, which stands in Kyrgyzstan, while Khan-Tengri (the 'Lord of the Spirits'), the highest peak in Kazakhstan, is a marble-capped pyramid of 7,010m (23,000ft) and one of the most popular climbs for experts. Because of the dry climate, the snowline is far higher than elsewhere in the world, and is generally above 3,350m (11,000ft). The western Tien Shan contain beautiful landscapes, including cedar forests, snowcapped mountain peaks, and deep canyons. Khan Tengri straddles the border between Kazakhstan and Kyrgyzstan, and is a mecca not just for climbers but for hikers and riders, too, who make for the lower slopes. Inylchek glacier lies here and is almost 60km (37 miles) in length: it holds Merzbacher Lake in its centre. Other beautiful lakes in the region include the three Kolsai Lakes, known as the pearls of the northern Tien Shan, while Lake Marakol is claimed to be as picturesque as Lake Baikal.

HUANGSHAN MOUNTAIN

China

Formed 100 million years ago by movement in the Earth's crust and subsequently carved out by glaciers, this multi-peaked, granite range is known collectively as Huangshan Mountain. Situated in the south of Anhui Province, in eastern China, 77 of Huangshan's peaks reach heights above 1,000m (3,300ft), and 72 are poetically named, the three highest being called 'Lotus', 'Bright Summit' and 'Celestial'. Listed by UNESCO in 1990, the peaks have their own, individual beauty – some slender and graceful, others majestic and craggy, and all swathed in a multitude of trees, particularly pines, some of which are over 1,000 years old. Forces of nature have shaped these trees – they grow from crevices in the rock face, cling to the edges of steep cliffs, and overhang deep, dark valleys. Some have roots so twisted that they look like mythical creatures. Amongst the trees, streams rush and babble – the area is known for its waterfalls, hot springs and natural pools. Pathways twist and turn around the peaks, which are often shrouded in mist and cloud. Many of the peaks rise above cloud level, and visitors can see fascinating light phenomena as they look down on the clouds from above. This is a natural work of art, known for centuries and immortalized by poets and painters from Li Bai (701–762) through the master painters of the Qing Dynasty, to the modern day. There are over 1,500 species of flora here, and every season has a different look. Spring brings a mass of bright wildflowers; summer is voluptuous and verdant; in autumn, the maples and other deciduous species blaze red, yellow and purple, before falling in the path of winter and its frosty world of silver, white and grey.

HOW TO GET THERE:
By road from Huangshan.
WHEN TO GO:
Any time of year.
NEAREST TOWN:
Huangshan 72km (45 miles).

DON'T MISS
Celestial Peak.

THE THREE GORGES

China

HOW TO GET THERE:
Fly to Chongqing, then
take a cruise.
WHEN TO GO:
October to March.
NEAREST TOWN:
Chongqing, at the southern
end of the Three Gorges.

Situated in Hubei province, roughly at the halfway point of the Yangtze river, is the famously scenic area of the Three Gorges. The Qutang Gorge is 8km (5 miles) long, never more than 100m (330ft) wide, with almost vertical cliff walls rising up into the clouds. Wu Gorge is 45km (28 miles) long, and lined with such fantastic cliffs that legend tells of the goddess Yao Ji and her sisters having to turn some wicked river dragons into mountains. Finally, there is Xiling Gorge, at 66km (41 miles) the longest of the three, and historically considered the most dangerous to navigate. This area is not only spectacular to look at, but is also bursting with cultural history and many important archaeological sites. For 90 years Chinese governments have been considering putting a dam in these gorges, and the resulting construction, completed in 2006 and fully operational by 2012, is the largest hydroelectric river dam in the world. It has caused enormous controversy. Proponents point to the clean electricity it will provide, desperately needed by the booming economy, and say that it will help to control the ever more frequent flooding that occurs on the Yangtze river. Opponents point to the one-million-plus displaced people, the loss of hundreds of archaeological sites, 13 cities, 140 towns and 1,352 villages and the damage to the ecosystem. It will be some years before we know whether this was a brilliant idea, or a disastrous one.

HOW TO GET THERE:
By road from Kunming. Bus
tours are available.
WHEN TO GO:
Year-round.
NEAREST TOWN:
Kunming 96km (60 miles).

YOU SHOULD KNOW

Bus tours run from Kunming, and there are a number of hotels in the area.

Right: The Shilin Stone Forest in China.

THE SHILIN STONE FOREST

China

Spread over 350 sq km (140 sq miles) in Yunnan province, these extraordinary limestone needles emerging vertically from the ground look like an ancient, petrified forest. The rocks are more than 270 million years old, and local legend says the forest was created when a young woman was forbidden to marry her love – she rebelled by turning herself into stone. Caused by the dissolution of limestone over millennia, the tall rocks seem to fall to the ground in the manner of stalagmites. Since 2007, two parts of the site, the Naigu Stone Forest and Suogeyi Village, have been UNESCO World Heritage Sites as part of the South China Karst. You can climb to the top of the stones for astonishing views, and roads wind around between the peaks, taking visitors to ever more unexpected and beautiful scenes.

MUZTAGH ATA

China

Muztagh Ata is a 7,546-m (24,757-ft) mountain peak on the northern edge of the Tibetan plateau, in China's Xinjiang province. Although it is only the second-highest peak in the Kunlun mountains, it is enormously popular with mountaineers. It towers over the Karakoram Highway, which runs from Kashi to Pakistan, and is only 24km (15 miles) from the Chinese border with Tajikistan – thus access to Muztagh Ata is reasonably simple, and it looks deceptively easy to climb. The first recorded attempt to climb this mountain was in 1894 by Sven Hedin, who was lulled into thinking it would be a relatively simple climb. Further official attempts were made in 1900, 1904 and 1947, all of which failed due to weather conditions. The first successful attempt was made by a party of Chinese and Russian climbers in 1956, and since then a great many successful climbs have been made. Muztagh Ata means 'Father of Ice Mountains', and it is easy to see why it was so named. The western and southern slopes are gently graduated, though divided into sections by deep, glacial troughs. The east and north faces, however, fall away from the summit ridge in precipitous, 2,100-m (7,000-ft) drops. Over 20 glaciers clothe the slopes, and the mountain has long, exposed areas that are bitterly cold, lashed by freezing winds and covered in deep, treacherous snow.

SICHUAN GIANT PANDA SANCTUARIES

China

Over 30 per cent of the world's giant pandas live within the Sichuan Sanctuaries in southwestern Sichuan province. Covering seven nature reserves and nine scenic parks in the Qionglai and Jiajin mountains, the sanctuaries form the largest contiguous habitat of these charming animals. Genetically, giant pandas are bears, although they do not hibernate and, unlike other bears, their eyes have vertical rather than round pupils. Despite having a carnivore's digestive tract, bamboo accounts for 99 per cent of their diet, and this is a major factor in their decline. As temperatures increase, pandas move higher, and only a few of the 25 bamboo species that they eat can thrive at high altitudes. Because it is low in nutrition, pandas need to eat some 13kg (30lbs) of bamboo shoots and leaves daily. Until recently it was thought that only 1,600 of these much-loved animals still existed in the wild, but thanks to conservation efforts, that number is increasing.

NAM CO LAKE
China

Situated in the Nyainqentanglha mountain range in Tibet, Nam Co Lake lies at an altitude of 4,627m (15,180ft), and is one of Tibet's three Holy Lakes.

Meaning 'Heavenly Lake' in Tibetan, Nam Co is a place of pilgrimage, and Buddhists come here, not only from all over China, but also from India, Nepal, Bhutan and Sikkim to complete a ritual walk around it. Dorje Gongzhama, the deity of the lake, is also the queen of the deity of Nyainqentanglha. Both were born in the Tibetan Year of the Sheep, and during the summer times of those years, more than any others, pilgrims come here to seek good luck and good harvests.

Measuring some 70km (44 miles) from east to west, 30km (19 miles) north to south and with a maximum depth of 33m (109ft), the lake can take anywhere from ten days to one month to circle, depending on how much time the pilgrim spends in contemplation and prayer en route. Four monasteries are situated around the lake, and there are ancient cave hermitages, too. This is a place of austere beauty — irregular in shape and strongly blue in colour, the water curves around the base of mountain slopes sparsely covered with vegetation. Several small islands dot the lake and in the past, towards the end of winter, pilgrims would walk across the frozen ice to an island and stay there in spiritual retreat until the waters froze again at the end of summer. To the north and west stand peak after peak of snow-covered mountains often hidden by mist, and changeable weather brings sudden snowstorms swirling and drifting across the lake.

HOW TO GET THERE:
By road from Lhasa.
WHEN TO GO:
June to September.
NEAREST TOWN:
Lhasa 420km (260 miles).

YOU SHOULD KNOW
Even if it is sunny and pleasant during the day, the temperature will plummet at night, so bring very warm clothing.

WULINGYIANG SCENIC AND HISTORIC INTEREST AREA

China

DON'T MISS
Puguang Temple and the grotto in the Yuhuang Cave.

Located in Hunan Province, Wulingyiang's 26,000-hectare (64,250-acre) site is one of the country's 40 most famous scenic spots and is inhabited by several tribal groups. Some three billion years ago this was an ancient sea, and today's landscape of eroded quartzite sandstone is the exposed and eroded seafloor. The region contains over 3,000 narrow sandstone pillars and peaks, and of these, over 1,000 rise to over 200m (656ft). In amongst them are waterfalls, streams and pools, deep valleys, ravines and complex limestone caves. Almost the entire region is forested – 99 per cent is covered with vegetation, including many rare species. Zhangjiajie National Forest is covered with primitive, subtropical forest. It boasts 191 types of tree, and is absolutely draped in flowers – orchids, azaleas and giant mountain lotus scent the air. The lobster flower, unique to the park, can change colour up to five times a day. Suoxiyu is the largest area of the park, with a creek running from east to west. The valley floor, made of yellow-green and dark green shale, contrasts with the upper slopes of dark red or grey quartzite and shale. Huanglong, or Yellow Dragon Cave, is thought to be one of the largest in China. On four levels, it contains an underground lake, two rivers, three waterfalls, 13 halls and 96 corridors. The Tianzi Mountain Reserve is at a much higher elevation and is rich with strangely shaped peaks and rocks. Famously covered in mist and fog, it is renowned for its beautiful views.

HOW TO GET THERE:
Fly to Changsha, then by road to Zhangjiajie.
WHEN TO GO:
September to May.
NEAREST TOWN:
Zhangjiajie (formerly Dayong) is close to the edge of Wulingyiang.

DON'T MISS
The Tibetan villages
and their
traditional culture.

JIUZHAIGOU VALLEY

China

HOW TO GET THERE:
From Chengdu by road or
by plane to Chuanzhusi
Township, then by road, or
by helicopter.
WHEN TO GO:
Spring or autumn.
NEAREST TOWN:
Zhangzha, at the exit
of the valley.

YOU SHOULD KNOW
This is a UNESCO World
Heritage and Biosphere Site.
An entry fee is payable.

Jiuzhaigou Valley, or the Valley of Nine Villages, is a remote nature reserve nestled within the mountains of northern Sichuan. It was not officially recognized by the authorities until 1972, but prior to that it was inhabited for centuries by Tibetan and Qiang peoples. Named after the nine stockaded villages once strung out along the valley, today only six remain, and its permanent inhabitants number fewer than 1,000. Jiuzhaigou Valley really consists of three Y-shaped gullies, surrounded by fabulous karst mountains. Covered in virgin forest of mixed broadleaf and conifer, the region looks lovely at any time of year but is absolutely glorious in the autumn, as the leaves turn to gold and crimson. This is a much-visited area, best known for its network of pristine alpine lakes. The valley lies on major fault lines, and earthquakes as well as glaciers have shaped its topography over millennia. The naturally formed glacial lakes were produced by a combination of rock falls and extremely high carbonate deposits that make their waters crystal clear. There are over 100 lakes in Jiuzhaigou Valley, in different shades of jade and turquoise. Here, too, are multi-layered waterfalls, splashing droplets like glistening pearls against the rock. It is home to endemic species of bamboo and rhododendron. It also shelters tiny populations of endangered giant panda and golden snub-nosed monkey,.

MOUNT EMEI SCENIC AREA

China

Mount Emei, 3,100m (10,230ft) in height, is to be found to the west of the Chengdu plain, in the province of Sichuan. This is not only a scenically beautiful area, with high plant diversity and many endemic species, but also the site of the first Buddhist temple in China, built in the 1st century AD. As Buddhism spread, more temples were built on the mountain, making it one of the most revered sites in the world. Today more than 100 temples and monasteries can be found here, many of which offer accommodation to visitors. The three summits of the mountain stand parallel to each other, making Emei recognizable from afar. Here you will find deep gorges, valleys, undulating hills, rivers, springs and waterfalls. Water erosion has formed various karstic features such as an underground river, caverns and the Shisungou karst forest. Five nature reserves are established here, and there are five vegetation belts, from subalpine coniferous forest and shrubs at the highest levels, to subtropical evergreen broadleafed forest at the base. Altogether, some 3,200 plants have been recorded, including more than 100 that are endemic. Around 2,300 animal species have been recorded, including a number of internationally threatened mammals, such as red pandas, Asiatic black bears, Asiatic golden cats and Tibetan macaques. Inscribed by UNESCO in 1996, the inscription includes the Leshan Giant Buddha Area, located 40km (25 miles) from Mount Emei. In 713AD, a monk named Haitong began carving the largest buddha in the world from the west cliff of Lingyun mountain. Located at the confluence of three rivers, the head of this giant buddha, 71m (234ft) tall, reaches the top of the mountain, and its feet rest by the water. If you are interested in Buddhism, there is a wonderfully rich cultural heritage to be found here.

THREE PARALLEL RIVERS OF YUNNAN

China

This national park is China's foremost region of biodiversity and superlative natural beauty, as well as being a showcase of the geological history of the area over the past 50 million years. Situated in the mountains of northwest Yunnan province, the park contains part of the upper reaches of the Yangtze, Mekong and Salween rivers. These are three of the greatest rivers in Asia, and they pour relentlessly through three deep, parallel gorges, surrounded by spectacular, glaciated peaks. Every type of landscape in the northern hemisphere exists here, apart from desert and ocean, and despite forming only 0.4 per cent of China's landmass, it contains over 20 per cent of the country's most important plants and 25 per cent of its animal species. The park contains 118 peaks with altitudes of over 5,000m (16,500ft). The highest is Mount Kawegbo at 6,740m (22,242ft), from which flows the extraordinary Mingyongqia glacier. All sorts of plants and animals live here, including many that are rare, threatened and endemic. That rarest of creatures, the snow leopard, haunts the upper reaches of the mountains in remote splendour.

TIANMUSHAN BIOSPHERE RESERVE

China

Tianmushan Biosphere Reserve is situated in southeast China, not far from Shanghai and Hangzhou. Covering 4,284 hectares (10,590 acres) of land, it lies on the watershed between the rivers Yangtze and Qiantanjiang. Known as the 'Kingdom of Big Trees', Tianmushan was inscribed as a UNESCO Biosphere Reserve in 1996 for its extensive and ancient forests and woodlands. The Biosphere Reserve comprises a number of different 'gardens' that focus on the conservation of rare and threatened species, as well as species of economic importance. Located close to heavily populated urban areas, it is a tourist magnet, and the revenue raised is put back into protecting and managing the area. The climate here is quite extreme, ranging from -20°C to 38°C (-4°F to 100°F), with rainfall of up to 1,870mm (74in) per year. The flora is incredibly diverse, including both evergreen and deciduous broadleafed, bamboo and coniferous forests, as well as marshes and aquatic plants. A little agriculture takes place here, as does managed, commercial forestry of bamboo, mulberry, medicinal plants and tea. However, Tianmushan is known above all for its fantastic, huge and ancient trees, many of them over 1,000 years old, including wild ginkgo biloba. One of these famous 'living fossils' is fondly known as 'the old dragon trying to fly'. Perched on the edge of a cliff, this tree consists of 15 trunks, the largest of which is 110cm (43in) in diameter.

MOUNT WUYI

China

DON'T MISS
The Ancient Xiamei
Folk Buildings.

HOW TO GET THERE:
By air from many major
Chinese cities, or by train
from Fuzhou or Xiamen.
WHEN TO GO:
October to March.
NEAREST TOWNS:
Wuyishan City 5km (3 miles)

Mount Wuyi, in Fujian province, is the most important area for biodiversity conservation, riverine beauty and archaeological significance in southeast China. The landscape has been formed by volcanic activity and eroded by water, and the Nine Bend river, running clear and deep, makes its way through a deep, dramatic gorge flanked by sheer, smooth, rock cliffs. Within this landscape of hills and gorges are a considerable number of ancient temples and monasteries, and although many of them are now completely ruined, the landscape is so perfect one could be looking at a classical Chinese painting. Mount Wuyi has been protected for 12 centuries, and is the cradle of Neo-Confucianism, a doctrine that was influential in the Far East for hundreds of years. In the 1st century BC, the rulers of the Han dynasty built a large walled city at nearby Chengcun, and this, as well as many other sites here, is of great archaeological significance. This is one of the most outstanding subtropical forests in the world. The vegetation is divided into 11 categories, the most common being evergreen broadleafed forest, and there is a wide diversity of fauna, too, including endangered species such as the South Chinese tiger, clouded leopard and mainland serow. There are three species here endemic to these mountains, including the bamboo snake. This is an area of almost otherworldly beauty. Drift through the Wuyi Canyon on a raft, gaze at fold upon fold of lush green mountains. Sit peacefully drinking a seriously delicious cup of tea, and meditate upon the marvellous nature of our planet.

HUANG LONG VALLEY

China

Huang Long valley is one of the most spectacular places in Sichuan province. Together with the nearby Muni Gorge, it is a World Heritage Site. Sichuan, the 'Land of Abundance', is bordered in the west by the Tibetan plateau, and it is in the Minshan range at the foot of the plateau that Huang Long lies. *Huang Long* means 'yellow dragon', and according to legend, about 4,000 years ago a great yellow dragon helped the Kia king, Xiayu, to remove floodwater by creating the Minjiang river. The king named the valley in honour of the dragon and had a temple built. More prosaically, the waters of the river have a golden hue because they carry dissolved calcium carbonate, which they deposit as they pass, and the valley could be said to resemble the tail of a dragon because it undulates through its gorge, following the path it has carved through faults in the limestone over the millennia. The spectacular gorge, about 250km (155 miles) from the provincial capital, Chengdu, is surrounded by primeval forests and dominated by snowcapped peaks. Its limestone formations are unique, and its massive waterfalls breathtaking. Its emerald-green lakes and thousands of multicoloured, calcium-carbonate-encrusted ponds are fed by melted snow from the mountain above and monsoon rains from May to September. The river has also carved out caves, and several of these contain spectacular stalactites. There are also warm springs just above the temples. The area is rich in wildlife, with a small population of giant pandas, lesser pandas, golden snub-nosed monkeys, brown bears, Asiatic black bears, Asiatic wild dogs, leopards, lynxes, three species of deer and possibly clouded leopards as well. More than 150 species of birds have been recorded here. Whether visitors believe the legend of the yellow dragon or not, this beautiful site will stay in their memories.

HOW TO GET THERE:
By air to Chengdu, then overland.
WHEN TO GO:
The weather is cold but dry in winter, while the monsoon season from May to September is hot and humid.
NEAREST TOWN:
Songpan Town 45km (28 miles).

YOU SHOULD KNOW
Minor earthquakes are not uncommon.

THE GOBI DESERT

Mongolia

HOW TO GET THERE:
By air to Ulaan Baator, then
by road (four-wheel drive).
WHEN TO GO:
June to September.
NEAREST TOWN:
Ulaan Baator is the
capital city.

The Gobi desert is a vast area in southern Mongolia covering 30 per cent of the entire country. It is largely made up of stony desert and gravel plains with rocky outcrops, but it also has mountains, grasslands, desert steppes, sand dunes and oases. This inhospitable landscape contains many rare and threatened species of flora and fauna and has been inhabited for centuries by nomadic herdsmen. For over 50 years the Gobi desert was off-limits to Westerners, only 're-opening' after the break up of the Soviet Union. The climate here is incredibly harsh – very little rain falls, and the wind blows almost continuously, carrying sand in its wake across hundreds of miles. The temperatures are extreme, reaching 40°C (104°F) in summer and -40°C (-40°F) in winter – in Eagle valley, the gorge remains frozen even on the hottest days. The Flaming Cliffs were named by the American paleontologist Roy Chapman Andrews when, in 1923, his team discovered the first nest of fossilized dinosaur eggs. These vivid, red, sandstone cliffs shelter an astonishing wealth of fossils that are providing the world with ever more evolutionary information. The region is rich with minerals – turquoise, agate, and crystal, as well as large deposits of copper and gold. There is also a sea of sand, stretching 180km (113 miles), with dunes reaching over 76m (250ft) high. This is named Hongor Els, or Singing Sands, as the perfectly round, smooth grains create a bizarre musical sound as they are blown across each other by the wind.

JEJU ISLAND LAVA TUBES

South Korea

Jeju Island is 130km (81 miles) off the southern coast of South Korea. A UNESCO World Heritage Site since 2007, this volcanic island has mountains, stunning coastal rock formations and the finest system of cave lava tubes in the world. With its multicoloured carbonate roofs and floors, dark-coloured lava walls and towers of petrified lava, it is an extraordinary sight. The tubes were natural conduits through which magma once flowed, and are now empty caves that are some of the largest in the world. The caves provide opportunities for scientific research, as well as being a popular tourist destination. Another volcanic feature of the island is the Cheju-do cliffs, which have tube-like formations similar to the Giant's Causeway in Northern Ireland. Situated in the middle of Jeju is Hallasan, the tallest mountain in South Korea and a dormant volcano, which rises 1,950m (6,396ft) above sea level. Its waterfalls, multi-shaped rock formations and lake-filled crater are outstandingly beautiful. The island is covered in volcanic rock and volcanic soil produced by Hallasan, which was formed over 25,000 years ago. There is a huge variety of animal and plant species on Jej, another reason for its importance as a natural reserve, and shellfish and animal fossils discovered in the area are very valuable as scientific resources. Stunning at any time of year, it is well worth a visit.

HOW TO GET THERE:
By boat from Busan or by air from Gimpo airport in Seoul.
WHEN TO GO:
Year-round.
NEAREST TOWNS:
Jeju and Seogwipo, both on the island.

YOU SHOULD KNOW
Jeju Island is the the largest island and the smallest province in South Korea.

AKIYOSHI-DO CAVE

Japan

HOW TO GET THERE:
By bus from the Shinkansen (Bullet Train) station in Yamaguchi.
WHEN TO GO:
Year-round; the cave temperature is a constant 17°C (63°F).
NEAREST TOWN:
Shuho 14km (9 miles).

Towards the southern tip of Honshu, Japan's main island, and northwest of Yamaguchi City, is Akiyoshidai, the largest karst formation in Japan. The landscape is quite extraordinary: it's literally a 350-million-year-old coral reef turned upside down, so that 130 sq km (50 sq miles) of otherwise pleasant, rolling grassland is dotted with great and small chunks of limestone full of marine fossils. Your imagination prompts comparisons like dragon's teeth, but most Japanese like to think of the rocks as grazing sheep. There's no such cultural anomaly about the region's much more spectacular underground treasures, and of these, nothing competes with Akiyoshi-do, the largest of 420 caves, and 300,000 years in the making. You enter Akiyoshi-do through a tall and narrow slit in the rock, at the bottom of the plateau where the river emerges from the karst. After a few paces with the water alongside booming in the rocky confines, the passage broadens to 100m (328ft), and the roof simply disappears beyond the reach even of floodlights. At the far end of this super-cathedral, the path rises away from the river and winds beside some of the most dramatic features of the cave's 10-km (6-mile) length. Try to come during the week when it is less crowded: the drama of the cave's enormity and colour is most effective when it's empty.

SHIRAKAMI-SANCHI FOREST

Japan

HOW TO GET THERE:
By Shinkansen (Bullet Train) to Akita City, then JR Gono sen (local train) via Higashinoshiro to Sirakamidaketozanguchi.
WHEN TO GO:
May to October.
NEAREST TOWNS:
Noshiro (Akita Pref.); Hirosaki (Aomori Pref.).

The Shirakami mountains straddle the border between Aomori and Akita, the two prefectures at the northwestern edge of Honshu, Japan's principal island. Untouched by glaciation, remote, and above all, protected by their extreme gradients from the threat of agriculture or forestry, the Shirakami are home to the biggest Japanese (Seibold's) beech forest anywhere, and the only one to remain virtually untouched by man. It stretches across a colossal 130,000 hectares (321,200 acres), but its core of 10,139 hectares (26 acres) has no trails or footpaths at all, and you need special permission to enter it. You can see why Shirakami is revered for its natural beauty by visiting the pure crystal Anmon-no-taki falls, the Dairakyo gorge, or the 33 lakes and marshes of Ju-ni-ko, of which the cobalt-blue Ao-ike pond is the acknowledged jewel.

DAISETSUZAN MOUNTAINS

Japan

Their name means 'Great Snowy Mountains', and they are also called 'the roof of Hokkaido'. Flanked by the Tokachi and Shikaribetsu ranges, the Daisetsuzan mountains form the majestic centrepiece of a trio of volcanic groups in north-central Hokkaido, collectively protected as the Daisetsuzan National Park.

HOW TO GET THERE:
By air/train/bus/car to Asahikawa via Sapporo; then bus/car to Asahidakeonsen.
WHEN TO GO:
Year-round.
NEAREST TOWN:
Asahikawa 30km (19 miles).

Each group consists of stratovolcanoes piled on top of one another: as one vent becomes active, it builds a peak, then stops until a new vent appears. It is a living landscape, evolving to the slow rhythm of a million-year-old pulse. The mineral-rich volcanic soil means that even at high altitudes there is an extraordinary wealth of mountain vegetation, and the fertile silt of steep valley floors supports numerous mountain villages. The Daisetsuzan massif typifies the region's rugged splendour. Japan's highest mountain, Asahi, towers over the highland plateau of Tomuraushi at 2,290m (7,511ft), where crystal streams carve rock-strewn gorges out of the alpine meadows and pasture. Loveliest of many is the 24-km (15-mile) Sounkyo gorge, just 50km (31 miles) from Hokkaido's second city, Asahikawa. The rock walls rise to 150m (492ft), with enchanting waterfalls (Ryusei-no-taki, Ginga-no-taki) tumbling down at intervals. Halfway along, at the resort of Sounkyo-onsen, a series of cable cars and chairlifts whisks you to well over 1,300m (4,264ft) up the mountainside for a sensational panoramic view of the forests, lakes, gorges, rock faces, and everywhere, the wispy trails of steam from the countless vents and hot springs. Such natural beauty is deservedly popular, and in every season. The Daisetsuzan mountains offer the best winter sports in Japan (and, experts say, the best powder-snow skiing in the whole world); and the sheer variety of walks, hikes, trails and vertical ascents can attract real crowds in summer and during the muted gold of autumn. Even so, it's easy to find space in the remote backcountry, where, amid such magnificence of nature, the biggest population is brown bears.

YOU SHOULD KNOW
Take sensible precautions about the brown bears in the backcountry.

MOUNT FUJI

Japan

The perfect cone of Mount Fuji overlooks the town of Fuji-Yoshida about 100km (60 miles) west of Tokyo, from where it can be seen on very clear days. At its most serene when covered with snow in winter, this is Japan's most sacred peak, in a land where people venerate the beauty of nature. An active stratovolcano that last erupted in 1707, it is instantly recognizable from the paintings of the Japanese master, Hokusai. At 3,776m (12,388ft), it is Japan's highest mountain. The full trip from Fuji-Yoshida to the summit takes up to 12 hours, so many people take the bus part of the way up and continue on foot from there. The routes are divided into 17 sections, or stations, and the buses go to the fifth station. There are four major routes from the fifth station and four from the foot of the mountain. Technically it is illegal to climb the mountain during winter without permission from the police. The peak season is in July and August, when many people make the climb at night so that they can stand at the summit to watch the sunrise over the beautiful landscape that surrounds the mountain. From below, their torches make bright, orange trails up the side of the mountain. For visitors who do not wish to make the climb up the mountain, the best views can be obtained from the shores of the lakes that surround it – Kawaguchi, Sai, Motosu, Shoji, Ashi and Yamanaka – but those who find the energy to do so will not regret it.

HOW TO GET THERE:
By road from Tokyo.
WHEN TO GO:
The peak season in July and August is very busy, but it is the only period when the huts are guaranteed to be open and the buses to operate.
NEAREST TOWN:
Fuji-Yoshida 10km (6 miles).

SHIRETOKO NATIONAL PARK

Japan

HOW TO GET THERE:
By air to Memanbetsu, then
by car to Utoro.
WHEN TO GO:
May to October.
NEAREST TOWNS:
Utoru and Rausu are
both within the park.

The Shiretoko peninsula juts 70km (44 miles) into the Sea of Okhotsk from the northeastern tip of Hokkaido. Roughly half of it is a complete wilderness, accessible only on foot or by boat. Mount Rausu on the east coast is the best known of Shiretoko's volcanoes, whose chain continues underwater and out to sea to resurface as Russia's Kuril Islands. Rausu town attracts visitors to its hot springs and to Makkausu cave, which wave action has coated with a unique, luminescent moss that glows eerily after nightfall. Rausu is famous for its harvest of edible kelp (a staple of soup stocks), but it's also the start of the 'Shiretoko traverse', the main hiking route to Utoro on the west coast. Ten kilometres (6 miles) north of Utoro brings you to the five lakes of the Shiretoko Go-Ko – quiet ponds surrounded by wild forest, each a perfect mirror for the rugged mountains. Just beyond are the Kamuiwakka-no-taki waterfalls, 32m (105ft) high. Hot spring water mixes with the river, and the falls descend in a series of hot plunge pools where you can bathe. It's breathtaking, beautiful and dramatic.

SHIKOTSU-TOYA NATIONAL PARK

Japan

HOW TO GET THERE:
By air/train/bus to Sapporo,
then by bus/car within
the park.
WHEN TO GO:
Year-round.
NEAREST TOWNS:
Sapporo, Muroran.

The Shikotsu-Toya National Park on the Pacific coast protects a full range of beautiful volcanic landscapes. The bubbling mud pools, crater lakes, steaming fissures, hot springs and sulphurous streams belie the natural peace of the wooded vales and mountain streams, the soaring rock faces, waterfalls and mossy ravines that inspire visitors' romantic imaginations. It's great that such natural loveliness should be easily accessible – but it does mean that the park can seem crowded. Even so, just an hour by bus from Sapporo you can bathe in sylvan solitude at the multiple Shiraito-no-taki waterfalls. From there, across the shifting panorama of the Nakayama Pass, you reach Lake Toya itself. Its almost exactly circular disc of crystal blue is in startling contrast to the intense green of the woods that crowd both its shoreline and Oshima, the miniature island cone set plumb in its centre. Less crowded than Toya, Lake Shikotsu is an even more beautiful caldera tucked between soaring cliffs – but the relative serenity of both is in marked contrast to the sulphurous frenzy of the hot springs surrounding Noboribetsu, Hokkaido's most popular spa, on the Pacific shore. You can bathe in more than 20 different kinds of hot mineral springs, at hundreds of sites all fed by the vents of Jigoku-dani ('Hell Valley'), a cauldron of steam, fumes and geyser columns that produces 10,000 tons of hot water every day.

AKAN NATIONAL PARK

Japan

In eastern Hokkaido, a dense, primeval forest covers a long ridge of volcanic peaks, craters, vents and hot springs, and between them lie three of Japan's loveliest lakes. Especially in autumn, when the red and gold of the subarctic forest frames the brilliant blues and greens of the water, Akan National Park adds visual romance to the natural beauty of somnolent vulcanology. Lake Akan itself benefits from the magnificent backdrop of Meakan and Oakan, two volcanoes to its south and east whose reflections are pierced by the many small islands in the lake, which often appears to be a bright green. The colour derives from the marimo, a very rare algae species that forms itself into beautiful, apple-green balls. Left to itself for several centuries, Lake Akan's marimo can reach the size of soccer balls – and at the Marimo Exhibition Centre on Churui-shima island, across from the little town of Akankohan, there's an underwater viewing room where you can see marimo balls, some hundreds of years old, bobbing up to the surface. Lake Kussharo, 50km (31 miles) from Akan, is the biggest of the lakes. The glory of its caldera is best seen from the Bihoro Pass on the north side, and includes the wooded island of Tomoshiri.

HOW TO GET THERE:
By car from Abashiri, Bihoro or Kushiro.
WHEN TO GO:
April to October.
NEAREST TOWNS:
Akankohan and Kawayu, both within the park.

LAKE ISSYK KUL

Kyrgyzstan

HOW TO GET THERE:
Bus or car from Bishkek (Kyrgyzstan) or from Almaty (Kazakhstan).
WHEN TO GO:
May to August.
NEAREST TOWNS:
Cholpon-Ata, Karakol.

In northern Kyrgyzstan lies Issyk Kul, the 'Pearl of the Tian Shan Mountains'. With the exception of Lake Titicaca in Bolivia/Peru, it's the biggest mountain lake in the world, with a shoreline nearly 700km (437 miles) long – big enough to create its own microclimate. It's fed by 118 rivers and streams, plus the meltwaters of the snowcapped peaks that surround it, but it never freezes because of the slightly saline hot springs bubbling up in its centre. Its name even means 'warm lake' in the Kyrgyz language. The lake's northern shore is a popular holiday resort. At Cholpon-Ata, the Soviet legacy of sanatoria and boarding houses is gradually being refurbished for the new generation of ecotourists and visitors keen to enjoy the beach life, hydrotherapy and mud baths for which the region is famous. Yet a taxi ride or an hour on horseback from Cholpon-Ata is the Grigorievskoye gorge, on the main hiking route to the lake from Almaty due north in Kazakhstan. Its rugged length and wild beauty is typical of the spectacular landscapes throughout the region.

PIK IMENI ISMAIL SAMANI

Tajikistan

HOW TO GET THERE:
By plane from Dushanbe to Khorog, then by helicopter or on foot.
WHEN TO GO:
Best climbing months are June, July and August.
NEAREST TOWNS:
Khorog 100km (62 miles), Karaat 80km (50 miles).

Better known as Pik Kommunizma, its name until 1998, or Pik Stalin (until 1962), or Pik Garmo (until 1933), Pik Imeni Ismail Samani is the highest peak in the Pamir mountains of east Tajikistan. It is a huge craggy mountain, oozing glaciers despite towering over a dry, barren region. Its rock is poor and its approach a crumbling, difficult scramble on snow and ice, but at 7,495m (24,584ft), the highest in the region, its summit is a magnet for climbers. High, cold and remote, the Pamir range is at the hub of Asia, and remains one of the least explored areas of the world. The bulk of it lies in the east Tajik region of Gorno-Badakhshan. It's often said that these are political as much as geographical 'badlands', but reaching the Pamirs is worth it. From Dushanbe, the Tajik capital, you ascend through lush valleys past beautiful, turquoise lakes.

K2 AND THE KARAKORAM RANGE

Pakistan

DON'T MISS
The view from Concordia.

HOW TO GET THERE:
By plane or bus from Islamabad to Skardu, by car to Askole, then on foot to Concordia.
WHEN TO GO:
April to September.
NEAREST TOWN:
Askole.

The Karakoram range is the greatest consolidation of high mountains in the world. The sinister beauty of hundreds of peaks, spires and fluted ridges makes a spectacular setting for the 60 giants over 7,000m (22,960ft) crammed into an area of 160 sq km (100 sq miles); and even these are just a backdrop to the overlord of the Karakoram, K2. The second-highest mountain in the world at 8,611m (28,252ft), K2 owes its notoriety as 'the savage mountain' to the extraordinary symmetry of its granite pyramidal summit. Each face drops a sheer 2,800m (9,184ft) in under 4km (2.5 miles). Standing proud from the Qogir glacier below, it is treacherously steep and exposed to extremes of hailstorms, blizzards and sudden, violent winds that frequently pluck climbers off its icy glaze. Beyond K2 lie Pakistan's borders with India and China and an ocean of snow, so the best approach is from Skardu, Pakistan's Balti capital. A hair-raising, eight-hour drive through dust and grit to the typical Balti village of Askole is a prelude to a trek of several days. Each step reveals a more impressive panorama, until, after crossing the rubble and moraine debris of the huge Baltoro glacier, you reach Concordia. It's not a village, but a view: from this junction of three major glaciers, framed by peaks in serried ranks to left and right, K2 rears up in all its solitary, massive grandeur.

TRANGO TOWERS

Pakistan

Some of the highest cliffs in the world are in northeastern Pakistan in the Karakoram mountain range. The Trango Towers are one such group, a family of rock towers that rise 1km (0.6 miles) above the other granite spires in the ridge. They have an elevation of more than 6,200m (20,336ft) above sea level, a sight that's just too tempting for intrepid climbers and base-jumpers. The towers are situated in to the north of Baltoro glacier in Gilgit-Baltistan, an autonomous territory in the north of Pakistan. They are part of the Baltoro Muztagh, a sub-range of the Karakoram range. Every year, a number of expeditions from all over the world travel to Karakoram to visit these granite cliffs that offer some of the most challenging rock climbing on the planet. The highest point in the group is the summit of Great Trango Tower at 6,286m (20,608ft), the east face of which features the world's greatest nearly vertical drop. Just northwest of Great Trango is the Trango Tower, at 6,239m (20,470ft), often called 'Nameless Tower', and north of this is a smaller rock spire known as 'Trango Monk'. Overall, the Trango Towers group has seen some of the most difficult and significant climbs ever accomplished, due to the combination of altitude, total height of the routes, and the steepness of the rock. They are an extraordinary sight.

VALLEY OF FLOWERS

India

HOW TO GET THERE:
By car to Joshimath, then
on foot.
WHEN TO GO:
June to September.
NEAREST TOWN:
Pulna 12km (7.5 miles) south
of park entrance.

The Valley of Flowers in the Paspawati valley is an outstandingly beautiful, high-altitude Himalayan valley cherished by botanists for a century, and by Hindu mythology for much longer. Almost everything about it is rare. In less than 2,500 hectares (6,178 acres) it contains over 600 specifically sub-, mid- and high-alpine species, including the Himalayan maple and the blue poppy among five unknown elsewhere, 31 officially endangered others, and 45 medicinal plants in daily local use. The fauna is just as magnificently special, and it is no surprise that such a wonderful work of nature should be a place of major pilgrimage. Because the valley is so easily accessible, thousands visit the shrines here every year. But no camping is allowed in the valley, and no other facilities impinge on its pristine natural bounty – visitors are accompanied by a local guide who steers them clear of the most sacred flowers.

BORRA CAVES

India

HOW TO GET THERE:
By train or road from Visag.
WHEN TO GO:
November and December.
NEAREST TOWN:
Araku Hill Station 15km
(9 miles).

The Borra caves spread across 2 sq km (1.25 sq miles) of the Anatigiri Hills, their colossal formations hewn out of the limestone by the Ghostani river over a million years. In one cave you can hear the torrent rushing above you; in another, you can see it disappear into a hole in the rock at your feet, then peer over a precipice and watch it emerge 90m (292ft) below you. Some caverns feel like artfully lit cathedrals – and the religious association is reinforced by local tribal worship of certain legendary features within them. At festival times, crowds flock to the Shivalingam stalagmite over which hangs Khamdenu, the stalactite idol of a cow whose dripping udder is said to be the source of the Ghostani river. Around the caves it is wild and rugged, an impossibly beautiful landscape that is at its best in the Araku valley north of the Borra caves. Araku's lush meadows, streams and waterfalls are home to 19 tribal cultures, distinguished by the dramatic colours of their dress code and spectacular songs and dances. These are not performed just for visitors' entertainment: they are the tribal rituals that give the many religious legends of the Borra caves their living significance. Getting there by train is a splendid event in itself. The slow, winding journey from the beaches of Visag – 110km (69 miles) over five hours – rises through coffee plantations and the thick vegetation of the Eastern Ghats. This is the highest broad-gauge railway in India, and it stops both at the Borra caves and Araku.

THAR DESERT

India

HOW TO GET THERE:
By rail or road from Delhi
to Jaisalmer (17 hours),
then by camel.
WHEN TO GO:
November to March.
NEAREST TOWN:
Jaisalmer 65km (41 miles)
to Desert Park.

The Thar is known as the Great Indian Desert. Approximately 800km (500 miles) long and 400km (250 miles) wide, it stretches from the Indus and Sutlej rivers of east Pakistan to the Aravalli ranges of northwest India. Despite its extreme aridity, it's the most densely populated desert in the world. It harbours thousands of small towns and villages, and Rajasthan boasts some of India's most beautiful and famous cities, like Jaipur, Jaisalmer and Jodhpur. They are jewels of Rajput grandeur in a landscape of the living colour of swaying saris and tribal dress. Jaisalmer sits in the heart of the Thar. Its palaces, forts and temples are typical of the desert cities' magic and brilliance. At sunset, their pink sandstone reflects a glow so intense that Jaisalmer is called the 'golden city'. From here you can ride a camel into the shifting dunes, broken rocks and scrub that characterize the desert's harshness. Swirls of dust shimmer in the midday heat – but when moonlight defines every wind-ridge in the great dunes, the starry silence broken only by the shuffle of hoofs in the sand, the desert is a place of eerie romance. To the south is the Thar Desert National Park, which brings together elements of all the desert's moods. It includes three lakes, the only permanent waterholes, and the Sudashri Forest Post, which is a magnet for rare desert species.

HOW TO GET THERE:
By boat and rickshaw
from Canning.
WHEN TO GO:
September to March.
NEAREST TOWN:
Gosaba 50km (31 miles).

DON'T MISS
The cruise down
many of the creeks.

SUNDARBANS ROYAL BENGAL TIGER RESERVE

India

A World Heritage Site, the Sundarbans Reserve forms the core of the vast Ganges delta in west Bengal. Here the silt deposits of a continent form islands connected to the mainland by a series of labyrinthine waterways choked with tangled mangroves. Half the world's species and 80 per cent of all India's mangrove swamps make these the most fecund marshes on the planet, able to support the biggest concentration of tigers along with many other animals and birds. Twice a day the mangroves flood with the tide, making access especially difficult. The Sundarbans tigers have long adapted to this amphibious habitat. They are adept swimmers, can survive in and on brackish water, and are known to feed on fish and turtles as well as their usual prey. Their proliferation is a measure of the reserve's success in limiting poaching and human activities such as fishing and the collection of wood and forest produce.

KAZIRANGA NATIONAL PARK

India

On the banks of the Brahmaputra river in the extreme northeast of India in Assam, the 430 sq km (269 sq miles) of the Kaziranga National Park, a maze of forests, swamps and tall thickets of elephant grass, provide the ideal habitat for the Indian one-horned rhino. There are more here than anywhere else, along with a large population of Indian elephants, barasingha and hog deer, sloth bears, tigers, leopards, capped langurs, hoolock gibbons, wild boar, jackals, buffalos, pythons and jungle otters. It is a breathtaking vision of the teeming potential of successful wilderness parks. In winter, huge numbers of migratory birds descend on the lakes and marshes. Greylag geese, red-crested pochard, gadwall and northern shoveller are among those splashing down to join the oriental honey buzzard, brahminy kite, white-tailed and Pallas's fishing eagles, Himalayan griffon, and more than 100 other species already resident. The relatively open country makes watching the wildlife easy, and you can usually see all the major species within a single day. Early morning is best, when elephants resume their foraging and the grasslands are a magnet for circling raptors like the serpent eagle, searching for prey among the flashy kaleidoscope of storks, herons, pelicans and teal for whom the marshes are home. The park changes with the seasons – the major wildlife migrates to different areas within the park during the monsoon, for example, when the Brahmaputra overflows its banks. It is prudent to check in advance which areas are accessible, and whether permits may be necessary.

HOW TO GET THERE:
By plane to Jorhat, then by road.
WHEN TO GO:
November to April.
NEAREST TOWN:
Jorhat 95km (59 miles).

YOU SHOULD KNOW
You can ride elephants (with mahouts) through the park.

NANDA DEVI BIOSPHERE RESERVE

India

The Garwhal Himalaya range stretches north from Haridwar past increasingly remote villages, alpine pastures and dense virgin forests until it enters a vast bowl in the hills known as the Outer Sanctuary of Nanda Devi. To the west is Nanda Devi itself, at 7,816m (25,643ft) India's second-highest mountain, a natural fortress surrounded by an unbroken ridge wall never lower than 6,000m (19,400ft). This Inner Sanctuary is breached only by the spectacular Rishi Ganga gorge, a long chasm of tumbled rock along which the dense clumps of fir, juniper and rhododendron trees give way to arid scrub and the Nanda Devi glacier. Visitors must stop here. The unrivalled magnificence of the panorama is compensation enough – but this wilderness is of far more than ecological significance. The area is revered as one of the holiest places in India, the source of the Mother River, Ganges. The national park surrounding Nanda Devi rewards the considerable effort it takes to get there. Against the constantly changing backdrop of multiple snowcapped peaks, you pass 312 floral species among the grasses, alpine mosses and lichens. Warblers, grosbeaks, rose finches and ruby-throats are among 80 species of birds, and this is one of few regions where you might actually see bears, leopard, langur, musk deer and the fabled snow leopard. Global rarity is almost commonplace here.

KATHMANDU VALLEY

Nepal

The town of Kathmandu is the capital, but it is the Kathmandu valley, as a whole, that is the political, commercial and cultural hub of Nepal. It's roughly oval, encircled by green-terraced hills and dotted by clusters of red-tiled roofs. It luxuriates in its ancient fertility, a natural showcase for an equally rich culture, art and traditional way of life. Until very recently, it was still said that the valley held as many temples and shrines as it did houses, but the rapid urbanization of the last three decades now threatens its survival as a unique, living, breathing entity developed over more than 2,000 years. The valley holds three towns of great historic significance: Kathmandu, Lalitpur (Patan) and Bhaktapur (Bhadgaon). Each is a treasure-trove of golden temples, enigmatic buddhas and fabulous artefacts.

SAGARMATHA NATIONAL PARK

Nepal

In Sanskrit it means 'Mother of the Universe', and Sagarmatha is the modern Nepali name for both Mount Everest as a whole, and for the park in eastern Nepal that covers 1,148 sq km (718 sq miles) of Himalayan ecological zone. The park's dramatic mountains, glaciers and deep valleys are dominated by the southern half of Everest, which soars up to the border with Tibet and forms the watershed between central Asia and the Indian Ocean. At 8,848m (29,021ft) Sagarmatha is the top of the world, its familiar, iconic summit guarded by six other peaks over 6,000m (19,680ft) and surrounded by gorges and rugged terrain that never drops below 2,845m (9,331ft). Lower down, forests of juniper, birch and silver fir trees provide a spring and monsoon showcase for the brilliant colours of flowering rhododendrons, and a protective habitat for 118 species of birds such as the blood pheasant and yellow-billed chough. Large mammals like the musk deer and Himalayan tahr are common, along with the jackal, weasel, marten, common langur and black bear. It's also occasional home to the snow leopard and lesser panda. That they exist at all is witness to the still relatively pristine alpine and mountain ecology, now under threat from the tourism it needs for its own protection. The park's HQ and visitor centre is in the village of Namche Bazaar, a focal point of the Sherpa culture predominant in eastern Nepal. Most visitors enter the park here (there's a southern entrance just north of Mondzo, a hamlet one day's hike from the airstrip at Lukla), and you have only to walk a few paces from Namche's buildings to claim the incredible mountian view as your own: the chain of Lhotse, Nuptse, Cho-Oyu, Thamserku and Amadablam standing homage to the ultimate peak of Everest itself.

DON'T MISS
Khumbu Glacier;
Sherpa culture in
Syangboche.

HOW TO GET THERE:
By plane from Kathmandu to
Lukla, then a two-day hike
to Namche; by helicopter to
Syangboche (one-hour walk
from Namche), the world's
highest airstrip.
WHEN TO GO:
October to November,
March to May.
NEAREST TOWN:
Namche Bazaar.

KANGCHENJUNGA

Nepal/Sikkim

With the tallest of its five peaks at 8,586m (28,162ft), Kangchenjunga is the world's third-highest mountain. It straddles the eastern border of Nepal with Sikkim, the autonomous region of India, and is as famous for its dramatic beauty as it is feared for its dangerous power over those who live in its foothills. The mountain is honoured by the Sikkimese as a deity, and the religious association is so strong that seasoned mountaineers refuse to desecrate Sikkimese sensibilities, turning back a few feet short of Kangchenjunga's actual summit. Despite its fearsome weather – roaring ice avalanches, hailstorms, flash floods and sudden blizzards – the mountain offers the best of any access to the Himalayas' unique flora and fauna. It's only 74km (46 miles) as the eagle flies, but a whole world away from Darjeeling's subtropical tea plantations. The contrast between lush lowlands, the band of alpine meadows and the forbidding majesty of the icy peaks with Mount Everest in the background could not be more dramatic. But the best approach to Kangchenjunga and the Himalayas in general is from Nepal. You can trek (with varying degrees of difficulty) from the tiny airstrip at Taplejung to the South Face base camp at Ramche. Actually climbing Kanchenjunga is notoriously difficult, and requires an official permit either from Nepal or Sikkim. Even trekking in the region is subject to strict rules, and it's usually best to join a guided party.

YALA NATIONAL PARK

Sri Lanka

Yala National Park, otherwise known as Ruhunu, in southeastern Sri Lanka, is the most-visited national park in the country and the best place in which to see large mammals. The landscape is mainly flat, with rocky outcrops of up to 245m (800ft) rising suddenly upwards. A seasonal river, the Menik Ganga, and four seasonal streams carry away the monsoon waters, and there are rock pools and natural water holes, essential for wildlife. To the southeast of the park, there are small patches of riverine forest, mangroves, pristine beaches, sand dunes and the sea. Inscriptions found in this region date back to the 2nd century BC, but nothing has been found that is later than 10th century AD. It would seem that the human population departed at that time, leaving the mature, secondary forest that we see today to cover their tracks. Much of the area consists of thorny scrub forest, allowing visitors a really good chance of seeing wildlife.

SINHARAJA FOREST RESERVE
Sri Lanka

HOW TO GET THERE:
By air to Colombo,
then by road.
WHEN TO GO:
January to April and
August to September.
NEAREST TOWN:
Ratnapura 44km (27 miles).

YOU SHOULD KNOW
Leeches can be a problem.

One of the jewels of Sri Lanka, the Sinharaja Forest Reserve lies in the southwest of the island and is its last remnant of pristine tropical rainforest. It provides a last home for such rare animals as wild boar, barking deer, giant squirrels, civets, porcupines, mongoose, purple-faced langurs and extremely elusive leopards. This area is precious because it holds so many species of plants that no longer occur anywhere else in the world, as the forests around them have been cut down. Sinharaja has been declared a UNESCO World Heritage Site because of the importance and rarity of its plants. There are two main habitats within the reserve – tropical lowland rainforest and tropical wet evergreen forest – and more than half of the major plant species here are found nowhere else. The dense forests are home to many species of birds, among them Sri Lankan blue magpie, white-headed starling, orange-billed babbler, red-faced malkoha and the extremely rare green-billed coucal. Among the other creatures that enjoy the lush green wilderness are hump-nosed and green pit vipers and many amphibians, including tree frogs.

PHONG NHA-KE BANG NATIONAL PARK

Vietnam

Phong Nha-Ke Bang National Park is in central Vietnam, in Quang Binh province. This is the narrowest part of the country, abutting Laos to the west, with the sea to the east only 42km (26 miles) away. It is one of the world's two largest limestone regions, and the oldest in Asia. There is an ongoing plan between Vietnam and Laos to jointly manage their adjacent nature reserves, which, if combined, would form the largest karst forest in southeast Asia. Designated a UNESCO World Heritage Site in 2003, the park preserves a wonderfully complex system of limestone caves, tunnels, grottos and rock formations, as well as some of the longest underground rivers in the world. The Phong Nha cave, the park's main visitor attraction, is probably the most spectacular of those explored so far, and contains amazing giant speleothems. Tourboats can venture 1,500m (4,900ft) inside. The region is covered with tropical forest, much of it primary, which provides habitat for a diverse range of flora and fauna, including 13 species endemic to Vietnam and one species endemic to this site.

HOW TO GET THERE:
By road.
WHEN TO GO:
Spring and early summer.
NEAREST TOWN:
Dong Hoi 50km (31 miles).

YOU SHOULD KNOW
The park has been earmarked as a major tourist attraction, but currently it is very difficult to visit as an independent traveller.

HALONG BAY

Vietnam

HOW TO GET THERE:
By boat or kayak.
WHEN TO GO:
Spring and early summer.
NEAREST TOWNS:
Halong City, Hong Gai
and Cam Pha are all
on Halong Bay.

This utterly beautiful bay is one of Asia's most perfect natural wonders. A heavenly combination of sky, water and stone, it seems almost to be an enormous artwork created by the inhabitants of another world. Halong Bay means 'The Bay of the Descending Dragon', and legend has it that long ago, during an invasion by the Chinese, dragons came to defend the land, spitting out thousands of pearls as they descended, each of which turned into a jade island upon hitting the water. These islands formed a defensive barrier into which the invader's ships crashed and sank. Halong Bay is situated in the Gulf of Tonkin, close to the border between Vietnam and China, and it contains about 2,000 islands. Dating back millions of years, they are the remnants of a limestone mountain range that was submerged by the sea, leaving the karst seascape of today. The islands are mainly topped by impenetrable jungle, and the elements continue to erode them into ever more fanciful shapes, echoed by names such as Elephant and Wallowing Buffalo. Many islands contain caves and grottoes; some are almost hollow. Wooden Stakes cave is the largest of these, and is accessed by 90 rock-hewn steps. Archaeological sites have been found, containing so many artefacts that collectively they have been accorded the term 'Halong Culture' – meaning the Neolithic Age culture of northeastern, coastal Vietnam. There are fishing communities here, who inhabit floating villages and make a living from the fish that swim in these clear blue waters.

THE MARBLE MOUNTAINS

Vietnam

HOW TO GET THERE:
By road from Da Nang.
WHEN TO GO:
Spring and early summer.
NEAREST TOWN:
Da Nang 12km (7.5 miles).

To the west of Da Nang, facing towards the East China Sea, stand five mountains that appear to have risen together from the surrounding plain. These are the Marble mountains, formed in fact from both marble and limestone, and riven with passages, tunnels and caves. The mountains are famous for traditional stone carving, and in the nearby village of Dong Hai, 600 families earn their livelihood from carving statues and making jewellery and artefacts such as chess sets. The mountains each have different shades of marble – pinks, whites and browns – but excavating rock directly from them has now been banned. Today the local craftsmen work with material that has been quarried elsewhere, while their children act as guides to the visitors, hoping to be able to sell a souvenir or two for their trouble. Thuy Son is the highest mountain, and has carved steps to the top that lead to the Tham Thia pagoda and the Huyen Khong cave.

THE MEKONG DELTA

DON'T MISS
The spectacle of
the colonies of birds.

Vietnam

With a length of 4,160km (2,585 miles), the Mekong river is the 12th-longest in the world. Rising high on the Tibetan plateau, it descends across southwestern China, through Laos and along its border with Thailand, across Cambodia and Vietnam to discharge into the South China Sea. The delta itself is usually regarded as starting in Phnom Penh in Cambodia, where the river divides in two, and then further splits to form the 'Nine Dragons', as the channels are known. The delta itself is the result of the deposition of silt washed down by the river and in places the land is reclaiming up to 150m (500ft) of land from the sea each year. The silt makes this a highly fertile region, so it is important to the nation's economy and is densely populated in places, but it is still possible to get away from the crowds and explore the nature reserves and the wildlife that inhabits this flat land of mangrove swamps and melaleuca trees. Twenty-three species of mammals, six amphibians, 35 reptiles, 386 species and subspecies of birds and 260 fish have been recorded. The quieter areas of the Mekong delta are an unexpectedly beautiful find in a crowded land.

HOW TO GET THERE: By road from Ho Chi Minh City.
WHEN TO GO: The monsoon season is from late May to September and is best avoided.

THE BOLAVEN PLATEAU

Laos

HOW TO GET THERE:
By road from Pakse.
WHEN TO GO:
November to May.
NEAREST TOWN:
Pakse 30km (19 miles).

DON'T MISS
Elephant treks
from Tad Lo.

High above the humid Mekong river valley, in southern Laos, is an area of flat, fertile land known as the Bolaven plateau. Its average altitude of 600m (1,980ft) provides it with a cool, pleasant climate, and rivers tumble down from it on all sides, producing numerous beautiful waterfalls. There are several tribal groups living on the plateau, which is named after the largest of them, the Laven. The area has long been cultivated on a small scale using traditional methods, but in the early 20th century, a Frenchman called Jean Dauplay realized it was perfect coffee-growing country and introduced the bean to Laos, bringing it from Vietnam. The region was heavily bombed by the USA during the Vietnam War in the 1960s and 1970s, but today it produces some of the finest and most expensive coffee beans in the world, with a distinctive taste. There are also many tea plantations, vegetables, spices and orchards growing here – even raspberries and strawberries are successful in this climate. Two of the best-known waterfalls in the area are Tad Lo and Tad Fan. The former, whilst not a particularly high fall, has both upper and lower cascades in a beautiful forest setting, with cool, clear swimming holes, and smooth granite rocks on which to relax.

NAKAI-NAM THEUN NATIONAL BIODIVERSITY CONSERVATION AREA

Laos

HOW TO GET THERE:
By road from Route 8B.
WHEN TO GO:
November, after the monsoon.
NEAREST TOWN:
Nakai 10km (6 miles).

In 1993 the government of Laos created 18 National Biodiversity Conservation Areas, the largest of which is Nakai-Nam Theun. This area is now considered to be the world's most significant biodiversity conservation area, partly due to its complex range of habitats – including evergreen, montane beech, cloud and riverine forest, the Annamite mountains, which separate Laos from Vietnam, and the Nakai plateau. Much of the area is pristine forest, and is home to well over 400 species of bird. Nakai-Nam Theun is best known for its large mammals, many of which are threatened, making the populations here particularly crucial. There are many rare cats here: tigers, clouded leopards, marbled cats, Asiatic golden cats and many more. It is also home to most of Laos's Asiatic elephants and gaurs. There are nine species of primate, including the most important population of red-shanked douc in the world and, in 1999, the striped rabbit, a new species, was discovered here. A major hydropower project is planned for this region, but the Lao and Vietnamese governments are considering forming some manner of super-reserve in order to protect it.

MEKONG RIVER VALLEY

Laos

The Mekong river, which rises in Tibet and empties into the South China Sea, runs through very nearly the entire length of Laos, and has an almost spiritual significance for Lao people. About 75 per cent of Laos is made up of remote mountains and plateaux and this, combined with it being a landlocked country, means that the Mekong is deeply important. It is used not only as a source of food and water, but also for travelling on, although as more roads are built, more people use them. The river is home to over a thousand species of fish, which provide about 80 per cent of the protein that most Lao people eat. It is home to the largest freshwater fish in the world, the giant catfish, as well as the endangered Irrawaddy dolphin. The river swells enormously during the monsoon and leaves behind it wonderfully rich sediment, ensuring extremely fertile riverbanks and flood plains. Virtually all of the rice grown in Laos comes from the southern flood plain, and the two largest cities, Vientiane, the capital, and Savannakhet, are situated on the river's edge.

HOW TO GET THERE: By air or overland to Laos.
WHEN TO GO: November to April.
NEAREST TOWNS: Luang Prabang, Vientiane, Savannakhet and Pakse are all situated on the Mekong river.

KUANG SI FALLS

Laos

The Kuang Si falls are situated some 30km (19 miles) south of Luang Prabang, in northern Laos. It is a beautiful, wide and generous waterfall that cascades down over limestone tiers and through a number of calm, shallow pools. The calcite deposits that have covered and rounded the tiers give the water an extraordinary pale milky-blue cast.

At the lower level a pretty park has been landscaped, with seats and picnic tables all arranged to give the best views of both the falls and the surrounding forest. A forest trail leads upwards to the top of the falls, following the path of the stream, and those who take this come upon a second tier of the falls where the natural pool is fine for swimming. Venture behind the curtain of water and you will discover a cave that goes back for 10m (33ft). Back on the trail, continue scrambling to the top and you will find the stream that feeds the falls surrounded by forest and with a meadow beyond. The view down the 60-m (197-ft) fall is gorgeous, framed with flowering forest shrubs and trees, and swathes of bougainvillea. Just before you reach the falls you pass by the picturesque village of Ban Ta Baen, with its charming wooden stilt houses, colourful chilies arranged on the roofs to dry, and beautifully situated on the river with its clear bathing pools and mini-waterfalls. The sound of water splashing and tinkling is calming, and birdsong and the laughter of children add to the rural charm of this idyllic spot.

YOU SHOULD KNOW
A small entry fee is payable.

DON'T MISS
Ban Ta Baen village.

CALLAO CAVE

Philippines

The Callao cave complex is located in the Penablanca Protected Landscape and Seascape region in the province of Cagayan, to the northeast of Luzon Island. This is an area of great ecological importance, containing the last of the Philippines' old growth forest, the Cagayan river – the longest river in the country – and a coastline that is home to unique coastal and marine ecosystems. In recognition of the importance of this region, President Gloria Arroyo expanded the protected area from 4,136 hectares (10,220 acres) to over 118,000 hectares (291,600 acres), connecting it to the northern Sierra Madre National Park and thus creating a conservation area that is larger than Switzerland. Amongst the animals that are now safeguarded are three critically endangered species, and many that are threatened. Callao is an amazing, seven-chambered cave, each chamber having natural light that filters through crevices in the rock. During the Second World War, the Japanese Occupational Forces are thought to have used the cave as a camp.

TUBBATAHA REEF

Philippines

The Tubbataha Reef is situated in the middle of the Sula Sea, to the east of the island of Palawan. It is composed of two atolls separated by four nautical miles of water. North Reef is a continuous, oblong reef platform that completely encloses a sandy lagoon. South Reef is narrower, triangular in shape, and also encloses a sandy lagoon. On its southern tip, a solar-powered lighthouse stands, providing a convenient perch for various seabirds. The Sula Sea contains over 30 per cent of the world's coral reefs, and Tubbataha are the finest in the Philippines, and a must for serious divers. This remote spot became known for its 'walls' – areas where the shallow reef suddenly plunges sharply down. These walls contain caves and crevices and are rich with coral cover. Large fish such as dog-tooth tuna and snappers are abundant here, as well as most species of Pacific reef fish in all their glorious shapes and colours. Underwater visibility is often up to 30m (99ft), and this protected habitat absolutely teems with life. Other, larger species also found here include manta rays, sharks and endangered sea turtles, which lay their eggs on the coral sand beaches. During the 1980s and 1990s, Tubbataha Reef was damaged by illegal fishing practices, including the use of dynamite. However, since 1994 all fishing in the Marine Park has been halted, and the conservation measures put in place have led to a remarkable and entirely natural regeneration.

PUERTO-PRINCESA SUBTERRANEAN RIVER NATIONAL PARK

Philippines

The Puerto-Princesa National Park is situated in the St Paul mountains, on the northwest coast of Palawan island. Over 90 per cent of the park consists of karst topography – sharp, limestone ridges and rounded peaks around Mount St Paul. The hills are largely covered with lush, tropical forest, dominated by hardwood species and home to several endemic mammals. At the coast are mangrove swamps, and offshore there are coral reefs and beds of seagrass where endangered dugong have been recorded. The main feature of the park, however, is the subterranean river. This rises some 2km (1.25 miles) southwest of Mount St Paul and then winds its way underground for some 8km (5 miles) before flowing out into the sea at St Paul's Bay. The river, which is navigable, is known as St Paul's Cave. Highly unusual, it passes through huge domed caverns up to 60m (198ft) high and 120m (396ft) wide, containing major formations of speleothems. The river is also of particular interest because it empties into the sea – thus having a sweetwater to saltwater ecosystem. The lower portion is brackish and tidal, producing a unique habitat, and the large passages and chambers through which it passes are home to sizeable populations of swiftlets and eight species of bat. Palawan's flora and fauna are more closely related to that of Borneo than the rest of the Philippines, having once been joined to mainland Asia.

KHAO SOK ANCIENT RAINFOREST

Thailand

Khao Sok National Park is situated in Thailand's southern peninsula, roughly halfway between the two coasts, in Surat Thani province. Its limestone crags are covered by the largest area of pristine rainforest in southern Thailand, and possibly the oldest in the world, dating back 180 million years. The forest here has more in common with that of Malaysia than that of northern Thailand, being taller, denser, darker and more humid. This is the wettest region in the country, receiving monsoon rains of up to 3.5m (12ft) per year from both the Andaman Sea to the west and the Gulf of Thailand to the east. Home to a variety of flora and fauna, it is possibly best known for the rare and bizarre flower, rafflesia kerrii. This is the second-largest bloom in the world, with a diameter of almost 1m (3.3ft). The flower itself is rather unattractive, exuding a truly unpleasant smell that attracts its pollinator. The Chao Lam Lake is picture-book perfect, with karst islands and towering limestone peaks that surround the emerald waters in which they are reflected.

SIMILAN ARCHIPELAGO REEFS

Thailand

The Similan Archipelago is truly one of Thailand's most precious treasures, and the reefs around them provide some of the best underwater scenery in the world.

A National Marine Park, the nine granite islands themselves are virtually uninhabited, save for park officials and organized dive-tour groups. The Thai navy has a presence on one of the islands, where it protects a sea turtle reserve, and the youngest daughter of the present king has a house on another. This has helped the marine park escape some of the worst excesses of damage caused by fishermen, such as dynamiting the reefs for an extra big catch. The eastern shores are well protected from the monsoon storms, and have white sandy beaches and gently sloping reefs providing wonderful snorkelling territory. The western side catches the full force of the winds and the waves of the Andaman Sea, and the underwater scenery is much more dramatic: granite boulders covered in coral seem to have been hurled into the sea where they have formed arches and passages, cliffs and caves anywhere between 2m to 30m (7ft to 98ft) deep. The fantastic, convoluted shapes of the many different corals teem with rich and varied marine life. Shoals of vividly coloured fish such as angelfish, butterfly fish and many more form and swirl around and through forests of sea anemones and sea fans that sway gently in the currents. These, although strong, keep the reefs clear of sand and thus provide crystal-clear views of this magical underwater world.

HOW TO GET THERE:
By boat from Phuket, Thap Lamu or Hat Khao Lak.
WHEN TO GO:
December to May.
NEAREST TOWN:
Khao Lak, two hours by speedboat.

YOU SHOULD KNOW
Entry fee payable. The park office, visitor centre and all accommodation is on Ko Miang. Or join a 'live aboard' trip.

KHAO PHRA THAEO

Thailand

HOW TO GET THERE:
By road from Phuket.
WHEN TO GO:
All year round, but best
between November and May.
NEAREST TOWN:
Phuket 20km (12.5 miles).

Phra Thaeo National Park is situated some 20km (12.5 miles) north of Phuket town, and is a compact area of well-forested hills and valleys that encompasses a river with two splendid waterfalls, Bang Pae and Ton Sai. However, far and away its most important feature is the Gibbon Rehabilitation Centre. In years gone by, white-handed, or lar, gibbons were indigenous to Phuket island, and the forest canopy was busy with these most athletic of tree-dwelling mammals. Lar gibbons are black- or brown-bodied creatures, with a white frame around their faces. They are largely fruit-eating, but supplement their diet with leaves, insects, invertebrates and the occasional lizard. Gibbons are the only primate, other than man, to live in permanent, monogamous families. They communicate with other groups by whooping and screaming together, and these 'duets' can be heard up to five miles away. Gibbons are such charming creatures that they make very desirable pets, with the result that they are now an endangered species and protected by law in Thailand. The rehabilitation centre is doing an excellent job of rescuing pet gibbons, which even now can be found chained up at guesthouses and bars in Phuket, rehabilitating them and putting them back into the wild. The project makes for a fascinating visit, but don't expect to get up close to a lar gibbon here – their contact with humans is kept to a minimum while they are reintegrated with their forest home.

HOW TO GET THERE:
By train or road to Pak Chong
from Bangkok, then by road
to the forest complex.
WHEN TO GO:
November to May.
NEAREST TOWN:
Pak Chong 23km (14 miles).

DONG PHAYAYEN-KHAO YAI FOREST COMPLEX

Thailand

Inscribed as a UNESCO World Heritage Site in 2005, the Dong Phayayen-Khao Yai Forest Complex comprises four national parks and a wildlife sanctuary, spanning 230km (144 miles) from Khao Yai and east to the Cambodian border. The complex contains seven major types of rainforest, the dominant being tropical, evergreen rainforest, which covers almost 75 per cent of the entire area. There are wild rivers and rushing streams, with scores of waterfalls and gorges on the southern side of the range. This large protected area provides habitats for an enormous amount of flora and fauna that are under pressure elsewhere. Around 50km (31 miles) of hiking trails wind through the forest, an extraordinary place of towering trees draped in lianas, mosses and epiphytes. There are huge numbers of flowering trees and shrubs, and wild orchids bloom in profusion. The forest is never quiet: gibbons hoot, cicadas click continuously, apes chatter in the trees and birds constantly trill and whistle. At dusk you can watch over one million bats as they leave their cave at the edge of the park to feed.

TONLE SAP

Cambodia

Tonle Sap, which means 'large freshwater river', is a hugely important lake and river system in Cambodia, and the largest freshwater lake in southeast Asia. The lake is drained by the Tonle Sap river into the Mekong, near Phnom Penh. This is one of the largest inland fisheries in the world, providing the main source of protein for much of the population, and a livelihood for over one million people. Moreover, it is a breeding ground and nursery area for fish that subsequently migrate into the Mekong, from which two million tons of fish are harvested each year. For much of the year the lake is only 1m (3.3ft) deep. During the monsoon, however, a unique phenomenon occurs: the flow of the Tonle Sap river is reversed due to the vast quantities of water pouring into the Mekong. The area of the lake increases fivefold, and the depth increases to almost 10m (33ft). This inundates the swamp forest that surrounds the lake, and by the time the waters subside and the flow changes direction again, fish are carried back down to the Mekong and the area is left covered with a rich layer of silt.

RATANAKIRI

Cambodia

The remote northeastern province of Ratanakiri, in Cambodia, is a world unto itself. Almost untouched by modernity, it is home to 12 separate tribal groups, collectively known as the Khmer Loeu, who make up over 80 per cent of the inhabitants of the region. There is virtually no electricity or running water here, and no paved roads: thus the indigenous population live in very much the same way as their forefathers. Ratanakiri is rural – much of it is rolling hills and fields, with heavily forested mountains close to its border with Vietnam. Around the provincial capital, Banlung, are large plantations of cashews, coffee, peanuts and rubber trees, but several of the Khmer Loeu tribes still live mainly in the mountains and forests, practising traditional slash and burn agricultural methods and hunting with crossbows and poison darts. Banlung makes a good base from which to explore the hill-tribe villages, but there are other attractions nearby including numerous waterfalls. Probably the best-known attraction is Yak Loum Lake, which lies in the caldera of an ancient volcano. Almost perfectly circular and surrounded by lush rainforest vegetation and large trees, the lake is perfect for swimming.

CORAL REEFS AND THE EYE OF THE MALDIVES

Maldives

The Maldive islands are located 480km (300 miles) southwest of Cape Cormorin, on the southern tip of India. Consisting of 26 large atolls containing 1,190 islands, they run 648km (405 miles) from north to south, and 130km (81 miles) east to west, a double chain lying within the central area. Only 200 of the islands are inhabited and, of these, some 88 are exclusive holiday resorts.

The geomorphology of the Maldivian islands is unusual. An atoll is a coral formation surrounding a circular lagoon, but these lagoons, many of which are very large, are dotted with other, smaller, ring-shaped reefs, each surrounding its own sandy lagoon. These are known locally as 'faros', and this formation is known as the Eye of the Maldives. Natural channels, allowing the free movement of fish and currents between the lagoons and the open sea, cut through each reef. The islands are formed from coral sand and are very low lying, averaging no more than 2m (7ft), with vegetation mainly consisting of coconut palms and mangroves. Just take a look, however, beneath the surface of the turquoise sea and you will find glorious, dazzling coral gardens teeming with multicoloured fish. The diving and snorkelling here are the main attraction. Long term, the Maldives are under threat. Climate change is already adversely affecting the coral, which can only thrive at temperatures from 24 to 27°C (75 to 81°F), and the natural phenomena of El Niño and La Niña have caused severe bleaching to some of the formations. Sea levels are also rising, and although preventative work is being done, it seems that these fairy-tale coral islands will surely slip beneath the surface of the sea in the not too distant future.

MOUNT KINABALU

Malaysia

HOW TO GET THERE:
Travel by bus or hire car
from Kota Kinabalu.
WHEN TO GO:
The mountain is driest
between February and
April, but it is in a tropical
climate so expect showers
whenever you go.
NEAREST TOWN:
Kota Kinabalu 88km
(55 miles).

Mount Kinabalu is the tallest mountain between the Himalayas and New Guinea, towering above the rainforest at 4,095m (13,432ft). It is a relatively young mountain and is still growing at a rate of 5mm (0.2in) per year. It is climbed over two days, and you must have a guide if you're climbing to the summit. The climb starts off steadily as winding stairs cut into the mountainside sweep through rainforest. Pitcher plants pepper the side of the footpath and, along with other flora in the area, earned the park UNESCO World Heritage Site status. Accommodation on the mountain is varied, with Laban Rata being by far the best. The second part of the climb begins at around 2am and the final stage of the mountain is rocky and high enough to cause altitude sickness. As the sky becomes brighter and the clouds begin to burn away at around 6am, the hard climb and the tiredness are worth it: you are on top of the world with the best seat in the house.

NIAH CAVES, SARAWAK

Malaysia

Niah caves, one of the largest limestone caves in the world, are part of the Niah National Park, which is located near the coast between Miri and Bintulu in northern Sarawak. Excavations in the 1950s and 1960s proved the caves to be of great archaeological significance, after the discovery of a human skull revealed that the caves had been home to humans 40,000 years ago. Reaching the caves is not for the fainthearted: you first have to take a boat across the Sungai Niah, then it's a 3-km (2-mile) trek along a plank walk that winds through the rainforest. Add to that the humidity of the rainforest and crocodiles in the river, and it can be a little daunting. The Great Cave is the main attraction, with a roof 75m (246ft) high and the mouth of the cave measuring 250m (820ft) across. Green algae covers the rocks that litter the cave floor, creating an enchanting display that glows green in the jungle sunlight. Make sure you bring a torch, as the light soon disappears in the vastness of the cave.

HOW TO GET THERE: Travel by bus or hire a car. Three hours
from the waterfront at Bintulu or two hours from Miri.
WHEN TO GO: Witness the birds'-nest-collecting season
between August and December, and from January to March.
NEAREST TOWN: Batu Niah 3.5km (2 miles).

THE CAVES OF GUNUNG MULU NATIONAL PARK

Malaysia

Gunung Mulu National Park, Sarawak's largest national park, is home to extensive, world-renowned limestone caves. Set in 530 sq km (205 sq miles) of tropical rainforest comprising the peaks of Gunung Mulu and Gunung Api, the park boasts sandstone and limestone formations and a diverse range of flora and fauna. Gunung Mulu was awarded UNESCO World Heritage Site status in 2000 in recognition of its significant geomorphic characteristics and biodiversity. For the more adventurous, there are extensive caving and trekking available. Underground chambers stretching to 51km (32 miles) include the largest cave chamber in the world – the spectacular Sarawak Chamber. To date, 310km (193 miles) of passages have been charted but it is believed that there are many more yet to be discovered. The Deer, Lang, Clearwater and Wind caves are all known as the Show Caves, and each has its own very individual atmosphere. They can all be reached by the 3-km (2-mile) plank walk from park headquarters that winds through primary jungle.

HOW TO GET THERE:
Fly from Miri, Maurudi and Limbang.
WHEN TO GO:
Gunung enjoys a very high rate of rainfall all year round, but avoid the period from October to March when it is particularly heavy during monsoon season.
NEAREST TOWN:
Miri 110km (70 miles) away, with its good flight connections, is the best place to use as a base.

HOW TO GET THERE:
There is a 3-km (2-mile) boardwalk from Gunung Mulu Park HQ to the cave.
WHEN TO GO:
Make sure you arrive with enough time to explore the cave before dusk at 5pm.
NEAREST TOWN:
Miri 110km (70 miles).

YOU SHOULD KNOW
Be prepared to be showered with guano, the smell of which can make your eyes water.

DEER CAVE BAT ROOST

Malaysia

Deer Cave, the largest cave passage in the world, is part of the cave system of Gunung Mulu National Park. The cave is a self-contained world with a huge forest growing inside as well as a river, hills and valleys. This terrain sustains a huge population of somewhere between two and five million bats. There are at least 12 species of bat inside the cave, the most prolific being the wrinkle-nosed bat. These chattering, squealing creatures line the walls and ceiling of the cave throughout the day then leave the cave in a billowing black cloud, streaking across the sky to feed on insects in the jungle. Their guano lines the cave floor in great dunes, 6m (20ft) deep in some places. The surface is alive, teeming with millions of insects ranging from cockroaches and scorpions to earwigs and giant cave centipedes. Be sure to bring a torch, as the cave is deep and the floor is teeming with insects that will crunch underfoot if you're not careful.

THE HEART OF BORNEO

Malaysia

HOW TO GET THERE:
The area is huge so you have a choice of visiting Kalimantan, Sabah, Brunei Darussalam or Sarawak.
WHEN TO GO:
Go from March to October to avoid the monsoon.
NEAREST TOWNS:
Bintulu for Sarawak, or Kota Kinabalu in Sabah, Tanjung Selor in Kalimantan and Temburong in Brunei.

DON'T MISS
Trekking in the dense jungle of the Bario Loop.

Home to 6 per cent of the world's biodiversity, the Heart of Borneo is 220,000 sq km (85,000 sq miles) of largely unspoilt equatorial rainforest spanning the highlands and foothills of Brunei, Sarawak and Sabah. The diverse land is made up of lush jungle, mangroves, mountains, rivers, swamps and limestone peaks and is an area of immense beauty and uncharted territory. This is one of only two places in the world where rhinos, elephants and orangutans coexist, and new species are being found at a rate of three every month – 360 new species have been discovered in the last ten years. Indigenous tribes encompassing over 30 ethnic groups still live in the area, sustained by 14 of the 20 rivers that flow through this vast space. Living from the land and nurturing ancient traditions, these diverse cultures need the protection of the rainforest to ensure their survival and preservation of a unique way of life.

UJONG KULONG NATIONAL PARK

Indonesia

HOW TO GET THERE:
By road and boat from Jakarta or Labuhan.
WHEN TO GO:
April to August.
NEAREST TOWN:
Labuhan 50km (31 miles).

A nature reserve since the early 1920s, Ujong Kulon National Park encompasses some 500 sq km (193 sq miles) of the southwestern tip of Java, Indonesia's most populous island and home to the country's capital city, Jakarta. The park is situated on a peninsula and it includes several islands, amongst them the notorious volcanoes of Krakatoa and Anak Krakatoa. Krakatoa blew itself apart in August 1883 in one of the world's greatest eruptions. The sound could be heard in Queensland, Australia over 4,000km (6,400 miles) away, and the resulting tidal waves were traced as far away as France. Anak Krakatoa, literally 'child of Krakatoa', emerged from the sea in 1928. Uniquely interesting to scientists, it provides the perfect opportunity to study its colonization by the plant and animal species that have found their way across from the mainland. Some 30 years ago Ujong Kulon was upgraded to national park status, when it was recognized that its unique ecosystem supports the most concentrated array of species, together with a spectacular combination of habitats – sandy beaches, swamps, mangroves, estuarine shallows, river valleys, hills, grasslands and lowland rainforest – in any Javan reserve. It is home to a wealth of birds and also to the estuarine crocodile. There are leopards, civet cats, flying foxes and green turtles, but the rarest animal it shelters is the endangered Javan rhinoceros, a one-horned rhino that may only exist here.

MOUNT BROMO

Indonesia

HOW TO GET THERE:
By train or bus from Surubaya, or hire a car.
WHEN TO GO:
April to November.
NEAREST TOWN:
Ngadisari 3km (2 miles).

YOU SHOULD KNOW

The temperature may be several degrees below zero during the dry season, so bring warm clothing. It can get hot very quickly after the sun rises.

At 2,329m (7,641ft), Mount Bromo is not the highest peak in the Tengger massif, but it is the most well-known. Its stunning beauty lies in its incredible setting: this smoking crater sits in a sea of sand inside the Bromo Tengger Semeru National Park in east Java, and offers spectacular views over a dramatic landscape. It's actually a small, active volcano inside the much-larger caldera of an ancient, extinct volcano. The massif area is one of the most-visited tourist attractions in east Java, and Mount Bromo sits in the middle of a vast plain called the 'Sea of Sand', a protected nature reserve since 1919. The typical way to visit it is from the nearby mountain village of Cemoro Lawang. From there it is possible to walk to the volcano in about 45 minutes, but you can also take an organized jeep tour, which includes a stop at the viewpoint on Mount Penanjakan which reaches 2,770m (9,088ft). The eerie landscape has spurned countless legends and myths, and the volcano is a point of pilgrimage for Javanese Hindus who congregate here every year for the Kasada festival, during which offerings of vegetables, chickens and money are thrown into the crater. Depending on the degree of volcanic activity, the Indonesian Centre for Volcanology and Disaster Hazard Mitigation sometimes issues warnings against visiting, so find out before you go.

KOMODO NATIONAL PARK

Indonesia

HOW TO GET THERE:
By air to Labuanbajo from
Bali, then by boat.
WHEN TO GO:
April to October.
NEAREST TOWN:
Labuanbajo 35km (22 miles).

Komodo National Park was established in 1980 to protect the ancient monitor lizards of the same name, and was inscribed on the World Heritage List in 1991. The three islands are surrounded by one of the world's best marine environments, and are becoming increasingly popular dive sites. However, it is the dragons that are the lure for most visitors to these barren, volcanic islands in Indonesia's Lesser Sundas. Guided tours take tourists to hot spots during the morning or late afternoon, when the lizards are active. During the heat of the middle of the day, they burrow in the dry streambed to keep cool. These prehistoric predators can grow up to 3m (10ft) in length. Despite their stumpy looking legs they can run as fast as a dog and, given the opportunity, could eat a human. Visitors are advised to keep an eye out for their foot- and tail-prints in the sand when on the beautiful beaches in the sandy bays. They have also been spotted swimming from island to island.

LORENTZ NATIONAL PARK

Indonesia

Lorentz National Park is the largest in southeast Asia. Situated in the Indonesian province of Papua (western New Guinea), it is the sole area of the world where a continuous, intact transect, from a tropical marine environment, through lowland wetlands and right up to the snowy mountain peaks, is protected. New Guinea's main mountain range is on the edge of the Pacific and Australian tectonic plates, and it is one of only three areas in the world where equatorial glaciers still exist. Puncak Jaya, at 4,884m (16,117ft), is not only Indonesia's highest mountain, but also the highest between the Himalayas and the Andes. The entire region is covered in pristine forest, much of which has never been explored or mapped. People have lived here for over 25,000 years. Today, some 6,300 people from eight indigenous groups live within the park boundaries, and there are perhaps 50 small villages, accessible only by foot and the occasional missionary airstrip. These people are mainly traditional hunter-gatherers, who do a little subsistence farming on the steep hillsides.

HOW TO GET THERE: By plane or boat to Jayapura, then by plane.
WHEN TO GO: May to October.
NEAREST TOWN: Most visitors are based in Wamena, in the Baliem Valley, which has an airstrip.

BUKIT BARISAN MOUNTAINS, SUMATRA

Indonesia

The Bukit Barisan are a range of mountains running almost the entire length of Sumatra's western side, from Aceh in the north to Lampung in the south, forming the spine of this huge island. It comprises three national parks, collectively known as the Tropical Rainforest Heritage of Sumatra, and was listed by UNESCO in 2004. Some 70 million years ago, when tectonic plate collision raised the Himalayas, the Barisan mountains were also forced upwards along the west coast of the island. Here the mountains often meet the shoreline, while east of the range lie low hills, plains and swamps. The terrain consists mainly of densely forested volcanoes, many of which are still active, and includes, at 3,800m (12,540ft), the highest volcanic peak in Indonesia, Mount Kerinci. This fabulous mountain range is rich in habitat. Several large rivers rise here and many streams; there are extraordinary lakes such as Lake Toba, Kelimutu Crater Lake and Lake Gunung Tujuh, the highest in southeast Asia, stunning waterfalls, hot springs, smoke-belching fumeroles and complex cave systems. Above all, Bukit Barisan protects over 10,000 plant species, more than 200 mammals, 22 of which are Asian and not found elsewhere in Indonesia and 15 of which are found solely in Indonesia. This is home to orangutans and Asian elephants and is almost the last refuge of the critically endangered Sumatran tiger and Sumatran rhino. Illegal logging, forest clearance for agriculture and poaching are the main threats to wildlife here, and UNESCO's protection is essential to conserve Bukit Barisan for future generations.

HOW TO GET THERE:
Plane or ferry to Medan, or plane to Padang, then by road.
WHEN TO GO:
May to September north of the equator; March to August south of the equator.
NEAREST TOWNS:
Towns and villages are scattered throughout the mountains and up and down the coast.

MOUNT EREBUS

Antarctica

The world's southernmost active volcano, Mount Erebus, looms over the American research station of McMurdo and New Zealand's Scott Base, both of which are sited at the southern end of Hut Point Peninsula on Ross Island. Discovered by the British explorer James Ross in 1841, it was climbed in 1908 by members of Ernest Shackleton's expedition. Since the early 1970s, the volcano has been under observation – since 1980, continuously so, via a network of six seismic stations. For about six weeks each year, from November

to January, scientists ascend the slopes to their camp at 3,476m (11,400ft) for active fieldwork. The summit of Mount Erebus, at 3,794m (12,444ft), is almost invariably crowned with clouds of vapour. Unusually it has an outer crater, within which lies a smaller crater containing a lake of churning, molten lava. Explosions within the lake lob lava bombs that can land up to 1.6km (1 mile) away. The volcano's sides are dotted with fumaroles, or ice chimneys, up to 18m (60ft) high. These are formed by heat from within melting the snow to form a cave, from which escaping steam freezes the moment it hits the air. Scientists are attempting to discover whether these warm ice caves could ever have supported life. Glaciers extend from the volcano to the edges of the island. The Erebus glacier tongue is between 50 and 300m (164 and 984ft) thick and grows every year, stretching several kilometres beyond the island into the bay.

HOW TO GET THERE:
Unless you are a scientist you are unlikely to visit Ross Island. However, a limited number of cruise ships visit Antarctica.
WHEN TO GO:
During the Antarctic summer.

YOU SHOULD KNOW
The average temperature here is -20°C (-4°F) during summer and -60°C (-76°F) during winter.

INDEX

INDEX

PICTURE CREDITS